Studying Culture

Studying Culture

An Introductory Reader

Second Edition

Edited by

Ann Gray
Senior Lecturer in Cultural Studies,
University of Birmingham

and

Jim McGuigan
Senior Lecturer in Sociology,
Loughborough University

A member of the Hodder Headline Group
LONDON

First published in Great Britain in 1993
This impression reprinted in 2003 by
Arnold, a member of the Hodder Headline Group,
338 Euston Road, London NW1 3BH

Distributed in the United States of America by
Oxford University Press Inc.,
198 Madison Avenue, New York, NY 10016

The advice and information in this book is believed to be true and accurate at
the date of going to press, but neither the authors nor the publisher can accept
any legal responsibility or liability for any errors or omissions.

British Library Cataloguing in Publication Data
A catalogue entry for this book is available from the British Library

Library of Congress Cataloging-in-Publication Data
Studying culture: an introductory reader/edited by Ann Gray and
Jim McGuigan—2nd ed.
p.   cm.
Includes bibliographical references and index.
ISBN 0-340-67688-4 (pbk.)
1. Popular culture 2. Culture. 3. Great Britain—
Civilization—1945- 1. Gray, Ann, 1946- II. McGuigan, Jim,
CB430.S78 1997

306—dc21   97-14189
                                              CIP

ISBN 0 340 67688 4

6 7 8 9 10

Composition by Phoenix Photosetting, Chatham, Kent

Contents

Section 4   Social selves and public policy

Acknowledgements

When we decided to construct a reader in Cultural Studies we knew it would be fun. Making such a compilation of selected texts has an affinity with picking a list of favourite records, novels, films or whatever. Yet little did we imagine how difficult and occasionally tortuous a project we had embarked upon. We have chopped and changed the selection so many times that we have now lost count of quite how many times. Also, when for one reason or another a piece had to be removed we found it impossible merely to slot in a substitute; the unbalancing effect was normally too great. In the end, however, we believe that the selection of writings presented here constitutes a fair representation of cultural studies, and possibly a better one than all the previous selections that we had to discard or modify drastically, which is not to say it is definitive: that would be impossible in any event. Some of the items are cut for reasons of space or in order to bring out the argument more sharply. These cuts are marked by the convention of [. . .]. We apologise to those authors who may feel this has distorted their work. It is, of course, to the authors we have drawn upon that we owe the greatest acknowledgement, all of whom have taught us something and whose works, we believe, exemplify the best of cultural studies. The particular selection of texts has been very much influenced by our learning from students, especially adult education students, initially at the Workers' Educational Association in Leeds and subsequently tutoring on the Open University's Popular Culture course in the mid-1980s.

Ann Gray and Jim McGuigan
March 1997

The editors and publishers would like to thank the following for permission to use copyright material in this book:

HarperCollins Publishers Limited, and Farrar, Straus & Giroux, Inc. for the extract from 'The rhetoric of the image' from *Image/music/text* by Roland Barthes, translated by Stephen Heath (Fontana, 1977), English translation copyright © 1977 by Stephen Heath. Reprinted by permission of Hill and Wang, a division of Farrar, Straus & Giroux, Inc.; Routledge Ltd for 'The New Petite Bourgeoisie' from *Distinction* by Pierre Bourdieu (Routledge, 1984); Macmillan Press Ltd for Erica Carter, 'Alice in the consumer wonderland' from Angela McRobbie and Mica Nava (eds), *Gender and generation*

(Macmillan, 1984); New Left Review for 'European cities, the informational society, and the global economy' by Manuel Castells, from *New Left Review* no. 204, March/April 1994; the author of Phil Cohen, 'Subcultural conflict and working-class community' reprinted from *Working papers in cultural studies 2* (Centre for Contemporary Cultural Studies, University of Birmingham, Spring 1972); the authors and Pion Ltd for 'The city as studio; the world as back lot: the impact of vertical disintegration on the location of the motion picture industry' by Susan Christopherson and Michael Storper, from *Environment and Planning D: Society and Space*, vol. 4 (1986); Routledge Ltd for 'Cultural studies from the viewpoint of cultural policy' by Stuart Cunningham, from Graeme Turner (ed.) *Nation, culture, text – Australian cultural and media studies* (Routledge, 1993); the author for Liz Curtis, 'Echoes of the present – the Victorian press and Ireland', from *Truth: the first casualty* (Information on Ireland, 1978); Verso for Mike Davis, 'The view from futures past', from *City of quartz – excavating the future of Los Angeles* (Verso/NLB, London and New York, 1990); the authors and Broadcast for Richard Dyer, Terry Lovell and Jean McCrindle, 'Soap opera and women' reprinted from *Edinburgh International Television Festival 1977 – Official Programme* (Broadcast, 1977); Verso for 'Can Cinderella become a citizen?' from *Cinderella goes to market – citizenship, gender and women's movements in East Central Europe* by Barbara Einhorn (Verso, 1993); Routledge for Nicholas Garnham, 'Concepts of culture' from *Cultural Studies*, Vol. 1, No. 1, Methuen & Co; Routledge for Marie Gillespie, 'Technology and tradition', from *Cultural Studies*, Vol. 3, No. 2; Routledge for Paul Gilroy, 'Black and white on the dance floor' from *There ain't no black in the Union Jack* (Hutchinson, 1987); the Council of Europe for Stuart Hall, 'The television discourse – encoding and decoding', © Council of Europe, first published in *Education and Culture* No. 25, 1974; the author and the Institute of Contemporary Arts for Stuart Hall, 'Minimal selves', from *Identity: the real me – postmodernism and the question of identity* (ICA Documents 6, 1987) pp. 44–6, © Stuart Hall and the ICA; Verso for Fredric Jameson, 'Postmodernism and consumer society', reprinted from E. Ann Kaplan (ed.), *Postmodernism and its discontents* (Verso/NLB, London and New York, 1988) pp. 213–29; the author and *Marxism Today* for Doreen Massey, 'A global sense of place', first published in *Marxism Today*, June, 1991; the author for Kobena Mercer, 'Just looking for trouble – Robert Mapplethorpe and fantasies of race' reprinted from Lynne Segal and Mary McIntosh (eds), *Sex exposed – sexuality and the pornography debate* (Virago, 1992); Australian Journal of Communication for Graham Murdock, 'Cultural studies at the crossroads' from *Australian Journal of Communication* No. 16 (December, 1989); 'The Institute of Race Relations for Jan Nederveen Pieterse, 'Fictions of Europe', from *Race and Class* Vol. 32, No. 3, (1991); the author for Bhikhu Parekh, 'Between holy text and moral void', reprinted from *New Statesman* (24 March 1989); the author and Routledge Ltd for 'An invitation to a sociology of stories' from *Telling sexual stories – power, change and social worlds* by Ken Plummer (Routledge, 1995); the author and Routledge Ltd for 'a problematic – speaking the self' from *Sexing the self – gendered positions in cultural studies* by Elspeth Probyn (Routledge, 1993); Verso and the University of North Carolina Press for the extract from *Reading the romance: women, patriarchy, and popular literature* by

Janice Radway (Verso, 1987), copyright © 1991 by the University of North Carolina Press, used by permission of the publisher; Pantheon Books for the extract from *Orientalism* by Edward W. Said, © 1978 by Edward W. Said, reprinted by permission of Pantheon Books, a division of Random House, Inc., Routledge for the extract from Edward W. Said, *Orientalism*, (Routledge and Kegan Paul, 1978); the New Left Review for 'Empowering technology: the exploration of cyberspace' by Julian Stallabrass from *New Left Review* no. 211, May/June 1995, also published in *Gargantua – manufactured mass culture* by Julian Stallabrass (Verso, 1996); the author and the Watkins/Loomis Agency for 'Nihilism in Black America' by Cornel West, published in Gina Dent (ed.) *Black popular culture* (Bay Press, 1992), originally published in *Dissent* (Spring 1991); Merryn Williams for Raymond Williams, 'Culture is ordinary' reprinted from N. McKenzie (ed.), *Convictions* (MacGibbon and Kee, 1958); Marion Boyars Publishers Ltd for the extract from Judith Williamson, *Decoding Advertisements* (Marion Boyars, 1978); Open University Press for Paul Willis, 'Symbolic creativity' from *Common Culture* (Open University Press, 1990).

Every effort has been made to trace copyright holders of material reproduced in this book. Any rights not acknowledged here will be acknowledged in subsequent printings if notice is given to the publisher.

Introduction

This book aims to introduce cultural studies by offering a particular selection of more or less 'classic' readings. Such an offering obliges the editors to address the question: 'what is cultural studies?' That is a perfectly reasonable question to be posed by a newcomer to the field, and it is newcomers to the field who are inevitably positioned as the ideal readers of an introductory textbook. The book, however, also aims to address those already familiar with the field of study who may feel they have been journeying through a terrain for which there is no agreed map. This is not, of course, to say there are no maps, the best known being Stuart Hall's original efforts (1980a, 1980b). Since Hall mapped out the field according to the distinction between the paradigms of 'culturalism' and 'structuralism', his own neo-Gramscian synthesis of 'hegemony theory' and a series of 'post-structuralist' variants, the field has expanded and become much more diverse than it was at the end of the 1970s (Grossberg *et al.*, 1992).

Although the question as posed is reasonable, there is no easy or satisfactory way of answering it. It is one of those questions which tends to come up against evasions and, at best, to spawn other questions, questions that are much more pertinent than the desire to achieve comfort by fixing too precisely the coordinates of an unruly and rapidly developing field of study. We do not intend to evade the question, but we also believe there is no single answer that would not do violence to the values of openness. Ours is a particular version by virtue of being a selection shaped by educational considerations derived from our own experiences of studying and teaching cultural studies over several years. We think this book can be useful to students and tutors by facilitating a provisional entry into the field.

To prefix 'cultural studies' with 'British' (Turner, 1990) produces a particularly narrow answer to our question. It is true that the term 'cultural studies' became current in Britain during the late 1960s and early 1970s with specific reference to its institutional siting at Birmingham University in the Centre for Contemporary Cultural Studies, founded in 1964 by Professor of English, Richard Hoggart, and presided over in the 1970s by Stuart Hall as Director. This centre of international repute, now superseded by the Birmingham Department of Cultural Studies, drew upon a tradition of study which emerged in the post-Second-World-War period in British adult education (Williams, 1989). Out of the discipline of English inspired by Raymond Williams (1958) and the little-recorded efforts of many other adult education tutors, important questions were being asked, mainly by working-class mature students, about the relations between 'culture' and 'society', concerns which broke the bounds of traditional disciplines such as literature and history and had a difficult and sometimes deeply troubled association with newer social scientific disciplines, most notably sociology.

For sociologists schooled in a positivistic mode, cultural studies seemed far too soft, concerned with the interpretation of meanings, reminiscent of literary criticism but encroaching upon the grounds of the social: qualitative in approach rather than 'scientifically' quantitative. Richard Hoggart's *The uses of literacy* (1957), drawing on his own experience of growing up in the industrial North of England, 'read' everyday working-class life, customs and habits as though they were literary texts, opening up the study of popular culture and applying the interpretive procedures of the humanities to the stuff of social science. In this sense, cultural studies had more in common with anthropology than with the survey research methods and statistical analyses of mainstream sociology. Its great precursor was Mass Observation, a movement of the 1930s and 1940s which sought to turn the anthropological gaze inwards from colonial subjects exclusively to register indigenous subjects (Jeffrey, 1978; Stanton, 1996). A further complementary strand was that of 'history from below', represented at the time most profoundly by Edward Thompson's *The making of the English working class* (1963). These precursors and complementarities to cultural studies, as it was forming, are not anthologized in this book. To leave Hoggart and Thompson out is indeed strange, but it is because of limitations of space and to the stronger claims, at present, of more immediately usable material for understanding contemporary cultural practices that we omit them. To represent this 'culturalist' current, we have included Raymond Williams's less well-known essay from 1958, 'Culture is ordinary', which in its polemical title encapsulates most sharply the cardinal impulse of what became understood as 'cultural studies' in Britain and in the English-speaking world generally, the stress on 'lived experience' and the recovery of 'the popular' from its denigration or sentimentalization by cultural elitists (McGuigan, 1992). We also believe that Williams is the single most important figure in the original formation of cultural studies, although Hall played a larger role in establishing it as a curriculum subject, particularly by fusing the British tradition of 'culturalism' with the French tradition of 'structuralism', represented initially in this anthology by Roland Barthes's essay from 1964, 'The rhetoric of the image'.

The linguistic turn in cultural studies during the 1970s, inspired by structural linguistics (Saussure, 1974), Levi-Strauss's (1968) structural anthropology and Barthes's (1972) semiological readings of contemporary popular culture, relates to the broader answer to the question 'what is cultural studies?'; seen in retrospect, it was something of an imperialistic project. It was not only associated with the pretensions of structuralism, since 'culture' could be conceived from an historical materialist perspective, after economy and polity, as 'the third instance of the social whole' (Mulhern, 1980, p. 32), clustering together all sense-making practices. There is a consistency here with structuralism's systematic retotalization of academic enquiry in general and especially with its promise to colonize the humanities and social sciences entirely with a universalistic method and with its startling claims that language speaks us and, because everything is discursive, is therefore inseparable from the subterranean operations of language (Lane, 1970). This is not the context in which to evaluate the structuralist project and its legacy for cultural studies: briefly, the crucial point is that cultural studies, for a moment, seemed to be out to capture the whole field of 'the cultural', to hegemonize its own intellectual leadership. That rationalist takeover bid did not succeed. The traditional disciplines changed but were not displaced. Literary criticism, for example, became increasingly redefined according to the new literary theory (Eagleton, 1983) and, for another example, sociology took on board the cultural to a greater extent, particularly in the encounter with postmodernism towards the end of the 1980s (see, for instance, Lash, 1990). The resultant outcome of cultural studies' bid for hegemony, however, was to leave it peculiarly boundless. Unlike older disciplines, and some of the newer ones, proponents of cultural studies are reluctant to enclose their terms of reference with definitional precision: everything remains up for grabs. There is also an enormous resistance to the very idea of disciplinarity and its connotations of policing the borders of knowledge. Cultural studies, broadly speaking, can still be said, however, to be concerned with anything that is meaningful, usually seen in connection to power relations.

There is an additional way of trying to pin cultural studies down: institutionally and, to some extent, spatially. Cultural studies crept in from the margins, accompanied by other subjects (communication, film, media studies), to become institutionalized within the academy and to spread, in one form or another, throughout the educational system. We now have undergraduate degrees variously named which either mark themselves out explicitly as cultural studies or which are placed in some implicitly cognate relationship to it. For instance, communication studies, which led the way at this level, is frequently all but cultural studies in name or includes the cultural studies 'perspective' as one amongst any number of disciplinary contributions to an umbrella subject. Many students reading this book will be on programmes of study not named cultural studies but for which the book is undoubtedly relevant. And, on the school curriculum, there are now numerous and varied courses in communication, cultural and media studies.

Cultural studies has latterly gone international. Its reception, especially in Australia and North America, decentred what was once a distinctly British field of study that had been obsessed, arguably, with the peculiarities of the British, bringing continental rationalist theory to bear upon localized empirical objects, for example, upon the succession of spectacular youth subcultures, one of Britain's major exports to the rest of the world. It is debatable whether cultural studies has become *de*centred or, instead, *re*centred in the US university system, as a symposium held at the University of Illinois, drawing together stars in the firmament to ponder the past, present and future of cultural studies, would suggest (Grossberg *et al.*, 1992). The claims of feminism, black politics, the discourses of 'the other', however, were already decentring British cultural studies politically from its narrowly national and social-class preoccupations. These political interventions and their theoretical consequences have guided our selection of material. For

American students, Patrick Brantlinger's *In Crusoe's footprints* (1990) provides a useful articulation of cultural studies with American studies that may offset the necessarily British-rootedness of this particular collection.

This book, in effect, traces the developments outlined above, beginning with Raymond Williams's challenge to cultural elitism from within the tradition of 'English' criticism, through to writings that illustrate the internationalization of cultural studies and into our final section which introduces two of the major themes emerging across the many manifestations of 'cultural studies' in the 1990s: that of 'the self' and how it can be understood as an articulation of the social, historical and cultural; and, equally pressing in a time of massive global upheaval, the issue of 'public policy'. The authors variously address questions of the 'inner' worlds of self and identity, theoretically and methodologically, and those of citizenship, global economic power, urban deprivation and consumption and, significantly, in our view, end with a critical exploration of the recent entries into 'cyberspace' and the often Utopian claims made on its behalf.

By tracking through a dense forest of theoretical perspectives and analytical applications, not all of them compatible with one another, we aim to provide a sense of what cultural studies has been and might yet become. The selection slightly marginalizes the textual in favour of the lived. This reflects both the availability of other readers, particularly those concerned with visual and literary media, which foreground the textual (supplemented by the psychoanalytic) and which do not need yet further replication, for the time being at least, and our own predilections, which are more ethnographically inclined and policy orientated. The book represents, then, a comparatively sociological 'take' on cultural studies, though probably unrecognizably so to many sociologists. It may, therefore, be more accurate to describe this selection as one which foregrounds the social with the partial aim of redressing the balance in that direction.

References

Barthes, R. 1972: *Mythologies*. London: Paladin.

Brantlinger, P. 1990: *In Crusoe's footprints – cultural studies in Britain and America*. London/New York: Routledge.

de Saussure, F. 1974: *Course in general linguistics*. London: Fontana.

Eagleton, T. 1983: *Literary theory – an introduction*. Oxford: Basil Blackwell.

Grossberg, L., Nelson, C. and Treichler, P. (eds) 1992: *Cultural studies*. London/New York: Routledge.

Hall, S. 1980a: Cultural studies – two paradigms. *Media, Culture & Society*, vol. 4(2).

Hall, S. 1980b: Cultural studies and the centre – some problematics and problems. In Hall, S., Hobson, D., Lowe, A. and Willis, P. (eds), *Culture, media, language*. London: Hutchinson.

Hoggart, R. 1957: *The uses of literacy*. London: Chatto & Windus.

Jeffrey, T. 1978: *Mass observation – a short history*. Birmingham CCCS Occasional Paper.

Lane, M. (ed.) 1970: *Structuralism – a reader*. London: Jonathan Cape.

Lash, S. 1990: *Sociology of postmodernism*. London/New York: Routledge.

Levi-Strauss, C. 1968: *Structural anthropology*. London: Penguin Books.

McGuigan, J. 1992: *Cultural populism*. London/New York: Routledge.

Mulhern, F. 1980: Notes on culture and cultural struggle. *Screen Education* no. 34, London: Society for Education in Film and Television.

Stanton, G. 1996: Ethnography, anthropology and cultural studies: links and connections. In Curran, J., Morley, D. and Walkerdine, V. (eds), *Cultural studies and communications*. London: Arnold.

Thompson, E.P. 1963: *The making of the English working class*. London: Victor Gollancz.

Turner, B. 1990: *British cultural studies – an introduction*. London: Unwin Hyman.

Williams, R. 1958: *Culture and society*. London: Chatto & Windus.

Williams, R. 1989: *The politics of modernism*. London: Verso.

Editors' note

In some of the earlier pieces in this Reader the term 'man' is used to refer to both men and women in a manner common until feminism's questioning of patriarchal language impacted upon academic discourse. The problem is signalled now rather than marked in every instance.

Section 1

Some foundations

Reference has already been made to the problems of definition in relation to cultural studies and the same can be said of any attempt to construct a history of a field of study, which the term 'foundations' would seem to imply. It is true that there could be many different histories accounting for the development of cultural studies, but the most common one begins with the 'triumvirate' of Richard Hoggart, Raymond Williams and Edward Thompson, more remarkable for their differences than this traditional grouping would imply but who, writing in the late 1950s in Britain, shared at the very least a common questioning of academic values and disciplines, in particular those entrenched within English and History. However, our selection here is less concerned with constructing a coherent or chronological narrative through cultural studies than with seeking to indicate a number of interventions, often from the margins, which at their best cause disjunctures and dislocations in the development of the field of study.

Writing in 1958, **Raymond Williams** insisted that 'Culture is ordinary' and forced the first important shift into a new way of thinking about the symbolic dimensions of our lives. Thus, 'culture' is wrested from that privileged space of artistic production and specialist knowledge into the lived experience of the everyday.

In following with **Roland Barthes**'s 'The rhetoric of the image', originally published in France in 1964, we are recognizing the impact of the body of work known as 'structuralism' in the development of cultural studies, although its impact reverberated through many disciplines. Structuralism and, particularly in this instance, semiology were seen to offer the potential for a rigorous mode of analysis, especially of the visual image, but also of other texts and social practices. This was an analysis which, with its emphasis on the underlying structures of texts and practices, was seen to provide a necessary distance which the more experiential and humanistic versions of cultural studies lacked.

Although semiotics offered a method of textual analysis, attempts were made to go beyond this limited focus. The essay by **Stuart Hall** provides a

1

model for understanding the textual construction of meaning *and* the practice of reading, or decoding, the text. This model was taken up most notably
by David Morley in his study of the popular magazine programme,
Nationwide (1980). Here Hall introduces a sociological dimension to the question of 'reading' (a term used in relation to all texts) and this piece also serves
to place television as a key object of study.

This focus is returned to and expanded in the paper presented to the
Edinburgh International Television Festival in 1977 by **Richard Dyer**, **Terry
Lovell** and **Jean McCrindle** on women's viewing of and representation in
the soap opera genre, who insist that popular television should be taken seriously and, further, demand that genres specifically addressed to a female
audience should be critically examined. This was an important intervention
from which followed a number of studies of soap opera in particular (Allen,
1985; Ang, 1985; Brunsdon, 1981; Dyer *et al.*, 1981; Geraghty, 1990; Hobson,
1982; Modleski, 1982) and also of female genres more generally and the
female audience. The theme of soap opera and women provided an important bridge between the sociologically based media studies and feminist
work within film theory, producing fruitful attempts to work with often
incompatible theoretical frameworks (Brown, 1990; Brunsdon, 1986;
Gamman and Marshment, 1988; Kuhn, 1984; Mattelart, 1986; Pibram, 1988;
Seiter *et al.*, 1989; Taylor, 1989.)

Edward Said's ground-breaking book *Orientalism*, the introduction to
which is printed here, opens up a very different set of questions – those of
'race' and ethnicity, which were being raised elsewhere in a range of contexts – but, more broadly, using a Foucauldian framework, he points to the
operations of power in the Eurocentric constructions of the 'Orient' across
many sites of knowledge production. The consequences of these dense accu-
mulations of 'referential power' constituting myths of the Orient in the culture at large were never more sharply focussed than during the Gulf War of
1991 when the global dimensions of 'race' and 'otherness' and the crippling
consequences of Orientalism were exposed in all public, and many private,
discursive sites (Kabbani, 1986; Norris, 1992.)

The inclusion of **Nicholas Garnham**'s paper presented to the Greater
London Council in 1983 is to introduce an often neglected dimension of culture within the field of mainstream cultural studies, that is, the constitution
and formation of the cultural industries, the intensification of cultural distribution, and therefore access to audiences, and what contribution cultural
studies can offer to policy making. This important level of analysis is rendered absent in most studies of cultural consumption.

Janice Radway's introduction to the British publication of her influential
work *Reading the romance* usefully reminds us of the importance of the context of intellectual production whilst outlining her study of American
romance readers as an 'interpretive community'. Whilst Radway's auto-cri-
tique is important (see also Radway, 1988), *Reading the romance* remains as
one of the few examples of a multi-layered analysis of a hugely popular fictional genre and its readers.

This section ends with a note of caution and critique from **Graham
Murdock** in which he registers a problem for the future of cultural studies.
The metaphor of the 'crossroads' is nicely ironic in its allusion to the highly

popular and much analysed British soap opera of the same name (no longer on-air) given his critique of the tendencies in recent work within cultural studies, those of populism and a critical pluralism, its British focus and its tendency to ignore questions of political economy. What he, and others, have signalled is the danger in the slippage from 'ordinariness' to 'banality' (Morris, 1988) in cultural studies and the need to reflect constantly on our frameworks and objects of study.

References

Allen, R. 1985: *Speaking of soap operas*. Chapel Hill, NC: University of North Carolina Press.

Ang, I. 1985: *Watching Dallas: soap opera and the melodramatic imagination*. London: Methuen.

Brown, M.E. 1990: *Television and women's culture*. London: Sage.

Brunsdon, C. 1981: *Crossroads*: notes on soap opera. *Screen* **22**(4).

Brunsdon, C. (ed.) 1986: *Films for women*. London: British Film Institute.

Dyer, R., Geraghty, C., Lovell, T., *et al.* 1981: *Coronation Street*. London: British Film Institute.

Gamman, L. and Marshmant, M. (eds) 1988: *The female gaze: women as viewers of popular culture*. London: The Women's Press.

Geraghty, C. 1990: *Women and soap opera*. Oxford: Polity Press.

Hobson, D. 1982: *Crossroads: the drama of a soap opera*. London: Methuen.

Kabbani, R. 1986: *Europe's myths of Orient*. London: Pandora.

Kuhn, A. 1984: Women's genres. *Screen* **25**(1).

Mattelart, M. 1986: *Women, media, crisis*. London: Comedia.

Modleski, T. 1982: *Loving with a vengeance*. Hamden, CT: Shoestring Press.

Morley, D. 1980: *The nationwide audience*. London: British Film Institute.

Morris, M. 1988: Banality in cultural studies. *Block* no. 14.

Norris, C. 1992: *Uncritical theory – postmodernism, intellectuals and the Gulf War*. London: Lawrence & Wishart.

Pibram, E.D. (ed.) 1988: *Female spectators*. London: Verso.

Radway, J. 1988: Reception study: ethnography and the problem of dispersed audience, and nomadic subjects. *Cultural Studies* 2(3).

Seiter, E., Borchers, H., Kreutzner, G. and Warth, E.M. (eds) 1989: *Remote control: TV audiences and cultural power*. London: Routledge.

Taylor, H. 1989: *Scarlett's women: Gone with the Wind and its female fans*. London: Virago.

Further reading

Kuhn, A. 1982: *Women's pictures: feminism and cinema*. London: Routledge & Kegan Paul.

Morley, D. 1986: *Family television*. London: Comedia.

Williams, R. 1965: *The long revolution*. Harmondsworth: Penguin Books.

Williams, R. 1974: *Television: technology and cultural form*. London: Fontana.

Williams, R. 1976: *Keywords: a vocabulary of culture and society*. London: Fontana.

Williams, R. 1980: *Problems in materialism and culture: selected essays*. London: New Left Review.

Williams, R. 1981: *Politics and letters: interviews with New Left Review*. London: Verso.
Williams, R. 1983: *Towards 2000*. London: Chatto & Windus.

1

Culture is ordinary

Raymond Williams

Originally published in N. McKenzie (ed.): *Convictions* (MacGibbon and Kee, 1958); reprinted in R. Williams: *Resources of hope* (Verso, 1989).

The bus stop was outside the cathedral. I had been looking at the Mappa Mundi, with its rivers out of Paradise, and at the chained library, where a party of clergymen had got in easily, but where I had waited an hour and cajoled a verger before I even saw the chains. Now, across the street, a cinema advertised the *Six-Five Special* and a cartoon version of *Gulliver's Travels*. The bus arrived, with a driver and a conductress deeply absorbed in each other. We went out of the city, over the old bridge, and on through the orchards and the green meadows and the fields red under the plough. Ahead were the Black Mountains, and we climbed among them, watching the steep fields end at the grey walls, beyond which the bracken and heather and whin had not yet been driven back. To the east, along the ridge, stood the line of grey Norman castles; to the west, the fortress wall of the mountains. Then, as we still climbed, the rock changed under us. Here, now, was limestone, and the line of the early iron workings along the scarp. The farming valleys, with their scattered white houses, fell away behind. Ahead of us were the narrower valleys: the steel-rolling mill, the gasworks, the grey terraces, the pitheads. The bus stopped, and the driver and conductress got out, still absorbed. They had done this journey so often, and seen all its stages. It is a journey, in fact, that in one form or another we have all made.

I was born and grew up halfway along that bus journey. Where I lived is still a farming valley, though the road through it is being widened and straightened, to carry the heavy lorries to the north. Not far away, my grandfather, and so back through the generations, worked as a farm labourer until he was turned out of his cottage and, in his fifties, became a roadman. His sons went at thirteen or fourteen on to the farms, his daughters into service. My father, his third son, left the farm at fifteen to be a boy porter on the railway, and later became a signalman, working in a box in this valley until he died. I went up the road to the village school, where a curtain divided the two classes – Second to eight or nine, First to fourteen. At eleven I went to the local grammar school, and later to Cambridge.

Culture is ordinary: that is where we must start. To grow up in that country was to see the shape of a culture, and its modes of change. I could stand on the mountains and look north to the farms and the cathedral, or south to the smoke and the flare of the blast furnace making a second sunset. To grow up in that family was to see the shaping of minds: the learning of new skills, the shifting of relationships, the emergence of different language and ideas. My grandfather, a big hard labourer, wept while he spoke, finely and excitedly, at the parish meeting, of being turned out of his cottage. My father, not long before he died, spoke quietly and happily of when he had started a trade-union branch and a Labour Party group in the village, and, without bitterness, of the 'kept men' of the new politics. I speak a different idiom, but I think of these same things.

Culture is ordinary: that is the first fact. Every human society has its own shape, its own purposes, its own meanings. Every human society expresses these, in institutions, and in arts and learning. The making of a society is the finding of common meanings and directions, and its growth is an active debate and amendment under the pressures of experience, contact, and discovery, writing themselves into the land. The growing society is there, yet it is also made and remade in every individual mind. The making of a mind is, first, the slow learning of shapes, purposes, and meanings, so that work, observation and communication are possible. Then, second, but equal in importance, is the testing of these in experience, the making of new observations, comparisons, and meanings. A culture has two aspects: the known meanings and directions, which its members are trained to; the new observations and meanings, which are offered and tested. These are the ordinary processes of human societies and human minds, and we see through them the nature of a culture: that it is always both traditional and creative; that it is both the most ordinary common meanings and the finest individual meanings. We use the word culture in these two senses: to mean a whole way of life – the common meanings; to mean the arts and learning – the special processes of discovery and creative effort. Some writers reserve the word for one or other of these senses; I insist on both, and on the significance of their conjunction. The questions I ask about our culture are questions about our general and common purposes, yet also questions about deep personal meanings. Culture is ordinary, in every society and in every mind.

Now there are two senses of culture – two colours attached to it – that I know about but refuse to learn. The first I discovered at Cambridge, in a teashop. I was not, by the way, oppressed by Cambridge. I was not cast down by old buildings, for I had come from a country with twenty centuries of history written visibly into the earth: I liked walking through a Tudor court, but it did not make me feel raw. I was not amazed by the existence of a place of learning; I had always known the cathedral, and the bookcases I now sit to work at in Oxford are of the same design as those in the chained library. Nor was learning, in my family, some strange eccentricity; I was not, on a scholarship in Cambridge, a new kind of animal up a brand-new ladder. Learning was ordinary; we learned where we could. Always, from those scattered white houses, it had made sense to go out and become a scholar or a poet or a teacher. Yet few of us could be spared from the immediate work; a price had been set on this kind of learning, and it was more, much more, than we could individually pay. Now, when we could pay in common, it was a good, ordinary life.

I was not oppressed by the university, but the teashop, acting as if it were one of the older and more respectable departments, was a different matter. Here was culture, not in any sense I knew, but in a special sense: the outward and emphatically visible sign of a special kind of people, cultivated people. They were not, the great majority of them, particularly learned; they practised few arts; but they had it, and they showed you they had it. They are still there, I suppose, still showing it, though even they must be hearing rude noises from outside, from a few scholars and writers they call – how comforting a label is! – angry young men. As a matter of fact there is no need to be rude. It is simply that if that is culture, we don't want it; we have seen other people living.

But of course it is not culture, and those of my colleagues who, hating the teashop, make culture, on its account, a dirty word, are mistaken. If the people in the teashop go on insisting that culture is their trivial differences of behaviour, their trivial variations of speech habit, we cannot stop them, but we can ignore them. They are not that important, to take culture from where it belongs.

Yet, probably also disliking the teashop, there were writers I read then, who went into the same category in my mind. When I now read a book such as Clive Bell's *Civilisation*, I experience not so much disagreement as stupor. What kind of life can it be, I wonder, to produce this extraordinary fussiness, this extraordinary decision to call certain things culture and then separate them, as with a park wall, from ordinary people and ordinary work? At home we met and made music, listened to it, recited and listened to poems, valued fine language. I have heard better music and better poems since; there is the world to draw on. But I know, from the most ordinary experience, that the interest is there, the capacity is there. Of course, farther along that bus journey, the old social organization in which these things had their place has been broken. People have been driven and concentrated into new kinds of work, new kinds of relationship; work, by the way, which built the park walls, and the houses inside them, and which is now at last bringing, to the unanimous disgust of the teashop, clean and decent and furnished living to the people themselves. Culture is ordinary: through every change let us hold fast to that.

The other sense, or colour, that I refuse to learn, is very different. Only two English words rhyme with culture, and these, as it happens, are sepulture and vulture. We don't yet call museums or galleries or even universities culture-sepultures, but I hear a lot, lately, about culture-vultures (man must rhyme), and I hear also, in the same North Atlantic argot, of do-gooders and highbrows and superior prigs. Now I don't like the teashop, but I don't like this drinking-hole either. I know there are people who are humourless about the arts and learning, and I know there is a difference between goodness and sanctimony. But the growing implications of this spreading argot – the true cant of a new kind of rogue – I reject absolutely. For, honestly, how can anyone use a word like 'do-gooder' with this new, offbeat complacency? How can anyone wither himself to a state where he must use these new flip words for any attachment to learning or the arts? It is plain that what may have started as a feeling about hypocrisy, or about pretentiousness (in itself a two-edged word), is becoming a guilt-ridden tic at the mention of any serious standards whatever. And the word 'culture' has been heavily compromised by this conditioning: Goering reached for his gun; many reach for their chequebooks; a growing number, now, reach for the latest bit of argot.

'Good' has been drained of much of its meaning, in these circles, by the exclusion of its ethical content and emphasis on a purely technical standard; to do a good job is better than to be a do-gooder. But do we need reminding that any crook can, in his own terms, do a good job? The smooth reassurance of technical efficiency is no substitute for the whole positive human reference. Yet men who once made this reference, men who were or wanted to be writers or scholars, are now, with every appearance of satisfaction, advertising men, publicity boys, names in the strip newspapers. These men were given skills, given attachments, which are now in the service of the most brazen money-grabbing exploitation of the inexperience of ordinary people. And it is these men – this new, dangerous class – who have invented and disseminated the argot, in an attempt to influence ordinary people – who because they do real work have real standards in the fields they know – against real standards in the fields these men knew and have abandoned. The old cheapjack is still there in the market, with the country boys' half-crowns on his reputed packets of gold rings or watches. He thinks of his victims as a slow, ignorant crowd, but they live, and farm, while he coughs behind his portable stall. The new cheapjack is in offices with contemporary *décor*, using scraps of linguistics, psychology and sociology to influence what he thinks of as the mass mind. He too, however, will have to pick up and move on, and meanwhile we are not to be influenced by his argot; we can simply refuse to learn it. Culture is ordinary. An interest in learning or the arts is simple, pleasant and natural. A desire to know what is best, and to do what is good, is the whole positive nature of man. We are not to be scared from these things by noises. There are many versions of what is wrong with our culture. So far I have tried only to clear away the detritus which makes it difficult for us to think seriously about it at all. When I got to Cambridge I encountered two serious influences which have left a very deep impression on my mind. The first was Marxism, the second the teaching of Leavis. Through all subsequent disagreement I retain my respect for both.

The Marxists said many things, but those that mattered were three. First, they said that a culture must be finally interpreted in relation to its underlying system of production. I have argued this theoretically elsewhere[1] – it is a more difficult idea than it looks – but I still accept its emphasis. Everything I had seen, growing up in that border country, had led me towards such an emphasis: a culture is a whole way of life, and the arts are part of a social organization which economic change clearly radically affects. I did not have to be taught dissatisfaction with the existing economic system, but the subsequent questions about our culture were, in these terms, vague. It was said that it was a class-dominated culture, deliberately restricting a common inheritance to a small class, while leaving the masses ignorant. The fact of restriction I accepted – it is still very obvious that only the *deserving* poor get much educational opportunity, and I was in no mood, as I walked about Cambridge, to feel glad that I had been thought deserving; I was no better and no worse than the people I came from. On the other hand, just because of this, I got angry at my friends' talk about the ignorant masses: one kind of

Communist has always talked like this, and has got his answer, at Poznan and Budapest, as the imperialists, making the same assumption, were answered in India, in Indo-China, in Africa. There is an English bourgeois culture, with its powerful educational, literary and social institutions, in close contact with the actual centres of power. To say that most working people are excluded from these is self-evident, though the doors, under sustained pressure, are slowly opening. But to go on to say that working people are excluded from English culture is nonsense; they have their own growing institutions, and much of the strictly bourgeois culture they would in any case not want. A great part of the English way of life, and of its arts and learning, is not bourgeois in any discoverable sense. There are institutions, and common meanings, which are in no sense the sole product of the commercial middle class; and there are art and learning, a common English inheritance, produced by many kinds of men, including many who hated the very class and system which now take pride in consuming it. The bourgeoisie has given us much, including a narrow but real system of morality; that is at least better than its court predecessors. The leisure which the bourgeoisie attained has given us much of cultural value. But this is not to say that contemporary culture is bourgeois culture: a mistake that everyone, from Conservatives to Marxists, seems to make. There is a distinct working-class way of life, which I for one value – not only because I was bred in it, for I now, in certain respects, live differently. I think this way of life, with its emphases of neighbourhood, mutual obligation, and common betterment, as expressed in the great working-class political and industrial institutions, is in fact the best basis for any future English society. As for the arts and learning, they are in a real sense a national inheritance, which is, or should be, available to everyone. So when the Marxists say that we live in a dying culture, and that the masses are ignorant, I have to ask them, as I asked them then, where on earth they have lived. A dying culture, and ignorant masses, are not what I have known and see.

What I had got from the Marxists then, so far, was a relationship between culture and production, and the observation that education was restricted. The other things I rejected, as I rejected also their third point, that since culture and production are related, the advocacy of a different system of production is in some way a cultural directive, indicating not only a way of life but new arts and learning. I did some writing while I was, for eighteen months, a member of the Communist Party, and I found out in trivial ways what other writers, here and in Europe, have found out more gravely: the practical consequences of this kind of theoretical error. In this respect, I saw the future, and it didn't work. The Marxist interpretation of culture can never be accepted while it retains, as it need not retain, this directive element, this insistence that if you honestly want socialism you must write, think, learn in certain prescribed ways. A culture is common meanings, the product of a whole people, and offered individual meanings, the product of a man's whole committed personal and social experience. It is stupid and arrogant to suppose that any of these meanings can in any way be prescribed; they are made by living, made and remade, in ways we cannot know in advance. To try to jump the future, to pretend that in some way you *are* the future, is strictly insane. Prediction is another matter, an offered meaning, but the only thing we can say about culture in an England that has socialized its means of production is that all the channels of expression and communication should be cleared and open, so that the whole actual life, that we cannot know in advance, that we can know only in part even while it is being lived, may be brought to consciousness and meaning.

Leavis has never liked Marxists, which is in one way a pity, for they know more than he does about modern English society, and about its immediate history. He, on the other hand, knows more than any Marxist I have met about the real relations between art and experience. We have all learned from him in this, and we have also learned his version of what is wrong with English culture. The diagnosis is radical, and is rapidly becoming orthodox. There was an old, mainly agricultural England, with a traditional culture of great value. This has been replaced by a modern, organized, industrial state, whose characteristic institutions deliberately cheapen our natural human responses, making art and literature into desperate survivors and witnesses, while a new mechanized vulgarity sweeps into the centres of power. The only defence is in education, which will at least keep certain things alive, and which will also, at least in a minority, develop ways of thinking and feeling which are competent to understand what is happening and to maintain the finest individual values. I need not add how widespread this diagnosis has become, though little enough acknowledgement is still made to Leavis himself. For my own part, I was deeply impressed by it; deeply enough for my ultimate rejection of it to be a personal crisis lasting several years.

For, obviously, it seemed to fit a good deal of my experience. It did not tell me that my father and grandfather were ignorant wage-slaves; it did not tell me that the smart, busy, commercial culture (which I had come to as a stranger, so much so that for years I had violent headaches whenever I passed through London and saw underground advertisements and evening newspapers) was the thing I had to catch up with. I even made a fool of myself, or was made to think so, when after a lecture in which the usual point was made that 'neighbour' now does not mean what it did to Shakespeare, I said – imagine! – that to me it did. (When my father was dying this year, one man came in and dug his garden; another loaded and delivered a lorry of sleepers for firewood; another came and chopped the sleepers into blocks; another – I don't know who, it was never said – left a sack of potatoes at the back door; a woman came in and took away a basket of washing.) But even this was explicable; I came from a bit of the old society, but my future was Surbiton (it took me years to find Surbiton, and have a good look at it, but it's served a good many as a symbol – without having lived there I couldn't say whether rightly). So there I was, and it all seemed to fit.

Yet not all. Once I got away, and thought about it, it didn't really fit properly. For one thing I knew this: at home we were glad of the Industrial Revolution, and of its consequent social and political changes. True, we lived in a very beautiful farming valley, and the valleys beyond the limestone we could all see were ugly. But there was one gift that was overriding, one gift which at any price we would take, the gift of power that is everything to men who have worked with their hands. It was slow in coming to us, in all its effects, but steam power, the petrol engine, electricity, these and their host of products in commodities and services, we took as quickly as we could get them, and were glad. I have seen all these things being used, and I have seen the things they replaced. I will not listen with patience to any acid listing of them – you know the sneer you can get into plumbing, baby Austins, aspirin, contraceptives, canned food. But I say to these Pharisees: dirty water, an earth bucket, a four-mile walk each way to work, headaches, broken women, hunger and monotony of diet. The working people, in town and country alike, will not listen (and I support them) to any account of our society which supposes that these things are not progress: not just mechanical, external progress either, but a real service of life. Moreover, in the new conditions, there was more real freedom to dispose of our lives, more real personal grasp where it mattered, more real say. Any account of our culture which explicitly or implicitly denies the value of an industrial society is really irrelevant; not in a million years would you make us give up this power.

So then the social basis of the case was unacceptable, but could one, trying to be a writer, a scholar, a teacher, ignore the indictment of the new cultural vulgarity? For the plumbing and the tractors and the medicines could one ignore the strip newspapers, the multiplying cheapjacks, the raucous triviality? As a matter of priorities, yes, if necessary; but was the cheapening of response really a consequence of the cheapening of power? It looks like it, I know, but is this really as much as one can say? I believe the central problem of our society, in the coming half-century, is the use of our new resources to make a good common culture; the means to a good, abundant economy we already understand. I think the good common culture can be made, but before we can be serious about this, we must rid ourselves of a legacy from our most useful critics – a legacy of two false equations, one false analogy, and one false proposition.

The false proposition is easily disposed of. It is a fact that the new power brought ugliness: the coal brought dirt, the factory brought overcrowding, communications brought a mess of wires. But the proposition that ugliness is a price we pay, or refuse to pay, for economic power need no longer be true. New sources of power, new methods of production, improved systems of transport and communication can, quite practically, make England clean and pleasant again, and with much more power, not less. Any new ugliness is the product of stupidity, indifference, or simply incoordination; these things will be easier to deal with than when power was necessarily noisy, dirty, and disfiguring.

The false equations are more difficult. One is the equation between popular education and the new commercial culture: the latter proceeding inevitably from the former. Let the masses in, it is said, and this is what you inevitably get. Now the question is obviously difficult, but I can't accept this equation, for two reasons. The first is a matter of faith: I don't believe that the ordinary people in fact resemble the normal description of the masses, low and trivial in taste and habit. I put it another way: that there are in fact no masses, but only ways of seeing people as masses. With the coming of industrialism, much of the old social organization broke down and it became a matter of difficult personal experience that we were constantly seeing people we did not know, and it was tempting to mass them, as 'the others', in our minds. Again, people were physically massed, in the industrial towns, and a new class structure (the names of our social classes, and the word 'class' itself in this sense, date only from the Industrial Revolution) was practically imposed. The improvement in communications, in particular the development of new forms of multiple transmission of news and entertainment, created unbridgeable divisions between transmitter and audience, which again led to the audience being interpreted as an unknown mass. Masses became a new word for mob: the others, the unknown, the unwashed, the crowd beyond one. As a way of knowing other people, this formula is obviously ridiculous, but, in the new conditions, it seemed an effective formula – the only one possible. Certainly it was the formula that was used by those whose money gave them access to the new communication techniques; the lowness of taste and habit, which human beings assign very easily to other human beings, was assumed, as a bridge. The new culture was built on this formula, and if I reject the formula, if I insist that this lowness is not inherent in ordinary people, you can brush my insistence aside, but I shall go on holding to it. A different formula, I know from experience, gets a radically different response.

My second reason is historical: I deny, and can prove my denial, that popular education and commercial culture are cause and effect. I have shown elsewhere that the myth of 1870 – the Education Act which is said to have produced, as its children grew up, a new cheap and nasty press – is indeed myth. There was more than enough literacy, long before 1870, to support a cheap press, and in fact there were cheap and really bad newspapers selling in great quantities before the 1870 Act was heard of. The bad new commercial culture came out of the social chaos of industrialism, and out of the success, in this chaos, of the 'masses' formula, not out of popular education. Northcliffe did few worse things than start this myth, for while the connection between bad culture and the social chaos of industrialism is significant, the connection between it and popular education is vicious. The Northcliffe Revolution, by the way, was a radical change in the financial structure of the press, basing it on a new kind of revenue – the new mass advertising of the 1890s – rather than the making of a cheap popular press, in which he had been widely and successfully preceded. But I tire of making these points. Everyone prefers to believe Northcliffe. Yet does nobody, even a Royal Commission, read the most ordinarily accessible newspaper history? When people do read the history, the false equation between popular education and commercial culture will disappear for ever. Popular education came out of the other camp, and has had quite opposite effects.

The second false equation is this: that the observable badness of so much widely distributed popular culture is a true guide to the state of mind and feeling, the essential quality of living, of its consumers. Too many good men have said this for me to treat it lightly, but I still, on evidence, can't accept it. It is easy to assemble, from print and cinema and television, a terrifying and fantastic congress of cheap feelings and moronic arguments. It is easy to go on from this and assume this deeply degrading version of the actual lives of our contemporaries. Yet do we find this confirmed, when we meet people? This is where 'masses' comes in again, of course: the people *we* meet aren't vulgar, but God, think of Bootle and Surbiton and Aston! I haven't lived in any of those places; have you? But a few weeks ago I was in a house with a commercial traveller, a lorry driver, a bricklayer, a shopgirl, a fitter, a signalman, a nylon operative, a domestic help (perhaps, dear, she is your very own treasure). I hate describing people like this, for in fact they were my family and family friends. Now they read, they watch, this work we are talking about; some of them quite critically, others with a good deal of pleasure. Very well, I read different things, watch different entertainments, and I am quite sure why they are better. But could I sit down in that house and make this equation we are offered? Not, you understand, that shame was stopping me; I've learned, thank you, how to behave. But talking to my family, to my friends, talking, as we were, about our own lives, about people, about feelings, could I in fact find this lack of quality we are discussing? I'll be honest – I looked; my training has done that for me. I can only say that I found as much natural fineness of feeling, as much quick discrimination, as much clear grasp of ideas within the range of experience as I have found anywhere. I don't altogether understand this, though I am not really surprised. Clearly there is something in the psychology of print and image that none of us has yet quite grasped. For the equation looks sensible, yet when you test it, in experience – and there's nowhere else you can test it – it's wrong. I can understand the protection of critical and intelligent reading: my father, for instance, a satisfied reader of the *Daily Herald*, got simply from reading the company reports a clear idea, based on names, of the rapid development of combine and interlocking ownership in British industry, which I had had made easy for me in two or three academic essays; and he had gone on to set these facts against the opinions in a number of articles in the paper on industrial ownership. That I understand; that is simply intelligence, however partly trained. But there is still this other surprising fact: that people whose quality of personal living is high are apparently satisfied by a low quality of printed feeling and opinion. Many of them still live, it is true, in a surprisingly enclosed personal world, much more so than mine, and some of their personal observations are the finer for it. Perhaps this is enough to explain it, but in any case, I submit, we need a new equation, to fit the observable facts.

Now the false analogy, that we must also reject. This is known, in discussions of culture, as a 'kind of Gresham's Law'. Just as bad money will drive out good, so bad culture will drive out good, and this, it is said, has in fact been happening. If you can't see, straight away, the defect of the analogy, your answer, equally effective, will have to be historical. For in fact, of course, it has not been happening. There is more, much more bad culture about; it is easier, now, to distribute it, and there is more leisure to receive it. But test this in any field you like, and see if this has been accompanied by a shrinking consumption of things we can all agree to be good. The editions of good literature are very much larger than they were; the listeners to good music are much more numerous than they were; the number of people who look at good visual art is larger than it has ever been. If bad newspapers drive out good newspapers, by a kind of Gresham's Law, why is it that, allowing for the rise in population, *The Times* sells nearly three times as many copies as in the days of its virtual monopoly of the press, in 1850? It is the law I am questioning, not the seriousness of the facts as a whole. Instead of a kind of Gresham's Law, keeping people awake at nights with the now orthodox putropian nightmare, let us put it another way, to fit the actual facts: we live in an expanding culture, and all the elements in this culture are themselves expanding. If we start from this, we can then ask real questions: about relative rates of expansion; about the social and economic problems raised by these; about the social and economic answers. I am working now on a book[2] to follow my *Culture and Society*, trying to interpret, historically and theoretically, the nature and conditions of an expanding culture of our kind. I could not have begun this work if I had not learned from the Marxists and from Leavis; I cannot complete it unless I radically amend some of the ideas which they and others have left us.   [. . .]

Notes

1 *Culture and Society* (1958).
2 *The Long Revolution* (1961).

2

The rhetoric of the image

Roland Barthes

French original, 'Rhetorique de l'image', *Communications* 1, 1964; English translation by Stephen Heath in R. Barthes: *Image/music/text* (Fontana, 1977).

According to an ancient etymology, the word *image* should be linked to the root *imitari*. Thus we find ourselves immediately at the heart of the most important problem facing the semiology of images: can analogical representation (the 'copy') produce true systems of signs and not merely simple agglutinations of symbols? Is it possible to conceive of an analogical 'code' (as opposed to a digital one)? We know that linguists refuse the status of language to all communication by analogy – from the 'language' of bees to the 'language' of gesture – the moment such communications are not doubly articulated, are not founded on a combinatory system of digital units as phonemes are. Nor are linguists the only ones to be suspicious as to the linguistic nature of the image; general opinion too has a vague conception of the image as an area of resistance to meaning – this is the name of a certain mythical idea of Life: the image is re-presentation, which is to say ultimately resurrection, and, as we know, the intelligible is reputed antipathetic to lived experience. Thus from both sides the image is felt to be weak in respect of meaning: there are those who think that the image is an extremely rudimentary system in comparison with language and those who think that signification cannot exhaust the image's ineffable richness. Now even – and above all if – the image is in a certain manner the *limit* of meaning, it permits the consideration of a veritable ontology of the process of signification. How does meaning get into the image? Where does it end? And if it ends, what is there *beyond*? Such are the questions that I wish to raise by submitting the image to a spectral analysis of the messages it may contain. We will start by making it considerably easier for ourselves: we will only study the advertising image. Why? Because in advertising the signification of the image is undoubtedly intentional; the signifieds of the advertising message are formed *a priori* by certain attributes of the product and these signifieds have to be transmitted as clearly as possible. If the image contains signs, we can be sure that in advertising these signs are full, formed with a view to the optimum reading: the advertising image is *frank*, or at least emphatic.

15

Figure 2.1   Panzani advertisement.

The three messages

Here we have a Panzani advertisement [Figure 2.1]: some packets of pasta, a tin, a sachet, some tomatoes, onions, peppers, a mushroom, all emerging from a half-open string-bag, in yellows and greens on a red background.[1] Let us try to 'skim off' the different messages it contains.

The image immediately yields a first message whose substance is linguistic; its supports are the caption, which is marginal, and the labels, these being inserted into the natural disposition of the scene, *'en abyme'*. The code from which this message has been taken is none other than that of the French language; the only knowledge required to dicipher it is a knowledge of writing and French. In fact, this message can itself be further broken down, for the sign *Panzani* gives not simply the name of the firm but also, by its assonance, an additional signified, that of 'Italianicity'. The linguistic message is thus twofold (at least in this particular image): denotational and connotational. Since, however, we have here only a single typical sign,[2] namely that of articulated (written) language, it will be counted as one message.

Putting aside the linguistic message, we are left with the pure image (even if the labels are part of it, anecdotally). This image straightaway provides a series of discontinuous signs. First (the order is unimportant as these signs are not linear), the idea that what we have in the scene represented is a return from the market. A signified which itself implies two euphoric values: that of the freshness of the products and that of the essentially domestic preparation for which they are destined. Its signifier is the half-open bag which lets the provisions spill out over the table, 'unpacked'. To read this first sign requires only a knowledge which is in some sort implanted as part of the habits of a very widespread culture where 'shopping around for oneself' is opposed to the hasty stocking up (preserves, refrigerators) of a more 'mechanical' civilization. A second sign is more or less equally evident; its signifier is the bringing together of the tomato, the pepper and the tricoloured hues (yellow, green, red) of the poster; its signified is Italy or rather *Italianicity*. This sign stands in a relation of redundancy with the connoted sign of the linguistic message (the Italian assonance of the name *Panzani*) and the knowledge it draws upon is already more particular; it is a specifically 'French' knowledge (an Italian would barely perceive the connotation of the name, no more probably than he would the Italianicity of tomato and pepper), based on a familiarity with certain tourist stereotypes. Continuing to explore the image (which is not to say that it is not entirely clear at the first glance), there is no difficulty in discovering at least two other signs: in the first, the serried collection of different objects transmits the idea of a total culinary service, on the one hand as though Panzani furnished everything necessary for a carefully balanced dish and on the other as though the concentrate in the tin were equivalent to the natural produce surrounding it; in the other sign, the composition of the image, evoking the memory of innumerable alimentary paintings, sends us to an aesthetic signified: the *'nature morte'* or, as it is better expressed in other languages, the 'still life'[3]; the knowledge on which this sign depends is heavily cultural. It might be suggested that, in addition to these four signs, there is a further information pointer, that which tells us that this is an advertisement and which arises both from the place of the image in the magazine and from the emphasis of the labels (not to mention the caption). This last information, however, is co-extensive with the scene; it eludes signification insofar as the advertising nature of the image is essentially functional: to utter something is not necessarily to declare *I am speaking*, except in a deliberately reflexive system such as literature.

Thus there are four signs for this image and we will assume that they form a coherent whole (for they are all discontinuous), require a generally cultural knowledge, and refer back to signifieds each of which is global (for example, *Italianicity*), imbued with euphoric values. After the linguistic message, then, we can see a second, iconic message. Is that the end? If all these signs are removed from the image, we are still left with a certain informational matter; deprived of all knowledge, I continue to 'read' the image, to 'understand' that it assembles in a common space a number of identifiable (nameable) objects, not merely shapes and colours. The signifieds of this third message are constituted by the real objects in the scene, the signifiers by these same objects photographed, for, given that the relation between thing signified and image signifying in analogical representation is not 'arbitrary' (as it is in language), it is no longer necessary to dose the relay with a third term in the guise of the psychic image of the object. What defines the third message is precisely that the relation between signified and signifier is quasi-tautological; no doubt the photograph involves a certain arrangement of the scene (framing, reduction, flattening) but this transition is not a *transformation* (in the way a coding can be); we have here a loss of the equivalence characteristic of true sign systems and a statement of quasi-identity. In other words, the sign of this message is not drawn from an institutional stock, is not coded, and we are brought up against the paradox (to which we will return) of a *message without a code*. This peculiarity can be seen again at the level of the knowledge invested in the reading of the message; in order to 'read' this last (or first) level of the image, all that is needed is the knowledge bound up with our perception. That knowledge is not nil, for we need to know what an image is (children only learn this at about the age of four) and what a tomato, a string-bag, a packet of pasta are, but it is a matter of an almost anthropological knowledge. This message corresponds, as it were, to the letter of the image and we can agree to call it the literal message, as opposed to the previous symbolic message.

If our reading is satisfactory, the photograph analysed offers us three messages: a linguistic message, a coded iconic message, and a non-coded iconic message. The linguistic message can be readily separated from the other two, but since the latter share the same (iconic) substance, to what extent have we the right to separate them? It is certain that the distinction between the two iconic messages is not made spontaneously in ordinary reading: the viewer of the image receives *at one and the same time* the perceptual message and the cultural message, and it will be seen later that this confusion in reading corresponds to the function of the mass image (our concern here). The distinction, however, has an operational validity, analogous to that which allows the distinction in the linguistic sign of a signifier and a signified (even though in reality no one is able to separate the 'word' from its meaning except by recourse to the metalanguage of a definition). If the distinction permits us to describe the structure of the image in a simple and coherent fashion and if this description paves the way for an explanation of the role of the image in society, we will take it to be justified. The task now is thus to reconsider each type of message so as to explore it in its generality, without losing sight of our aim of understanding the overall structure of the image, the final inter-relationship of the three messages. Given that what is in question is not a 'naive' analysis but a structural description,[4] the order of the messages will be modified a little by the inversion of the cultural message and the literal message; of the two iconic messages, the first is in some sort imprinted on the second: the literal message appears as the *support* of the 'symbolic' message. Hence, knowing that a system which takes over the signs of another system in order to make them its signifiers is a system of connotation,[5] we may say immediately that the literal image is *denoted* and the symbolic image *connoted*. Successively, then, we shall look at the linguistic message, the denoted image, and the connoted image.

The linguistic message

Is the linguistic message constant? Is there always textual matter in, under, or around the image? In order to find images given without words, it is doubtless necessary to go back to partially illiterate societies, to a sort of pictographic state of the image. From the moment of the appearance of the book, the linking of text and image is frequent, though it seems to have been little studied from a structural point of view. What is the signifying structure of 'illustration'? Does the image duplicate certain of the informations given in the text by a phenomenon of redundancy or does the text add a fresh information to the image? The problem could be posed historically as regards the classical period with its passion for books with pictures (it was inconceivable in the eighteenth century that editions of La Fontaine's *Fables* should not be illustrated) and its authors such as Menestrier who concerned themselves with the relations between figure and discourse.[6] Today, at the level of mass communications, it appears that the linguistic message is indeed present in every image: as title, caption, accompanying press article, film dialogue, comic strip balloon. Which shows that it is not very accurate to talk of a civilization of the image – we are still, and more than ever, a civilization of writing,[7] writing and speech continuing to be the full terms of the informational structure. In fact, it is simply the presence of the linguistic message that counts, for neither its position nor its length seem to be pertinent (a long text may only comprise a single global signified, thanks to connotation, and it is this signified which is put in relation with the image). What are the functions of the linguistic message with regard to the (twofold) iconic message? There appear to be two: *anchorage* and *relay*.

As will be seen more clearly in a moment, all images are polysemous; they imply, underlying their signifiers, a 'floating chain' of signifieds, the reader able to choose some and ignore others. Polysemy poses a question of meaning and this question always comes through as a dysfunction, even if this dysfunction is recuperated by society as a tragic (silent, God provides no possibility of choosing between signs) or a poetic (the panic 'shudder of meaning' of the Ancient Greeks) game; in the cinema itself, traumatic images are bound up with an uncertainty (an anxiety) concerning the meaning of objects or attitudes. Hence in every society various techniques are developed intended to *fix* the floating chain of signifieds in such a way as to counter the terror of uncertain signs; the linguistic message is one of these techniques. At the level of the literal message, the text replies – in a more or less direct, more or less partial manner – to the question: *what is it?* The text helps to identify purely and simply the elements of the scene and the scene itself; it is a matter of a denoted description of the image (a description which is often incomplete), or, in Hjelmslev's terminology, of an *operation* (as opposed to connotation).[8] The denominative function corresponds exactly to an *anchorage* of all the possible (denoted) meanings of the object by recourse to a nomenclature [. . .]. When it comes to the 'symbolic message', the linguistic message no longer guides identification but interpretation, constituting a kind of vice which holds the connoted meanings from proliferating, whether towards excessively individual regions (it limits, that is to say, the projective power of the image) or towards dysphoric values. An advertisement (for *d'Arcy* preserves) shows a few fruits scattered around a ladder; the caption (*'as if from your own garden'*) banishes one possible signified (parsimony, the paucity of the harvest) because of its unpleasantness and orientates the reading towards a more flattering signified (the natural and personal character of fruit from a private garden); it acts here as a counter-taboo, combating the disagreeable myth of the artificial usually associated with preserves. Of course, elsewhere than in advertising, the anchorage may be ideological and indeed this is its principal function; the text *directs* the reader through the signifieds of the image, causing him to avoid some and receive others; by means of an often subtle *dispatching*, it remote-controls him towards a meaning chosen in advance. In all these cases of anchorage, language clearly has a function of elucidation, but this elucidation is selective, a metalanguage applied not to the totality of the iconic message but only to certain of its signs. The text is indeed the creator's (and hence society's) right of inspection over the image; anchorage is a control, bearing a responsibility – in the face of the projective power of pictures – for the use of the message. With respect to the liberty of the signifieds of the image, the text has thus a *repressive* value' and we can see that it is at this level that the morality and ideology of a society are above all invested.

Anchorage is the most frequent function of the linguistic message and is commonly found in press photographs and advertisements. The function of relay is less common (at least as far as the fixed image is concerned); it can be seen particularly in cartoons and comic strips. Here text (most often a snatch of dialogue) and image stand in a complementary relationship; the words, in the same way as the images, are fragments of a more general syntagm and the unity of the message is realized at a higher level, that of the story, the anecdote, the diegesis (which is ample confirmation that the diegesis must be treated as an autonomous system).[10] While rare in the fixed image, this relay-text becomes very important in film, where dialogue functions not simply as elucidation but really does advance the action by setting out, in the sequence of messages, meanings that are not to be found in the image itself. Obviously, the two functions of the linguistic message can co-exist in the one iconic whole, but the dominance of the one or the other is of consequence for the general economy of a work. When the text has the diegetic value of relay, the information is more costly, requiring as it does the learning of a digital code (the system of language); when it has a substitute value (anchorage, control), it is the image which detains the informational charge and, the image being analogical, the information is then 'lazier': in certain comic strips intended for 'quick' reading the diegesis is confided above all to the text, the image gathering the attributive informations of a paradigmatic order (the stereotyped status of the characters); the costly message and the discursive message are made to coincide so that the hurried reader may be spared the boredom of verbal 'descriptions', which are entrusted to the image, that is to say to a less 'laborious' system.

The denoted image

We have seen that in the image, properly speaking, the distinction between the literal message and the symbolic message is operational; we never encounter (at least in advertising) a literal image in a pure state. Even if a totally 'naive' image were to be achieved, it would immediately join the sign of naivety and be completed by a third – symbolic – message. Thus the characteristics of the literal message cannot be substantial but only relational. It is first of all, so to speak, a message by eviction, constituted by what is left in the image when the signs of connotation are mentally deleted (it would not be possible actually to remove them for they can impregnate the whole of the image, as in the case of the 'still life composition'). This evictive state naturally corresponds to a plenitude of virtualities: it is an absence of meaning full of all the meanings. Then again (and there is no contradiction with what has just been said), it is a sufficient message, since it has at least one meaning at the level of the identification of the scene represented; the letter of the image corresponds in short to the first degree of intelligibility (below which the reader would perceive only lines, forms, and colours), but this intelligibility remains virtual by reason of its very poverty, for everyone from a real society always disposes of a knowledge superior to the merely anthropological and perceives more than just the letter. Since it is both evictive and sufficient, it will be understood that from an aesthetic point of view the denoted image can appear as a kind of Edenic state of the image; cleared utopianically of its connotations, the image would become radically objective, or, in the last analysis, innocent.

This utopian character of denotation is considerably reinforced by the paradox already mentioned, that the photograph (in its literal state), by virtue of its absolutely analogical nature, seems to constitute a message without a code. Here, however, structural analysis must differentiate, for of all the kinds of image only the photograph is able to transmit the (literal) information without forming it by means of discontinuous signs and rules of transformation. The photograph, message without a code, must thus be opposed to the drawing which, even when denoted, is a coded message. The coded nature of the drawing can be seen at three levels. Firstly, to reproduce an object or a scene in a drawing requires a set of *rule-governed* transpositions; there is no essential nature of the pictorial copy, and the codes of transposition are historical (notably those concerning perspective). Secondly, the operation of the drawing (the coding) immediately necessitates a certain division between the significant and the insignificant: the drawing does not reproduce *everything* (often it reproduces very little) without its ceasing, however, to be a strong message; whereas the photograph, although it can choose its subject, its point of view and its angle, cannot intervene *within* the object (except by trick effects). In other words, the denotation of the drawing is less pure than that of the photograph, for there is no drawing without style. Finally, like all codes, the drawing demands an apprenticeship (Saussure attributed a great importance to this semiological fact). Does the coding of the denoted message have consequences for the connoted message? It is certain that the coding of the literal prepares and facilitates connotation since it at once establishes a certain discontinuity in the image: the 'execution' of a drawing itself constitutes a connotation. But at the same time, insofar as the drawing displays its coding, the relationship between the two messages is profoundly modified: it is no longer the relationship between a nature and a culture (as with the photograph) but that between two cultures; the 'ethic' of the drawing is not the same as that of the photograph.

In the photograph – at least at the level of the literal message – the relationship of signifieds to signifiers is not one of 'transformation' but of 'recording', and the absence of a code clearly reinforces the myth of photographic 'naturalness': the scene *is there*, captured mechanically, not humanly (the mechanical is here a guarantee of objectivity). Man's interventions in the photograph (framing, distance, lighting, focus, speed) all effectively belong to the plane of connotation; it is as though in the beginning (even if utopian) there were a brute photograph (frontal and clear) on which man would then lay out, with the aid of various techniques, the signs drawn from a cultural code. Only the opposition of the cultural code and the natural non-code can, it seems, account for the specific character of the photograph and allow the assessment of the anthropological revolution it represents in man's history. The type of consciousness the photograph involves is indeed truly unprecedented, since it establishes not a consciousness of the *being-there* of the thing (which any copy could provoke) but an awareness of its *having-been-there*. What we have is a new space–time category: spatial immediacy and temporal anteriority, the photograph being an illogical conjunction between the *here-now* and the *there-then*. It is thus at the level of this denoted message or message without code that the *real unreality* of the photograph can be fully understood: its unreality is that of the *here-now*, for the photograph is never experienced as illusion, is in no way a *presence* (claims as to the magical character of the photographic image must be deflated); its reality that of the *having-been-there*, for in every photograph there is the always stupefying evidence of *this is how it was*, giving us, by a precious miracle, a reality from which we are sheltered. This kind of temporal equilibrium (*having-been-there*) probably diminishes the projective power of the image (very few psychological tests resort to photographs while many use drawings): the *this was so* easily defeats the *it's me*. If these remarks are at all correct, the photograph must be related to a pure spectatorial consciousness and not to the more projective, more 'magical' fictional consciousness on which film by and large depends. This would lend authority to the view that the distinction between film and photograph is not a simple difference of degree but a radical opposition. Film can no longer be seen as animated photographs: the *having-been-there* gives way before a *being-there* of the thing; which omission would explain how there can be a history of the cinema, without any real break with the previous arts of fiction, whereas the photograph can in some sense elude history (despite the evolution of the techniques and ambitions of the photographic art) and represent a 'flat' anthropological fact, at once absolutely new and definitively unsurpassable, humanity encountering for the first time in its history *messages without a code*. Hence, the photograph is not the last (improved) term of the great family of images; it corresponds to a decisive mutation of informational economies.

At all events, the denoted image, to the extent to which it does not imply any code (the case with the advertising photograph), plays a special role in the general structure of the iconic message which we can begin to define (returning to this question after discussion of the third message): the denoted image naturalizes the symbolic message, it innocents the semantic artifice of connotation, which is extremely dense, especially in advertising. Although the *Panzani* poster is full of 'symbols', there nonetheless remains in the photograph, insofar as the literal message is sufficient, a kind of natural *being-there* of objects: nature seems spontaneously to produce the scene represented. A pseudo-truth is surreptitiously substituted for the simple validity of openly semantic systems; the absence of code disintellectualizes the message because it seems to found in nature the signs of culture. This is without doubt an important historical paradox: the more technology develops the diffusion of information (and notably of images), the more it provides the means of masking the constructed meaning under the appearance of the given meaning.

Rhetoric of the image

It was seen that the signs of the third message (the 'symbolic' message, cultural or connoted) were discontinuous. Even when the signifier seems to extend over the whole image, it is nonetheless a sign separated from the others: the 'composition' carries an aesthetic signified, in much the same way as intonation although suprasegmental is a separate signifier in language. Thus we are here dealing with a normal system whose signs are drawn from a cultural code (even if the linking together of the elements of the sign appears more or less analogical). What gives this system its originality is that the number of readings of the same lexical unit or *lexia* (of the same image) varies according to individuals. In the *Panzani* advertisement analysed, four connotative signs have been identified; probably there are others (the net bag, for example, can signify the miraculous draught of fishes, plenty, etc.). The variation in readings is not, however, anarchic; it depends on the different kinds of knowledge – practical, national, cultural, aesthetic – invested in the image and these can be classified, brought into a typology. It is as though the image presented itself to the reading of several different people who can perfectly well co-exist in a single individual: *the one lexia mobilizes different lexicons*. What is a lexicon? A portion of the symbolic plane (of language) which corresponds to a body of practices and techniques.[11] This is the case for the different readings of the image: each sign corresponds to a body of 'attitudes' – tourism, housekeeping, knowledge of art – certain of which may obviously be lacking in this or that individual. There is a plurality and a co-existence of lexicons in one and the same person, the number and identity of these lexicons forming in some sort a person's *idiolect*.[12] The image, in its connotation, is thus constituted by an architecture of signs drawn from a variable depth of lexicons (of idiolects); each lexicon, no matter how 'deep', still being coded, if, as is thought today, the *psyche* itself is articulated like a language; indeed, the further one 'descends' into the psychic depths of an individual, the more rarified and the more classifiable the signs become – what could be more systematic than the readings of Rorschach tests? The variability of readings, therefore, is no threat to the 'language' of the image if it be admitted that that language is composed of idiolects, lexicons and subcodes. The image is penetrated through and through by the system of meaning, in exactly the same way as man is articulated to the very depths of his being in distinct languages. The language of the image is not merely the totality of utterances emitted (for example at the level of the combiner of the signs or creator of the message), it is also the totality of utterances received:[13] the language must include the 'surprises' of meaning.

Another difficulty in analysing connotation is that there is no particular analytical language corresponding to the particularity of its signifieds – how are the signifieds of connotation to be named? For one of them we ventured the term *Italianicity*, but the others can only be designated by words from ordinary language (*culinary preparation, still life, plenty*); the metalanguage which has to take charge of them at the moment of the analysis is not specialized. This is a difficulty, for these signifieds have a particular semantic nature; as a seme of connotation, 'plenty' does not exactly cover 'plenty' in the denoted sense; the signifier of connotations (here the profusion and the condensation of the produce) is like the essential cipher of all possible plenties, of the purest idea of plenty. The denoted word never refers to an essence for it is always caught up in a contingent utterance, a continuous syntagm (that of verbal discourse), oriented towards a certain practical transitivity of language; the seme 'plenty', on the contrary, is a concept in a pure state, cut off from any syntagm, deprived of any context and corresponding to a sort of theatrical state of meaning, or, better (since it is a question of a sign without a syntagm), to an *exposed* meaning. To express these semes of connotation would therefore require a special metalanguage and we are left with barbarisms of the *Italianicity* kind as best being able to account for the signifieds of connotation, the suffix *-icity* deriving an abstract noun from the adjective: *Italianicity* is not Italy, it is the condensed essence of everything that could be Italian, from spaghetti to painting. By accepting to regulate artificially – and if needs be barbarously – the naming of the semes of connotation, the analysis of their form will be rendered easier.[14] These semes are organized in associative fields, in paradigmatic articulations, even perhaps in oppositions, according to certain defined paths or, as A.J. Greimas puts it, according to certain semic axes.[15] *Italianicity* belongs to a certain axis of nationalities, alongside Frenchicity, Germanicity or Spanishicity. The reconstitution of such axes – which may eventually be in opposition to one another – will clearly only be possible once a massive inventory of the systems of connotation has been carried out, an inventory not merely of the connotative system of the image but also of those of other substances, for if connotation has typical signifiers dependent on the different substances utilized (image, language, objects, modes of behaviour) it holds all its signifieds in common: the same signifieds are to be found in the written press, the image or the actor's gestures (which is why semiology can only be conceived in a so to speak total framework). This common domain of the signifieds of connotation is that of *ideology*, which cannot but be single for a given society and history, no matter what signifiers of connotation it may use.

To the general ideology, that is, correspond signifiers of connotation which are specified according to the chosen substance. These signifiers will be called *connotators* and the set of connotators a *rhetoric*, rhetoric thus appearing as the signifying aspect of ideology. Rhetorics inevitably vary by their substance (here articulated sound, there image, gesture or whatever) but not necessarily by their form; it is even probable that there exists a single rhetorical *form*, common for instance to dream, literature and image.[16] Thus the rhetoric of the image (that is to say, the classification of its connotators) is specific to the extent that it is subject to the physical constraints of vision (different, for example, from phonatory constraints) but general to the extent that the 'figures' are never more than formal relations of elements. This rhetoric could only be established on the basis of a quite considerable inventory, but it is possible now to foresee that one will find it in some of the figures formerly identified by the Ancients and the Classics;[17] the tomato, for example, signifies *Italianicity* by metonymy and in another advertisement the sequence of three scenes (coffee in beans, coffee in powder, coffee sipped in the cup) releases a certain logical relationship in the same way as an asyndeton. It is probable indeed that among the metabolas (or figures of the substitution of one signifier for another),[18] it is metonymy which furnishes the image with the greatest number of its connotators, and that among the parataxes (or syntagmatic figures), it is asyndeton which predominates.

The most important thing, however, at least for the moment, is not to inventorize the connotators but to understand that in the total image they constitute *discontinuous* or better still *scattered traits*. The connotators do not fill the whole of the lexia, reading them does not exhaust it. In other words (and this would be a valid proposition for semiology in general), not all the elements of the lexia can be transformed into connotators; there always remaining in the discourse a certain denotation without which, precisely, the discourse would not be possible. Which brings us back to the second message or denoted image. In the *Panzani* advertisement, the Mediterranean vegetables, the colour, the composition, the very profusion rise up as so many scattered blocks, at once isolated and mounted in a general scene which has its own space and, as was seen, its 'meaning': they are 'set' in a syntagm *which is not theirs and which is that of the denotation*. This last proposition is important for it permits us to found (retroactively) the structural distinction between the second or literal message and the third or symbolic message and to give a more exact description of the naturalizing function of the denotation with respect to the connotation. We can now understand that *it is precisely the syntagm of the denoted message which 'naturalizes' the system of the connoted message*. Or again: connotation is only system, can only be defined in paradigmatic terms; iconic denotation is only syntagm, associates elements without any system: the discontinuous connotators are connected, actualized, 'spoken' through the syntagm of the denotation, the discontinuous world of symbols plunges into the story of the denoted scene as though into a lustral bath of innocence.

It can thus be seen that in the total system of the image the structural functions are polarized: on the one hand there is a sort of paradigmatic condensation at the level of the connotators (that is, broadly speaking, of the symbols), which are strong signs, scattered, 'reified'; on the other a syntagmatic 'flow' at the level of the denotation – it will not be forgotten that the syntagm is always very close to speech, and it is indeed the iconic 'discourse' which naturalizes its symbols. Without wishing to infer too quickly from the image to semiology in general, one can nevertheless venture that the world of total meaning is torn internally (structurally) between the system as culture and the syntagm as nature: the works of mass communications all combine, through diverse and diversely successful dialectics, the fascination of a nature, that of story, diegesis, syntagm, and the intelligibility of a culture, withdrawn into a few discontinuous symbols which men 'decline' in the shelter of their living speech.

Notes

1 The *description* of the photograph is given here with prudence, for it already constitutes a metalanguage. The reader is asked to refer to the reproduction.
2 By *typical sign* is meant the sign of a system insofar as it is adequately defined by its substance: the verbal sign, the iconic sign, the gestural sign are so many typical signs.
3 In French, the expression *nature morte* refers to the original presence of funereal objects, such as a skull, in certain pictures.
4 'Naive' analysis is an enumeration of elements; structural description aims to grasp the relation of these elements by virtue of the principle of the solidarity holding between the terms of a structure: if one term changes, so also do the others.
5 Cf. Barthes, R. 1964: Eléments de sémiologie. *Communications* 4, 130 (trans. Elements of semiology, London 1967 and New York 1968, 89–92).
6 Menestrier, 1684: *L'Art des emblèmes*.
7 Images without words can certainly be found in certain cartoons, but by way of a paradox; the absence of words always covers an enigmatic intention.
8 Barthes, R. 1964: Eléments de sémiologie, 131–2 (trans., 90–4).
9 This can be seen clearly in the paradoxical case where the image is constructed according to the text and where, consequently, the control would seem to be needless. An advertisement which wants to communicate that in such and such a coffee the aroma is 'locked in' the product in powder form and that it will thus be wholly there when the coffee is used depicts above this proposition a tin of coffee with a chain and padlock round it. Here, the linguistic metaphor ('locked in') is taken literally (a well-known poetic device); in fact, however, it is the image which is read first and the text from which the image is constructed becomes in the end the simple choice of one signified among others. The repression is present again in the circular movement as a banalization of the message.
10 Cf. Bremond, C. 1964: 'Le message narratif'. *Communications* 4.
11 Cf. Greimas, A.J. 1959: Les problèmes de la description mécanographique. *Cahiers de Lexicologie* 1, 63.
12 Cf. Barthes, R. 1964: Eléments de sémiologie, p. 96 (trans., 21–2).
13 In the Saussurian perspective, speech (utterances) is above all that which is emitted, drawn from the language-system (and constituting it in return). It is necessary today to enlarge the notion of language (*langue*), especially from the semantic point of view: language is the 'totalizing abstraction' of the messages emitted *and received*.
14 *Form* in the precise sense given it by Hjelmslev (cf. Barthes, R. 1964: Eléments de sémiologie, p. 105 [trans., 39–41]), as the functional organization of the signifieds among themselves.[']
15 Greimas, A.J. 1964: Cours de Sémantique. Notes roneotyped by the Ecole Normale Supérieure de Saint-Cloud.
16 Cf. Benveniste, E. 1956: Remarques sur la fonction du langage dans la découverte freudienne. *La psychanalyse* 1, 3–16 (reprinted in 1966: *Problèmes de linguistique générale*. Paris, Chapter 7; translated in 1971: *Problems of general linguistics*. Coral Gables, FL).

17 Classical rhetoric needs to be rethought in structural terms (this is the object of a work in progress); it will then perhaps be possible to establish a general rhetoric or linguistics of the signifiers of connotation, valid for articulated sound, image, gesture, etc. See L'ancienne rhétorique (Aide-mémoire). *Communications* **16**, 1970.

18 We prefer here to evade Jakobson's opposition between metaphor and metonymy for if metonymy by its origin is a figure of contiguity, it nevertheless functions finally as a substitute of the signifier, that is, as a metaphor.

3

The television discourse – encoding and decoding

Stuart Hall

From *Education and Culture*, no. 25 (UNESCO, 1974).

The 'object' of production practices and structures in television is the production of a *message*: that is, a sign-vehicle, or rather sign-vehicles of a specific kind, organized, like any other form of communication or language, through the operation of codes, within the syntagmatic chains of a discourse. The apparatus and structures of production issue, at a certain moment, in the form of a symbolic vehicle constituted within the rules of 'language'. It is in this 'phenomenal form' that the circulation of the 'product' takes place. Of course, the transmission of this symbolic vehicle also requires its material substratum – videotape, film, the transmitting and receiving apparatus, etc. But it is primarily in this symbolic form that the reception of the 'product', and its distribution between different segments of the audience, takes place. Once accomplished, the translation of that message into societal structures must be made again for the communication circuit to be completed. Thus, whilst in no way wanting to limit research to 'following only those leads which emerge from content analyses',[1] we must recognize that the symbolic form of the message has a privileged position in the communicative exchange: and that the moments of 'encoding' and 'decoding', though only 'relatively autonomous' in relation to the communicative process as a whole, are *determinate* moments. The raw historical event cannot in that form be transmitted by, say, a television newscast. It can only be signified within the aural–visual form of a televisual language. In the moment when the historical event passes under the sign of language, it is subject to all the complex formal 'rules' by which language signifies. To put it paradoxically, the event must become a 'story' before it can become a *communicative event*. In that moment of 'encoding', the formal sub-rules of language are 'in dominance', without, of course, subordinating out of existence the historical event so signified, or the historical consequences of the event having been signified in this way. The 'message-form' is the necessary form of the appearance of the event in its passage from source to receiver. Thus, the transposition into and out of the 'message-form' or the meaning-dimension (or mode of exchange of the message) is not a random 'moment', which we can take up or ignore for the sake of convenience or simplicity. The 'message-form' is a determinate moment, though, at another level, it comprises the surface-movements of the communications system only, and requires, at another stage of the analysis, to be integrated into the essential relations of communication of which it forms only a part.

From this general perspective, we may crudely characterize the communicative exchange as follows. The broadcasting organizations, with their institutional structures and networks of production, their organized routines and technical infrastructures, are required to produce the programme. Production, here, initiates the message. Production and reception of the television message are not identical, but they are related: they are differentiated moments within the totality formed by the communicative process as a whole.

Though we know the television programme is not a behavioural input, like a tap on the knee-cap, it seems to have been almost impossible for researchers to conceptualize the communicative process without lapsing back into one or other variant of low-flying behaviourism. Yet, by now, it should have been firmly established, as Gerbner has remarked, that representations of violence on the TV screen 'are not violence but messages about violence'.[2]

Take, for example, the simple-structure, early (and now children's) TV Western, modelled on the early Hollywood B-feature genre Western; with its clear-cut, good/bad Manichean moral universe, its clear social and moral designation of villain and hero, the clarity of its narrative line and development, its iconographical features, its clearly-registered climax in the violent shoot-out, chase, personal show-down, street or bar-room duel, etc. For long, on both British and American TV, this form constituted the predominant drama-entertainment genre. In quantitative terms, such films/programmes contained a high ratio of violent incidents, deaths, woundings, etc. Whole gangs of men, whole troops of Indians, went down nightly to their deaths. Researchers – Himmelweit among others – have, however, suggested that the structure of the early TV/B-feature Western was so clear-cut, its action so conventionalized, stylized, that most children (boys rather earlier than girls, an interesting finding in itself) soon learned to recognize and 'read' it like a 'game': a 'cowboys-and-Injuns' game. It was therefore further hypothesized that Westerns with this clarified structure were less likely to trigger the aggressive imitation of violent behaviour or other types of aggressive 'acting-out' than other types of programmes with a high violence ratio which were not stylized. But it is worth asking what this recognition of the Western as a 'symbolic game' means or implies: how does this transform our research conceptualizations and perspectives?

Conventionalizing the Western means that a set of extremely tightly-coded 'rules' exist whereby stories of a certain recognizable type, content and structure can be easily encoded within the Western form. What is more, these 'rules of encoding' were so diffused, so symmetrically shared as between producer and audience, that the 'message' was likely to be decoded in a manner highly symmetrical to that in which it had been encoded. This reciprocity of codes is, indeed, precisely what is entailed in the notion of stylization or 'conventionalization', and the persistence of such reciprocal codes over time is, of course, what defines or makes possible the existence of a *genre*. Such an account, then, takes the encoding/decoding moments properly into account, and the case appears an unproblematic one.

The violent element or string in the narrative structure of the simple-structure Western – shoot-out, brawl, ambush, bank-raid, fist-fight, wounding, duel or massacre – like any other semantic unit in a structured discourse, cannot signify anything on its own. It can only signify in terms of the structured meanings of the message as a whole. Further, its signification depends on its relation – or the sum of the relations of similarity and difference – with other elements or units. Burgelin³ has long ago, and definitively, reminded us that the violent or wicked acts of a villain only mean something in relation to the presence/absence of good acts.

We must now add that the meaning of the violent act or episode cannot be fixed, single and unalterable, but must be capable of signifying different values depending on how and with what it is articulated. As the signifying element, among other elements, in a discourse, it remains *polysemic*. Indeed, the way it is structured in its combination with other elements serves to delimit its meanings within that specified field, and effects a 'closure', so that a *preferred meaning* or reading is suggested. There can never be only one single, univocal and determined meaning for such a lexical item; but, depending on how its integration within the code has been accomplished, its possible meanings will be organized within a scale which runs from *dominant* to *subordinate*. And this, of course, has consequences for the other – the reception – end of the communicative chain: there can be no law to ensure that the receiver will take the preferred or dominant meaning of an episode of violence in precisely the way in which it has been encoded by the producer.

The presence of the code has the effect of displacing the meaning of single episodes from one category to another. Thus, within the structure of the programme as a whole, the violent episode may contain a message or make a proposition, not about violence but about conduct, or even about professionalism, nor perhaps even about the relation of professionalism to character. And here we recall Robert Warshow's intuitive observation that, fundamentally, the Western is not 'about' violence but about codes of conduct . . .

Thus, drawing attention to the symbolic/linguistic/coded nature of communications, far from boxing us into the closed and formal universe of signs, precisely opens out into the area where cultural content, of the most resonant but 'latent' kind, is transmitted: and especially the manner in which the interplay of codes and content serves to *displace* meanings from one frame to another, and thus to bring to the surface in 'disguised' forms, the repressed contents of a culture.

Let us turn now to a different area of programming, and a different aspect of the operation of codes. The televisual sign is a peculiarly complex one, as we know. It is a visual sign with strong, supplementary aural–verbal support. It is one of the iconic signs, in Peirce's sense.

As Eco has convincingly argued, iconic signs 'look like objects in the real world', to put it crudely (e.g. the photograph or drawing of a /cow/, and the animal /cow/), because they 'reproduce the conditions of perception in the receiver'.⁴ These conditions of 'recognition' in the viewer constitute some of the most fundamental perceptual codes which all culture-members share. Now, because these perceptual codes are so widely distributed, denotative visual signs probably give rise to less 'misunderstandings' than linguistic ones. A lexical inventory of the English language would throw up thousands of words which the ordinary speaker could not denotatively comprehend: but provided enough 'information' is given, culture-members would be able or be competent to decode, denotatively, a much wider range of visual signifiers. In this sense, and at the denotative level, the visual sign is probably a more universal one than the linguistic sign. Similarly, whereas, in societies like ours, linguistic competence is very unequally distributed as between different classes and segments of the population (predominantly, by the family and the education system), what we might call 'visual competence', at the denotative level, is more universally diffused. (It is worth reminding ourselves, of course, that it is not, in fact, 'universal', and that we are dealing with a spectrum: there are kinds of visual representation, short of the 'purely abstract', which create all kinds of visual puzzles for ordinary viewers: e.g. cartoons, certain kinds of diagrammatic representation, representations which employ unfamiliar conventions, types of photographic or cinematic cutting and editing, etc.) It is also true that the iconic sign may support 'misreadings' simply because it is so 'natural', so 'transparent'. Mistakes may arise here, not because we as viewers cannot literally decode the sign (it is perfectly obvious what it is a picture of), but because we are tempted, by its very 'naturalization', to 'misread' the image for the thing it signifies. With this important proviso, however, we would be surprised to find that the majority of the television audience had much difficulty in literally or denotatively identifying what the visual signs they see on the screen refer to or signify. Whereas most people require a lengthy process of education in order to become relatively competent users of the language of their speech community, they seem to pick up its visual-perceptual codes at a very early age, without formal training, and are quickly competent in its use.

The visual sign is, however, also a *connotative sign*. And it is so pre-eminently within the discourses of modern mass communication. The level of connotation of the visual sign, of its contextual reference, of its position in the various associative fields of meanings, is precisely the point where the denoted sign intersects with the deep semantic structures of a culture, and takes on an ideological dimension. In the advertising discourse, for example, we might say that there is almost no 'purely denotative' communication. Every visual sign in advertising 'connotes' a quality, situation, value or inference which is present as an implication or implied meaning, depending on the connotational reference. We are all probably familiar with Barthes's example of the 'sweater', which, in the rhetoric of advertising and fashion, always connotes, at least, 'a warm garment' or 'keeping warm', and thus by further connotative elaboration, 'the coming of winter' or 'a cold day'. In the specialized sub-codes of fashion, 'sweater' may connote 'a fashionable style of *haute-couture*', or, alternatively, 'an informal style of dress'. But, set against the right background, and positioned in the romantic sub-code, it may connote a 'long autumn walk in the woods'.[5] Connotational codes of this order are, clearly, structured enough to signify, but they are more 'open' or 'open-ended' than denotative codes. What is more, they clearly contract relations with the universe of ideologies in a culture, and with history and ethnography. These connotative codes are the 'linguistic' means by which the domains of social life, the segmentations of culture, power and ideology are made to signify. They refer to the 'maps of meaning' into which any culture is organized, and those 'maps of social reality' have the whole range of social meanings, practices and usages, power and interest 'written in' to them.

Literal or denotative 'errors' are relatively unproblematic. They represent a kind of noise in the channel. But 'misreadings' of a message at the connotative or contextual level are a different matter. They have, fundamentally, a societal, not a communicative, basis. They signify, at the 'message' level, the structural conflicts, contradictions and negotiations of economic, political and cultural life. The first position we want to identify is that of the *dominant or hegemonic code*. (There are, of course, many different codes and sub-codes required to produce an event within the dominant code.) When the viewer takes the connoted meaning from, say, a television newscast or current affairs programme, full and straight, and decodes the message in terms of the reference-code in which it has been coded, we might say that the viewer is operating inside the dominant code. This is the ideal-typical case of 'perfectly transparent communication', or as close as we are likely to come to it 'for all practical purposes'.

Next (here we are amplifying Parkin's model), we would want to identify the *professional code*. The professional code is 'relatively independent' of the dominant code, in that it applies criteria and operations of its own, especially those of a technico-practical nature. The professional code, however, operates within the 'hegemony' of the dominant code. The hegemonic interpretations of the politics of Northern Ireland, or the Chilean coup or the Industrial Relations Bill are given by political elites: the particular choice of presentational occasions and formats, the selection of personnel, the choice of images, the 'staging' of debates, etc. are selected by the operation of the professional code.[6] How the broadcasting professionals are able to operate with 'relatively autonomous' codes of their own, while acting in such a way as to reproduce (not without contradiction) the hegemonic signification of events, is a complex matter which cannot be further spelled out here. It must suffice to say that the professionals are linked with the defining elites not only by the institutional position of broadcasting itself as an 'ideological apparatus',[7] but more intimately by the structure of *access* (i.e., the systematic 'over-accessing' of elite personnel and 'definitions of the situation' in television). It may even be said that the professional codes serve to reproduce hegemonic definitions specifically by not overtly biasing their operations in their direction: ideological reproduction therefore takes place here inadvertently, unconsciously, 'behind men's backs'. Of course, conflicts, contradictions and even 'misunderstandings' regularly take place between the dominant and the professional significations and their signifying agencies.

The third position we would identify is that of the *negotiated code*. Majority audiences probably understand quite adequately what has been dominantly defined and professionally signified. The dominant definitions, however, are hegemonic precisely because they represent definitions of situations and events which are 'in dominance' and which are *global*. Dominant definitions connect events, implicitly or explicitly, to grand totalizations, to the great syntagmatic views-of-the-world: they take 'large views' of issues: they relate events to 'the national interest' or to the level of geopolitics, even if they make these connections in truncated, inverted or mystified ways. The definition of a 'hegemonic' viewpoint is (a) that it defines within its terms the mental horizon, the universe of possible meanings of a whole society or culture; and (b) that it carries with it the stamp of legitimacy – it appears coterminous with what is 'natural', 'inevitable', 'taken for granted' about the social order. Decoding within the *negotiated version* contains a mixture of adaptive and oppositional elements: it acknowledges the legitimacy of the hegemonic definitions to make the grand significations, while, at a more restricted, situational level, it makes its own ground-rules, it operates with 'exceptions' to the rule. It accords the privileged position to the dominant definition of events, whilst reserving the right to make a more negotiated application to 'local conditions', to its own more *corporate* situation. This negotiated version of the dominant ideology is thus shot through with contradictions, though these are only on certain occasions brought to full visibility. Negotiated codes operate through what we might call particular or situated logics: and these logics arise from the differential position of those who occupy this position in the spectrum, and from their differential and unequal relation to power.

The simplest example of a negotiated code is that which governs the response of a worker to the notion of an industrial relations bill limiting the right to strike, or to arguments for a wages freeze. At the level of the national-interest economic debate, he may adopt the hegemonic definition, agreeing that 'we must all pay ourselves less in order to combat inflation', etc. This, however, may have little or no relation to his willingness to go on strike for better pay and conditions, or to oppose the industrial relations bill at the level of his shop-floor or union organization. We suspect that the great majority of so-called 'misunderstandings' arise from the disjunctures between hegemonic-dominant encodings and negotiated-corporate de-codings. It is just these mismatches in the levels which most provoke defining elites and professionals to identify a 'failure in communications'. Finally, it is possible for a viewer perfectly to understand both the literal and connotative inflection given to an event, but to determine to decode the message in a globally contrary way. He detotalizes the message in the preferred code in order to retotalize the message within some alternative framework of reference. This is the case of the viewer who listens to a debate on the need to limit wages, but who 'reads' every mention of 'the national interest' as 'class interest'. He is operating with what we must call an *oppositional code*. One of the most significant political moments (they also coincide with crisis-points within the broadcasting organizations themselves for obvious reasons) is the point when events which are normally signified and decoded in a negotiated way begin to be given an oppositional reading.

The question of cultural policies now falls, awkwardly, into place. When dealing with social communications, it is extremely difficult to identify as a neutral, educational goal, the task of 'improving communications' or of 'making communications more effective', at any rate once one has passed beyond the strictly denotative level of the message. The educator or cultural policy-maker is performing one of his most partisan acts when he colludes with the resignification of real conflicts and contradictions as if they were simply kinks in the communicative chain. Denotative mistakes are not structurally significant. But connotative and contextual 'misunderstandings' are, or can be, of the highest structural significance. To interpret what are in fact essential elements in the systematic distortions of a socio-communications system as if they were merely technical faults in transmission is to misread a deep-structure process for a surface phenomenon. The decision to intervene in order to make the hegemonic codes of dominant elites more effective and transparent for the majority audience is not a technically neutral but a political one. To 'misread' a political choice as a technical one represents a type of unconscious collusion with the dominant interests, a form of 'technological rationality' to which social science researchers are all too prone. Though the sources of such mystification are both social and structural, the actual process is greatly facilitated by the operation of discrepant codes. It would not be the first time that scientific researchers had 'unconsciously' played a part in the reproduction of hegemony, not by openly submitting to it, but simply by operating the 'professional bracket'.

Notes

1 Halloran, 1975: Understanding television. *Screen Education* no. 14 (Spring).
2 Gerbner, 1970: Violence in TV drama: a study of trends and symbolic functions. Annenberg School, University of Pennsylvania.
3 Burgelin, O. 1968: 'Structural analysis and mass communications'. *Studies in broadcasting* no. 6. Nippon Hoso Kyokai.
4 Eco, U. 1965: Towards a semiotic inquiry into the television message, *Working papers in cultural studies* 3, Birmingham Centre for Contemporary Cultural Studies.
5 Barthes, R. 1971: Rhetoric of the image. In *Working papers in cultural studies* 1, Birmingham Centre for Contemporary Cultural Studies, University of Birmingham. [Editors' note: a longer version of Barthes' article which is indicated in this reader.]
6 Cf. Hall, S. 1972: External/internal dialectic in broadcasting. In *Fourth Symposium on Broadcasting*, Department of extra-mural studies, University of Manchester.
7 Cf. Althusser, L. 1971: Ideological stage apparatuses. In *Lenin and philosophy, and other essays*. New Left Books.

4

Soap opera and women

Richard Dyer, Terry Lovell and Jean McCrindle

From *Edinburgh International Television Festival 1977 – Official Programme* (Broadcast, 1977).

[. . .] We are not yet in a situation where all criticism assumes that the world of women is as important as the world of men, leave alone that the separation of the two worlds ought to be broken down; and until we are, polemical papers specifically about women and largely written by them have to be produced.

Why then turn to soap opera? We did begin to analyse the marginality or absence or distortion of women in high drama and this is still something that needs to be done. But we decided instead to look closely at the only form of television drama that has been traditionally defined as drama for women and about women and watched by women. As a major output on television, particularly commercial television (and the link with advertising and women as consumers is obvious), how does it define the experience that it offers to its female audience and what are the limits and possibilities of this kind of dramatic form from the point of view of a critical feminism? We are trying to analyse the ways in which representations of women in soap opera reproduce and reinforce the subordination of women in contemporary society and to explore possible strategies for women directors and writers struggling in their work against the prevailing sexism of the media.

'Coronation Street', which is the soap opera we have done most work on up to date, has become Granada's nostalgic look back to the 1950s before affluence and consumerist ethics corrupted working-class values of togetherness and community (Hilda Ogden is always being laughed at for her attempts to keep up to date with her interior decorating and getting the names of the trends wrong – 'my murial'). Middle-class television directors, script writers and producers clearly find it much easier to identify with a supposedly more sympathetic working class than they can find around on the contemporary scene. This nostalgia for the past also affects the American series 'The Waltons', which, unlike 'Coronation Street', is trying to recreate not a working-class street, but a rural extended family living also before the days of affluence, in fact in the depression, and expressing strong family ideology to the point of throat-hurting efficacy. Granny looks like the picture on the oatcakes packet; mom is lovely, gentle, morally supportive, still loves dad and runs the large farm kitchen where the most important ritual of family life takes place – the evening meal. Dad works hard at his own business, helped by grandad, loves mom, calms her down if she gets upset by the children, is tolerant, wise and prepared to learn from the insufferable John Boy when American ideals of honesty and integrity are being undermined by unscrupulous politicians, etc., etc. It has the same nauseating message each week and yet each week this utopia exercises its charm over children and women and probably even some men. We are still trying to understand why and we deal with this aspect later in the paper.

Obviously very different representations of women are being shown if a comparison is made between 'Coronation Street' and 'The Waltons'. The first obvious fact about the women in 'Coronation Street' is how many of them are strong, independent women from whom much of the action is generated – Ena Sharples, Elsie, Bet, Rita, Annie Walker – only one of them has found a man to stay around and producer Bill Podmore says he is worried because marriage so easily diminishes characters in a serial.

But these women not only dominate much of the narrative, they also do not live in nuclear families and rarely have children living with them – hence a whole era that 'The Waltons' depends on for narrative momentum is missing on 'Coronation Street' since these are women without children. Presumably this is partly the problem of employing child actors over such long numbers of years and the family consequently has always to be the grown up family as in 'Crossroads' where they run the motel and garage, or else small babies can be occasionally shown as they are always just about to go off to bed!

The other effect of the absence of children is that almost all the women in soap operas work outside the home; they work in service jobs – cleaning, typing, shop-keeping, waitressing, running the pub, motel, boutique, office. In fact work in these fictional worlds is not large-scale factory production where the sexual division of labour has condemned women to the most trivial, monotonous, unskilled, degraded, low-paid jobs – work for the scriptwriters of soap operas is petty bourgeois jobs for men and women alike with all the values that go with self-made, self-employed, hard-working, individualized workers. Mike Baldwin's machinists are made to look like selfish, grasping, parochial, demanding wage workers in comparison with his concern with 'the national interest' (in this case simply that he has another factory down South that he has to worry about). The Ogdens are the epitome of the feckless working class and the message about work that comes through is that it is your fault for being lazy and inadequate if you end up like Stan. Hence, the men and women of 'Coronation Street' are much more identified with their work than can be true for the majority of the audience who watch and this echoes the nostalgia of the programme for the days of a supposedly more humane and less alienating work ethic.

This is not to say that class difference is absent from 'Coronation Street' – Annie Walker talks posh, Hilda always has her hair in curlers, Ken Barlow wears middle-class clothes – but these differences are a source of humour and are easily transcended by the community as they are in 'The Archers' on radio – it's as if 'Coronation Street' were a village in an urban setting.

We are still trying to work out what the implications of these images are for us as feminists and our theory still needs to be integrated into our empirical observations.

Our theoretical orientation is difficult to characterize, as we did not begin with any strongly partisan position in relation to contemporary debates. Our position has evolved in the course of our work and is still so doing. We shared the assumption that the general frame of reference which had most to offer was Marxism, especially the Marxist concept of ideology. We read and discussed recent developments in that area associated with the work of Louis Althusser and his followers, and we looked at the attempts to apply Althusserian and psychoanalytic concepts and theories to film. While recognizing that this work is still in its infancy and may yet produce a satisfactory approach to film, we yet found this work confused and confusing and at such a high level of abstraction as to be of little immediate relevance to our problems. In particular we could not accept the unremitting hostility of this approach to all forms of realism. This anti-realism too easily slides over into hostility to all or most popular forms and conventions. We wanted to study soap opera precisely because it *is* popular, it *is* for and about women, it *is not* prestigious and we wanted to discover why it gives pleasure to millions of people and to relate that to its ideological effects.

Our interest in soap opera and what it could become does not mean that we do not find it at present largely contemptible. Although it is for and about women it is dominated at the point of production by men and it gives us male definitions of women and how they relate to each other and to men. And in relation to the fundamental areas of reproduction (family) and production (work) soap opera's representations of women have to be uncompromisingly attacked. And yet it does have strengths and possibilities, as the Susi Hush episodes of 'Coronation Street' demonstrate. By its very nature it does have to validate positively what women are and achieve in the sphere of the world to which they are confined – that is, soap opera validates *relationships*; it is *not* about social structures, material realists, physical strength, dramas of career or struggles for power.

In looking at the ways in which representations of women are conceived within soap opera and the fictional limits of these representations we are conscious of the difficulty of ascertaining exactly how the audience 'reads' the ideology that emerges. We are certainly not suggesting a simple identification or distanciation. The multiplicity of feminine images is much greater, we would suggest, in television than in film or the other visual arts, and obviously reactions to these representations will vary according to class, age, place in the family, ideological formation and individual biography. But the need for women to see themselves mirrored in the society's representations is often much greater than for men due to women's marginality in the political, economic and power structures. As feminists we would support attempts to show women coping with their marginality not just in series like 'Helen, A Woman of Today' but also within the more conventionalized genres like the soap opera.

We have taken soap opera to mean a certain kind of serial drama on television. While it does not have the tight definition of a genre such as the Western or the sonnet, there are some overall similarities that bind the various programmes into a distinctive television kind.

They are set in small-scale interiors – the pub, the home, the rooms of the motel, the corner shop, the farmhouse. Sequences shot in exteriors or large public buildings are unusual or felt as exceptional, like the day in the country, or a character's uneasy encounter with officialdom. Even 'The Waltons', which is frequently shot out of doors, or 'Emmerdale Farm', manages to render the farm and the surrounding countryside mere extensions of the family nest. Camera style tends to be simple, not drawing attention to itself, and interaction between characters is stressed rather than interiority. Most soap operas are continuous, although not necessarily ('General Hospital', 'The Waltons'), and they either have a self-contained story in each episode or a multi-linear narrative with several plot strands interweaving ('Coronation Street', 'Crossroads'). They usually contain a range of equally important characters but Meg in 'Crossroads' and John Boy in 'The Waltons' are partial exceptions to this.

For this paper we have watched the following current soap operas: 'Coronation Street', 'Rooms', 'Emmerdale Farm', 'General Hospital', 'Crossroads', 'The Waltons'. If we were to discuss them in detail then differences between them would obviously emerge which would require much more close analysis than we have yet had time for. We are concerned with soap operas as entertainment, as escapism, as pleasurable experience as well as where many people including children learn and see how fictional characters cope with personal relationships. We would like to suggest looking at this form of entertainment under the following headings – validation, reassurance and utopianism.

Validation

In *The Uses of Literacy*, Richard Hoggart writes:

> The overriding interest in the close detail of the human condition is the first pointer to an understanding of working class art. To begin with, working class art is essentially a 'showing' (rather than an 'exploration'), a presentation of what is known already. It starts from the assumption that human life is fascinating in itself.

And this is surely a description of soap opera – the pleasure it takes in the close detail of life, its sense of familiarity (one feels sorry when Elsie receives the letter from her husband about the divorce and cries) and even its predictability, the transparency of the characters. Hoggart's stress on art that 'presents' rather than 'explores' points to one of the prime ways in which soap opera is entertaining – namely that it validates everyday life as it is lived. This can have positive functions. Any way of life is richer for having a language (including images, stories, ways of speaking and interacting) in which to talk about itself.

Given that one of the major sources of such language in this society is television and given that the language of television is still largely expressive of bourgeois man, any programme that even half adequately offers a repository of images for women and the working class which doesn't just treat them as comic or victims is going to be pleasurable for those groups (although obviously since these programmes are not made by women or the working class then the pleasure is complex). Secondly, television grants such a language public recognition; it validates it beyond the immediate confines of the home and the local community. And thirdly, the humanistic emphasis of Hoggart's position, for all its current unfashionability, is not easily sneered at – the problem is that this validation procedure also involves several less admirable effects.

Hoggart has often been accused, rightly, of speaking of the working class in general and yet of describing in fact only a particular section of it – what is generally referred to as 'the respectable working class' – and predominantly through his view of the female culture of the class. Thus he omits for instance the experience of work, trade unions and other aspects of working-class life, including the more organized and politicized aspects and the more masculine aspects. Our concern here is not primarily with working-class culture (though 'The Uses of Literacy' at times reads like a description of 'Coronation Street') but with female culture, but the same general point can be made. That is, just as Hoggart took part of the working class for the whole, so soap opera takes part of women's lives for the whole of them.

The second weakness of Hoggart's approach is the unproblematic use of notions such as 'human life', 'the everyday', as if how we live our daily lives was not itself structured by both material realities and the patterns of ideology. This too is the problem with soap opera, for in its loving recreation of 'the close detail of the human condition', it takes how life is for humans now as the way things always have been and always will be. (Nor is it very hard for soap opera to do this, since the myth of motherhood and life-giver – the person who attends to men's very basic physiological needs – depends upon thinking of women as being outside of history, neither determined by the historically specific structures of a given society, nor having a hand in the transformation of that society as of now.) In other words, while it is possible to validate and recognize the achievements of people – women – in 'their' sphere of the world, it is less so to mask the fact that this is nonetheless culturally and historically specific. Women's lives are changing and changing dramatically – in their intimate day-to-day existence as well as in relation to wider structures such as work and trade unions or the state and these changes are also affecting the way men relate to these aspects; and the danger for soap opera is that it too easily slips back into nostalgia for the old ways. ('The Waltons' specifically recreates this supposed past of the extended family where work and the home were still one and men and women's roles still predetermined.)

Reassurance

Where entertainment-as-validation is concerned above all to celebrate the achievements of the way people live now, reassurance is more concerned with exploring the problems people face and providing resolutions fictionally. To have one's problems recognized publicly and then resolved during the experience of the drama is reassuring. Soap opera is endlessly founded on this simple narrative structure and the drawbacks are obvious. Problems in life are frequently intractable for psychological, and social and other reasons and this kind of reassurance, that everything will turn out for the best etc., is false. On the other hand it might be possible to use reassurance in more interesting and stimulating ways – resolving problems more collectively perhaps.

Related to this is one of the fundamental problems for most soap operas. The reassurance pattern depends upon narrative closure – when the drama ends, the problem must end too. But soap opera does not end; their whole point is their ongoing open-endedness. Although in practice the writing adheres to the demand for narrative closure, one can always feel when one plot strand has come to the end – nonetheless the open-endedness of the form can present difficulties for the reassurance mode, problems that could be utilized effectively to suggest the real nature of the society in which people live.

Utopianism

By utopianism we are not so much thinking of the representation of ideal worlds – though this can be the case – as of the presentation of ideal *feeling*. Entertainment embodies the feelings that would be characteristic of an ideal world; it makes you experience utopia even if it does not show you either how utopia would be organized or how to get there.

The various utopian feelings that entertainment most typically embodies can be categorized as abundance, energy, intensity, transparency and community. Of these it is the last three that most characterize soap opera's utopianism. By intensity is meant the whole-hearted, unambiguous, all-out experience of feeling, taking one's emotions to their fullest pitch, without holding back, and laying oneself on the line emotionally. In soap opera it is above all women who bear this quality, and soap opera has taken over from show business in general the strong women types embodied by such as Meg in 'Crossroads', Elsie Tanner in 'Coronation Street'. By transparency, we refer to the way that relationships between people in soap opera are free from manipulation (except of a fairly obvious kind) – and plots may often be about the reassuring discovery of falsehood which effectively renders a relationship transparent, ambivalent, game-playing. People know where they are with each other. Community is fairly obvious in its meaning – a close, warm sense of togetherness, a network of relationships which depend on assumed trust rather than intellectual or other forms of communication. As noted before, community is central to the very definition of soap opera; even non-communities – families in 'The Waltons' and 'The Cedar Tree', workplaces in 'General Hospital' and 'Emmerdale Farm' – are rendered as communities, caring, rallying round, supportive.

It may seem strange that we have emphasized the radical possibilities of soap opera and yet our theoretical work suggests good reasons for this.

Marxist theory draws a central distinction between the use-value and exchange-value of commodities. Capitalist commodity production is the production of exchange-value in order to accumulate capital. It is the accumulation of capital which is the dynamic of capitalism, not production of socially useful objects. As such the capitalist is indifferent to use-value, and useful qualities of the articles produced.

Nevertheless a capitalist system of production has certain requirements for its continuation of viability. These requirements we shall refer to as the conditions of existence of capitalism. One aspect of this is the dominance of bourgeois ideology – that is to say, an ideology favourable in its effects to the reproduction of capitalist social relations. We accept that popular forms are rooted in the dominant ideology. But capitalism has no automatic means of ensuring that the media produce bourgeois ideological effects. Ideological production is always hazardous, uncertain and contradictory and we cannot know for certain what will be uncovered in any given product of the media from an ideological point of view. Ideological production always escapes full surveillance and this is especially true where ideological production is penetrated by capital.

Media women and men are not as such producing ideology. They are producing films, television programmes, books, etc. These are all bearers of ideology but they are each different and cannot be reduced to mere ideology. Viewers and spectators do not watch soap operas to consume bourgeois ideology but to be entertained. The producers of ideology are therefore in the first place constrained by the need to entertain – to produce a use-value that is wanted by the consumer, rather than the use-value (ideology) which is needed by capitalism. These two things may, but need not, overlap. They may and probably will come into contradiction with each other at times. Characteristically it may be precisely when capital and the accumulation of capital become the dynamic principle of cultural production (as with commercial TV and radio) that the ideological functions secured by that production escape social control and become problematic. There is, by this argument, good reason to hope for more possibilities within the despised area of commercial television than from the more state-controlled BBC sector.

5

Orientalism

Edward Said

From his *Orientalism* (Routledge and Kegan Paul, 1978; Penguin, 1985).

On a visit to Beirut during the terrible civil war of 1975–1976 a French journalist wrote regretfully of the gutted downtown area that 'it had once seemed to belong to . . . the Orient of Chateaubriand and Nerval'. He was right about the place, of course, especially so far as a European was concerned. The Orient was almost a European invention, and had been since antiquity a place of romance, exotic beings, haunting memories and landscapes, remarkable experiences. Now it was disappearing; in a sense it had happened, its time was over. Perhaps it seemed irrelevant that Orientals themselves had something at stake in the process, that even in the time of Chateaubriand and Nerval Orientals had lived there, and that now it was they who were suffering; the main thing for the European visitor was a European representation of the Orient and its contemporary fate, both of which had a privileged communal significance for the journalist and his French readers.

Americans will not feel quite the same about the Orient, which for them is much more likely to be associated very differently with the Far East (China and Japan, mainly). Unlike the Americans, the French and the British – less so the Germans, Russians, Spanish, Portuguese, Italians, and Swiss – have had a long tradition of what I shall be calling *Orientalism*, a way of coming to terms with the Orient that is based on the Orient's special place in European Western experience. The Orient is not only adjacent to Europe; it is also the place of Europe's greatest and richest and oldest colonies, the source of its civilizations and languages, its cultural contestant, and one of its deepest and most recurring images of the Other. In addition, the Orient has helped to define Europe (or the West) as its contrasting image, idea, personality, experience. Yet none of this Orient is merely imaginative. The Orient is an integral part of European *material* civilization and culture. Orientalism expresses and represents that part culturally and even ideologically as a mode of discourse with supporting institutions, vocabulary, scholarship, imagery, doctrines, even colonial bureaucracies and colonial styles. In contrast, the American understanding of the Orient will seem considerably less dense, although our recent Japanese, Korean, and Indochinese adventures ought now to be creating a more sober, more realistic 'Oriental' awareness. Moreover, the vastly expanded American political and economic role in the Near East (the Middle East) makes great claims on our understanding of that Orient.

It will be clear to the reader (and will become clearer still throughout the many pages that follow) that by Orientalism I mean several things, all of them, in my opinion, interdependent. The most readily accepted designation for Orientalism is an academic one, and indeed the label still serves in a number of academic institutions. Anyone who teaches, writes about, or researches the Orient – and this applies whether the person is an anthropologist, sociologist, historian, or philologist – either in its specific or its general aspects, is an Orientalist, and what he or she does is Orientalism. Compared with *Oriental studies* or *area studies*, it is true that the term *Orientalism* is less preferred by specialists today, both because it is too vague and general and because it connotes the high-handed executive attitude of nineteenth-century and early-twentieth-century European colonialism. Nevertheless books are written and congresses held with 'the Orient' as their main focus, with the Orientalist in his new or old guise as their main authority. The point is that even if it does not survive as it once did, Orientalism lives on academically through its doctrines and theses about the Orient and the Oriental.

Related to this academic tradition, whose fortunes, transmigrations, specializations, and transmissions are in part the subject of this study, is a more general meaning for Orientalism. Orientalism is a style of thought based upon an ontological and epistemological distinction made between 'the Orient' and (most of the time) 'the Occident'. Thus a very large mass of writers, among whom are poets, novelists, philosophers, political theorists, economists, and imperial administrators, have accepted the basic distinction between East and West as the starting point for elaborate theories, epics, novels, social descriptions, and political accounts concerning the Orient, its people, customs, 'mind', destiny, and so on. This Orientalism can accommodate Aeschylus, say, and Victor Hugo, Dante and Karl Marx. A little later in this introduction I shall deal with the methodological problems one encounters in so broadly construed a 'field' as this.

The interchange between the academic and the more or less imaginative meanings of Orientalism is a constant one, and since the late eighteenth century there has been a considerable, quite disciplined – perhaps even regulated – traffic between the two. Here I come to the third meaning of Orientalism, which is something more historically and materially defined than either of the other two. Taking the late eighteenth century as a very roughly defined starting point Orientalism can be discussed and analyzed as the corporate institution for dealing with the Orient – dealing with it by making statements about it, authorizing views of it, describing it, by teaching it, settling it, ruling over it: in short, Orientalism as a Western style for dominating, restructuring, and having authority over the Orient. I have found it useful here to employ Michel Foucault's notion of a discourse, as described by him in *The archaeology of knowledge* and in *Discipline and punish*, to identify Orientalism. My contention is that without examining Orientalism as a discourse one cannot possibly understand the enormously systematic discipline by which European culture was able to manage – and even produce – the Orient politically, sociologically, militarily, ideologically, scientifically, and imaginatively during the post-Enlightenment period. Moreover, so authoritative a position did Orientalism have that I believe no one writing, thinking, or acting on the Orient could do so without taking account of the limitations on thought and action imposed by Orientalism. In brief, because of Orientalism the Orient was not (and is not) a free subject of thought or action. This is not to say that Orientalism unilaterally determines what can be said about the Orient, but that it is the whole network of interests inevitably brought to bear on (and therefore always involved in) any occasion when that peculiar entity, 'the Orient', is in question. How this happens is what this book tries to demonstrate. It also tries to show that European culture gained in strength and identity by selling itself off against the Orient as a sort of surrogate and even underground self.

Historically and culturally there is a quantitative as well as a qualitative difference between the Franco-British involvement in the Orient and – until the period of American ascendancy after World War II – the involvement of every other European and Atlantic power. To speak of Orientalism therefore is to speak mainly, although not exclusively, of a British and French cultural enterprise, a project whose dimensions take in such disparate realms as the imagination itself, the whole of India and the Levant, the Biblical texts and the Biblical lands, the spice trade, colonial armies and a long tradition of colonial administrators, a formidable scholarly corpus, innumerable Oriental 'experts' and 'hands', an Oriental professorate, a complex array of 'Oriental' ideas (Oriental despotism, Oriental splendour, cruelty, sensuality), many Eastern sects, philosophies, and wisdoms domesticated for local European use – the list can be extended more or less indefinitely. My point is that Orientalism derives from a particular closeness experienced between Britain and France and the Orient, which until the early nineteenth century had really meant only India and the Bible lands. From the beginning of the nineteenth century until the end of World War II France and Britain dominated the Orient and Orientalism; since World War II America has dominated the Orient, and approaches it as France and Britain once did. Out of that closeness, whose dynamic is enormously productive even if it always demonstrates the comparatively greater strength of the Occident (British, French, or American), comes the large body of texts I call Orientalist. [. . .]

I have begun with the assumption that the Orient is not an inert fact of nature. It is not merely *there*, just as the Occident itself is not just *there* either. We must take seriously Vico's great observation that men make their own history, that what they can know is what they have made, and extend it to geography: as both geographical and cultural entities – to say nothing of historical entities – such locales, regions, geographical sectors as 'Orient' and 'Occident' are man-made. Therefore as much as the West itself, the Orient is an idea that has a history and a tradition of thought, imagery, and vocabulary that have given it reality and presence in and for the West. The two geographical entities thus support and to an extent reflect each other.

Having said that, one must go on to state a number of reasonable qualifications. In the first place, it would be wrong to conclude that the Orient was *essentially* an idea, or a creation with no corresponding reality. When Disraeli said in his novel *Tancred* that the East was a career, he meant that to be interested in the East was something bright young Westerners would find to be an all-consuming passion; he should not be interpreted as saying that the East was *only* a career for Westerners. There were – and are – cultures and nations whose location is in the East, and their lives, histories, and customs have a brute reality obviously greater than anything that could be said about them in the West. About that fact this study of Orientalism has very little to contribute, except to acknowledge it tacitly. But the phenomenon of Orientalism as I study it here deals principally, not with a correspondence between Orientalism and Orient, but with the internal consistency of Orientalism and its ideas about the Orient (the East as career) despite or beyond any correspondence, or lack thereof, with a 'real' Orient. My point is that Disraeli's statement about the East refers mainly to that created consistency, that regular constellation of ideas as the pre-eminent thing about the Orient, and not to its mere being.

A second qualification is that ideas, cultures, and histories cannot seriously be understood or studied without their force, or more precisely their configurations of power, also being studied. To believe that the Orient was created – or, as I call it, 'Orientalized' – and to believe that such things happen simply as a necessity of the imagination, is to be disingenuous. The relationship between Occident and Orient is a relationship of power, of domination, of varying degrees of a complex hegemony, and is quite accurately indicated in the title of K.M. Panikkar's classic *Asia and Western dominance*. The Orient was Orientalized not only because it was discovered to be 'Oriental' in all those ways considered commonplace by an average nineteenth-century European, but also because it *could be* – that is, submitted to being – *made* Oriental. There is very little consent to be found, for example, in the fact that Flaubert's encounter with an Egyptian courtesan produced a widely influential model of the Oriental woman; she never spoke of herself, she never represented her emotions, presence, or history. *He* spoke for and represented her. He was foreign, comparatively wealthy, male, and these were historical facts of domination that allowed him not only to possess Kuchuk Hanem physically but to speak for her and tell his readers in what way she was 'typically Oriental'. My argument is that Flaubert's situation of strength in relation to Kuchuk Hanem was not an isolated instance. It fairly stands for the pattern of relative strength between East and West, and the discourse about the Orient that it enabled.

This brings us to a third qualification. One ought never to assume that the structure of Orientalism is nothing more than a structure of lies or of myths which, were the truth about them to be told, would simply blow away. I myself believe that Orientalism is more particularly valuable as a sign of European–Atlantic power over the Orient than it is as a veridic discourse about the Orient (which is what, in its academic or scholarly form, it claims to be). Nevertheless, what we must respect and try to grasp is the sheer knitted-together strength of Orientalist discourse, its very close ties to the enabling socio-economic and political institutions, and its redoubtable durability. After all, any system of ideas that can remain unchanged as teachable wisdom (in academies, books, congresses, universities, foreign-service institutes) from the period of Ernest Renan in the late 1840s until the present in the United States must be something more formidable than a mere collection of lies. Orientalism, therefore, is not an airy European fantasy about the Orient, but a created body of theory and practice in which, for many generations, there has been a considerable material investment. Continued investment made Orientalism, as a system of knowledge about the Orient, an accepted grid for filtering through the Orient into Western consciousness, just as that same investment multiplied – indeed, made truly productive – the statements proliferating out from Orientalism into the general culture.

Gramsci has made the useful analytic distinction between civil and political society in which the former is made up of voluntary (or at least rational and non-coercive) affiliations like schools, families, and unions, the latter of state institutions (the army, the police, the central bureaucracy) whose role in the polity is direct domination. Culture, of course, is to be found operating within civil society, where the influence of ideas, of institutions, and of other persons works not through domination but by what Gramsci calls consent. In any society not totalitarian, then, certain cultural forms predominate over others, just as certain ideas are more influential than others; the form of this cultural leadership is what Gramsci has identified as *hegemony*, an indispensable concept for any understanding of cultural life in the industrial West. It is hegemony, or rather the result of cultural hegemony at work, that gives Orientalism the durability and the strength I have been speaking about so far. Orientalism is never far from what Denys Hay has called the idea of Europe, a collective notion identifying 'us' Europeans as against all 'those' non-Europeans, and indeed it can be argued that the major component in European culture is precisely what made that culture hegemonic both in and outside Europe: the idea of European identity as a superior one in comparison with all the non-European peoples and cultures. There is in addition the hegemony of European ideas about the Orient, themselves reiterating European superiority over Oriental backwardness, usually overriding the possibility that a more independent, or more sceptical thinker, might have had different views on the matter.

In a quite constant way Orientalism depends for its strategy on this flexible *positional* superiority which puts the Westerner in a whole series of possible relationships with the Orient without ever losing him the relative upper hand. And why should it have been otherwise, especially during the period of extraordinary European ascendancy from the late Renaissance to the present? The scientist, the scholar, the missionary, the trader, or the soldier was in, or thought about, the Orient because he *could be there*, or could think about it, with very little resistance on the Orient's part. Under the general heading of knowledge of the Orient, and within the umbrella of Western hegemony over the Orient during the period from the end of the eighteenth century, there emerged a complex Orient suitable for study in the academy, for display in the museum, for reconstruction in the colonial office, for theoretical illustration in anthropological, biological, linguistic, racial, and historical theses about mankind and the universe, for instances of economic and sociological theories of development, revolution, cultural personality, national or religious character. Additionally, the imaginative examination of things Oriental was based more or less exclusively upon a sovereign Western consciousness out of whose unchallenged centrality an

Oriental world emerged, first according to general ideas about who or what was an Oriental, then according to a detailed logic governed not simply by empirical reality but by a battery of desires, repressions, investments, and projections. [. . .]

And yet, one must repeatedly ask oneself whether what matters in Orientalism is the general group of ideas overriding the mass of material – about which who could deny that they were shot through with doctrines of European superiority, various kinds of racism, imperialism, and the like, dogmatic views of 'the Oriental' as a kind of ideal and unchanging abstraction? – or the much more varied work produced by almost uncountable individual writers, whom one would take up as individual instances of authors dealing with the Orient. In a sense the two alternatives, general and particular, are really two perspectives on the same material: in both instances one would have to deal with pioneers in the field like William Jones, with great artists like Nerval or Flaubert. And why would it not be possible to employ both perspectives together, or one after the other? Isn't there an obvious danger of distortion (of precisely the kind that academic Orientalism has always been prone to) if either too general or too specific a level of description is maintained systematically?

My two fears are distortion and inaccuracy, or rather the kind of inaccuracy produced by too dogmatic a generality and too positivistic a localized focus. In trying to deal with these problems I have tried to deal with three main aspects of my own contemporary reality that seem to me to point the way out of the methodological or perspectival difficulties I have been discussing, difficulties that might force one, in the first instance, into writing a coarse polemic on so unacceptably general a level of description as not to be worth the effort, or, in the second instance, into writing so detailed and atomistic a series of analyses as to lose all track of the general lines of force informing the field, giving it its special cogency. How then to recognize individuality and to reconcile it with its intelligent, and by no means passive or merely dictatorial, general and hegemonic context?

I mentioned three aspects of my contemporary reality: I must explain and briefly discuss them now, so that it can be seen how I was led to a particular course of research and writing.

1. *The distinction between pure and political knowledge.* It is very easy to argue that knowledge about Shakespeare or Wordsworth is not political whereas knowledge about contemporary China or the Soviet Union is. My own formal and professional designation is that of 'humanist', a title which indicates the humanities as my field and therefore the unlikely eventuality that there might be anything political about what I do in that field. Of course, all these labels and terms are quite unnuanced as I use them here, but the general truth of what I am pointing to is, I think, widely held. One reason for saying that a humanist who writes about Wordsworth, or an editor whose specialty is Keats, is not involved in anything political is that what he does seems to have no direct political effect upon reality in the everyday sense. A scholar whose field is Soviet economics works in a highly charged area where there is much government interest, and what he might produce in the way of studies or proposals will be taken up by policymakers, government officials, institutional economists, intelligence experts. The distinction

between 'humanists' and persons whose work has policy implications, or political significance, can be broadened further by saying that the former's ideological colour is a matter of incidental importance to politics (although possibly of great moment to his colleagues in the field, who may object to his Stalinism or fascism or too easy liberalism), whereas the ideology of the latter is woven directly into his material – indeed, economics, politics, and sociology in the modern academy are ideological sciences – and therefore taken for granted as being 'political'.

Nevertheless the determining impingement on most knowledge produced in the contemporary West (and here I speak mainly about the United States) is that it be nonpolitical, that is, scholarly, academic, impartial, above partisan or small-minded doctrinal belief. One can have no quarrel with such an ambition in theory, perhaps, but in practice the reality is much more problematic. No one has ever devised a method of detaching the scholar from the circumstances of life, from the fact of his involvement (conscious or unconscious) with a class, a set of beliefs, a social position, or from the mere activity of being a member of a society. These continue to bear on what he does professionally, even though naturally enough his research and its fruits do attempt to reach a level of relative freedom from the inhibitions and the restrictions of brute, everyday reality. For there is such a thing as knowledge that is less, rather than more, partial than the individual (with his entangling and distracting life circumstances) who produces it. Yet this knowledge is not therefore automatically nonpolitical. [. . .]

... Orientalism is not a mere political subject matter or field that is reflected passively by culture, scholarship, or institutions; nor is it a large and diffuse collection of texts about the Orient; nor is it representative and expressive of some nefarious 'Western' imperialist plot to hold down the 'Oriental' world. It is rather a *distribution* of geopolitical awareness into aesthetic, scholarly, economic, sociological, historical, and philological texts; it is an *elaboration* not only of a basic geographical distinction (the world is made up of two unequal halves, Orient and Occident) but also of a whole series of 'interests' which, by such means as scholarly discovery, philological reconstruction, psychological analysis, landscape and sociological description, it not only creates but also maintains; it *is*, rather than expresses, a certain *will* or *intention* to understand, in some cases to control, manipulate, even to incorporate, what is a manifestly different (or alternative and novel) world; it is, above all, a discourse that is by no means in direct, corresponding relationship with political power in the raw, but rather is produced and exists in an uneven exchange with various kinds of power, shaped to a degree by the exchange with power political (as with a colonial or imperial establishment), power intellectual (as with reigning sciences like comparative linguistics or anatomy, or any of the modern policy sciences), power cultural (as with orthodoxies and canons of taste, texts, values), power moral (as with ideas about what 'we' do and what 'they' cannot do or understand as 'we' do). Indeed, my real argument is that Orientalism is – and does not simply represent – a considerable dimension of modern political-intellectual culture, and as such has less to do with the Orient than it does with 'our' world.

The kind of political questions raised by Orientalism, then, are as follows: What other sorts of intellectual, aesthetic, scholarly, and cultural energies went into the making of an imperialist tradition like the Orientalist one? How did philology, lexicography, history, biology, political and economic theory, novel-writing, and lyric poetry come to the service of Orientalism's broadly imperialist view of the world? What changes, modulations, refinements, even revolutions take place within Orientalism? What is the meaning of originality, of continuity, of individuality, in this context? How does Orientalism transmit or reproduce itself from one epoch to another? In fine, how can we treat the cultural, historical phenomenon of Orientalism as a kind of *willed human work* – not of mere unconditioned ratiocination – in all its historical complexity, detail, and worth without at the same time losing sight of the alliance between cultural work, political tendencies, the state, and the specific realities of domination? Governed by such concerns a humanistic study can responsibly address itself to politics *and* culture. But this is not to say that such a study establishes a hard-and-fast rule about the relationship between knowledge and politics. My argument is that each humanistic investigation must formulate the nature of that connection in the specific context of the study, the subject matter, and its historical circumstances.

2. *The methodological question.* In a previous book[1] I gave a good deal of thought and analysis to the methodological importance for work in the human sciences of finding and formulating a first step, a point of departure, a beginning principle. A major lesson I learned and tried to present was that there is no such thing as a merely given, or simply available, starting point: beginnings have to be made for each project in such a way as to *enable* what follows from them. Nowhere in my experience has the difficulty of this lesson been more consciously lived (with what success – or failure – I cannot really say) than in this study of Orientalism. The idea of beginning, indeed the act of beginning, necessarily involves an act of delimitation by which something is cut out of a great mass of material, separated from the mass, and made to stand for, as well as be, a starting point, a beginning; for the student of texts one such notion of inaugural delimitation is Louis Althusser's idea of the *problematic*, a specific determinate unity of a text, or group of texts, which is something given rise to by analysis. Yet in the case of Orientalism (as opposed to the case of Marx's texts, which is what Althusser studies) there is not simply the problem of finding a point of departure, or problematic, but also the question of designating which texts, authors, and periods are the ones best suited for study. [. . .]

... What German Orientalism had in common with Anglo-French and later American Orientalism was a kind of intellectual *authority* over the Orient within Western culture. This authority must in large part be the subject of any description of Orientalism, and it is so in this study. Even the name *Orientalism* suggests a serious, perhaps ponderous style of expertise; when I apply it to modern American social scientists (since they do not call themselves Orientalists, my use of the word is anomalous), it is to draw attention to the way Middle East experts can still draw on the vestiges of Orientalism's intellectual position in nineteenth-century Europe.

There is nothing mysterious or natural about authority. It is formed, irradiated, disseminated; it is instrumental, it is persuasive; it has status, it establishes canons of taste and value; it is virtually indistinguishable from certain ideas it dignifies as true, and from traditions, perceptions, and judgements it forms, transmits, reproduces. Above all, authority can, indeed must, be analyzed. All these attributes of authority apply to Orientalism, and much of what I do in this study is to describe both the historical authority in and the personal authorities of Orientalism.

My principal methodological devices for studying authority here are what can be called *strategic location*, which is a way of describing the author's position in a text with regard to the Oriental material he writes about, and *strategic formation*, which is a way of analyzing the relationship between texts and the way in which groups of texts, types of texts, even textual genres, acquire mass, density, and referential power among themselves and thereafter in the culture at large. I use the notion of strategy simply to identify the problem every writer on the Orient has faced: how to get hold of it, how to approach it, how not to be defeated or overwhelmed by its sublimity, its scope, its awful dimensions. Everyone who writes about the Orient must locate himself vis-à-vis the Orient; translated into his text, this location includes the kind of narrative voice he adopts, the type of structure he builds, the kinds of images, themes, motifs that circulate in his text – all of which add up to deliberate ways of addressing the reader, containing the Orient, and finally, representing it or speaking on its behalf. None of this takes place in the abstract, however. Every writer on the Orient (and this is true even of Homer) assumes some Oriental precedent, some previous knowledge of the Orient, to which he refers and on which he relies. Additionally, each work on the Orient *affiliates* itself with other works, with audiences, with institutions, with the Orient itself. The ensemble of relationships between works, audiences, and some particular aspects of the Orient therefore constitutes an analyzable formation – for example, that of philological studies, of anthologies of extracts from Oriental literature, of travel books, of Oriental fantasies – whose presence in time, in discourse, in institutions (schools, libraries, foreign services) gives it strength and authority. [. . .]

. . . I believe it needs to be made clear about cultural discourse and exchange within a culture that what is commonly circulated by it is not 'truth' but representations. It hardly needs to be demonstrated again that language itself is a highly organized and encoded system, which employs many devices to express, indicate, exchange messages and information, represent, and so forth. In any instance of at least written language, there is no such thing as a delivered presence, but a *re-presence*, or a representation. The value, efficacy, strength, apparent veracity of a written statement about the Orient therefore relies very little, and cannot instrumentally depend, on the Orient as such. On the contrary, the written statement is a presence to the reader by virtue of its having excluded, displaced, made supererogatory any such *real thing* as 'the Orient'. Thus all of Orientalism stands forth and away from the Orient: that Orientalism makes sense at all depends more on the West than on the Orient, and this sense is directly indebted to various Western techniques of representation that make the Orient visible, clear, 'there' in discourse about it. And these representations rely upon institutions, traditions, conventions, agreed-upon codes of understanding for their effects, not upon a distant and amorphous Orient. [. . .]

3. *The personal dimension.* In the *Prison notebooks* Gramsci says: 'The starting-point of critical elaboration is the consciousness of what one really is, and is "knowing thyself" as a product of the historical process to date, which has deposited in you an infinity of traces, without leaving an inventory.' The only available English translation inexplicably leaves Gramsci's comment at that, whereas in fact Gramsci's Italian text concludes by adding, 'therefore it is imperative at the outset to compile such an inventory'.

Much of the personal investment in this study derives from my awareness of being an 'Oriental' as a child growing up in two British colonies. All of my education, in those colonies (Palestine and Egypt) and in the United States, has been Western, and yet that deep early awareness has persisted. In many ways my study of Orientalism has been an attempt to inventory the traces upon me, the Oriental subject, of the culture whose domination has been so powerful a factor in the life of all Orientals. This is why for me the Islamic Orient has had to be the centre of attention. Whether what I have achieved is the inventory prescribed by Gramsci is not for me to judge, although I have felt it important to be conscious of trying to produce one. Along the way, as severely and as rationally as I have been able, I have tried to maintain a critical consciousness, as well as employing those instruments of historical, humanistic, and cultural research of which my education has made me the fortunate beneficiary. In none of that, however, have I ever lost hold of the cultural reality of, the personal involvement in having been constituted as, 'an Oriental'.

The historical circumstances making such a study possible are fairly complex, and I can only list them schematically here. Anyone resident in the West since the 1950s, particularly in the United States, will have lived through an era of extraordinary turbulence in the relations of East and West. No one will have failed to note how 'East' has always signified danger and threat during this period, even as it has meant the traditional Orient as well as Russia. In the universities a growing establishment of area-studies programmes and institutes has made the scholarly study of the Orient a branch of national policy. Public affairs in this country include a healthy interest in the Orient, as much for its strategic and economic importance as for its traditional exoticism. If the world has become immediately accessible to a Western citizen living in the electronic age, the Orient too has drawn nearer to him, and is now less a myth perhaps than a place crisscrossed by Western, especially American, interests.

One aspect of the electronic, postmodern world is that there has been a reinforcement of the stereotypes by which the Orient is viewed. Television, the films, and all the media's resources have forced information into more and more standardized moulds. So far as the Orient is concerned, standardization and cultural stereotyping have intensified the hold of the nineteenth-century academic and imaginative demonology of 'the mysterious Orient'. This is nowhere more true than in the ways by which the Near East is grasped. Three things have contributed to making even the simplest perception of the Arabs and Islam into a highly politicized, almost raucous matter: one, the history of popular anti-Arab and anti-Islamic prejudice in the West, which is immediately reflected in the history of Orientalism; two, the struggle between the Arabs and Israeli Zionism, and its effects upon American Jews as well as upon both the liberal culture and the population at large; three, the almost total absence of any cultural position making it possible either to identify with or dispassionately to discuss the Arabs or Islam. Furthermore, it hardly needs saying that because the Middle East is now so identified with Great Power politics, oil economics, and the simple-minded dichotomy of freedom-loving, democratic Israel and evil, totalitarian, and terroristic Arabs, the chances of anything like a clear view of what one talks about in talking about the Near East are depressingly small.

My own experiences of these matters are in part what made me write this book. The life of an Arab Palestinian in the West, particularly in America, is disheartening. There exists here an almost unanimous consensus that politically he does not exist, and when it is allowed that he does, it is either as a nuisance or as an Oriental. The web of racism, cultural stereotypes, political imperialism, dehumanizing ideology holding in the Arab or the Muslim is very strong indeed, and it is this web which every Palestinian has come to feel as his uniquely punishing destiny. It has made matters worse for him to remark that no person academically involved with the Near East – no Orientalist, that is – has ever in the United States culturally and politically identified himself wholeheartedly with the Arabs; certainly there have been identifications on some level, but they have never taken an 'acceptable' form as has liberal American identification with Zionism, and all too frequently they have been radically flawed by their association either with discredited political and economic interests (oil-company and State Department Arabists, for example) or with religion.

The nexus of knowledge and power creating 'the Oriental' and in a sense obliterating him as a human being is therefore not for me an exclusively academic matter. Yet it is an *intellectual* matter of some very obvious importance. I have been able to put to use my humanistic and political concerns for the analysis and description of a very worldly matter, the rise, development, and consolidation of Orientalism. Too often literature and culture are presumed to be politically, even historically, innocent; it has regularly seemed otherwise to me, and certainly my study of Orientalism has convinced me (and I hope will convince my literary colleagues) that society and literary culture can only be understood and studied together. In addition, and by an almost inescapable logic, I have found myself writing the history of a strange, secret sharer of Western anti-Semitism. That anti-Semitism and, as I have discussed it in its Islamic branch, Orientalism resemble each other very closely is a historical, cultural, and political truth that needs only to be mentioned to an Arab Palestinian for its irony to be perfectly understood. But what I should like also to have contributed here is a better understanding of the way cultural domination has operated. If this stimulates a new kind of dealing with the Orient, indeed if it eliminates the 'Orient' and 'Occident' altogether, then we shall have advanced a little in the process of what Raymond Williams has called the 'unlearning' of 'the inherent dominative mode'.[2]

Notes

1 *In my beginnings: intention and method* (1975).
2 *Culture and society* (1958), p. 376.

Editors' note

In this extract, specialist and mainly historical references to 'the Orient' have been removed.

6

Concepts of culture – public policy and the cultural industries

Nicholas Garnham

Originally published as a discussion paper by the Greater London Council in 1983; reprinted in the GLC's *The state of the art or the art of the state?* (1985) and in *Cultural Studies*, vol. 1, no. 1 (1987).

To mobilize the concept of the cultural industries as central to an analysis of cultural activity and of public cultural policy is to take a stand against a whole tradition of idealist cultural analysis. This tradition, well delineated in the British form, for instance, by Raymond Williams in *Culture and society*, defines culture as a realm separate from, and often actively opposed to, the realm of material production and economic activity.

This is important for our present purposes because, in general, public cultural policies have evolved from within that tradition. Public intervention, in the form of subsidy, is justified on the grounds (1) that culture possesses inherent values, of life enhancement or whatever, which are fundamentally opposed to and in danger of damage by commercial forces; (2) that the need for these values is universal, uncontaminated by questions of class, gender and ethnic origin; and (3) that the market cannot satisfy this need.

A further crucial component of this ideology is the special and central status attributed to the 'creative artist' whose aspirations and values, seen as stemming from some unfathomable and unquestionable source of genius, inspiration or talent, are the source of cultural value. The result of placing artists at the centre of the cultural universe has not been to shower them with gold, for artistic poverty is itself an ideologically potent element in this view of culture, but to define the policy problem as one of finding audiences for their work, rather than vice versa. When audiences cannot be found, at least at a price and in a quantity which will support the creative activity, the market is blamed and the gap is filled by subsidy.

It is important to note that most of those on the left who have challenged this dominant view of culture as élitist have themselves tacitly if not explicitly accepted the remaining assumptions of the tradition they were rejecting. Indeed, in my view this in part accounts for their limited success in shifting the terms of the policy debate and the effortless ease with which they have been incorporated.

One result of this cultural policy-making tradition has been to marginalize public intervention in the cultural sphere and to make it purely reactive to processes which it cannot grasp or attempt to control. For, while this tradition has been rejecting the market, most people's cultural needs and aspirations are being, for better or worse, supplied by the market as goods and services. If one turns one's back on an analysis of that dominant cultural process, one cannot understand either the culture of our time or the challenges and opportunities which that dominant culture offers to public policy makers.

We can get some idea of the relative orders of magnitude between public-sector expenditure on cultural activity and private, market expenditure if we compare the £673.8 million of public expenditure on libraries, museums and galleries and other cultural activities in the United Kingdom in 1981–2 with the £15 538 million of 1982 consumer expenditure on recreation, entertainment and education, and with the total media advertising expenditure in 1982 of £3 216 million. [. . .]

An analysis of culture structured around the concept of the cultural industries, on the other hand, directs our attention precisely at the dominant private market sector. It sees culture, defined as the production and circulation of symbolic meaning, as a material process of production and exchange, part of, and in significant ways determined by, the wider economic processes of society with which it shares many common features.

Thus, as a descriptive term, 'cultural industries' refers to those institutions in our society which employ the characteristic modes of production and organization of industrial corporations to produce and disseminate symbols in the form of cultural goods and services, generally, although not exclusively, as commodities. These include newspapers, periodical and book publishing, record companies, music publishers, commercial sports organizations, etc. In all these cultural processes, we characteristically find at some point the use of capital-intensive, technological means of mass production and/or distribution, highly developed divisions of labour and hierarchical modes of managerial organization. [. . .]

Consumption time

For most people, cultural consumption is confined to a so-called free time, the extension of which is limited by the material necessities of work and sleep. If we assume a working week (including travel) of 45 hours and sleep time of 48 hours per week, that leaves 75 hours per week in which all other activities have to be fitted. On average, 20 hours per week are taken up by TV viewing.

Cultural consumption is particularly time-consuming in the sense that the most common and popular form of culture, namely narrative and its musical equivalent, are based upon manipulation of time itself, and thus they offer deep resistances to attempts to raise the productivity of consumption time. This scarcity of consumption time explains:

1) the acute competition for audiences in the cultural sector;
2) the tendency to concentrate cultural consumption in the home, thus cutting out travel time;

3) as recent Swedish studies have shown, a sharp rise in the unit cost of each minute of consumption time, in particular as investment on domestic hardware increases while the time for using such hardware does not. Thus in Sweden between 1970 and 1979 time spent listening to music rose by 20 per cent while the cost rose by 86 per cent, with each hour of listening costing 55 per cent more.

The labour market

The various cultural industries compete in the same market for labour. Individual film-makers, writers, musicians or electricians may move in their work from film, to television, to live theatre. The electronic engineer may work in manufacturing or broadcasting. The journalist may work in newspapers, periodicals, radio or television.

This unified labour market is reflected in trade-union organizations. The Association of Cinematograph, Television and Allied Technicians (ACTT) organizes across film, television and radio, the National Union of Journalists (NUJ) across newspapers, books, magazines, radio and television. The Musicians' Union members work in film, radio, television and records as well as live performances, and so on.

As a result of these levels of integration within the cultural sector, a shift in one place affects the structure of the whole sector. The introduction of a new television channel, such as Channel 4, restructures the broadcasting, film and advertising market in specific ways. Even more, of course, will this be the case with cable and satellite services. The introduction of a new colour supplement has repercussions upon the finances of other publications, but may well also have cross-effects on broadcasting revenue. The same holds true for public intervention. One needs to be aware that one may be playing a zero-sum game, and that all options are not simultaneously open.

A classic example of this interaction and of the ways in which the dynamics of the private sector impact on the public sector is the relation between ITV and BBC. Because ITV holds a monopoly of television advertising, and because there has in general been a high demand for this commodity, extra broadcasting hours mean, for ITV, extra revenue, more efficient utilization of plant and thus higher profit. There has therefore been steady pressure from ITV, in common with commercial broadcasting systems throughout the world, to expand the hours of broadcasting – pressure which has been successful. For the BBC, on the other hand, expansion of hours leads to increases in costs with no increase in revenue. They have, however, been forced to respond to ITV because of the need to compete for audiences, thus increasing the pressure to spend more public money on broadcasting if the balance between public and private sectors is to be maintained.

The structure and dynamics of the cultural industries

The particular economic nature of the cultural industries can be explained in terms of the general tendencies of commodity production within the capitalist mode of production as modified by the special characteristics of the cultural commodity. Thus we find competition driving the search for profits via increased productivity, but it takes specific forms.

There is a contradiction at the heart of the cultural commodity. On the one hand, there is a very marked drive towards expanding the market share or the form this takes in the cultural sector, audiences. This is explained by the fact that in general, because one of the use-values of culture is novelty or difference, there is a constant need to create new products which are all in a sense prototypes. That is to say, the cultural commodity resists that homogenization process which is one of the material results of the abstract equivalence of exchange to which the commodity form aspires. This drive for novelty within cultural production means that in general the costs of reproduction are marginal in relation to the costs of production (the cost of each record pressing is infinitesimal compared to the cost of recording, for instance). Thus the marginal returns from each extra sale tend to grow, leading in turn to a powerful thrust towards audience maximization as the preferred profit maximization strategy.

On the other hand, the cultural commodity is not destroyed in the process of consumption. My reading of a book or watching of a film does not make it any less available to you. Moreover, the products of the past live on and can be relatively easy and cheaply reproduced anew. Thus it has been difficult to establish the scarcity on which price is based. And thus cultural goods (and some services, such as broadcasting, for technical reasons) tend towards the condition of a public good. Indeed, one can observe a marked tendency, where they are not *de jure* so treated, for consumers to so treat them *de facto* through high levels of piracy, as is now the case with records, video cassettes and books. (It should be noted that this in its turn relates to another contradiction in the cultural sphere, on which I shall comment shortly, between the producers of cultural hardware and software. It is the development of a market in cheap reproduction technology that makes piracy so difficult to control.) In contradiction, then, to the drive to maximize audiences, a number of strategies have had to be developed for artificially limiting access in order to create scarcity.

The drive to audience maximization leads to the observed tendency towards a high level of concentration, internationalization and cross-media ownership in the cultural industries. The strategies to limit access have taken a variety of forms:

1) Monopoly or oligopolistic controls over distribution channels, sometimes, as in broadcasting, linked to the state. One often finds here a close relationship between commercial interests and those of state control.
2) An attempt to concentrate the accumulation process on the provision of cultural hardware – e.g. radio and television receivers, hi-fi, VCRs, etc. – with the programmes, as in the early days of British broadcasting, as necessary loss-leaders. The rationale for the introduction of cable in the UK is an example of this.
3) The creation of the audience as a commodity for sale to advertisers, where the cultural software merely acts as a free lunch. This has proved

itself the most successful solution; both the increased proportion of advertising to sales revenue in the press and periodicals market, culminating in the growth of free newspapers and magazines, and the steady expansion of wholly advertising-financed broadcasting services, are indications of this.

4) The creation of commodities, of which news is the classic example, which require constant reconsumption.

Audiences, cultural repertoire and distribution

The third key characteristic of the cultural commodity lies in the nature of its use-values. These have proved difficult if not impossible to pin down in any precise terms, and demand for them appears to be similarly volatile. As I have already remarked, culture is above all the sphere for the expression of difference. Indeed, some analysts would claim that cultural goods are pure positional goods, their use-value being as markers of social and individual difference. While this aspect of culture merits much deeper and more extended analysis, it is only necessary here to draw one key conclusion, namely that demand for any single cultural product is impossible to predict. Thus the cultural industries, if they are to establish a stable market, are forced to create a relationship with an audience or public to whom they offer not a simple cultural good, but a cultural repertoire across which the risks can be spread. For instance, in the record industry only 1 in 9 singles and 1 in 16 LPs makes a profit, and 3 per cent of the output can account for up to 50 per cent of turnover. Similarly, in films the top ten films out of 119 in the UK market in 1979 took 32 per cent of the box-office receipts and the top 40 took 80 per cent.

Thus the drive to audience maximization, the need to create artificial scarcity by controlling access and the need for a repertoire bring us to the central point in this analysis. *It is cultural distribution, not cultural production, that is the key locus of power and profit*. It is access to distribution which is the key to cultural plurality. The cultural process is as much, if not more, about creating audiences or publics as it is about producing cultural artefacts and performances. Indeed, that is why that stress upon the cultural producers that I noted earlier is so damaging.

We need to recognize the importance, within the cultural industries and within the cultural process in general, of the function which I shall call, for want of a better word, editorial: the function not just of creating a cultural repertoire matched to a given audience or audiences but at the same time of matching the cost of production of that repertoire to the spending powers of that audience. These functions may be filled by somebody or some institution referred to variously as a publisher, a television channel controller, a film distributor, etc. It is a vital function totally ignored by many cultural analysts, a function as creative as writing a novel or directing a film. It is a function, moreover, which will exist centrally within the cultural process of any geographically dispersed society with complex division of labour.

Taking these various factors into account, we are now in a position to understand why our dominant cultural processes and their modes of organization are the way they are. The newspaper and the television and radio schedule are montages of elements to appeal to as wide a range of readers, viewers and listeners as possible. The high levels of concentration in the international film, record and publishing industries are responses to the problem of repertoire. The dominance of broadcast television stems from its huge efficiency as a distribution medium, with its associated economies of scale.

For this reason, the notion that the new technologies of cable and VCR are fragmenting the market rather than shifting the locus of oligopolistic power needs to be treated with caution, since there are strict limits to how far such fragmentation can go economically.

The hierarchy of cultural industries

As I have noted, power in the cultural sector clusters around distribution, the channel of access to audiences. It is here that we typically find the highest levels of capital intensity, ownership concentration and multinationaliza- tion, the operation of classic industrial labour processes and relations of production with related forms of trade-union organization. These characteristics are exhibited to their highest degree in the manufacture of the hardware of cultural distribution, especially domestic hardware. This is a sub-sector increasingly dominated by a few Japanese corporations such as Matsushita, Sony, Sanyo, Toshiba and Hitachi, together with Eastman Kodak, Philips and RCA. The major UK firm of this type is Thorn-EMI.

Then there are the major controllers of channels of software distribution, often closely linked to specific modes of reproduction, such as record pressing or newspaper printing. In non-print media there is again a high level of concentration and internationalization, and US firms dominate, owing to the large size of the domestic US market. Here we find some of the same firms as in hardware, e.g. RCA, Thorn-EMI and Philips joined by firms such as Warner, CBS, Time-Life, Gulf-Western and MCA. The multinationalization of print media has been limited by barriers of language. None the less, apart from the high levels of concentration in the national UK market, with three groups controlling 74 per cent of daily newspaper circulation, two of these groups – News International and Reed International – have extensive foreign interests.

The increasing tendency in this field, as an extension of the principle of repertoire, is the formation of multi-media conglomerates. Examples are Pearson-Longman and Thorn-EMI in the UK, who own interests across a number of media, thus enabling them both to exploit the same product, be it a film, a book or a piece of music, across several media, and also to expand the principles of risk-spreading not only across a range of consumer choice in one medium, but also across consumers' entire range of cultural choice. The development of such centres of cultural powers also, of course, raises barriers to entry.

Around these centres of power cluster groups of satellites. These satellites can be either small companies, for instance independent production companies in relation to Channel 4, or individual cultural workers such as freelance journalists, writers, actors and film directors. In these satellite sectors we find high levels of insecurity, low levels of profitability, low levels of unionization and, where they exist, weak trade-union organizations. Often labour is not waged at all, but labour power is rented out for a royalty.

The existence of this dependent satellite sector fulfils a very important function for the cultural industries because it enables them to shift much of the cost and risk of cultural research and development off their own shoulders and on to this exploited sector, some of which is then indeed supported from the public purse. It also enables them to maintain a consistently high turnover of creative cultural labour without running the risk of labour unrest or bearing the cost of redundancy or pension payments. Their cup brimmeth over when, as is often the case, the workers themselves willingly don this yoke in the name of freedom.

The market and culture

[. . .] One last general analytical question must be raised: what should be our attitude to the relation between the market and the cultural process? There is that general tradition, to which I alluded at the beginning of this paper, which regards culture and the market as inherently inimical. This view is powerfully reinforced within the socialist tradition by opposition to the capitalist mode of production.

I think it is crucial, however, to separate the concept of the market from the concept of the capitalist mode of production, that is to say from a given structure of ownership and from the special features derived from labour as a market commodity. In terms of this relationship between consumers, distributors and producers of cultural goods and services, the market has much to recommend it, provided that consumers enter that market with equal endowments and that concentration of ownership power is reduced, controlled or removed. However, we must be clear that removal of the power vested in private or unaccountable public ownership will not remove the need for the function I have described as editorial, whether such a function is exercised individually or collectively. It also has to be stressed that even within the capitalist mode of production the market has, at crucial historical junctures, acted as a liberating cultural force. One thinks of the creation of both the novel and the newspaper by the rising bourgeoisie in the eighteenth century and of working men's clubs and the working-class seaside holiday in the late nineteenth century.

Indeed, the cultural market, as it has developed in the last 150 years in the UK as a substitute for patronage in all its forms, cannot be read either as a destruction of high culture by vulgar commercialism or as a suppression of authentic working-class culture, but should be read as a complex hegemonic dialectic of liberation and control – which makes an analysis, for instance, of the role of broadcasting and of the BBC public-service tradition so difficult.

What analysis of the cultural industries does bring home to us is the need to take the question of the scarcity and thus of the allocation of cultural resources seriously, together with the question of audiences – who they are, how they are formed and how they can best be served. For it needs to be said that the only alternative to the market which we have constructed, with the partial exception of broadcasting, has tended either simply to subsidize the existing tastes and habits of the better-off or to create a new form of public culture which has no popular audience; cultural workers create for the only audience they know, namely the cultural bureaucrats who pay the bill and upon whom they become psychologically dependent even while reviling them. [. . .]

7

Reading *Reading the romance*

Janice Radway

Introduction to the English edition of her *Reading the romance* (Verso, 1987); the book was originally published in the USA by University of North Carolina Press in 1984.

It seems especially fitting that a book about the *particular* nature of the relationship between audiences and texts, which was itself initially conceived for and addressed to a specific community of readers, should require a new introduction precisely at the moment that it is to be offered to a new and different set of readers situated in another social context. Indeed, in reading *Reading the romance* for the first time since the manuscript was completed, in preparation for offering it to a British audience, I have been struck by how much the book's argument is a product of my own intellectual history and that of the community I intended and hoped to address. As a consequence, these new remarks will constitute something of an apologia for the book's limitations and an effort to secure a particular reading in the British context.[1] I want to situate and explain the polemic of *Reading the romance* because I suspect that the book's early theoretical claim to be doing something new will seem odd to a British audience, which will also particularly note the absence of certain references and concepts. Despite those absences, however, *Reading the romance* does take up specific questions that have preoccupied British feminists and cultural studies scholars for some time. Thus I would like to highlight those questions, consider how and why they were posed as they were in *Reading the romance*, and explore their similarity to and differences from the questions posed by British scholars working on subcultures and the culture of women and girls. Finally, I would like to say something about the political implications of *Reading the romance* as I now understand them, because they have been articulated more clearly for me by my continuing engagement with the work of British feminists and cultural studies scholars.

British readers of *Reading the romance* will note immediately that the book's theoretical argument is directed generally to American Studies scholars working in the United States (although this latter qualification is not stated specifically) and more particularly to those who take literature as their primary object of concern. The resulting preoccupation with the question of what a literary text can be taken as evidence for may seem a peculiar and oblique focus for a book that has largely been read as a contribution to feminist scholarship or as a contribution to discussions within communications theory about the status of the reader and the nature of mass cultural consumption.[2] This latter fact simply demonstrates, however, that whatever her intentions no writer can foresee or prescribe the way her book will develop, be taken up, or read. Neither can she predict how it will transform her, I might add, a subject to which I will return. Still, I think it will be helpful to know something about the immediate personal and intellectual situation which served as the polemical ground and orienting context for the writing of *Reading the romance* because I think it goes a long way toward explaining why the book was eventually hijacked by its own theory and subject and, *en route* to its intended destination, gradually found itself directed to another.

As much as the theoretical argument of chapter one is the product of an intellectual quarrel, so too is it the product of an institutional and political one as well. It was born of the fact that I had been hired in 1977 by the American Civilization Department at the University of Pennsylvania, which has been known within the American Studies community in the United States for its particular challenge to an earlier American Studies orthodoxy. That orthodoxy, formed in the late 1940s and early 1950s, developed as part of the reaction to the hegemony of New Criticism in American English departments. Disturbed by the extreme preoccupation with formalist criticism in an historical context that seemed to cry out for a consideration once again of what constituted 'the American', certain students of the national literature began to reassert the validity of an enterprise that would reunite the classic American literary texts with the historical context within which they were conceived. Resulting largely in an alliance between literary scholars and intellectual historians, the impulse led to the creation of American Studies programmes and departments which, whatever their differences with more traditional English departments, at least still assumed that the most reliable and complex record of the American past could be found in the country's 'greatest' works of art.[3]

In opposition to such claims, however, the American Civilization Department at Pennsylvania began to elaborate a critique of the assumption that works selected on the basis of their aesthetic achievement would necessarily be representative of the large sections of the population that had never read such books. Writing within the framework prescribed by the social sciences and preoccupied therefore with questions of evidentiary validity and statistical representivity, my future colleagues (who were not, for the most part, literary critics) argued that while 'elite' literature might be taken as evidence for the beliefs of a particular section of the American population, assertions based upon it could not easily be extrapolated to wholly different classes or ethnic groups. They argued that if accurate statements were to be made about more 'ordinary' Americans, the popular literature produced for and consumed by large numbers ought to become the primary focus of culturally-oriented scholarship.[4]

I was hired, then, because much of my graduate work had been preoccupied with popular literature of one sort or another. That work had been directed by Russel Nye, one of the first serious scholars of American popular culture in the United States.[5] Although Nye was himself trained as an historian, he worked within the English Department at Michigan State University. Therefore, under his tutelage, its American Studies programme articulated the need for the study of popular culture even though it remained theoretically more traditional than that at Pennsylvania. The methods of analysis it taught were still primarily those of formal analysis and textual exegesis. Thus I went to Pennsylvania as a student of popular culture but also as a literary critic. *Reading the romance* clearly demonstrates that provenance in the conversations it chooses to join.

By the time I arrived in the department my colleagues had turned away somewhat from statistical models for the study of society and behaviour and had elaborated instead a complex rationale for the use of ethnographic methods in the effort to make sense of American culture. Drawing on anthropology rather than sociology, they argued that cultural investigation must always take account of spatial and temporal specificity. Thus they moved from what Stuart Hall and others have called the 'literary–moral' definition of culture to an anthropological one, defining it as the whole way of life of a historically and temporally situated people.[6] The department's essential graduate seminars were structured as ethnographies of particular communities which were studied synchronically and in depth. Interestingly enough, these were initiated at almost the same time as investigators at the Birmingham Centre for Contemporary Cultural Studies [CCCS], prompted by arguments made by Raymond Williams, E.P. Thompson, Hall, and others, were turning to ethnographic methods in their effort to study the necessary 'struggle, tension, and conflict' between subcultures or different ways of life.[7] Because this latter move originated within the well-developed Marxist tradition in Britain, even the earliest work at the Centre made an effort to consider the nature of the relationship between ethnographic investigation of behaviour and cultural meaning and ideological analysis of the structures of determination.[8] Although the turn to ethnography in American Studies was prompted by a concern with the relationship (if not the struggle) between subgroups within a complex society and by an interest in the relationship between behaviour and 'belief systems', the relative weakness of the Marxist tradition in the USA meant that most of the early work did not explicitly engage debates over ideology or the place of specifically cultural production in securing the domination of one group over another.

In any case, the ethnographic turn began to have relevance for me when I simultaneously began to engage with the theoretical work developing within the literary critical community on the reader and semiotic conceptions of the literary text. I grappled with this work as a result of discussions carried on within the Penn Semiotics Seminar which was heavily influenced by Dell Hymes, Erving Goffman, and Barbara Herrnstein Smith, among others. Thus, even as I was attempting to respond to my departmental colleagues' questions about what a literary text could be taken as evidence for, I was being gradually convinced by the theoretical arguments about the social and hence variable nature of semiotic processes. If one could talk of the necessity for ethnographies of speaking, I saw no reason why one shouldn't also assume that as speech varied across space and over time so, too, reading must as well. If this was true and one could discover how actual communities actually read particular texts, I thought I saw a way to answer my colleagues' questions about the evidentiary status of literature. If reading varied spatially and temporally and one did wish to use literature in an effort to reconstruct culture, it would be necessary to connect particular texts with the communities that produced and consumed them and to make some effort to specify how the individuals involved actually constructed those texts as meaningful semiotic structures. Hence my conclusion that what American Studies needed were ethnographies of reading.

Reading the romance was therefore conceived in response to a set of theoretical questions about literary texts. As a consequence, it was designed initially to see whether it was possible to investigate reading empirically so as to make 'accurate' statements about the historical and cultural meaning of literary production and consumption. The decision to move beyond the various concepts of the inscribed, ideal, or model reader and to work with actual subjects in history was thus a product of the difficult questions that had been put to me by colleagues trained in the social science tradition and in culture theory. The resulting empiricism of *Reading the romance*, embodied most obviously in its claim that empirically-based ethnographies of reading should replace *all* intuitively conducted interpretation in cultural study, precisely because such empiricism would guarantee a more *accurate* description of what a book meant to a given audience, was thus a function of my situation within the American Studies intellectual community as it carried on the familiar debate about the relative merits of 'scientific' as opposed to 'literary' methods in cultural study.[9]

The book that resulted did not ultimately sustain its initial project, however, because the activity of actually 'doing ethnography' produced many surprises, not the least of which was the realization that even ethnographic description of the 'native's' point of view must be an interpretation or, in words adapted from Clifford Geertz, my own construction of my informants' construction of what they were up to in reading romances. This, of course, will not be news to anyone familiar with anthropological method or with the ethnographic work of the CCCS, but it was something I only really discovered in the course of attempting to write the ethnography. I tried to acknowledge this point in the introduction to the American edition which, like so many others, was substantially revised after all the other chapters were completed. I attempted to do this by proclaiming openly my feminism and by acknowledging that it had affected the way I evaluated or reacted to my subject's self-understanding. However, I now think that my initial preoccupation with the empiricist claims of social science prevented me from recognizing fully that even what I took to be simple descriptions of my interviewee's self-understandings were produced through an internal organization of data and thus mediated by my own conceptual constructs and ways of seeing the world.[10]

I would therefore now want to agree with Angela McRobbie when she states flatly that 'representations are interpretations'.[11] As she goes on to say, they can never be pure mirror images of some objective reality but exist always as the result of 'a whole set of selective devices, such as highlighting, editing, cutting, transcribing and inflecting'. Consequently, I no longer feel that ethnographies of reading should *replace* textual interpretation completely because of their greater adequacy to the task of revealing an objective cultural reality. Rather, I think they should become an essential and necessary component of a multiply-focussed approach that attempts to do justice to the ways historical subjects understand and partially control their own behaviour while recognizing at the same time that such behaviour and self-understanding are limited if not in crucial ways complexly determined by the social formation within which those subjects find themselves.

In practice, if not perhaps in theory, I think *Reading the romance* actually does make an effort to do this in large part because my attempts to deal with literary production and consumption as complex social processes were affected by my first serious engagement with Marxist literary theory. That engagement had been prompted initially by Jerry Palmer's suggestion that I might want to read Terry Eagleton's *Criticism and ideology*.[12] This initiated the pursuit of a trail of bibliographic references through the Marxist literature on ideology, an intellectual move that was reinforced by my ongoing reading in feminist literature as I began to grapple with the social situations of the women who were sharing their perceptions with me. The question of determination was thus posed for me by my attention to the material and social context within which romance reading generally occurs.

I had first taken up the subject of romances in graduate school as part of my dissertation on the differences between 'popular' and 'elite' literature.[13] Searching for a way to trace the variable use of generic conventions across these evaluative categories, I chose the gothic romance because my participation in a feminist consciousness-raising group had made me curious about feminist scholarly writing and I saw the study of the romance as a way to engage with this literature. Thus I hoped to bring together my feminist 'personal' life with my supposedly non-gendered academic work which, until that point, had not focussed on women. This decision set in motion a slow, imperfect, often painful process of transformation which only really gathered impetus in the actual writing of *Reading the romance* some six to seven years later, when the difficulties of accounting for the complexities of actual romance reading produced a more intense and personal engagement with feminist theory and its analysis of women's situation. That engagement was fostered by the romance readers' eloquence about their own lives. Even as I began to see myself in their accounts of themselves and thus to admit my identification with them, feminist writers helped me to analyze women's situation and to begin to trace its various determinants. Thus, another of the major surprises produced by doing ethnographic work was my own growing politicization. This politicization had not proceeded very far, however, at the time I began writing, and that fact, along with my preoccupation with the methodological questions about how to conduct the cultural study of literature, caused me to misread earlier feminist work on the romance resulting in a blindness to the continuity between my own arguments and those of scholars such as Tania Modleski and Ann Barr Snitow.[14]

As a consequence, the way the study was formulated and carried out was largely a function of my first theoretical concerns, concerns that I formulated at the outset within the terms of literary critical debates. Since I was assuming from the start with reader theorist Stanley Fish that textual interpretations are constructed by interpretive communities using specific interpretive strategies, I sought to contrast the then-current interpretation of romances produced by trained literary critics with that produced by fans of the genre.[15] Thus, in going into the field, I still conceived of reading in a limited fashion *as interpretation* and saw the project largely as one focussing on the differential interpretation of texts. It was only when the Smithton women repeatedly answered my questions about the meaning of romances by talking about the meaning of romance *reading* as a social event in a familial context that the study began to intersect with work being carried on in Britain.

What is so striking to me now is the way in which the romance readers themselves and their articulation of their concerns pushed me into a consideration of many of the same issues then preoccupying Paul Willis, David Morley, Charlotte Brunsdon, Angela McRobbie, Dorothy Hobson and many others.[16] Indeed, it was the women readers' construction of the act of romance reading as a 'declaration of independence' that surprised me into the realization that the meaning of their media-use was multiply determined and internally contradictory and that to get at its complexity it would be helpful to distinguish analytically between the significance of the *event* of reading and the meaning of the *text* constructed as its consequence. Although I did not then formulate it in so many words, this notion of the event of reading directed me towards a series of questions about the uses 'to which a particular text is put, its function within a particular conjuncture, in particular institutional spaces, and in relation to particular audiences'.[17] What the book gradually became, then, was less an account of the way romances as texts were interpreted than of the way romance reading as a form of behaviour operated as a complex intervention in the ongoing social life of actual social subjects, women who saw themselves first as wives and mothers.

As a consequence, *Reading · the romance* bears striking similarities to Dorothy Hobson's *Crossroads*, to the work on the TV programme 'Nationwide' by David Morley and Charlotte Brunsdon, and to Angela McRobbie's work on the culture of working-class girls. Although the central problematic of the book is not formulated in the languages they employ, nor is their work cited specifically, *Reading the romance* shares their preoccupation with questions about the degree of freedom audiences demonstrated in their interaction with media messages and their interest in the way such cultural forms are embedded in the social life of their users. The theoretical position taken up in the book is quite close to Dorothy Hobson's conclusion that 'there is no overall intrinsic message or meaning in the work', and that 'it comes alive and communicates when the viewers add their own interpretation and understanding to the programme'.[18] Indeed, because I agreed at the outset with Stanley Fish's claim that textual features are not an essential structure upon which an interpretation is hung but rather produced *through* the interpretive process, I think the theoretical position of *Reading the romance* is also close to Hobson's additional observation that 'there can be as many interpretations of a programme [or text] as the individual viewers bring to it'.[19] However, the book argues additionally that whatever the theoretical possibility of an infinite number of readings, in fact, there are patterns or regularities to what viewers and readers bring to texts and media messages in large part because they acquire specific cultural competencies as a consequence of their particular social location. Similar readings are produced, I argue, because similarly located readers learn a similar set of reading strategies and interpretive codes which they bring to bear upon the texts they encounter.

Reading the romance turns to Fish's notion of 'interpretive communities' to theorize these regularities and then attempts to determine whether the Smithton women operate on romances as an interpretive community that is somehow different from the community of trained literary scholars. However, because Fish developed the notion of the interpretive community only to account for varying modes of literary criticism within the academy, that is, to account for the differing interpretations produced by Freudian, Jungian, mythic, or Marxist critics, the concept is insufficiently theorized to deal with the complexities of social groups or to explain how, when, and why they are constituted precisely *as* interpretive communities. Thus it cannot do justice to the nature of the connection between social location and the complex process of interpretation. It is inadequate finally to the task of explaining determination.

The question of determination and regularities became immediately relevant to the research, however, because the group I examined was relatively homogeneous. Not only did the women give remarkably similar answers to my questions about romances, but they referred constantly and *voluntarily* to the connection between their reading and their daily social situation as wives and mothers. I thus theorized the correlation between their patterned answers and their similar social location by resorting to the explanatory constructs of feminist theory, to the notion of 'patriarchal marriage' in particular. Not only have I used the concept to account for the social situation within which their reading occurs and thus employed it to make sense of their reading as an intervention within that situation, but I have also projected it back in time as a social form and, with the help of the psychoanalytic theories of Nancy Chodorow, used it to explain the construction of desire responsible for their location and their partial dissatisfaction with it, which itself leads ultimately to repetitive romance reading.

While I now feel this reification of patriarchal marriage was helpful in generating detailed knowledge about the ways in which romances engage these women, I also think it permitted me to avoid certain crucial theoretical questions about the precise mechanisms of determination. Had I designed the study comparatively, perhaps some of the issues David Morley has raised in his critical postscript to *The 'Nationwide' audience* might have come more prominently to the fore.[20] He points there in particular to the inadequacies he sees in his own earlier discussion of the determinations upon meaning produced by the effectivity of the traditional sociological/structural variables – age, sex, race and class. Many of the problems Morley identifies in his work with respect to this problem are also present in mine. Whereas he notes his excessive concentration on the single variable of class and the rather simple way in which the concept itself was constructed, so I might point in my own study to the exclusive preoccupation with gender and to the use of a rather rigid notion of patriarchy. Indeed I would now want to organize an ethnography of romance reading comparatively in order to make some effort to ascertain how other sociological variables like age, class, location, education and race intersect with gender to produce varying, even conflicting engagements with the romance form. It might also be interesting to study similarly situated women who are non-romance readers in an effort to locate the absence (or perhaps the addition) of certain discursive competencies which render the romance incomprehensible, uninteresting, or irrelevant.

Whatever the sociological weaknesses of *Reading the romance,* I continue to feel that the particular method (or aggregate of methods) employed there to map the complexities of the romance's 'purchase' on this small group of women can serve as a starting point for further discussion and perhaps for future analysis. I think this true, in part, because the understanding of reading that is worked out in the course of the discussion is close to the very useful generic or discursive model Morley has recommended in place of the earlier encoding–decoding formulation. I don't mean simply to imply here that *Reading the romance* does what Morley calls for, although there are some striking similarities between what he recommends and the set of procedures the Smithton women's observations eventually pushed me toward. Rather, I want to suggest that his thoughtful comments in the postscript can usefully be employed to identify some of the other insufficiently theorized steps in my own analysis and thus might be used to extend and improve it.

Having identified what he takes to be the principal sociological problems with his earlier work on the 'Nationwide' audience, Morley suggests that audience research might be more successful if it turned to a genre-based theory of interpretation and interaction instead of to a simple encoding–decoding model. Such a theory, he observes, might more adequately theorize the process of reading as a complex and interrelated series of actions which involves questions of relevance/irrelevance and comprehension/incomprehension in addition to that of ideological agreement. A theory in which genre is conceived as a set of rules for the production of meaning, operable both through writing and reading, might therefore be able to explain why certain sets of texts are especially interesting to particular groups of people (and not to others) because it would direct one's attention to the question of how and where a given set of generic rules had been created, learned, and used. This genre framework would focus attention on interdiscursive formations, that is, on questions about the kinds of cultural competencies that are learned as a consequence of certain social formations and how those are activated and perpetuated within and through multiple, related genres or discourses. Thus, just as one might want to ask what sorts of social grammars prepare working-class kids to understand Kung-fu movies and to find them interesting, so one might also want to ask what competencies prepare certain women to recognize romances as relevant to their experience and as potential routes to pleasure.

Although *Reading the romance* does not use Morley's terms, it does work toward a kind of genre theory as he conceives it. To begin with, it attempts to understand how the Smithton women's social and material situation prepares them to find the act of reading attractive and even necessary. Secondly, through detailed questioning of the women about their own definition of romance and their criteria for distinguishing between ideal and failed versions of the genre, the study attempts to characterize the structure of the particular narrative the women have chosen to engage because they find it especially enjoyable. Finally, through its use of psychoanalytic theory, the book attempts to explain how and why such a structured 'story' might be experienced as pleasurable by those women as a consequence of their socialization within a particular family unit. I would like to elaborate briefly on each of these moments in *Reading the romance* in order to prepare the reader for what she or he will find in the subsequent pages and point to issues which would repay further exploration.

Most of the first half of *Reading the romance* is devoted to a discussion of the social and material situation within which romance reading occurs. Thus I initially survey the collection of social forces resulting in the mass production of romances in the 1970s and '80s, which are marketed in ways particularly appropriate to women, that is, through mail order and at commercial outlets largely frequented by them.[21] Although the move is analogous to Dorothy Hobson's detailed effort to explore the production of *Crossroads*, I have not gone so far as to investigate the professional ideologies informing the writing and editing of romances as she has done with the soap opera. The text does, however, recognize the importance of the romance writing community even to readers, because the Smithton women made it absolutely clear that they understood themselves to be reading particular and individual authors, whose special marks of style they could recount in detail, rather than identical, factory-produced commodities. Despite the mediations of the publishing industry, romance reading was seen by the women as a way of participating in a large, exclusively female community. Were I conducting this study today, I would want to compare the meaning and significance of the romance as it is inserted in the day-to-day existence of both writers and readers, for such a move might demonstrate the problems inherent in a simple reading off of cultural meaning or ideology from a single text.[22]

Turning from the particular processes impinging on production which create the conditions of possibility for regular romance purchases, *Reading the romance* then attempts a parallel look at the conditions organizing women's private lives which likewise contribute to the possibility of regular romance reading. It is in this context that I distinguish analytically between the event of reading and the text encountered through the process. I found it necessary to do so, the reader will discover, because the Smithton women so insistently and articulately explained that their reading was a way of temporarily refusing the demands associated with their social role as wives and mothers. As they observed, it functioned as a 'declaration of independence', as a way of securing privacy while at the same time providing companionship and conversation. In effect, what chapters two and three try to do as a result is to unpack the significance of the phrase 'escape' by taking it somewhat more literally than have most analysts of the media in order to specify the origin and character of the distance the women find it necessary to maintain between their 'ordinary' lives and their fantasies.[23] I have therefore tried to take seriously the dual implications of the word escape, that is, its reference to conditions left behind and its intentional projection of a utopian future.

It is this move, I think, that specifically relates *Reading the romance* to Hobson's *Crossroads* work, to her work on housewives, and to McRobbie's work on the culture of working-class girls. Indeed there are remarkable similarities to the way all of the women who contributed to these studies use traditionally female forms to resist their situation *as women* by enabling them to cope with the features of the situation that oppress them. Thus, just as the adolescent girls studied by McRobbie manipulate the culture of femininity to 'combat the class-based and oppressive features of the school' and the housewives in Hobson's study rely on radio and TV to address their extreme loneliness, so the romance readers of Smithton use their books to erect a barrier between themselves and their families in order to declare themselves temporarily off-limits to those who would mine them for emotional support and material care. What the reader will find in chapter three, then, is an effort to explore the myriad ways in which the simple act of taking up a book addresses the personal costs hidden within the social role of wife and mother. I try to make a case for seeing romance reading as a form of individual resistance to a situation predicated on the assumption that it is women alone who are responsible for the care and emotional nurturance of others. Romance reading buys time and privacy for women even as it addresses the corollary consequence of their situation, the physical exhaustion and emotional depletion brought about by the fact that no one within the patriarchal family is charged with *their* care. Given the Smithton women's highly specific reference to such costs, I found it impossible to ignore their equally fervent insistence that romance reading creates a feeling of hope, provides emotional sustenance and produces a fully visceral sense of well-being.

It was the effort to account for the ability of romance reading to address the women's longing for emotional replenishment that subsequently directed my attention to the cultural conditions that had prepared the women to choose romances from among all the other books available to them. Thus I found myself wondering how, given the particular 'needs' the event of reading seemed to address for the Smithton women, the romance story itself figured in this conjuncture. I began to wonder what it was about the romance heroine's experience that fostered the readers' ability to see her story as interesting and accounted for their willingness to seek their own pleasure through hers precisely at the moment when they were most directly confronting their dissatisfaction with traditionally structured heterosexual relationships. What contribution did the narration of a romance make to their experience of pleasure? Why didn't the Smithton women choose to read detective stories, Westerns or bestsellers in their precious private moments?

In thus searching for a way to link a specific desire with a particularly chosen route to the fulfilment of that desire, I turned to psychoanalytic theory in general and to Nancy Chodorow's feminist revision of Freud in particular. Her work seemed relevant in this context because it insistently focussed on the precise manner in which the social fact of parenting by women constitutes a female child with an ongoing need for the style of care associated originally with her primary parent, that is, with her mother. What I was trying to explain was the fact that the Smithton women apparently felt an intense need to be nurtured and cared for and that despite their universal claim to being happily married (a claim I did not doubt), that need was not being met adequately in their day-to-day existence. Romance reading, it appeared, addressed needs, desires, and wishes that a male partner could not. Chodorow's work looked useful precisely because it theorized an asymmetrical engendering process constituting women and men in profoundly mismatched ways. That work appeared additionally relevant when an investigation of the romances the Smithton women like best revealed that the heroines they most appreciated were virtually always provided with the kind of attention and care the Smithton women claimed to desire and further that the hero's ministrations were nearly always linked metaphorically with maternal concern and nurturance. Thus I found Chodorow's theories attractive because they could account for the ongoing search for the *mother* that I detected in the Smithton women's discussion of the act of romance reading and in their preferences for particular examples of the genre.

Chodorow's revision of the psychoanalytic account of the family romance was interesting to me, in other words, because it postulated in women an ongoing, unfulfilled longing for the mother even after the oedipal turn to the father and heterosexuality had been negotiated. Although Chodorow's principal argument was that the tripartite internal object configuration with which women are therefore endowed is addressed by a woman's subsequent turn to mothering and to her child (an argument that might be taken to imply that the constructed desire for the preoedipal mother may be met through particular social arrangements), it seemed to me that what the Smithton readers were saying about romance reading indicated that in fact not even the activity of mothering could satisfy that lack or desire for the women, at least for some women.[24] I thought this might be true because so much of what the women consciously said and unconsciously revealed through their evaluative procedures pointed to the centrality of the fact that in ideal romances the hero is constructed androgynously. Although the women were clearly taken with his spectacularly masculine phallic power, in their voluntary comments and in their revealed preferences they emphasized equally that his capacity for tenderness and attentive concern was essential as well. Chodorow's theories seemed helpful because of their capacity to explain what I thought of as the twin objects of desire underlying romance reading, that is, the desire for the nurturance represented and promised by the preoedipal mother and for the power and autonomy associated with the oedipal father. Romance reading, it seemed to me, permitted the ritual retelling of the psychic process by which traditional heterosexuality was constructed for women, but it also seemed to exist as a protest against the fundamental inability of heterosexuality to satisfy the very desires with which it engendered women.[25]

Reading the romance turns to Chodorow's revision of psychoanalytic theory in order to explain the construction of the particular desires that seem to be met by the *act* of romance reading. However, it additionally uses that theory to explore the psychological resonance of the romantic *narrative* itself for readers so constructed and engendered, a narrative which is itself precisely about the process by which female subjectivity is brought into being within the patriarchal family. Psychoanalysis is thus used also to explain why the story hails these readers, why they believe it possible to pursue their own pleasure by serving as witness to the romantic heroine's achievement of hers. What the psychoanalytically based interpretation reveals is the deep irony hidden in the fact that women who are experiencing the consequences of patriarchal marriage's failure to address their needs turn to a story which ritually recites the history of the process by which those needs are constituted. They do so, it appears, because the fantasy resolution of the tale ensures the heroine's achievement of the very pleasure the readers endlessly long for. In thus reading the story of a woman who is granted adult autonomy, a secure social position, and the completion produced by maternal nurturance, all in the person of the romantic hero, the Smithton women are repetitively asserting to be true what their still-unfulfilled desire demonstrates to be false, that is, that heterosexuality can create a fully coherent, fully satisfied, female subjectivity.[26]

In the end, *Reading the romance* argues that romance reading is a profoundly conflicted activity centred upon a profoundly conflicted form. Thus the view of the romance developed here is similar to Valerie Walkerdine's account of girls' comics as a practice that channels psychic conflicts and contradictions in particular ways. It is also close to the view developed by Valerie Hey[27] as well as to that of Alison Light, who argues in her conclusion to her analysis of Daphne du Maurier's *Rebecca* that women's romance reading is 'as much a measure of their deep dissatisfaction with heterosexual options as of any desire to be fully identified with the submissive versions of femininity the texts endorse. Romance imagines peace, security and ease precisely because there is dissension, insecurity and difficulty.'[28] Light herself points to the crucial question raised by these fundamental ambiguities surrounding and infusing the act of romance reading, that is, to the crucial question of the ultimate effects the fantasy resolution has on the women who seek it out again and again. Does the romance's endless rediscovery of the virtues of a passive female sexuality merely stitch the reader ever more resolutely into the fabric of patriarchal culture? Or, alternatively, does the satisfaction a reader derives from the act of reading itself, an act she chooses, often in explicit defiance of others' opposition, lead to a new sense of strength and independence? *Reading the romance* ends without managing to resolve these questions, asserting that an adequate answer will come only with time and with careful investigation of the developmental trajectory of the lives of adult romance readers. However much I would like to resolve the issue here, once and forever, I continue to believe that such a resolution is theoretically impossible simply because the practices of reading and writing romance continue and their effects, even now, are not fully realized.

Recent critical work on the romance that focuses both on developments within the genre and within the changing profession of romance writing itself suggests that the recontainment of protest and the channelling of desire staged by the form have not been perfect enough to thwart all change. Indeed, Ann Jones has shown in an analysis of recent Mills & Boon romances that the genre has found it increasingly necessary to engage specifically with feminism.[29] She demonstrates that the contradictions within the genre have been intensified by a tendency to consolidate certain feminist agendas for women in the character of a working, independent heroine even while disparaging the women's movement itself, usually through the speeches of the hero. This 'conflict between feminism as emergent ideology and romance as a residual genre', contends Jones, produces three kinds of contradiction, including narrative discontinuity, irreconcilable settings, and inconsistency in realist dialogue.

I have found similar contradictions in recent American romances and have been struck by the urgency, indeed, by the near hysteria, with which romance authors assert that the newly active, more insistent female sexuality displayed in the genre is still most adequately fulfilled in an intimate, monogamous relationship characterized by love and permanence. Endless assertions of this claim are necessary because many of the more sexually explicit romances in lines such as Candlelight Ecstasy, Silhouette Desire, and Harlequin Temptation come very close to validating female desire and even to locating its origins within the woman herself. Many of the books in these lines, in fact, contain explicit depictions of premarital sexual relationships between hero and heroine and acknowledge that the heroine desires the hero as much as he does her and that she derives pleasure from the encounter. Yet in every case, these romances refuse finally to unravel the connection between female sexual desire and monogamous marriage. The stories therefore close off the vista they open up by virtue of their greater willingness to foreground the sexual fantasy at the heart of the genre. The editorial guidelines concerning the treatment of sex in Harlequin Temptations are illuminating in this context:

> Because this series mirrors the lives of contemporary women, realistic descriptions of love scenes should be included, provided they are tastefully handled. Each book should sustain a high level of sexual tension throughout, balanced by a strong story line. Sensuous encounters should concentrate on passion and the emotional sensations aroused by kisses and caresses rather than the mechanics of sex. Of course, the couple have to be obviously in love, with emphasis put on all that being in love entails. They should definitely consummate their relationship before the end of the story, at whatever point fits naturally into the plot. The love scenes may be frequent, but not overwhelming, and should never be gratuitously included.

It seems clear that while the sexually explicit romance of the '80s may begin positively to valorize female sexuality and thus to question the equation of femininity with virtue and virginity, it must nevertheless continue to motivate sexual activity through love. It does so by retaining the notion of passion as the natural and inevitable expression of a prior *emotional* attachment, itself dependent on a natural, biologically based sexual difference. Thus, as Jones has suggested, 'critiques of the double standard are now admissible; the notion that sexuality is socially constructed, variable, re-inventable rather than instinctive is not.'[30] Consequently, even the most progressive of recent romances continue to bind female desire to a heterosexuality constructed as the only natural sexual alliance, and thus continue to prescribe patriarchal marriage as the ultimate route to the realization of a mature female subjectivity.

The recuperation is clearly important, but again I feel that we must not allow it to blind us to the fact that the romance *is* being changed and struggled over by the women who write it. Indeed it is essential to note that in response to the creation of these sexually explicit romances, publishers have found it necessary to retain the more traditional 'sweet' romance and to create other new forms such as the 'evangelical', or 'inspirational' romance as it is called, for women who still cannot incorporate a more explicit sexuality into the ideology of love. Thus while some romance writers are perfectly willing to identify themselves as feminists, as Catherine Kirkland has found in her study of a local chapter of the Romance Writers of America, others vociferously assert that the romance is in fact the proper response to the havoc wrought by feminism on gender relations.[31] Furthermore, it cannot be said with any certainty whether the writers who are trying to incorporate feminist demands into the genre have been moved to do so by their recognition of the contradictions within the form itself or by the pressures exerted by developments in the larger culture. What does seem clear, however, is that the struggle over the romance is itself part of the larger struggle for the right to define and to control female sexuality. Thus, it matters enormously what the cumulative effects of the act of romance reading are on actual readers. Unfortunately, those effects are extraordinarily difficult to trace.

That the problem might be even more complicated than we think is suggested by Kirkland's discovery that most of the women in the group of romance writers she studied had been avid readers *before* they tried their hand at romance writing. Some of those women suggested that they turned to writing in order to intensify the fantasy experience they associated with the act of romance reading. Others, however, did so out of newfound confidence, which they attributed to romance reading, and which led to a desire to provide pleasure for other women. Romance reading, it would seem, profoundly changes at least some women by moving them to act and to speak in a public forum. Prompted to purchase their own word processor, to convert the former sewing-room into a study, and to demand time, not now for pleasure but for their own work, such women clearly begin to challenge in a fundamental way the balance of power in the traditional family. Of course this does not happen to all romance readers, but we should not discount it as an insignificant phenomenon since the crossover rate from consumer to producer seems to be unusually high within this genre. Indeed the romance boom could not continue to the extent it has were not thousands of women producing their own manuscripts and mailing them off regularly to Harlequin, Silhouette and Candlelight. Whether the satisfaction they derive from this activity ever prompts them to demand changes outside the privatized family environment is impossible to say but I am not willing to rule out the possibility. Indeed positive political strategies might be developed from the recognition that the practices of romance writing and reading continue, that they are fluid and actively being changed by both writers and readers, and that their final effects can neither be foreseen nor guaranteed in advance.

Such open-endedness, of course, immediately raises questions about specific modes of intervention, about how romance writers and readers, as well as feminist intellectuals, might contribute to the rewriting of the romance in an effort to articulate its founding fantasy to a more relevant politics. However, as many feminist theorists have acknowledged, to call for such a project from within the privileged space of the academy is highly problematic, since that call is almost inevitably grounded on a residual elitism which assumes that feminist intellectuals alone know what is best for all women. In this context, Angela McRobbie's admonition that academic feminists tend to 'underestimate the resources and capacities of [do]ordinary[dc] women and girls . . . to participate in their own struggles as women but quite autonomously' is well taken.[32] What is needed, I have come to feel, is a recognition that romance writers and readers are themselves struggling with gender definitions and sexual politics *on their own terms* and that what they may need most from those of us struggling in other arenas is our support rather than our criticism or direction. To find a way to provide such support, however, or alternatively to learn from romance writers and readers is not easy for we lack the space and channels for integrating our practices with theirs. Our segregation by class, occupation, and race, once again, works against us.

I am drawn finally to McRobbie's brilliant suggestion that it might be our traditional restriction to the arena of personal relations and our resultant penchant for talk about them that will enable us to come together as women and to explore both our common cause and our divergent agendas.[33] What we perhaps need most, then, is a place and a vocabulary with which to carry on a conversation about the meaning of such personal relations and the seemingly endless renewal of their primacy through the genre of romance. If we could begin to talk to each other from within our culture's 'pink ghetto', we might indeed learn how 'to make talk walk'.[34] We might learn how to activate the critical power that even now lies buried in the romance as one of the few widely shared womanly commentaries on the contradictions and costs of patriarchy.

Notes

1 Although I am still somewhat uncomfortable with the voice I have adopted here, in part because I fear this sort of discussion can be read as simple personal display, I have finally decided to use it because I agree with Angela McRobbie's argument in 'The politics of feminist research,' *Feminist Review* 12 (1982) that we must begin to acknowledge the ways in which our private, professional and intellectual lives intersect. Thus what I have tried to do is to indicate the ways in which my personal situation and insertion into already existing social institutions and theoretical conversations both served as the conditions of possibility for *Reading the romance* and structured its limitations.

2 See, for instance, Sandra Gilbert's review in the *New York Times Book Review* 30 December (1984).

3 For a comprehensive history of these debates, see Gene Wise, 'Paradigm dramas', *American Quarterly* 31 (1979), 293–337.

4 See, for instance, Murray Murphey, 'American civilization at Pennsylvania', *American Quarterly* 22 (Summer, 1970), 489–502.

5 See, for instance, *The unembarrassed muse: the popular arts in America*, New York: The Dial Press, 1970.

6 Stuart Hall, 'Cultural studies and the centre: some problematics and problems'. In *Culture, media, language: working papers in cultural studies, 1972–79*, London: Hutchinson, p. 19. See also his 'Cultural studies: two paradigms', *Media, Culture and Society* 2 (1980), 52–72.

7 Apparently, no one in my department knew at that time of the work carried out at the Birmingham Centre. I also remained unaware of this research until after I had completed *Reading the romance*. I cannot now recall exactly how I learned of British ethnographic studies of media use but I would like to express my great gratitude to Patrick Hagopian and Elaine Collins who directed my attention to many references, xeroxed chapters and articles in their possession not easily available in Philadelphia, and discussed all of it with me. Thanks also to Larry Grossberg for his more recent bibliographic help, criticism, and support.

8 I am thinking here of Paul Willis's early work, including his 'Notes on method' in *Culture, media, language* and his *Profane culture* as well as of the work by the Women's Studies Group at Birmingham collected in *Women take issue: aspects of women's subordination*, London: Hutchinson, 1978.

9 For a perceptive discussion of the dangers inherent in conceptualizing empirical work as objectively scientific and interpretive work as subjectively humanist and therefore as categorical opposites, see Lawrence Grossberg, 'Critical theory and the politics of research,' *Mass Communication Yearbook* 6 (Forthcoming).

10 Paul Willis, 'Notes on method', in *Culture media, language*, p. 90.

11 Angela McRobbie, 'The politics of feminist research', *Feminist Review* 12, 51.

12 See Palmer's *Thrillers: genesis and structure of a popular genre*, London: Edward Arnold, 1978; Terry Eagleton, *Criticism and ideology: a study in marxist literary theory*, London: New Left Books, 1976.

13 *A phenomenological theory of popular and elite literature*, PhD Dissertation, Michigan State University, 1977.

14 See, for instance, my comments throughout the introduction to the American edition. However, I should not minimize the fact that significant differences in method and political perspective, particularly with respect to the audience for mass culture, continue to separate my approach and that taken by Modleski. See, for instance, her introduction to the recent *Studies in entertainment: critical approaches to mass culture*, Bloomington, IN: University of Indiana, 1986, pp. ix–xix, where she specifically takes issue with the work of the 'Birmingham School' and related approaches to the study of mass culture and charges that work with being celebratory rather than critical.

15 See his *Is there a text in this class?: the authority of interpretive communities*, Cambridge, MA: Harvard University Press, 1980.

16 See the aforementioned titles by Willis and David Morley and Charlotte Brundson, *Everyday television: 'Nationwide'*, London: British Film Institute, 1978; David Morley, *The 'Nationwide' audience*, London: British Film Institute, 1980; Angela McRobbie, 'Working class girls and the culture of femininity,' in *Women take issue*, 96–108; 'Settling accounts with subcultures: a feminist critique', *Screen* 34 (Spring, 1980), 39–49; and '*Jackie*: an ideology of adolescent femininity', in Bernard Waites *et al.* (eds), *Popular culture past and present*, London (1982), 263–83; Dorothy Hobson, 'Housewives: isolation as oppression', in *Women take issue*, 79–95; and '*Crossroads': the drama of a soap opera*, London: Methuen, 1982.

17 David Morley, *The 'Nationwide' audience*, London: British Film Institute, 1980, p. 18.

18 Dorothy Hobson, '*Crossroads': the drama of a soap opera*, London: Methuen, 1982, p. 170.

19 Dorothy Hobson, *'Crossroads': the drama of a soap opera*, London: Methuen, 1982, p. 170.

20 David Morley, 'The "Nationwide" audience – a critical postscript', *Screen Education* **39** (Summer, 1981), 3–14.

21 I should perhaps note here that this boom was initiated in the USA by the Canadian firm of Harlequin Enterprises, which began its rise to prominence in mass market publishing by reprinting the romances of Mills & Boon in the 1950s and 1960s. The genre took off in the USA when Harlequin began to issue romance written by American women and when other firms simultaneously introduced explicit sex into the genre. The Smithton women did not confine themselves to a single kind of romance but read widely in the genre and appreciated many different variations.

22 On this point, see Grossberg's discussion in 'Critical theory and the politics of research', *Mass communications yearbook* **6** (1987).

23 The tendency to deplore the 'escapist' nature of popular fantasy seems much less pronounced in British work than in American. See, for instance, Valerie Walkerdine's sensitive discussion of the nature of fantasy escape for girls in 'Some day my prince will come: young girls and the preparation for adolescent sexuality', in Angela McRobbie and Mica Nava (eds), *Gender and generation*, London: Macmillan, 1984, 162–84.

24 The British reader will no doubt note that this did not lead me to reconsider Chodorow's work and its relation to object-relations theory. Walkerdine's comments in 'Some day my prince will come' (178–81) have since suggested to me that the revision romance reading caused me to propose in Chodorow's theory may be of more significance than I had thought. It may not be the case that mothering fails to work only for some (aberrant) women, but in fact that the struggle over gender identity is never resolved as she suggests, following Freud, Lacan, and Rose.

25 For a somewhat different use of Chodorow that also connects romance reading to the search for preoedipal merging, see Angela Mile's fascinating unpublished article, 'Confessions of a Harlequin reader: romance and the fantasy of male mothering'.

26 Cora Kaplan has recently advanced an argument which suggests that readers do not identify only with the romantic heroine but in fact identify in multiple and wandering fashion with the seducer, the seduced and the process of seduction itself. See 'The Thorn Birds: fiction, fantasy, femininity', in *Sea changes: feminism and culture*, London: Verso, 1986, 117–46. Although I found little evidence of this kind of multiple identification in the group I interviewed (at least at a conscious level), I have been told by many romance writers that the act of writing a romance is especially enjoyable because it gives them the opportunity to imagine themselves as the hero. It is also interesting to note that several American publishers of romances have recently permitted writers to experiment with the writing of a romance entirely from the hero's point of view. Thus, it might be possible that this sort of multiple identification actually varies from reader to reader and therefore can be increased by cultural or personal changes.

27 Valerie Hey, 'The necessity of romance', University of Kent at Canterbury, Women's Studies Occasional Papers, **3** (1983).

28 Alison Light, '"Returning to Manderley" – romance fiction, female sexuality and class', *Feminist Review* **16** (April, 1984), 7–25.

29 Ann Rosalind Jones, 'Mills & Boon Meets Feminism', in Jean Radford (ed.), *The progress of romance: the politics of popular fiction*, London: Routledge & Kegan Paul, 1986, 195–220.

30 Ann Jones, 'Mills & Boon meets feminism', p. 210.

31 Catherine Kirkland, *For the love of it: women writers and the popular romance*, PhD dissertation, University of Pennsylvania, 1984.
32 Angela McRobbie, 'The politics of feminist research', p. 53.
33 Angela McRobbie, 'The politics of feminist research', p. 57.
34 The phrases are Catherine Kirkland's and Angela McRobbie's, respectively.

8

Cultural studies at the crossroads

Graham Murdock

From *Australian Journal of Communication*, no. 16 (December 1989).

Abstract. This paper argues that if cultural studies is to maintain its intellectual vitality and its relevance to contemporary conditions and political debates, it needs to broaden its core concerns and establish new points of connection with work at the cutting edge of the social sciences.

Conceptual and methodological issues addressed include problems with ethnographic methodology; the commercial populism of the New Conservatism; the rejection of the 'dominant ideology' thesis and the development of 'critical pluralism'; the 'condition of England question' and the shifting relation between national, sub-national, and supranational cultural formations in the 1990s; and the need to integrate a critical political economy approach with the academic analyses of discourse.

Introduction

It is a truism, but nonetheless true, that what you see depends on where you stand and which direction you look in. My own view of the present state of cultural studies and its prospects is inevitably coloured by my experience of ten years of Thatcherism and of the ways in which it has reshaped the intellectual and political agenda in Britain. [. . .]

A set of broadly shared question marks is now beginning to form over the future of cultural studies, prompted by a general recognition that a crossroads has been reached and that it's time to take a long hard look at our central projects and preoccupations, at our dominant conceptualizations and preferred methodologies, and at the interventions we wish to make.

You don't have to subscribe to the more apocalyptic visions of postmodern theory to accept that the 1990s will be a decade of substantial realignment and change at the economic, political, and cultural levels both within nation states and within the world system as a whole. If cultural studies is going to have something distinctive and worthwhile to say about these shifts we will need to examine the intellectual baggage that we carry around with us and decide what to keep and what to throw away. To do this, we have to backtrack a little, and re-examine the projects, procedures, and politics which have shaped our practice up until now. I shall confine my remarks to work in Britain, not because I believe it is in any way privileged or paradigmatic, but because it highlights the conceptual and methodological issues we have to address particularly clearly.

British cultural studies' three projects

Cultural studies in Britain developed in reaction to the dominant definition of 'culture' bequeathed by the conservative tradition of cultural criticism, and challenged it at two basic levels.

In opposition to the identification of 'culture' with a particular selection of canonized texts and legitimized practices, it reasserted the anthropological conception of culture as all the ways in which people make sense of their situation and express these understandings. It was therefore as interested in the 'lived texts' of social rituals and social institutions as in artefacts. Where cultural criticism saw only an absence of 'culture' within the working class, cultural studies set out to uncover the variety and vitality of situated practices and beliefs, and to demonstrate their authentic roots in popular experience.

At the same time, it was clear that resources for meaning construction were not generated entirely within particular situations. Key elements were provided by the products promoted by the commercial cultural industries, by the discourses of state agencies and political parties, and by the paternalistic rhetorics of the public institutions such as schools, museums, and public broadcasting, which actively promoted the 'selective tradition'. Consequently, cultural studies' second major project was to show how these top-down initiatives worked ideologically to mobilize popular understanding and practice in the service of the asymmetric power relations between producers and consumers, government and citizens, and intellectuals and publics.

These two projects converged to produce a third, which was expressly concerned with the interplay between situated cultures and ideological formations, and particularly with the ways in which the first provides resources for negotiating, refusing, and resisting the second.

There are a range of problems with each of these strands, but in the space available here I want to concentrate on the issues that seem to me to be the most pressing as we enter the 1990s.

Everyday culture and popular creativity

Cultural studies' concerns with the active audience for commercially provided culture and the dialectical relations between concrete experience and mediated meaning have been elaborated in a wide range of studies, from Richard Hoggart's portrait of working-class culture between the Wars, through the successive waves of research on youth subcultures, popular decodings of televisual texts and women's pleasure, to the current vogue for studies of domestic consumption. Each of these literatures deserves detailed discussion, but for the moment I want to underline some basic problems with this whole tradition of work. The first has to do with the methods of inquiry employed.

Although cultural studies has taken over cultural anthropology's central focus on the making and taking of meaning in everyday life, it has not used properly ethnographic methods. There are some exceptions, most notably Paul Willis, but, by and large, empirical evidence has been gathered through casual observation, one-off interviews, and single group discussions. This produces 'thin' rather than 'thick' descriptions (Geertz, 1973), and means that interpretations are insufficiently contextualized.

This problem is particularly acute in instances such as Dick Hebdige's (1979) reading of youth subcultural styles, where the interpretations on offer are detached almost completely from the situational dynamics being analysed and from the self-understandings of participants. As a reading of 'lived texts' it has great elegance and panache, but as an account of how working-class youth subcultures actually developed and what they meant to their supporters, it contains a number of errors and misunderstandings that better ethnography could have avoided (see Hobbs, 1988; Chapter 6).

Even where direct evidence is available, as in Dorothy Hobson's work on housewives watching soap operas or David Morley's research on decoding, insufficient knowledge about the life situation and beliefs of the subjects often forces the analyses to explain particular readings by resorting to the general structural categories of class, gender, and ethnicity. To avoid this and generate more complex accounts of the social bases of everyday cultural activity we need not only better ethnographies but also bridging concepts that can link situations and formations, practices, and structures. [. . .] As I have argued elsewhere (Murdock, 1989a), Pierre Bourdieu's work provides a more productive starting point for this enterprise than de Certeau's currently fashionable writings. Whereas de Certeau focusses on the ways in which the 'procedures and ruses of consumers compose the network of an antidiscipline' (de Certeau, 1988, p. xv), Bourdieu underscores the inertia exerted by the prevailing structures of economic and symbolic capital and the ways they penetrate and organize everyday practice by regulating access to the competencies required for particular forms of consumption (Bourdieu, 1977, 1984).

From romanticism to populism

De Certeau's voluntaristic formulation reinforces the romanticism that has underpinned a good deal of work in cultural studies up until now. This stance has fuelled a continual search for signs of popular resistance against the regularities, routines, and ideologies of industrial capitalism. John Fiske, for example, is in no doubt at all that 'The culture of everyday life is best described through metaphors of struggle or antagonism: strategies opposed to tactics, the bourgeoisie by the proletariat; hegemony met by resistance, ideology countered or evaded; top-down power opposed by bottom-up power, social discipline faced with disorder' (Fiske, 1989, p. 47). There are several problems with this preference for refusal. Firstly, as Stanley Cohen has noted in relation to studies of youth subcultures, 'the constant impulse to decode only in terms of opposition and resistance means that instances are sometimes missed' when interpretations and practices are 'taken over intact from dominant commercial culture' (Cohen, 1980, p. xii). Secondly, and more importantly, the romantic celebration of consumer activity can easily support a stance which colludes (however unwittingly) with the commercial populism of the New Conservatism.

This is the case· with John Fiske's view that because successful programmes like 'Dallas' have to connect with the lives and values of a variety of social groups to retain a mass audience, there is no need to press for a production system committed to defending and extending programme diversity. Indeed, in his view, 'diversity of readings may best be stimulated by a greater homogeneity of programming' (Fiske, 1987, p. 319). This argument is fundamentally mistaken. Whilst it is self-evidently the case that prime-time programming has to provide multiple points of pleasure for a socially differentiated audience, the formats it employs clearly operate to regulate the range of discourses and presentations called into play in important ways, preferring some whilst marginalizing or excluding others. As a consequence there are identities, experiences, and forms of knowledge which are consistently pushed to or off the edge of the schedules. To argue otherwise is to accept commercial television's claim that it gives people what they want and need, and to undermine the case for new forms of public broadcasting that can address the full range of contemporary cultures. If John Fiske had been sitting in 10 Downing Street when· the relevant legislation was going through Parliament, Britain would never have launched Channel 4 with its statutory obligation to extend programme diversity, and the country would have missed the most significant attempt to engage with cultural plurality to date.

The view of audience members as first and foremost active consumers also helps to reinforce the New Conservatives' promotion of the marketplace as the fundamental sphere of liberty and of the freedom to choose between competing products as the core of individual rights. This conception operates to displace the alternative view of audience members as citizens with other entitlements, including rights of access to the full range of information, argument, and interpretation they need in order to understand their situation and to intervene to change it if they so choose. (See Murdock and Golding, 1989.) The question of citizenship – its nature and future – is set to become one of the key issues of the 1990s. If cultural studies is to make an effective intervention in this debate, it needs to recover its commitment to 'a more dense and participatory culture (and) not merely endorse the goals of greater individual freedom to choose' between cultural commodities and to develop counter interpretations and uses (Rustin, 1989, p. 68).

This involves a move away from the expressive individualism of some recent work on audiences back towards a more thorough engagement with the ways that meanings and identities are negotiated socially, and with the way that these grounded processes are structured by wider economic and ideological formations.

Critical pluralism and the contest of discourse

Recent work on ideology has been marked by a decisive and irreversible rejection of the 'dominant ideology' thesis in all its forms, and the development of what we can call 'critical pluralism'. This new perspective views the cultural field as the site of a continual struggle between competing discourses, each offering a particular way of looking at or speaking about the social world (or particular segments of it), and engaged in a contest for visibility and legitimacy across a range of social institutions. Whilst it accepts the pluralist stress on competition, it retains critical theory's insistence on the unequal nature of discursive struggles arising from the fact that some discourses are backed by greater material resources and have preferential access to the major means of publicity and policy-making. Consequently, to talk about the cultural field is 'to speak of a field of relations structured by power and difference' in which some discourses are more central and dominant than others, but where these 'positions are never permanently fixed' (Hall, 1989, p. 51). In a number of late capitalist societies, the commercial speech of the consumer system and the discourses of neo-conservatism enjoy a number of advantages. However, their command of popular consciousness cannot be guaranteed simply by their present ubiquity and centrality; it has to be constantly worked and struggled for.

Their success will largely depend on their ability to 'articulate' common sense, in the double sense of linking its separate and contradictory elements together in a functioning whole (in the same way that an articulated lorry is made up of a cab and a trailer that can be uncoupled), and of finding forms of rhetoric and signification that anchor this discursive formation convincingly in everyday experience (Grossberg, 1986, p. 53). Since the rise of Thatcherism provides a particularly rich instance of this process of 'articulation' in action, it has, not surprisingly, become a major focus of debate in Britain, and one in which Stuart Hall has played a leading role (see Hall and Jacques, 1983; Hall, 1988; Gamble, 1988). Underlying this discussion is an essentially simple question: how has Mrs Thatcher managed to get away with it?

Stuart Hall's work illustrates the strengths and weaknesses of approaching this question from within a cultural studies framework. The strengths are in the analysis of Thatcherism as a new discursive formation which combines the 'liberal discourses of the "free market" and economic man and the organic conservative themes of tradition, family, and nation, respectability, patriarchalism and order' (Hall, 1988, p. 2). The problems lie in the evaluation of its popular impact and Hall's relative lack of interest in the available evidence. Despite Thatcherism's acute orchestration of key themes in common-sense thinking, there is a good deal of evidence to suggest that it has been rather less successful in achieving hegemony in Hall's sense of the term (see Hall, 1988, p. 7) than his analysis would predict. Not only are Mrs Thatcher's electoral successes more plausibly explained as the outcome of pragmatic choices and the absence of a credible alternative government rather than as indications of popular support for Thatcherism (Hirst, 1989, Chapter 1), but recent research indicates that collectivist values have more than held their ground during the Thatcher years (Rentoul, 1989).

The rights and wrongs of these arguments, and their implications for political strategy, are mainly of interest to those of us living in Britain and hoping to see a change of government at the next General Election. But Hall's work on Thatcherism also points to another, deeper, problem with cultural studies as it is currently constituted. This has to do with its continuing fixation with the state of the nation.

Cultural studies and the condition of England

The British tradition of cultural criticism was always strongly linked to what came to be known as 'the condition of England question'. The question was this: how was it possible to construct a common culture in a situation where the uneven growth of industrial capitalism was creating deep class divisions and where organized religion was losing its always slim hold over the popular imagination. The conservative response was to embark on a general 'invention of tradition' (Hobsbawn and Ranger, 1983) designed to provide new symbols and rituals of nationhood that would bind the country together in an imagined community, strong enough to displace the solidarities of class, region, and locality. The construction of a selective cultural tradition which embodied the essential qualities of 'Englishness' in their 'highest' form was an integral part of this project (Dodd, 1986).

Although cultural studies expressly set out to deconstruct this formation of nation and people, it has inevitably ended up working within its general framework. Indeed, a good deal of work in British cultural studies can be read as a series of meditations on 'the condition of England' devoted to interrogating national ideologies and exploring the counter formations of class, and to a lesser extent region. As a consequence it has had little to say about the explosive growth of transnational culture. However, there is little doubt that questions about the shifting relation between national, subnational, and supranational cultural formations will play a much more prominent role in the 1990s.

Coming to terms with the multinationals and multiculturalism

Interest in the transnational circulation of representations has grown over the last decade as a result of three main factors. Firstly, the spread of new communications technologies, particularly video cassette recorders and satellite television, has enabled the Hollywood studios, the major advertising agencies, and the multinational entrepreneurs of the moving image to get around many of the regulations governing national broadcasting and cinema systems and open up new markets for their products. Secondly, this process has been given an added boost in many countries by the enthusiasm for privatization policies (Murdock, 1989b). Thirdly, there is now considerable interest in exploring the cultural implications of groupings such as the European Community and the Pacific Rim.

The dynamics of globalization are of course more complex than the cruder characterizations of 'cultural imperialism' allow for. To argue that they impose alien cultures on indigenous peoples simply revives the 'dominant ideology' thesis. It is more productive to see them as changing the terms of existing struggles by introducing new discursive formations and new points of identity and pleasure and by facilitating new kinds of cultural practice. Understanding how these dynamics are worked through at the level of everyday life and how they impinge on the ideological strategies employed in nation building is one of the central tasks for cultural studies in the coming decade.

This does not mean abandoning studies of particular local conditions. On the contrary, if we are to avoid facile generalizations and comparisons we need the widest possible range of research on specific situations. At the same time, in an era when every country is locked into an emerging world cultural system, knowledge of how that system works provides an indispensable context for interpreting and explaining situated activity. We must learn how to think globally while acting locally, and put some energy into developing concepts and forms of writing which will explicate the links between knowable communities and larger systems (see Marcus and Fischer, 1986, Chapter 4).

One powerful experiential connection between national conditions and the world system operates through exile, migration, and resettlement. These movements have assumed particular significance in the post-colonial era and have made multiculturalism a key issue for a growing number of societies, including Britain.

Within cultural studies writings Britain's black population has frequently been celebrated as a source of white style or empathized with as victims of racism, but until comparatively recently their own cultural strategies remained mostly uncharted. Consequently, black students coming to the area often experienced its analyses of the national condition as a 'morbid celebration of England and Englishness from which blacks (were) systematically excluded' (Gilroy, 1987, p. 12). This situation has now changed as a new generation of black British intellectuals has begun to speak from within black British experience and to interrogate the cultural legacy of empire from the other end of the colonial chain. Even so, the issues posed by Britain's transition to a multicultural society remain inadequately theorized and only partially integrated into cultural studies' core projects. Nor is this simply a British problem.

Although it expressly sets out to challenge the prevailing belief in 'a monolithic Australian culture' by revealing the 'richness and diversity' of the country's lived cultures, Fiske, Hodge and Turner's recent book, *Myths of Oz* (1987), offers no sustained analysis of the new ethnic communities and their complex relations to white Australia. Yet here, as elsewhere in the post-colonial world, questions of national culture and identity can no longer be adequately posed, let alone answered, without taking the dynamics of a multicultural formation fully into account.

Coming to terms with political economy

The other major problem with contemporary cultural studies is its continuing refusal to incorporate a critical political economy of culture.

True, there have been some recent moves in this direction, but as recent writings on postmodernism show all too clearly, there is still some way to go before a theoretical synthesis is achieved. At the moment, work on the postmodern condition falls into two broad categories. There is a burgeoning literature on the emergence of postmodernist forms of representation and aesthetics. There is also a growing volume of commentary on the transition from a Fordist economic regime to one organized around flexible accumulation, in which information and communication systems come to play a central role as factors of production. As yet, however, there have been few attempts to theorize the possible linkages between these two movements, and most of these have come from social scientists, rather than from cultural studies (e.g. Lash and Urry, 1987; Harvey, 1989).

The need for cultural studies to take the insights of critical political economy seriously is clearly signalled by the popularity of the notion of 'cultural industries' which is now to be found peppering the speeches and reports of politicians and policy-makers as well as academics. Its currency points to a growing awareness that the cultural industries are both similar to and different from other industries. On the one hand, they are clearly organized industrially in specifiable ways and are part of the general productive system. On the other hand, the goods they manufacture – the movies, ads, and TV shows – are unlike the products of other industries in that they play a pivotal role in organizing the images and discourses through which we make sense of the world. They do not simply make commodities; they make available the repertoire of meanings through which the social world, including the world of commodities, is understood and acted on. It is not enough simply to acknowledge this duality (see Fiske 1989, Chapter 2), we need to conceptualize the relations between the material and discursive organization of culture without reducing one to the other.

It is precisely this focus on the *interplay* between the symbolic and the economic which distinguishes a political economy approach from one ground solely in academic economics. Where economists are primarily interested in how the cultural industries work as part of the bounded domain of 'the economy', political economy is concerned to show how different ways of financing and organizing cultural production (and production in general) have traceable consequences for the range of discourses and representations in the public domain and their accessibility to audiences. Neo-conservatives see markets as the best guarantor of diverse production and consumer choice. Those like myself, in the critical camp, point to the distorting effects of inequalities in the distribution of wealth and income and argue for positive public intervention to underwrite plurality and public access.

In principle, many of those working in cultural studies accept the need for a critical political economy, but stop short of integrating its insights into their own analytical practice. Stuart Hall, for example, has recently argued that, although the structure of ownership and control is not 'a sufficient explanation of the way the ideological universe is structured, it is a *necessary starting point*' (Hall, 1986, p. 11) (my italics). Yet in another recent piece, he castigates critical political economists for having 'no conception of the struggle for meaning' and dismisses their analyses as crude and reductionist

(Hall, 1989, p. 50). This may be true of some variants (e.g. Herman and Chomsky, 1988, Chapter 1), but it is not a necessary consequence of pursuing critical political economy's core project. The sticking point is the vexed question of 'determination'.

Instead of persisting with Marx's original proposition that the economic determines 'in the last instance', with its implication that there is always a direct link between economic organization and cultural activity (however attenuated), we can adopt Stuart Hall's own very useful suggestion to think of the economic as determining in the 'first instance' (Hall, 1983). This immediately opens up the possibility of combining recent work in critical political economy with advances in the analyses of discourse. In my own recent work, for example, I have sought to argue firstly, that the changing economics of cultural production promotes certain cultural forms and practices at the expense of others (e.g. Murdock, 1989c), and secondly, that once in play, these cultural forms play a key role in organizing the contest of discourse on their own account by granting or withholding visibility and legitimacy (e.g. Schlesinger, Murdock and Elliott, 1983). A parallel argument that can be made for cultural consumption (see Murdock, 1989a).

Into the 1990s

I have argued that if cultural studies is to maintain its intellectual vitality and its relevance to contemporary conditions and political debates, it needs to broaden its core concerns and establish new points of connection with work at the cutting edge of the social sciences. There are a number of areas where social scientists are developing ideas which are directly relevant to cultural studies' main projects. Instances include sociological work on how the contest of discourses around key issues is organized (e.g. Hilgartner and Bosk, 1988; Gamson and Modigliani, 1989), and research in social psychology on the role of discourse and texts in the social constitution of identity (e.g. Shotter and Gergen, 1989). Cultural studies' relative isolation from these initiatives is one of the penalties of its emergence as a self-sustaining area of academic study with its own selective tradition of canonized texts. To counter this we need to recover the original interdisciplinary impetus and be more adventurous in crossing intellectual check-points.

We also need to restore cultural studies' commitment to making practical as well as academic interventions. This certainly involves arguing with policy-makers and contributing to debates on the funding and organization of cultural activity, but it also means renewing and developing the dialogue with the subjects of our inquiries, through adult and continuing education, public speeches, journalism, and programme making. The barriers to this enterprise arise not only from the crisis of intellectual practice [. . .] but also from the institutional crisis of the public sphere. If cultural studies is to contribute in a central way to the debates of the 1990s we will need to fight long and hard to defend and extend the spaces and resources that allow intellectual work and political debate to proceed independently of commercial pressures and the encroachments of state and government. If a decade of Thatcherism has taught us in Britain anything, it is this.

References

Bourdieu, P. 1977: *Outline of a theory of practice*. Cambridge: Cambridge University Press.
Bourdieu, P. 1984: *Distinction: a social critique of the judgement of taste*. London: Routledge & Kegan Paul.
Cohen, S. 1980: *Folk devils and moral panics: the creation of the mods and rockers*. Oxford: Martin Robertson.
de Certeau, M. 1988: *The practice of everyday life*, Berkeley, CA: University of California Press.
Dodd, P. 1986: Englishness and national culture. In Colls, R. and Dodd, P. (eds), *Englishness: politics and culture 1880–1920*. Beckenham: Croom Helm.
Fiske, J. 1987: *Television culture*. London: Methuen.
Fiske, J. 1989: *Understanding popular culture*. London: Unwin Hyman.
Fiske, J., Hodge, B. and Turner, G. 1987: *Myths of Oz: reading Australian popular culture*. Sydney: Allen & Unwin.
Gamble, A. 1988: *The free economy and the strong state: the politics of Thatcherism*. London: Macmillan.
Gamson, V.A. and Modigliani, A. 1989: Media discourse and public opinion on nuclear power: a constructionist approach. *American Journal of Sociology* 95(1), 1–37.
Geertz, C. 1973: *The interpretation of cultures*. New York: Basic Books.
Gilroy, P. 1987: *There ain't no black in the Union Jack: the cultural politics of race and nation*. London: Hutchinson.
Grossberg, L. 1986: On postmodernism and articulation: an interview with Stuart Hall. *Journal of Communication Inquiry* 10(2), 45–60.
Hall, S. 1983: The problem of ideology: Marxism without guarantees. In Matthews, B. (ed.), *Marx: a hundred years on*. London: Lawrence & Wishart, 57–85.
Hall, S. 1986: Media power and class power. In Curran, J. *et al.* (eds), *Bending reality: the state of the media*. London: Pluto Press, 5–14.
Hall, S. 1988: *The hard road to renewal: Thatcherism and the crisis of the left.* London: Verso.
Hall, S. 1989: Ideology and communication theory. In Dervin, B. *et al.* (eds), *Rethinking communication, volume one: paradigm issues*. London: Sage, 40–52.
Hall, S. and Jacques, K. (eds) 1983: *The politics of Thatcherism*. London: Lawrence & Wishart.
Harvey, D. 1989: *The condition of postmodernity*. Oxford: Basil Blackwell.
Hebdige, D. 1979: *Subculture: the meaning of style*. London: Methuen.
Herman, E. and Chomsky, N. 1988: *Manufacturing consent: the political economy of the mass media*. New York: Pantheon.
Hilgartner, S. and Bosk, C.L. 1988: The rise and fall of social problems: a public arenas model. *American Journal of Sociology* 94(1), 53–78.
Hirst, P. 1989: *After Thatcher*. London: Collins.
Hobbs, D. 1988: *Doing the business: entrepreneurship, the working class, and detectives in the East End of London*. Oxford: Oxford University Press.
Hobsbawn, E. and Ranger, T. (eds) 1983: *The invention of tradition*. Cambridge: Cambridge University Press.
Lash, S. and Urry, J. 1987: *The end of organised capitalism*. Cambridge: Polity Press.
Marcus, G.E. and Fischer, M. 1986: *Anthropology as cultural critique: an experimental movement in the human sciences*. Chicago, IL: University of Chicago Press.

Murdock, G. 1989a: Critical inquiry and activity. In Dervin, B. *et al.* (eds), *Rethinking communication, volume two: paradigm exemplars.* London: Sage, 226–49.

Murdock, G. 1989b: Redrawing the map of the communications industries: concentration and ownership in the era of privatisation. In Ferguson, M. (ed.) *Public communication: the new imperatives.* London: Sage (in press).

Murdock, G. 1989c: Televisual tourism: national image-making and international markets. In Thomsen, C.W. (ed.), *Cultural transfer or electronic imperialism?*. Heidelberg: Carl Winter Universitätsverlag, 171–84.

Murdock, G. and Golding, P. 1989: Information poverty and political inequality: citizenship in the age of privatised communication. *Journal of Communication* (in press).

Rentoul, J. 1989: *Me and mine: the triumph of the new individualism?*. London: Unwin Hyman.

Rustin, M. 1989: The politics of post-Fordism: or, the trouble with new times. *New Left Review* no. 175, 54–77.

Schlesinger, P., Murdock, G. and Elliott, P. 1983: *Televising 'terrorism': political violence in popular culture.* London: Comedia.

Shotter, J. and Gergen, K.J. 1989: *The texts of identity.* London: Sage.

Section 2

Difference and identity

This section includes works which in a variety of ways explore questions of difference and identity, with a certain emphasis on lived culture, and begins significantly with **Phil Cohen**'s seminal study which marked out one of the major trajectories of British cultural studies, that of youth culture and consumption. Rooted concretely in the East End of London, Cohen's piece discusses the consequences of economic planning of the mid-1960s for its inhabitants in terms of fragmentation and breakdown of the extended family and kinship networks, isolation and lack of communal space; a socio-ecology in which Commonwealth immigrants were scapegoated by a disorganized working class [see Cohen (1988) for his analysis of the complexities of class, race and youth (Bains and Cohen 1988)]. Turning specifically to young white working-class males, Cohen argues that youth subcultures, in their various forms, were responses to an experienced tension between the conflicting ideologies of the period: those of spectacular consumption and production, or work ethic. Substantively and theoretically this was the precursor of much important work by Cohen himself (Cohen, 1985, 1990; Robins and Cohen, 1978) but also of work which is more readily identified with the Centre for Contemporary Cultural Studies (CCCS) at Birmingham (Hebdige, 1979; Jefferson *et al.*, 1975; Willis, 1977), rather than Cohen's subsequent work (see also Schwartz [1990] for a contemporary analysis of London's East End Docklands).

If the early work of CCCS was preoccupied with the 'magical resolution' function of male youth subcultures, this formed the subject of strong feminist critique exemplified by the CCCS Women's Studies Group collection *Women take issue* published in 1978, but more specifically tackled by Angela McRobbie in 'Settling accounts with subcultures' (1980), in which she challenged the inherent masculinity of the studies of youth subculture then dominating the field, and in her concrete analysis of working-class girls and femininity (see also McRobbie, 1978, 1991). The feminist intervention in cultural studies has led to some of the most interesting and productive work in the field (Franklin *et al.*, 1991).

91

Erica Carter's interesting argument around young women and their relationship to consumerism and the market more generally owes much to that early feminist critique. She insists that the 'image industries' are acutely aware of gender difference which operates as a 'dominant variable for the construction of consumer groups', and takes the youth subcultural theorists to task for not recognizing this. She chooses to focus her study on the female consumer culture in post-war (West) Germany, and places youth studies in a broader, historical and national context.

The third piece indicates the second major challenge to British cultural studies in the 1980s: questions of 'race'. Here **Paul Gilroy** recovers the hidden history of African-Caribbean music in the dance halls of Britain and in particular shows how, through a series of exchanges and interactions, the politics of race have been lived out and transcended through popular musical forms, in the name of youth (see also Bains and Cohen 1988; CCCS, 1982.)

Theoretically informed by the post-structuralist challenges to the unified subject and developments within psychoanalysis, questions of identity have become quite central in recent cultural studies work, and **Stuart Hall**'s second piece included in this both exemplifies the twin focus of this trajectory: a politics of difference and a politics of reflexivity. Hall insists, however, that 'Who I am – the "real" me' – was formed in relation to a whole set of other narratives'. Identity for him is formed where subjectivity meets 'the narratives of history, of a culture'.

The 'Rushdie Affair' has, since 1989, brought a number of issues to the surface whilst provoking strange alliances amongst left, right and liberal intellectuals retaliating against the perceived unacceptable protests from the British Muslim community against the publication of *The Satanic Verses*. However, their most vociferous outrage was reserved for the *fatwa* of Ayatolla Khomeni, declared in 1989. **Bhikhu Parekh** looks closely at *The Satanic Verses* and seeks to understand both the authorial standpoint and the complexities of the book's reception within the fraught race relations of post-colonial Britain (Akhtar, 1989; Apignanesi and Maitland, 1989; Kabbani, 1989; Webster, 1990).

Small-scale qualitative research projects have remained an important feature of cultural studies, particularly British cultural studies (but see also Lull, 1990, 1991). **Marie Gillespie**'s 'ethnographic' study focuses on young British Asians and their parents and grandparents in Southall, West London, and on their relationship to a newer form of technology, the video cassette recorder. It reveals the complex use to which such technologies can be put and, surprisingly perhaps, shows how it maintains and reinforces the older cultural traditions of a community as well as the generational differences within it.

The final piece in this section, by **Kobena Mercer**, raises questions of the politics of representation, particularly in relation to pornography and race. Mercer takes issue with 'white' feminist antipornography polemics which on the one hand use the phenomenon of racial hatred as analogous to male violence and on the other can readily be taken up by the New Right in an allied call for censorship. Through his own changing readings of the controversial and challenging homoerotic images of black male nudes produced by the gay male photographer, Robert Mapplethorpe, Mercer draws our attention to his strategies of transgression across the boundaries of 'high' and 'low' (or popular) culture, fine art and pornography and calls for complexities of reading which resist fixity and simple accusations of 'racism'. Finally, Mercer places Mapplethorpe's subversive aesthetics within the deadly political climate of the AIDS crisis where new and fertile ground has appeared for the legitimacy of political homophobia and the spread of popular authoritarian tendencies across the Left–Right spectrum.

References

Akhtar, S. 1989: *Be careful with Muhammad! The Salman Rushdie affair*. London: Bellew.

Apignanesi, L. and Maitland, S. 1989: *The Rushdie file*. London: Fourth Estate.

Bains, H. and Cohen, P. 1988: *Multi-racist Britain*. London: Macmillan.

Cohen, P. 1985: *Rethinking the fourth question*, working papers. London: Post Sixteen Education Centre, University of London, Institute of Education.

Cohen, P. 1988: The perversions of inheritance – studies in the making of multi-racist Britain. In Cohen, P. and Baines, H. (eds), *Multi-racist Britain*. London: Macmillan.

Cohen, P. 1990: *Really useful knowledge*. Photography and Cultural Studies in Pre-vocational Education. London: Trentham Books.

CCCS 1982: *The Empire strikes back: race and racism in 70s Britain*, Centre for Contemporary Cultural Studies, University of Birmingham. London: Hutchinson.

Franklin, S., Lury, C. and Stacey, J. 1991: *Off-centre: feminism and cultural studies*. London: HarperCollins.

Hebdige, D. 1979: *Subculture: the meaning of style*, London: Methuen.

Jefferson, T. *et al.* (ed.) 1975: *Resistance through rituals*, Centre for Contemporary Cultural Studies, University of Birmingham. Republished 1976. London: Hutchinson.

Kabbani, R. 1989: *A letter to Christendom*. London: Virago.

Lull, J. 1990: *Inside family viewing*. London: Virago.

Lull, J. 1991: *China turned on*. London: Routledge.

McRobbie, A. 1978: Working class girls and the culture of femininity. In *Women take issue*. Birmingham: Women's Studies Group, Centre for Contemporary Cultural Studies, University of Birmingham.

McRobbie, A. 1980: Settling accounts with subcultures. In *Screen Education* **34**. Reprinted in Bennett, T., Martin, G., Mercer, C. and Woollacott, J. (eds), *Culture ideology and social process*. London: Batsford.

McRobbie, A. 1991: *Feminism and youth culture: from Jackie to Just Seventeen*. London: Macmillan.

Robins, D. and Cohen, P. 1978: *Knuckle sandwich – growing up in the working-class city*. London: Penguin Books.

Schwarz, B. 1991: Where horses shit a hundred sparrows feed – docklands and East London during the Thatcher years. In Corner, J. and Harvey, S. (eds), *Enterprise and heritage – cross currents of national culture*. London/New York: Routledge.

Webster, R. 1990: *A brief history of blasphemy – liberalism, censorship and 'The Satanic Verses'*. Southwold: Orwell Press.

Willis, P. 1977: *Learning to labour*. London: Saxon House.

WSG 1978: *Women take issue*. Birmingham: Women's Studies Group, Centre for Contemporary Cultural Studies, University of Birmingham.

Further reading

Bennet, T., Martin, G., Mercer, C. and Woollacott, J. (eds) 1981: *Culture, ideology and social process*. London: Batsford.

Campbell, B. 1984: *Wigan Pier revisited: poverty and politics in the eighties*. London: Virago.

Coward, R. 1984: *Female desire: women's sexuality today*. London: Paladin.

Corner, J. and Harvey, S. 1991: *Enterprise and heritage: cross-currents of national culture*. London/New York: Routledge.

Franklin, S., Lury, C. and Stacey, J. 1991: *Off-centre: feminism and cultural studies*. London: HarperCollins.

Gray, A. 1992: *Video playtime: the gendering of a leisure technology*. London: Routledge.

Hall, S. 1988: New ethnicities. In *Black film British cinema*. Document 7. London: Institute of Contemporary Arts.

Hebdige, D. 1988: *Hiding in the light: on images and things*. London: Routledge.

McRobbie, A. and McCabe, T. (eds) 1981: *Feminism for girls: an adventure*. London: Routledge & Kegan Paul.

Walkerdine, V. 1990: *Schoolgirl fictions*. London: Verso.

Winship, J. 1987: *Inside women's magazines*. London: Pandora Press.

9

Subcultural conflict and working-class community

Phil Cohen

From *Working Papers in Cultural Studies* 2 (Centre for Contemporary Cultural Studies, University of Birmingham, Spring 1972).

[. . .] The fifties saw the development of new towns and large estates on the outskirts of East London, Dagenham, Greenleigh etc., and a large number of families from the worst slums of the East End were rehoused in this way. The East End, one of the highest density areas in London, underwent a gradual depopulation. But as it did so, certain areas underwent a re-population, as they were rapidly colonized by a large influx of West Indians and Pakistanis. One of the reasons why these communities were attracted (in the weak sense of the word) to such areas is often called 'planning blight'. This concept has been used to describe what happens in the take-off phase of comprehensive redevelopment in the inner residential zones of large urban centres. The typical pattern is that as redevelopment begins, land values inevitably rise, and rental values fall; the most dynamic elements in local industry, who are usually the largest employers of labour, tend to move out, alongside the migrating families, and are often offered economic incentives to do so; much of the existing dilapidated property in the area is bought up cheaply by property speculators and the Rachman-type landlords, who are only interested in the maximum exploitation of their assets – the largest profits in the shortest time; as a result the property is often not maintained and becomes even further dilapidated. Immigrant families, with low incomes, and excluded from council housing, naturally gravitate to these areas, and their own trades and service industries begin to penetrate the local economy. This in turn accelerates the migration of the indigenous community to the new towns and estates. The only apparent exception to planning blight, in fact, proves the rule. For those few areas which are linked to invisible assets – such as possessing houses of 'character', i.e. late Georgian or early Victorian, or amenities such as parks – are actually bought up and improved, renovated for the new middle class, students, young professionals, who require easy access to the commercial and cultural centre of the city. The end result on the local community is the same; whether the neighbourhood is upgraded or downgraded, long-resident working-class families move out.

As the worst effects of the first phase, both on those who moved, and on

95

those who stayed behind, became apparent, the planning authorities decided to reverse their policy. Everything was now concentrated on building new estates on slum sites within the East End. But far from counteracting the social disorganization of the area, this merely accelerated the process. In analysing the impact of redevelopment on the community, these two phases can be treated as one. No one is denying that redevelopment brought an improvement in material conditions for those fortunate enough to be rehoused (there are still thousands on the housing list). But while this removed the tangible evidence of poverty, it did nothing to improve the real economic situation of many families, and those with low incomes may, despite rent rebate schemes, be worse off. But to this was added a new poverty – the impoverishment of working-class culture. Redevelopment meant the destruction of the neighbourhood, the breakdown of the extended kinship network, which [. . .] combined to exert a powerful force for social cohesion in the community. [. . .]

The first effect of the high density, high rise schemes, was to destroy the function of the street, the local pub, the corner shop, as articulations of communal space. Instead there was only the privatized space of the family unit, stacked one on top of each other, in total isolation, juxtaposed with the totally public space which surrounded it, and which lacked any of the informal social controls generated by the neighbourhood. The streets which serviced the new estates became thoroughfares, their users 'pedestrians', and by analogy so many bits of human traffic, and this irrespective of whether or not they were separated from motorized traffic. It's indicative of how far the planners failed to understand the human ecology of the working-class neighbourhood that they could actually talk about building 'vertical streets'! The people who had to live in them weren't fooled. As one put it – they might have running hot water and central heating, but to him they were still prisons in the sky. Inevitably the physical isolation, the lack of human scale and sheer impersonality of the new environment was felt worst by people living in the new tower blocks which have gradually come to dominate the East End landscape.

The second effect of redevelopment was to destroy what we have called 'matrilocal residence'. Not only was the new housing designed on the model on the nuclear family with little provision for large, low income families (usually designated as problem families!) and none at all for groups of young single people, but the actual pattern of distribution of the new housing tended to disperse the kinship network; families of marriage were separated from their families of origin, especially during the first phase of the redevelopment. The isolated family unit could no longer call on the resources of the wider kinship network, or of the neighbourhood, and the family itself became the sole focus of solidarity. This meant that any problems were bottled up within the immediate interpersonal context which produced them; and at the same time family relationships were invested with a new intensity, to compensate for the diversity of relationships previously generated through neighbours and wider kin. The trouble was that although the traditional kinship system which corresponded to it has broken down, the traditional patterns of socialization (of communication and control) continued to reproduce themselves in the interior of the family.

The working-class family was thus not only isolated from the outside, but undermined from within. There is no better example of what we are talking about than the plight of the so called 'housebound mother'. The street or turning was no longer available as a safe playspace, under neighbourly supervision. Mum, or Auntie, was no longer just round the corner to look after the kids for the odd morning. Instead the task of keeping an eye on the kids fell exclusively to the young wife, and the only safe playspace was the 'safety of the home'. Feeling herself cooped up with the kids, and cut off from the outside world, it wouldn't be surprising if she occasionally took out her frustration on those nearest and dearest! Only market research and advertising executives imagine that the housebound mother sublimates everything in her G-plan furniture, her washing machine or non-stick frying pans.

Underlying all this, however, there was a more basic process of change going on in the community, a change in the whole economic infrastructure of the East End.

In the late fifties, the British economy began to recover from the effect of the war, and to apply the advanced technology developed during this period to the more backward sectors of the economy. Craft industries and small-scale production in general were the first to suffer; automated techniques replaced the traditional hand skills and their simple division of labour. Similarly the economies of scale provided for by the concentration of capital resources meant that the small-scale family business was no longer a viable unit. Despite a long rearguard action many of the traditional industries, tailoring, furniture making, many of the service and distributive trades linked to the docks, rapidly declined, or were bought out. Symbolic of this was the disappearance of the corner shop; where these were not demolished by redevelopment, they were replaced by the larger supermarkets often owned by large combines. Even where corner shops were offered places in the redevelopment area often they could not afford the high rents. There was a gradual polarization in the structure of the labour force: on the one side the highly specialized, skilled and well-paid jobs associated with the new technology, and the high growth sectors that employed them; on the other the routine, dead end, low paid and unskilled jobs associated with the labour intensive sectors, especially the service industries. As might be expected, it was the young people, just out of school, who got the worst of the deal. Lacking openings in their fathers' trades, and lacking the qualifications for the new industries, they were relegated to jobs as vanboys, office boys, packers, warehousemen, etc., and long spells out of work. More and more people, young and old, had to travel out of the community to their jobs, and some eventually moved out to live elsewhere, where suitable work was to be found. The local economy as a whole contracted, became less diverse. The only section of the community which was unaffected by this was dockland, which retained its position in the labour market, and with it, its traditions of militancy. It did not, though, remain unaffected by the breakdown of the pattern of integration in the East End as a whole, vis-à-vis its sub-community structure. Perhaps this goes some way to explain the para-doxical fact that within the space of twelve months, the dockers could march in support of Enoch Powell, and take direct action for community control in the Isle of Dogs!

If someone should ask why the plan to 'modernize' the pattern of East End life should have been such a disaster, perhaps the only honest answer is that, given the macro-social forces acting on it, given the political, ideological, and economic framework within which it operated, the result was inevitable. For example many local people wonder why the new environment should be the way it is. The reasons are complex; they are political in so far as the system does not allow for any effective participation by local working-class community in the decision-making process at any stage or level of planning. The clients of the planners are simply the local authority or commercial developer who employs them. They are ideological in so far as the plans are unconsciously modelled on the structure of the middle-class environment, which is based on the concept of *property*, and *private ownership*, on individual differences of status, wealth, etc.; whereas the structure of the working-class environment is based on the concept of community, or collective identity, common lack of ownership, wealth, etc. Similarly needs were assessed on the norms of the middle-class nuclear family, rather than the extended working-class family, etc. But underpinning both these sets of reasons lie the basic economic factors involved in comprehensive redevelopment. Quite simply – faced with the task of financing a large housing programme, the local authorities were forced to borrow large amounts of capital, and also to design schemes which would attract capital investment to the area. This means that they have to borrow at the going interest rates, which in this country are very high, and that to subsidize housing, certain of the best sites have to be earmarked for commercial developers. A further and perhaps decisive factor is the cost of land, since very little of it is publicly owned and land values rise as the area develops.

All this means that planners have to reduce the cost of production to a minimum, through the use of capital intensive techniques – prefabricated and standardized components, allowing for semi-automated processes in construction. The attraction of high rise developments (tower blocks outside the trade) is not only that they meet these requirements, but they allow for certain economies of scale, such as the input costs of essential services, which can be grouped around a central core. As to 'non-essential' services, i.e. ones that don't pay, such as playspace, community centres, youth clubs and recreational facilities, these often have to be sacrificed to the needs of commercial developers, who of course have quite different priorities. Perhaps the best example of this happening is the notorious St Catherine's Dock scheme. This major contribution towards solving the East End's housing problem includes a yachting marina, a luxury hotel, luxury apartment blocks, and various cultural amenities for their occupants plus – a small section of low income accommodation, presumably to house the families of the low paid staff who will service the luxury amenities. And lest anyone becomes too sentimental about the existing site, Telford's warehouses etc., it should be mentioned that the original development was by the East India Company in the early nineteenth century, involved the destruction of the homes of thousands of poor families in the area, and met with such stiff opposition from them that it eventually required an Act of Parliament to get the scheme approved!

The situation facing East Enders at present, then, is not new. When the first tenements went up in the nineteenth century they raised the same objections from local people, and for the same very good reasons as their modern counterparts – the tower blocks. What *is* new is that in the nineteenth century the voice of the community was vigorous and articulate on these issues, whereas today, just when it needs it most, the community is faced with a crisis of indigenous leadership.

The reasons for this are already implicit in the analysis above. The labour aristocracy, the traditional source of leadership, has virtually disappeared along with the artisan mode of production. At the same time there has been a split in consciousness between the spheres of production and consumption. More and more East Enders are forced to work outside the area; young people especially are less likely to follow family traditions in this respect. As a result the issues of the workplace are no longer experienced as directly linked to community issues. Of course there has always been a 'brain drain' of the most articulate, due to social mobility. But not only has this been intensified as a result of the introduction of comprehensive schools, but the recruitment of fresh talent from the strata below – i.e. from the ranks of the respectable working class – has also dried up. For this strata, traditionally the social cement of the community, is also in a state of crisis.

The economic changes, which we have already described, also affected their position and as it were *de-stabilized it*. The 'respectables' found themselves caught and pulled apart by two opposed pressures of social mobility – downwards, into the ranks of the new suburban working-class elite. And more than any other section of the working class were caught in the middle of the two dominant but contradictory ideologies of the day: the ideology of spectacular consumption, promoted by the mass media, and the traditional ideology of production, the so-called work ethic which centred on the idea that a man's dignity, his manhood, even, was measured by the quantity or quality of his effort in production. If this strata began to split apart it was because their existing position had become untenable. Their bargaining power in the labour market was threatened by the introduction of new automated techniques, which eliminated many middle-range, semi-skilled jobs. Their economic position excluded them from entering the artificial paradise of the new consumer society; at the same time changes in the production process itself have made the traditional work ethic, the pride in the job, impossible to uphold. They had the worst of all possible worlds.

Once again this predicament was registered most deeply in and on the young. But here an additional complicating factor intervenes. We have already described the peculiar strains imposed on the 'nucleated' working-class family. And their most critical impact was in the area of parent/child relationships. What had previously been a source of support and security for both, now became something of a battleground, a major focus of all the anxieties created by the disintegration of community structures around them. One result of this was to produce an increase in early marriage. For one way of escaping the claustrophobic tensions of family life was to start a family of your own! And given the total lack of accommodation for young single people in the new developments, as well as the conversion of cheap rented accommodation into middle-class owner-occupied housing, the only practicable way to leave home was to get married. The second outcome of generational conflict (which may appear to go against the trend of early marriage, but in fact reinforced it) was the emergence of specific youth subcultures in opposition to the parent culture. And one effect of this was to weaken the links of historical and cultural continuity, mediated through the family, which had been such a strong force for solidarity in the working-class community. It is perhaps not surprising that the parent culture of the respectable working class, already in crisis, was the most 'productive' vis-à-vis subcultures; the internal conflicts of the parent culture came to be worked out in terms of generational conflict. What I think seems to happen is that one of the functions of generational conflict is to decant the kinds of tensions which appear face to face in the family and replace them by a generational specific symbolic system so that the tension is taken out of the interpersonal context and placed in a collective context, and mediated through various stereotypes which have the function of defusing the anxiety that interpersonal tension generates.

It seems to me that the latent function of subculture is this – to express and resolve, albeit 'magically', the contradictions which remain hidden or unresolved in the parent culture. The succession of subcultures which this parent culture generated can thus all be considered as so many variations on a central theme – the contradiction, at an ideological level, between traditional working-class puritanism, and the new hedonism of consumption; at an economic level between a future as part of the socially mobile elite, or as part of the new lumpen. Mods, parkers, skinheads, crombies, all represent, in their different ways, an attempt to retrieve some of the socially cohesive elements destroyed in their parent culture, and to combine these with elements selected from other class fractions, symbolizing one or other of the options confronting it.

It is easy enough to see this working in practice if we remember that subcultures are symbolic structures, and must not be confused with the actual kids who are their bearers and supports. Secondly a given lifestyle is actually made up of a number of symbolic subsystems, and it is the way these are articulated in the total lifestyle which constitutes its distinctiveness. There are basically four subsystems – and these can be divided into the relatively 'plastic' forms – dress and music, which are not directly produced by the subculture, but which are selected and invested with subcultural value in so far as they express its underlying thematic; and then the more 'infrastructural' forms – argot, and ritual, which are more resistant to innovation but of course reflect changes in the more plastic forms. I'm suggesting here that mods, parkers, skinheads, crombies are a succession of subcultures which all correspond to the same parent culture and which attempt to work out through a system of transformations, the basic problematic or contradiction which is inserted in the subculture by the parent culture. So you can distinguish three levels in the analysis of subcultures: one is historical analysis which isolates the specific problematic of a particular class fraction, in this case, the respectable working class; and secondly a structural or semiotic analysis of the subsystems and the way they are articulated and the actual transformations which those subsystems undergo from one subcultural moment to another; and thirdly the phenomenological analysis of the way the subculture is actually lived out by those who are the bearers and supports of the subculture. No real analysis of subculture is complete without all those levels being in place.

To go back to the diachronic string we are discussing, the original mod life style could be interpreted as an attempt to real-ize, *but in an imaginary relation*, the conditions of existence of the socially mobile white-collar worker. While their argot and ritual forms stressed many of the traditional values of their parent culture, their dress and music reflected the hedonistic image of the affluent consumer. The lifestyle crystallized in opposition to the rockers (viz. the famous riots in the early sixties) and it seems to be a law of subcultural evolution that its dynamic comes not only from the relations to its own parent culture, but from the relation to subcultures belonging to *other class fractions*, in this case the manual working class.

The next member of our string – the parkers or scooter boys – were in some senses a transitional form between the mods and skinheads. The alien elements introduced into music and dress by the mods were progressively de-stressed and the indigenous components of argot and ritual re-asserted as the matrix of subcultural identity. The skinheads themselves carried the process to completion. Their lifestyle in fact represents a systematic inversion of the mods – whereas the mods explored the upwardly mobile option, the skinheads explored the lumpen. Music and dress again became the central focus of the lifestyle; the introduction of reggae (the protest music of the West Indian poor) and the 'uniform' (of which more in a moment) signified a reaction against the contamination of the parent culture by middle-class values, and a re-assertion of the integral values of working-class culture – through its most recessive traits – its puritanism and chauvinism. This double movement gave rise to a phenomenon sometimes called 'machismo' – the unconscious dynamics of the work ethic translated into the out of work situation; the most dramatic example of this was the epidemic of 'queer bashing' across the country in '69/'70. The skinhead uniform itself could be interpreted as a kind of caricature of the model worker – the self image of the working class as distorted through middle-class perceptions; a metastatement about the whole process of social mobility. Finally the skinhead lifestyle crystallized in opposition both to the greasers (successors to the rockers) and the hippies – both subcultures representing a species of hedonism which the skinheads rejected.

Following the skinheads there emerged another transitional form variously known as crombies, casuals, suedes, etc. (the proliferation of names being a mark of transitional phases). They represent a movement back towards the original mod position, although this time it's a question of incorporating certain elements drawn from a middle-class *subculture* – the hippies, which the skinheads had previously ignored. But even though the crombies, etc. have adopted some of the external mannerisms of the hippy lifestyle, viz. dress, soft drug use, they still conserve many of the distinctive features of earlier versions of the subculture.

If the whole process as we've described it seems to be circular, forming a closed system, then this is because subculture, by definition, cannot break out of the contradiction derived from the parent culture, it merely transcribes its terms at a microsocial level, and inscribes them in an imaginary set of relations.

But there is another reason. Apart from its particular, thematic, contradiction, every subculture shares a general contradiction, which is inherent in its very conditions of existence. Subculture invests the weak points in the chain of socialization, between the family/school nexus, and integration into the work process which marks the resumption of the patterns of the parent culture for the next generation. But subculture is also a compromise solution, between two contradictory needs: the need to create and express *autonomy and difference* from parents, and by extension, their culture; and the need to maintain the security of existing ego defences, and the *parental identifications* which support them. For the initiate subculture provides a means of 'rebirth' without having to undergo the pain of symbolic death. The autonomy it offers is thus both real, but partial, and illusory, as a total 'way of liberation'. And far from constituting an improvised *rite de passage* into adult society, as some anthropologists have claimed, it is a collective and highly ritualized defence against just such a transition. And because defensive functions predominate, ego boundaries become cemented to subcultural boundaries. In a real sense subcultural conflict (i.e. greasers versus skinheads, mods versus rockers) serves as a displacement of generational conflict, both at a cultural level, and at an interpersonal level within the family. One consequence of this is to artificially foreclose the natural trajectory of adolescent revolt. For the kids who are caught up in the internal contradictions of a subculture, what began as a break in the continuum of social control can easily become a permanent hiatus in their lives. Although there is a certain amount of subcultural mobility, i.e. kids evolving from mods to parkers, or even switching subcultural affiliations, greasers 'becoming' skinheads, there are no career prospects as such! There are two possible solutions; one leads out of subculture into early marriage, and as we've said for working-class kids this is the normal solution. Alternatively subcultural affiliation can provide a way in to membership of one of the deviant subgroups, which exist in the margins of subculture, often adopt its protective colouration, but which nevertheless are not structurally dependent on it; such groups as pushers, petty criminals, junkies, even homosexuals.

This leads us into another contradiction inherent in subculture. Although as a symbolic structure it *does* provide a diffuse sense of affinity in terms of a common lifestyle, it does not in itself prescribe any crystallized group structure. We believe that it is through the function of *territoriality* that subculture becomes anchored in the collective reality of the kids who are its bearers, and who in this way become not just its passive support, but its conscious agents. Territoriality is simply the process through which environmental boundaries (and foci) are used to signify group boundaries (and foci) and become invested with a subcultural value. This is the function of football teams for the skinheads, for example. Territoriality is thus not only a way in which kids live subculture as a collective behaviour, but the way in which the subcultural group becomes rooted in the situation of its community. In the context of the East End it is a way of retrieving the solidarities of the traditional neighbourhood, destroyed by redevelopment. The existence of communal space is reasserted as the common pledge of group unity – you belong to the Mile End mob in so far as the Mile End belongs to you. Territoriality appears as a magical way of expressing ownership; for the Mile End is not owned by the people but by the property developers. Territorial division therefore appears within the subculture, and in the East End mirror many of the traditional divisions of sub-communities: Bethnal Green – Hoxton – Mile End – Whitechapel – Balls Pond Road, etc. Thus in addition to conflict between subcultures, there also exists conflict within them, on a territorial basis. Both these forms of conflict can be seen as displacing or weakening the dynamics of generational conflict, which is in turn a displaced form of the traditional parameters of class conflict. [. . .]

10

Alice in the consumer wonderland

Erica Carter

From Angela McRobbie and Mica Nava (eds), *Gender and generation* (Macmillan, 1984).

Changing gear: a reappraisal of the politics of style

> People say . . . well, what don't they say about teenagers?! They start with the accusation that we have no manners or sense of good behaviour, and that we're hopelessly lacking in all religious belief. Then we are told off, either for dressing too sloppily, or looking too old for our age . . . 'Either', we are told, 'you run around like tramps in floppy jackets buttoned up at the back and drainpipe trousers which are far too tight – or else you slavishly follow the latest fashion trends.'
> We would like for once to give our point of view . . . We teenagers have our own style. And that's what makes many people see red.
> (Advertisement for 'Triumph' underwear, *Bravo* magazine, no. 42, 1958)

Since the beginning of the 1970s, theorists of youth subcultures in Britain have appropriated the notion of 'style' from marketers of teenage fashion commodities, and mobilized it for their studies of oppositional subcultures in the post-war period. Recalling a tradition of cultural studies which reaches back to Richard Hoggart's *Uses of literacy* (Hoggart, 1957), early analysts of sub-cultural deviance and opposition[1] seem implicitly to share his distaste for the plastic glamour of commercialized youth culture; their gaze falls rather on visible subversions of dominant forms. The discordant notes sounded by Teds, rockers, mods, rastas or punks are seen to be pitched against the harmony of mass consumer culture; appropriating commodities from fashion, music and media industries, subcultural youths reassemble them into symbolic systems of their own which, if only at the moment of their birth, strike chords of disenchantment, rebellion and resistance. Like the phenomena which they examine, the analyses themselves are founded on a number of unspoken oppositions: conformity and resistance, harmony and rupture, passivity and activity, consumption and appropriation, femininity and masculinity.

In a discussion of sexism amongst the working-class lads of his 'Hammertown' study, Paul Willis finds himself slipping with ease into the discourse of consumerism.

> The male counter-school culture promotes its own sexism – even celebrates it as part of its overall confidence. Girls are pursued, sometimes roughly, for their

sexual favours, often dropped and labelled 'loose' when they are given. Girls are asked to be sexy and inviting as well as pure and monogamous; to be consumed and not to be consumed (Willis, 1977, p. 146).

In a study from which girls are largely absent, the moment of their appearance is profoundly significant. Girls, it seems, are written into youth cultural theory in the language of consumption; initially – though not, as we shall see, of necessity – as objects for consumption by men. Under the regime of Althusserian structuralism in British cultural theory, this led to the perception of girls at best as an absence, a silence, a lack which could perhaps only be filled in some separate world of autonomous female culture. Ideology was an 'instance', consumption a 'sphere', severed from its tangled roots in the social institutions with which structuralism was primarily concerned – the family, ideology and the repressive State. Feminist researchers then turned towards the family as the pivotal point around which the existence of teenage girls revolved.

> If women are marginal to the male cultures of work (middle and working class) it is because they are central and pivotal to a subordinate area, which mirrors, but in a complementary and subordinate way, the 'dominant' masculine arenas. They are 'marginal' to work because they are central to the subordinate, complementary sphere of the family (McRobbie and Garber, 1976, p. 211).

Following working-class girls into the closed arena of the family allowed the researchers of female culture privileged insights into the possibilities of specifically female cultural forms. So-called 'bedroom culture' was analogous to male subcultures, in that here too dominant signs and symbols were appropriated, reassembled and reproduced in homology[2] with an already existing set of social relations. In male youth subcultures, these homologies existed between the lived culture of a subordinate *class* and the symbolic systems through which its members made that culture 'mean'. In bedroom culture, gender relations overlaid, overlapped and took precedence over relations of race and class.

Yet the search for autonomous female cultural forms in the bedroom hideaways of teenage girls has been consistently dogged by nagging doubts as to the creative, productive and potentially subversive power of this mode of femininity. The study of 'teeny bopper culture', for example, was recognized as a key which might unlock the potentialities of specifically female forms; on the other hand, teenage adulation of male pop idols remained a symbol of the 'future general subordination' of adolescent girls (McRobbie and Garber, 1976, p. 219). One problem with taking subculture theory as a starting point for studies of female culture was that the homologies which 'profane culture' moulded and shaped for itself were always preformed – and more readily reformed at the slightest hint of female autonomy – by an ever-watchful capitalist market.

The spectacle of working-class subcultures erupted into a yawning gap between class relations as they are lived by working-class youth, and the classless categories according to which capitalist markets are structured. Ever since Warner's classic study of social class in America (Warner, 1960) the marketing establishment has measured consumers against typological grids on which 'class' appears primarily as an attribute of personal status and income; working-class subcultures are, in part, a raucous rejection of a consumer culture which has continually repressed the seamier side of class subordination from view. Gender, on the other hand, operates as a dominant variable for the structuring of consumer groups. Thus not only have market researchers developed a vast apparatus of consumer surveillance which ensures the immediate recuperation and reassimilation of new – or hitherto unheeded – facets of femininity; the 'image industries' (fashion, cosmetics, the female mass media) have also consistently drawn on these marketing data to produce symbolic representations which fit skintight to female experiences. Hence the difference in mood, tone and resonance of masculine and feminine revolts into style. Male 'semiological guerillas' plunder the symbolic treasure chests of consumer culture, recreating their booty as signifiers of resistance whose signifier – the disaffection of subordinate class fractions – was until recently banished from the symbolic landscape of the teenage mass market. Conversely, even the unpleasures of femininity find continual, if oblique, reflection in commodities on the female market, from perfect cures for the imperfections of the female body (slimming pills, aerobic outfits, beauty aids), to more expensive, and correspondingly drastic remedies for the psychic ailments of the female condition – from nerve-tonics to psychoanalysis, with Babycham to add a touch of sparkle.

Deviance, resistance, autonomy, revolt: in the sociological tradition of the academic Left, these are located beyond the hostile walls of an impassive monolith – the Market. Analyses of subcultural style represented an attempt to freeze commodities-as-signifiers into fixed relations of subversive opposition; the (re)marketing of punk safety-pins and crazy-colour hairstyles was dubbed a 'recuperation' – silencing, defeat. The first punk safety-pin to spill off the end of the mass production line did indeed dislodge punk from its anchorage in the adolescent culture of the urban working classes; yet at the same time, it carried the meanings and values of punk into a wider field of teenage mass culture, where its progress has yet to be properly charted.

If subculture theory has traditionally remained standing somewhat suspiciously on the sidelines of commercial youth culture, the same has not always been true of research into girls' culture. Women researchers have had to plunge, head-on at times, into the seething morass of capital flows, emerging with a proliferation of critiques of the commodities which pattern the fabric of girls' lives: advertising images, fashionable clothes, mass magazines, popular fiction. In feminist theory too, the theoretical terrain for a re-engagement with market mechanisms has been prepared since the beginning of the break with Althusser and structuralism. The market is not an institution with rigidly defined (if consistently subverted) hierarchies, structures, orders and conventions; neither is it a tightly-knit subculture whose practices and rituals can be traced onto frozen 'maps of meaning'. It is instead a vast machine for the regulation of interconnecting circulatory flows: the flow of capital and labour through the production process, the flows of money, commodities, visual and textual signifiers through the circuits of consumption unlocked by capital.

Recognizing market practices as constant and unbroken flows demands a similarly supple set of categories for their analysis; the homologies and oppositions of structuralist symbolic deconstructions offer only one of many routes into the fragmented and splintered realities of female consumption. Shifting onto more fluid epistemological ground will not entail a feminist farewell to subcultures: charting the labyrinth of female market practices, we will be led to girls and women within *and* outside subcultures, all of whom participate in the regulation and organization of market processes. The machine itself, if vast and apparently all-embracing, is never intrinsically monstrous; it is both manipulative and manipulated, controlled and controlling. Girls and women surface on a multitude of levels as both objects and agents of market processes: so, for example, the eighties boom in the second-hand rag trade owes its greatest debt to the 'nouvelle entrepreneuse' of New Wave subculture (and signals, incidentally, a successful attempt to divert fashion's commodity flows from their source in monopoly capitalist production).

An 'archaeology' of female consumption

Across the landscape of post-war mass markets, female consumers, too, emerge both as 'objects' (of market research, advertising campaigns, sexual consumption by men) and as active agents in consumption processes. The work presented in the following pages – studies of specific instances of female 'consumer culture' in post-war West Germany – represents a first step towards a latter-day 'archaeology' of female consumption; an attempt to grasp and represent aspects of female consumerism in all their myriad complexities; and an appeal for the postponement of premature outrage at the 'co-option', 'recuperation', 'objectification' of women and girls in post-war consumer culture.

The nascent Federal Republic of Germany may seem an unlikely point of departure. Yet the very distance between areas of study (in this case, both geographical and conceptual in nature) forces the disruption of established modes of understanding, pointing the way towards potentially more fertile theoretical terrain. In the first instance, looking at German attempts to build a new democracy out of the shattered ruins of Germany's Nazi past can shed light on processes which, in Britain, took on less visible forms. Germany in 1945 lacked the cosy security of the cultural institutions in which British democratic values were founded – from fair play in English cricket, to resonances of Empire in the British cup of tea. Analogous cultural forms and practices in post-war Germany resounded still with echoes of Nazism; meanwhile, the allied Western powers demanded tangible evidence of a decisive break with the totalitarian past. The West German constitution of 1949, then, was offered as an anchorage point for the fragile floating remnants of Weimar democracy; it contained, importantly, explicit guarantees of the equality of women and men before the law. The first section of the following study traces some of the processes whereby these constitutional promises came to be realized in the course of the 1950s. In practice, the explicit inscription of women as equal subjects in legal discourse was negotiated through their installation as consumers in a 'social market economy'; citizenship for women thus came to be defined through consumption on a capitalist mass market.

This, then, is a study of the ways in which the post-war market colonized and rooted itself in political discourses and institutions. The caesura of 1945 in Germany; attempts to suffocate a Nazi past under the cushion of consumer democracy; these may throw into sharper relief analogous developments in the consumerism of post-war Britain. Here as in Germany the middle-class housewife enacted her political enfranchisement through the exercise of economic rationality; choosing to buy or not to buy, to spend or to save, to covet or to shun.

Certainly in 1950s West Germany, this was part of the 'political' future to which teenage girls were widely urged to aspire; at the same time, the expanding market in teenage leisure commodities transported adolescent consumption into a separate dimension of 'symbolic' and 'hedonistic' pleasures (Woods, 1960). [. . .] I look at some aspects of fifties leisure consumption for girls; at the symbolic systems of teenage lifestyles; and at one specific instance of female mass consumption: artificial 'silk' stockings for teenage girls. Heavily laden though nylons may be with predetermined 'sexist' meanings, a cool appraisal of the actual mode of their consumptions reveals teenage girls engaged in the production of meanings and values more appropriate to their own needs. Nylon stockings, imported *en masse* from the USA, may appear simply as one of the more visible manifestations of American cultural hegemony. Yet a closer look at this one element in an emergent, and largely imported, teenage culture of consumption, points towards different questions to be asked of the process of consumption itself. Passive manipulation or active appropriation, escapist delusion or Utopian fantasy, consumerism can be all or none of these. [. . .]

Teenage girls in the consumer public

There are no simple connections to be made between women's position within relations of consumption for the fifties family, and the situation of adolescent girls as consumers on a mass teenage market. On the one hand, it was clearly the case that women taking up their new position of equality were seen to be lacking in the qualities necessary for democratic citizenship. Since women's assumed tendency to be over-emotional was said to hamper them in the exercise of rational consumer choice, it became the task of both state and private institutions (centrally, of course, the advertising establishment) to educate women into the required patterns of consumption.

There is, then, indeed a sense in which drives towards the end of the decade to initiate girls into new modes of consumption were simply preparing them for their entry into an adult female world. On the one hand, teenage consumption, revolving as it did around leisure commodities, was clearly distinct from that practised by housewives. Why, after all, should girls with a well-trained eye for fashionable colour combinations – the right shade of lipstick to set off matching gloves and shoes – necessarily be similarly adept at differentiating between an increasingly confusing variety of washing-powder brands?

Yet via the notion of the 'public', there are crucial links to be made. For the fifties housewives, one component of domestic labour – shopping – was lifted out of the enclaves of home and the local street, and transferred to the 'public' terrain of the supermarket and the neighbourhood or regional shopping centre. Abstract promises of a public identity for women as consumers took concrete form in the reorganization of public space around centralized loci of commodity exchange. Shops and stores gradually abandoned earlier styles of personal service, in favour of more up-to-date self-service methods. A number of stores introduced the so-called 'Kiebitz' system, displaying placards or badges which invited the customer to 'come in and look around', with no obligation to buy. Shop displays were reordered accordingly, with an emphasis on the commodity as image and spectacle; at the same time, posters and labels on or near individual articles drew the customers' attention to their particular advantages. Firms originally specializing in mail-order delivery expanded their department store chains; in urban centres in particular, specialist shops began to lose custom to larger department stores and supermarkets.

Developments in town planning further accelerated the centralization of the consumption process. West Berlin was particularly interesting in this respect; having sustained heavy bombing in the Second World War, the city centre was a blank page across which architects and town planners would write the forms of their social Utopias. In 1946 a town planning collective under the directorship of Hans Scharoun opened debates on the future of the city with an exhibition, 'Berlin plant' (Berlin plans). They proposed using the wide-open spaces left by bomb damage to break with previous traditions of high-density housing and closed communities in which living, sometimes also working-space, had been integrated with leisure facilities – the obligatory 'Eckkneipe' (local bar) – and other points of commodity exchange: the equally indispensable 'Tante-Emma-Laden' ('Aunt Emma's corner shop'). The post-war Berlin of Scharoun was to draw sharp boundaries between these diverse spheres of city life; strips of parkland and fast, wide roads were to divide off residential areas from commercial quarters, and from sites of work and leisure – including centralized shopping areas.

Through their integration into an expanding teenage market, adolescent girls were drawn in increasing numbers into this new public space. The new generation of young consumers were particularly attracted to self-service and department stores, where they were free to look, compare and admire at their leisure, with no immediate compulsion to buy. A 1957 Intermarket survey of West German consumer habits records the preference of teenagers for these more impersonal stores, as well as their predilection for the 'Americanized' off-the-peg fashions still regarded with suspicion by their older compatriots.

If girls are absent from subcultures, then, they become visible at the point of consumption. Working-class girls in particular have never been entirely absent from the street, the cinema or the dancehall; they have not lived a life of seclusion away from the eyes of predatory men. A favourite occupation of young female factory workers in 1950s West Germany was an evening stroll along main streets in search of excitement and the company of contemporaries. Again, it was shopping which drew them onto the street and into public life. In a series of sociological monographs published in 1958

(Wurzbacher and Jaide, 1958, pp. 169–70), Bärbel – fifteen-years-old at the time of the study, and employed since leaving school in a knitwear factory – relates how she is sent out every evening to fetch milk for the family (a duty she is only too happy to perform, since the dairy is a favourite meeting place for a large proportion of the local village youth).

> Here new films and the latest fashions are discussed. The boys at first set themselves a little apart, in order to be able to pass comment on the girls; later they make attempts to pick them up. This is a place for young people to talk together; this is the place where dates are made. There is always something going on at the dairy.

If the market offers itself to women and girls as a stage for the production of themselves as public beings, then it does so on particularly unfavourable terms. Bärbel's dairy was a meeting place for separate groups of boys and girls: the girls, whatever their own motives for assembling there, found themselves on display to boys angling for a date – or something more. It is this overwhelming power of men to position women as sexual prey that has made the feminist search for autonomous female subcultures so consistently difficult. Doubtless, though, the difficulty resides equally in the subculturalists' choice of object, cultural resistance being located chiefly in formal innovations by an adolescent avant-garde. If anything is to be learned about the lived realities of consumption, then we must shift the terms of the youth culture debate, looking first at the dominant forms of a supposedly conformist culture of consumerism (as well as its everyday subversions). One route into this project is the examination of teenage lifestyles: of their assemblage on the production line of commodities for the teenage market, and their deconstruction, appropriation, subversion and reassemblage by teenage girls themselves.

Girls in West Germany and the teenage dream

The word teenager first entered the German language in the 1950s, imported like chewing gum and Coca-Cola from the USA, and vibrant with connotations of crazy styles, zany humour, rock'n'roll parties, Elvis, James Dean, loud music and soft park-bench romance. Its partner, the 'Twen', arrived around the same time and is of somewhat more dubious origin. Signifying 'young people in their twenties', it relied on associations of Americanness ('false' ones, insofar as the 'Twen' does not exist outside Germany) to construct an image of the older, more responsible, but nonetheless fun-loving party-going free-spending twenty-year-old. The average marital age in late 1950s Germany was twenty-six, and the relatively high disposable income of unmarried 'Twens' made them particularly attractive to producers of consumer goods in the upper price range of the leisure market. A survey carried out by the DIVO Market Research Institute in 1961 estimated the disposable income of twenty-one to twenty-four-year-olds by 1960 at DM192 per month for men (compared with DM91 for seventeen to twenty-year-olds), and DM180 per month for women (compared with DM100 for their seventeen- to twenty-year-old counterparts).

It was on the teenage market, then, that girls represented a particularly attractive target group for the leisure industries. During their late teens (from the age of fifteen onwards) girls in general drew a higher income than boys, but dropped back below their male contemporaries on reaching the age of twenty. In part, this resulted from their greater store of 'cultural capital' (Bourdieu, 1967); girls leaving school in their mid-teens were likely to be initially better qualified for jobs requiring school certificates (Volksschulabschlüsse), while boys tended to make up for their lack of academic qualifications by entering an initially lower-paid apprenticeship or trainee post. The most lucrative section of the female market, then, was the group of 'Angestellte' (clerical and secretarial workers); their disposable income amounted to three or four times that of their grammar school and college counterparts, or of working-class girls in unskilled factory work. Girls on the margins of the middle income bracket were, in a sense, the deviants of marketing discourse, and 'Angestellte' the norm against which teenage market potential was measured.

To the marketing establishment, it was clear that the golden egg of the female market had to be cracked with care. The male leisure market offered no adequate model for marketing to girls for whom leisure and pleasure were elastic and unstable terms. Female consumption constantly slipped between the grey world of work on the one hand and, on the other, the glittering but (above all sexually) dangerous domain of unbounded hedonism. The leisure commodities favoured by boys offered pathways to present and immediate pleasures; for girls, on the other hand, so-called 'leisure' commodities embodied their more sober demands for future security in a precarious world. Girls in the middle to higher income brackets spent a significant portion of their income as unmarried females on collecting objects for their bottom drawer. This traditional female institution, having gone into decline in the austerity years of the forties and early fifties, celebrated its comeback towards the end of the decade, when girls began once again to collect bedclothes, table linen, crockery, cutlery, glassware – the accoutrements of the bourgeois domestic idyll. Teenage boys and young men, meanwhile, were busily buying motor-bikes, cars, cameras, sports equipment and other consumer durables: the only piece of technical equipment more highly favoured by female consumers was the typewriter (Scharmann, 1965, 33–8). Like the bottom drawer (which raised women's value on the marriage market) the typewriter represented an investment in a comfortable future, girls' production of themselves as desirable commodities on a competitive job market, and a key to the door of future financial security.

Private faces in public places

As girls and women entered the post-war market place, whole new areas of their lives began to become the 'public' property of marketing institutions. Modern surveillance systems were installed in shops and supermarkets for the observation and control of consumer behaviour: consumer panels were constituted as a source of information on attitudes to specific commodities and brands: 'in-depth' psychological testing came into vogue with the rise of motivation research. Investigations into consumer behaviour required a massive apparatus for the gathering and processing of data on consumer habits, preference, tastes and whims; hence the post-war boom in market research, when the five major West German institutes (DIVO, EMNID, GfM, IFD, INFRATEST) were founded in the space of as many years, between 1945 and 1950. The unifying principle of diverse market research techniques was the regulation of information flows, which were to proceed in one direction only: from the consumer upwards to the institutions of the image production industries. Here, data on consumers would be 'reprocessed', before being returned to them in the shape of commodity representations: product design, packaging, advertising, public relations. Until reaching the stage of its reproduction in these more palatable forms, knowledge of the consumer was channelled through scientific discourses within which she was placed only as object, never as subject of the consumption process. In commodity representations the situation was reversed. The same knowledge was used by the image industries to construct image commodities-as-symbols, from advertising images to fashionable clothes for a teenage mass market. First, however, it had to be 'translated' from the terms of social science into those of what may be called the 'commodity aesthetic' within which, importantly, consumers were replaced as subjects of consumption practices.

Since the second half of the nineteenth century, the proliferation and increasing differentiation of public images of and for women has been intimately bound up with their role as consumers. The effects of market research have been visible for almost a century in the newspaper industry; as early as the 1890s in America, newspapers began to extend society news and entertainment sections, after they discovered that women – the audience at whom these features were primarily aimed – carried the greatest potential as a future consumer market (Noelle, 1940, p. 92). Yet it was not until well into the 1950s that market research in Germany first turned its attention to the younger generation of female consumers. In 1959, the Gesellschaft für Marktforschung carried out a survey of 1500 male and female teenagers between the ages of fourteen and nineteen. The study was supplemented by further investigations in 1960, which aimed both 'to re-examine certain findings of the previous year' and 'to gain further basic insights into this important consumer group' (Scharmann, 1965, p. 17). While sociological and media research carried out earlier in the decade had confined itself to quantitative studies of adolescent leisure pursuits the GfM study was the first to focus specifically on the teenager as consumer and to attempt a broad sociometric analysis of teenage habits, preference and tastes.

In 1961, DIVO followed the GfM lead with a report commissioned by the advertising editors of *Bravo* magazine, a music, film, television, fashion and fiction teenage weekly which had been launched five years previously in 1956. By the early sixties, *Bravo* had already established itself as a leading light on the developing market for magazines aimed at a specifically teenage (male and female) readership. The 1961 survey aimed to spotlight the potential of the teenage market for the advertisers on whose revenue the magazine increasingly depended. *Bravo*, they argued, could operate as a bridge to span the gap between commodity producers, advertisers and consumers; its potential for success lay in its proven ability to capture and sustain a loyal readership amongst young people between the ages of twelve and twenty-four. In offering advertising space to the producers of commodities for a teenage market, it could ensure the dissemination of commodity representations amongst a teenage public constituted as such primarily through their role as consumers. *Bravo* readers, the publishers claim, are to be 'taken seriously' as consumers; for it is as such, they say, that teenagers primarily understand themselves.

> Confronted daily with literally hundreds of magazines and newspapers, young people may, it is true, pick up any one of them at any given time. Yet the only medium which will truly appeal to them is one which they feel is meant for and aimed only at them. They want, rightly, to be taken seriously enough for efforts to be made directly on their behalf. This is why *Bravo* has to be the way it is (DIVO, 1961).

In the face of moral outrage on the part of teachers, parents, academics and other guardians of Culture, Decency and Good Taste, *Bravo* was out to legitimize its own innovations in the field of popular taste. If teenagers were to assert themselves in a hostile world, they needed, it was argued, a mouthpiece through which their grievances could be aired, and it was in this capacity that *Bravo* offered its services, claiming itself to be the only forum in which teenage protest could – and should – find expression. The mode of teenage rebellion was to be not 'political' but aesthetic: 'We teenagers have our own style. And that's just what makes so many people see red' (Triumph advertisement, 1958). In the opening pages of the DIVO survey, *Bravo* then offered its services as an open site on which new teenage forms could be built and subsequently assembled into smoothly polished consumer lifestyles.

Girls in teenage lifestyle

The discourse of marketing defines lifestyles in terms of the specific configurations of commodity ownership which characterize particular consumer groups. In Germany, the Nürnberg Gesellschaft für Markt-forschung was the first marketing institute to develop its own theory of lifestyle; it was not until the mid-fifties that other market research establishments began to look in earnest to sources outside classical economics for more finely differentiated analyses of potential target groups. Taking up the work of Thorstein Veblen, Margaret Mead, Freud, Jung and others, consumption theorists now set about recuperating information gathered in the academic disciplines of cultural anthropology, sociology and psychology to feed the data banks of the capitalist market. Classical political economy had tended to neglect the consumer, or to consider consumption only in relation to the economics of commodity production and distribution. In opposition to this, the new wave of consumption theorists, with Bengler and Vershofen in Nürnberg as their avant-garde, argued consistently for a more sophisticated awareness of the social and aesthetic dimensions of commodity use. Wilhelm Vershofen proposed that the concept of commodity use value should be broken down into three analytical components: basic, or original use value; and social use value, measured against variables such as social prestige; and aesthetic use value, measured against given standards of social taste (Vershofen, 1954, p. 12). Members of the artistic and literary establishment were taken to task for their confinement of Culture to a discrete and autonomous sphere, floating freely above the colourless wasteland of everyday life. The mutual dependence of economy and culture was seen by Vershofen to take active form in the daily exercise of consumer choice, determined as much by aesthetic as by economic or socio-psychological considerations.

The aesthetic principle regulating consumer lifestyles was a unity of form which bound the separate elements through which they were constructed. Part of the function of teenage commodities was to provide aesthetic forms for a cultural 'space' (adolescent leisure culture) which was differently inhabited by female and male consumers. For middle-class and working-class girls, home, the workplace and the street, where they shopped in the daytime and strolled by night, were always simultaneously sites of labour and of leisure. For the female consumer, the focal point of leisure, pleasure and personal freedom is not traditionally any fixed geographical location, but the female body itself. It was therefore the 'image industries' – the female mass media, and fashion and cosmetics industries – which constituted the largest sector of the post-war market in leisure commodities for girls.

The unity of post-war consumer lifestyles demanded new forms, too, for the feminine woman, produced in part on the production lines of the fashion, cosmetics and beauty-care industries. A glance at 1950s fashion images shows designers engaged in the business of sculpting, shaping and moulding ever more imaginative feminine forms: in 1954, the H-line, in spring 1955, the A-line, Dior's 'sack' in 1957, the trapeze line in spring 1958, into 1959 with the Empire line. At the same time, rigorous beauty-care regimes ensured that female bodies slipped smoothly into these new forms. Young girls turning for advice to *Bravo*'s beauty-care columnist were taught techniques of body culture and maintenance whereby each part of the body could be separately shaped and trained. When skirt hems rose to just above the knee, attention was focussed on the female leg:

> From Paris comes the news that skirts are getting shorter – and short skirts show more leg! Are your legs in a fit state for public display? Nylon stockings show up every little blemish: do your stockings highlight the soft sheen of your well-cared-for skin . . . or is it the hard rough patches on thighs and knees which show up most? If it is, then something must be done at all costs! (*Bravo*, no. 10, 1958).

Tips on leg maintenance in *Bravo* between 1957 and 1959 included regular gymnastics, massage with 'slimming cream' (sic), visits to the chiropodist for sufferers from flat feet, lukewarm saltwater compresses for fat thighs, cycling for thin legs, trips to the doctor for red and inflamed skin. In conjunction with the beauty column, representations of women in the popular cultural discourses which traversed the pages of *Bravo* (film, television, fashion, rock and pop music and so on) reproduced certain common conventions of pose, gesture and body shape. For the perfect female leg, the general emphasis was on long, sweeping lines, further accentuated by high-heeled shoes tapering down to a pointed toe. Perfection was seen as embodied in particular representative female figures: Marlene Dietrich's legs, like Sophia Loren's hips and Brigitte Bardot's curves, were the talk of fifties beauty columns. Yet *Bravo* did not offer film star pin-ups as models of an ideal to which teenage girls should necessarily aspire; the ideal was displaced from visual representations, and located instead in the masculine gaze. 'Fashion has made skirts shorter', said the *Bravo* beauty tip in March 1958, 'More than ever, eyes are drawn to your legs'. That these were the eyes of men had been made clear in the same column in an earlier edition of the magazine, which sounded the following note of comfort for girls whose legs, despite hours of tortured beauty treatment, remained stubbornly inelegant.

> A lot of men – for whose sake, after all, we go to all this trouble – don't have anything against legs that are a little stocky. A true man doesn't fall in love with external appearances. And if he does, he's the wrong one for you! (*Bravo*, no. 44, 1957).

On the one hand, girls were exhorted to invest time and energy into the labour of body maintenance, grooming and careful dressing; on the other, the desired product of their labours remained persistently out of reach. The 'perfect female self' to which girls were urged to aspire was mirrored in the gaze of the men and boys with whom they shared their everyday lives; thus it remained unknowable, not signified in visual or textual representations, but in the ambiguous amorous attentions of men.

'Bravo girls' were offered one route out of this predicament; it led, not directly towards, but around and between the images of women which peopled the pages of the magazine. Mass media icons (film stars, fashion models, pop idols) were mediated to female readers by authoritative experts on fashion and beauty care – 'Ilse' in Triumph underwear advertisements, or 'Trixi' in *Bravo*'s own fashion column. The information they filtered down to the female reader concerned, not *what* she should look like, but instructions on *how* to make the best of her own resources. They celebrated not any single image of femininity but a set of aesthetic principles as possible instruments for the construction of a more beautiful self. Tailored to the modest resources of the 'Angestellte' who were *Bravo*'s most lucrative market, the mode of aesthetic production propagated here was rule by principles of sobriety, discretion, restraint, moderation and self-control.

> Our 'style' may perhaps tend at times to copy adult fashions. But in general it is still *more restrained, less changeable and less expensive* . . . Slaves to fashion? We're convinced . . . and we hope you are too – that that's the last thing we want to be (*Triumph* advertisement, *Bravo*, no. 42, 1958; author's emphasis).

'Consumption' as cultural practice

In the preceding sections of this survey of fifties consumer culture, I have outlined some of the ways in which capital organized commodity markets to expand the boundaries of female consumption. From this analysis of dominant forms, perspectives for future work on gender and consumption now begin to emerge. In the first instance, it is capital which dictates the forms which commodity consumption takes; yet the market remains dependent on the development by the female consumer of specific sets of social competences and skills: from the rational decision-making of the thrifty housewife, to teenage girls' production of themselves as aesthetic objects in the symbolic configurations of teenage lifestyles. The category of 'consumption' covers a multitude of sins: symbolic readings of commodity, representations, processes of sensual gratification, practices of economic and cultural exchange. The so-called 'sphere' of consumption can thus be dismantled into a multiplicity of complex forms, relations and practices, which operate on diverse and discrete market sites. On each of these 'levels' of consumption, female consumers engage differently with the market machine, activating multiple sets of functions, meanings and values in the commodities they consume. Rules and conventions governing these consumer practices are laid down in consumer law, advice and information; thus we have seen *Bravo*'s fashion advisors setting out implicit and explicit rules for the production of teenage style through the consumption of fashion commodities.

Analyses of these rules and conventions are indispensable to, yet at the same time inadequate for, feminist research into female practices of consumption. Highlighting the mechanisms of control which capital deploys, they fail to grasp the experiential quality of consumer culture for women and girls. Biographical narratives offer one way of bridging this gap, by tracing the paths whereby social subjects negotiate dominant forms; thus I have chosen to end this series of case studies in gender and consumer culture with two short narratives: a fictional filmic narrative, and a biography taken from an account of ethnographic field-work in the fifties. Positioned within radically different contexts, their common feature is the central significance accorded to one commodity: stockings. By 1961, nylon had swamped the young female market in West Germany; *Bravo*'s DIVO survey shows 85 per cent of 'Bravo girls' between the ages of twelve and twenty-four (compared with 80 per cent of non-readers in the same age group) to be wearing seamless stockings; the percentage of female *Bravo* readers who did not possess either Perlon or nylon stockings was nil (DIVO, 1961, p. 137). These figures can neither be read as indicators of girls' blind submission to the dictates of the market, nor do they signify female capitulation to fetishistic 'male' fantasy. The all-pervasiveness of synthetic silk stockings begs different questions: what were the sources of their popularity, and how were they actually 'consumed'?

Ninotchka

In the late fifties, *Bravo* ran a series of half-page advertisements for 'Opal' seamless stockings, depicting crossed female legs, long and sophisticated, emerging from the folds of an elegant black dress. Parallel to the 'Opal' campaign, the magazine carried reports on *Silk Stockings*, Cole Porter's musical remake of Ernst Lubitsch's *Ninotchka* (1939). In the fifties musical, Wim Sonneveld plays a Russian people's representative in Paris, whose loyalty to the Party is beginning to fade. Three Soviet commissars are ordered from Moscow to Paris: their mission – to rescue their colleague from the clutches of that decadent capital. When they in turn disappear, super-activist Ninotchka (Cyd Charisse) is sent on their trail. She soon recognizes the American, Edwin Canfield (Fred Astaire), as her main adversary; he, meanwhile, is amused, fascinated, but never convinced, by her fervent defence of socialism and the Soviet way of life. He guides her instead down the boulevards of Paris, knowing that no woman – 'above all no woman with the charms of Ninotchka' – can withstand the 'democratic temptations' of their dazzling window displays. The 'fortress Ninotchka' finally falls; she succumbs to the charms of Edwin, and of the Western world he represents.

> Moscow – and politics – have lost Ninotchka for ever. Silk stockings may be thin, but in the end and above all, they are more attractive than the best of political convictions (*Bravo*, no. 4, 1958).

Consumers of 'symbolic commodities' have preferred textual sources from which they draw the meanings with which those commodities are invested. *Bravo* is one such source for teenage consumers, and in 1958 it offered its readers a range of texts ('Opal' advertisements, fashion and beauty tips, reviews of *Silk Stockings*) in which synthetic silk (nylon or Perlon) stockings were encoded into new configurations of meaning. In part, these were drawn from the symbolic field of meanings around genuine silk, with its traditional associations of exoticism, sensuality, luxury and mystery: the legend of the Chinese princess said to have discovered the secret of the silkworm more than five thousand years ago: or the two sixth-century monks reputed to have smuggled the eggs of the silkworm out of China to the court of the Byzantine Emperor Justinian. But the additional glamour of the American nylon has specific origins elsewhere. On post-1945 black markets, American soldiers were well known as the main purveyors of nylon stockings; by the 1950s, poster graphics were using images of stockinged female legs for comparative representations of rising productivity rates in European countries. In popular representations of the Cold War period, the stocking became a dominant signifier of freedom, democracy and the American way of life; the musical *Silk Stockings* was Hollywood's contribution to this modern myth. In the *Silk Stockings* narrative, real anxieties over a simmering East–West conflict are played out in fantastic form across the female body. Ninotchka first becomes a 'true' woman through romantic association with a Western man – and through her consumption of fashion commodities for the feminine woman. In *Bravo*'s review, the resolution of the romantic narrative is couched in terms of military defeat ('the fortress Ninotchka ... falls'); in the person of Edwin Canfield, America emerges victorious, not only over Ninotchka herself, but over the red threat she represents.

Reconstructing the *Silk Stockings* narrative, *Bravo*'s review becomes instrumental in the production of a store of meanings around synthetic silk hose, from which teenage consumers might potentially have drawn. Those meanings cannot, however, simply be read off the *Bravo* text. Poststructuralist studies of narrative as complexly codified systems of representations (Barthes, 1975) have shown meaning to be the product of relationships between reader and text, and thus not an intrinsic characteristic of the narrative itself. In order to make sense of any given narrative, the reader engages differently with each of its multiple 'codes', reproducing in her/his signifying practices the relations of tension and contradiction which exist between those codes. In *Bravo's Silk Stockings* review, the so-called 'hermeneutic' and 'cultural' codes may be seen to produce just such contradictory meanings and values. The 'hermeneutic code' is the one which poses the central questions of the narrative, delaying the answers until the final moment of narrative resolution. The enigma of Ninotchka's narrative is the question of her possible transformation into a 'true' woman – a question answered at the end of the narrative in the language of female submission. Ninotchka capitulates to imperialist drives to colonize enemy continents, drives which are encapsulated here in the sexual passion of Edwin Canfield.

According to Barthes's definition in *S/Z*, the 'cultural code' of narrative refers the reader to meanings and values in the social world beyond the text. The social meaning of synthetic silk stockings is not exhausted in the *Bravo* narrative alone; indeed, connotations from other sources may badly disfigure the patterns of meaning constructed by 'internal' narrative codes (which are, in Barthesian terms, the hermeneutic and the semic codes). The following example of a second 1950s 'stocking narrative' shows one of the forms which these potentially oppositional meanings might take.

Annette

Between 1955 and 1957, a West German social worker, Renate Wald, put together a collection of biographical monographs of working-class factory girls, which were later published in Wurzbacher's [and Jaide's] *Die Junge Arbeiterin* (1958). She drew on a pool of ethnographic research conducted by a team of participant observers, all of whom had lived and worked as factory employees for a number of months or years.

One of the girls, Annette, works with her mother in a textile factory; an only child, she spends much of her 'leisure time' at home with the family, helping her mother around the house, or enjoying precious moments of lazy conversation when the chores are finally done. Annette's mother, wary of the dangers of possible sexual adventures, is unwilling to allow her to develop close friendships with young people of either sex; even female friendships, she fears, would ultimately lead to perilous encounters with the opposite sex. At the age of fifteen, Annette still amicably complies with her mother's wishes, remaining a model daughter in almost all respects. Even her taste in clothes is dictated by her mother's preferences for careful but unobtrusive dressing:

> She wears plain ... dark clothes; although she uses powder and lipstick, she does so with care and in moderation; her hair is well-groomed and simply styled. She has an air, not so much of homeliness, as of exceptional respectability (Wald, in Wurzbacher and Jaide, 1958, p. 161).

Although mother and daughter rarely clash, there is one niggling point of conflict. The Perlon stockings which Annette wears to work every day cannot stand the rigours of shopfloor labour; inevitably, she wears out two or three pairs a week. Since Annette spends her weekly pocket money on biscuits and sweets, her mother has constantly to replenish her stock of nylons out of the housekeeping money. Her acid comment on her daughter's prodigality: 'She oughtn't to spend so much on titbits to eat. There's plenty of fruit and sweets to be had at home' (p. 150). A striking characteristic of Annette's biography is the dreary regularity of her everyday life. Up at six in the morning to snatch a quick breakfast, stack the washing up, air the bedrooms and make the beds before setting out for work: nine hours at the production line: arriving back home at six-thirty in the evening to dust the rooms and clean the stairs before sitting down to eat with the family: retiring to bed by ten o'clock at the latest to recoup energy for the day ahead. Both at home and at the workplace, time, space, experience and action are regulated for Annette by institutions and agents of social control – the family and parents, the factory, overseers and management. In this context, Annette's conflict with her mother over stockings becomes more than a whimsical and inconsequential detail. A moment of disorder and disruption, it marks the displacement of potentially more grandiose demands for self-determination onto the only site where they may realistically be met. Annette is financially and emotionally dependent on the security of family life; she cannot allow herself prolonged struggles over points of generational difference. Repressed from the placid routine of everyday family life, these (inevitable) differences find expression in tangential conflicts and struggles.

It has been suggested that similar processes of displacement were in play in the formation of post-war youth subcultures (Cohen, 1972, p. 26). Yet subcultural resistance was no solution for Annette; isolated as she was from her contemporaries, her struggles necessarily took more minutely personal forms. Her conflicts with her mother centred on practices of day-to-day consumption – the money she wasted on frivolous treats, and her (mis)use of Perlon stockings. Perlon is made to be used and thrown away; mending stocking ladders is difficult, and diminishes aesthetic appeal. The 'built-in obsolescence' of Perlon stockings allowed Annette to use them to express an aberrant disregard for her mother's principle of moderation in all things, a principle to which she otherwise strictly adhered. Mass commodities demand to be consumed to excess: Annette, unconsciously perhaps, took them at their word.

Conclusion

As work on male youth subcultures has traced the 'hidden contradictions' which they 'magically resolve' (Hebdige, 1979, p. 18), so Annette's biography can shed light on some of the ways in which girls may live out the contradictions of their lives through an everyday culture of consumption. Her individual reformulation of the logic of built-in obsolescence took place *within* a teenage consumer culture; for her, hedonic consumption itself became a practice of refusal vis-à-vis dominant codes of social taste.

Feminists have commonly represented the 1950s as an age of repressive quiescence, in which women's disaffection with their feminine lot was successfully obscured and silenced. Since Betty Friedan's *Feminine Mystique* (1963), the blame for a widespread fifties' female malaise has been laid predominantly at the door of capitalist marketeers, to whom is ascribed the ability to dupe and seduce women into slavish submission to the authority of the market. But was 'consumerism' an adequate name for the problems of the female condition? Is there a hidden history of authentic female experience to be unearthed from beneath the glossy façade of fifties' femininity? Or could it not equally be the case that the façade itself 'speaks' the problems (and the delights) of the female condition? Consumerism not only offers, but also continually fulfils its promise of everyday solutions – albeit limited and partial ones – to problems whose origins may lie elsewhere. In post-war West Germany, women were constrained to search beyond national boundaries for female cultural forms untainted by aftertastes of Nazism. To don the accoutrements of an American female ideal – nylon stockings, scarlet lipstick, narrow skirts and high-heeled shoes – was in part to register a public disavowal of fascist images of femininity: scrubbed faces shining with health, sturdy child-bearing hips sporting seamed stockings and sensible shoes. Fifties consumerism, while it held many traps for women, nonetheless offered ways and means of negotiating a cultural history of militaristic discipline and rigorous control. Female 'resistance' of the period was perhaps not so much silenced, as pitched at a different level from earlier campaigns for women's equality (which in the fifties was proclaimed to have been achieved) or later feminist struggles against women's commoditization and objectification on a capitalist market. At specific moments in post-war history, the market has become a target for the rhetoric of a necessary and well-founded feminist opposition; yet in relation to the fifties – and possibly in the eighties too – there was, and is, little to be gained from 'oppositional' postures of aloof distaste.

> For me, the eighties are more than this: love the things that bring you down. I can't change things, I can't think plastic out of my world, so I try to turn the tables on it and see what's actually good about it. Do you see . . . I can drape myself with as much silk and linen as I want, and the plastic still won't go away. So I try to look at it differently. Love the things that bring you down (Annette Humpe, Ideal).

Notes

1 The seminal work in this field was Phil Cohen's 1972 study of 'Subcultural conflict and working-class community' (Birmingham, 1972). Other works to which both explicit and implicit reference will be made in the following pages include Hall and Jefferson (1976), Hebdige (1979), and Willis (1977).

2 The term 'homology' is used in subcultural theory to describe the 'degree of fit' between the structure of group experience and the cultural forms through which that experience is expressed. Thus for example in Paul Willis's studies of hippy and bike-boy culture, the music of each group was seen to exist in a relationship of 'homology' with its lifestyle and values. 'The preferred music must have the

potential, at least in its formal structure, to express meanings which resonate with other aspects of group life' (Willis, 'The cultural meaning of drug use', 1976, p. 106).

References

Barthes, R. 1975: *S/Z*. London: Jonathan Cape.

Bourdieu, P. 1967: Systems of education and systems of thought. *International Journal of Social Science* **XIX**(3).

Cohen, P. 1972: Subcultural conflict and working-class community. *Working Papers in Cultural Studies*, 2, Centre for Contemporary Cultural Studies, University of Birmingham.

DIVO (ed.) 1961: *Bravo-Leser stellen sich vor*. Munich: Kindler und Schiermeyer.

Hall, S. and Jefferson, T. (eds) 1976: *Resistance through rituals: youth subcultures in post-war Britain*. London: Hutchinson.

Hebdige, D. 1979: *Subcultures: the meaning of style*. London: Methuen.

Hoggart, R. 1957: *The uses of literacy*. Harmondsworth: Penguin Books.

McRobbie, A. and Garber, J. 1976: Girls and subcultures. In Hall, S. and Jefferson, T. (eds), *Resistance through rituals: youth subcultures in post-war Britain*. London: Hutchinson.

Noelle, E. 1940: *Massenbefragungen über Politik und Presse in USA*. Frankfurt-am-Main: Diesterweg.

Scharmann, D.-L. 1965: *Das Konsumverhalten von Jugendlichen*. Munich: Juventa.

Vershofen, W. 1954: Rationalisierung vom Verbraucher her. *Deutsche Wirtschaft im Querschnitt*. Beilage zu *Der Volkswirt*, no. 28.

Warner, W.L. 1960: *Social class in America*, Evanston, IL: Harper & Row.

Willis, P. 1976: 'The cultural meaning of drug use. In Hall, S. and Jefferson, T. (eds), *Resistance through rituals: youth subcultures in post-war Britain*. London: Hutchinson.

Willis, P. 1977: *Learning to labour: how working class kids get working class jobs*. London: Saxon House.

Woods, W. 1960: Psychological dimensions of consumer decision. *Journal of Marketing* **24**(3).

Wurzbacher, G. and Jaide, W. (eds) 1958: *Die junge Arbeiterin: Beiträge zur Sozialkunde und Jugendarbeit*. Munich: Juventa.

11

Black and white on the dance-floor

Paul Gilroy

From his *There ain't no black in the Union Jack* (Hutchinson, 1987).

[. . .] In July 1949, a *Picture Post* feature article by Robert Kee on 'The British colour bar' was illustrated by a photograph of a young couple and their child. The man was black and the woman was white. The caption beneath their picture was headlined 'a marriage that can lead to difficulties'. It revealed that the man, Herman McKay, was earning a living running a dance-band. In fact, the picture shows his wife helping him into his stage costume. The caption explained that he had been forced to adopt the pseudonym 'Alfonso Perez' as an essential part of this musical venture. This picture and its accompanying narrative vividly illustrate the way in which, from the beginning of post-war settlement, blacks were an ambiguous presence inside the popular culture of the 'host society'. Mr McKay was acceptable in the persona of 'Perez' the bandleader. He was welcome as a musician, as a producer of that culture, but the article implies that the informal but widespread colour bar would have excluded him as a customer from many of the places in which he worked as a performer.

The gradual transition from migrant to settler status involved a progression through a medley of different cultural forms. The early settlers were comparatively few in number (Peach, 1968) and beyond the British educations which were their colonial inheritance, they lacked a single cohesive culture which could bind them together. They set about creating it from the diverse influences which were available and which corresponded to their predicament. The dances, parties and social functions in which students, ex-service people and workers enjoyed themselves, reverberated to black musics drawn from the US and Africa as well as Latin America and the Caribbean. They jived and jitterbugged, foxtrotted and quickstepped, moving from one cultural idiom to another as the music changed. Class and occupational conflicts among the settlers as well as ethnic differences and the gender ratio[1] contributed to a degree of fragmentation. The student population concentrated in Bayswater, Kensington and North London diverged sharply from both the new workers who were beginning to make their homes in Brixton and Ladbroke Grove and the older seafaring community centred in the East End. The patterns of leisure generated by each relatively discrete group did not always overlap. Each in its own way combined black cultures from a variety of sources with those of the different white communities into which blacks were being drawn as a replacement population. Dancing was for many a primary leisure activity and, being couple centred, a sequence of conflicts based on whether blacks and whites could fraternize and touch in public began to develop.

Enrico Stennett, a young Jamaican political activist who had moved to Britain during 1947, achieved such notoriety for his prowess in the dance-halls of London that, after first being banned from the Lyceum, the Astoria, the Locarno and the Hammersmith and Wimbledon Palais, he was eventually hired by the management to perform exhibitions of jiving and jitterbugging to the delight of the white working-class crowds. This employment took him to ballrooms throughout the south of England and earned him £25 per week for three nights work. Unable to find a black woman to be his partner, Stennett discovered that dancing with white women provoked intense hostility from the management and sometimes violence. He and his white partner were contracted to leave immediately their exemplary performances ended lest other white women asked him to dance. Operating under the name 'Sugar', he and other young black dancers congregated at the Paramount ballroom in London's Tottenham Court Road. The Paramount rapidly became known as the dance-hall for black teenagers. 'Sugar' and other dance-floor hustlers working under names like 'The Magic Boots' and 'The Gladiator' equally quickly achieved a monopoly of the dance competitions organized by the ballroom owners.

> It was ironic to see, in an area of white people, you could not find one white male dancing. At the Paramount the atmosphere was always electric as the big bands jostled to play for us. . . . At these moments they could really enjoy their playing and by seeing the black people enjoying themselves to the full, it gave them more room for improvisation. . . . Alas there were no black women, but the Paramount was packed with young ladies coming in from the stockbroker belt of Surrey, Essex and Hampshire and other small villages and towns within a 60 mile radius of London.[2]

Stennett's account of the ballroom scene of the early 1950s is particularly valuable if read in conjunction with the autobiography of Leslie Thompson,[3] a black musician who worked in many of the biggest dance-bands during this period. Both testify to the ambiguous penetration of blacks into mainstream working-class leisure space. The contradictory nature of the black presence in those institutions is exemplified by Stennett's tale of the ways in which 'racial' hostility was tempered by the high status that derived from black pre-eminence on the dance-floor.

The different responses of whites along gender lines are also highly significant not only because they fracture the continuity of 'race' but also because of the centrality of miscegenation to the racist ideologies of the time. Stennett describes some of the conflicts which developed when white women were drawn into the unfolding antagonism between their black boyfriends and the police, who were particularly angered by the sight of black and white together. According to his account, both the police and the organized racist groups of the time felt that the association of white women with black men which was a marked feature of the Paramount sub-culture and actively discouraged by its management, degraded Britain as a whole.

Hostile police patrols and groups of racists would wait outside at closing time to assault and intimidate any black man they could find with a white woman.

> On one occasion I had left the Paramount dancehall alone and walked to the no. 1 bus stop in Warren Street. As I stood in a long queue of mostly women, I saw three African men with five English women enter a small café. They were not in the café more than five minutes when a gang of white men entered the café, pulled them outside and set about attacking them. The Africans were badly beaten so I rushed to the telephone to call the police. It was not long before they arrived in their cars and meat wagons. But the arrival of the police did not help the Africans. The leading police car blew his horn repeatedly giving the white men the chance to escape. They then proceeded to arrest the Africans. This did not go down well with the women in the queue. They set about the police attacking them physically with their stiletto heels as weapons. This resulted in many women being arrested along with the three Africans and taken to the police station off the Marylebone Road.[4]

Writing of the relationship between black men and white women at the time, Ras Makonnen (George Griffith) has suggested that a form of proto-feminism was to be found at the roots of women's support for the work of black political activists working in London.

> We recognised that the dedication of some of the girls to our cause was an expression of equal rights for women. One way of rejecting the oppression of men was to associate with blacks. To walk with a negro into a posh club like the Atheneum was to make this point. But many of them were vigorously attacked for this (Makonnen, 1973, p. 147).

It would appear that long before the advent of 'rock n'roll', the rise of soul, disco and reggae, the cultural institutions of the white working class were hosting an historic encounter between young black and white people. This meeting precipitated not only fear of the degeneration of the white 'race' in general and defilement of its womanhood in particular, but also the creation of a youth subculture in which black style and expertise were absolutely central. Indeed black supremacy within this subculture inverted in the most striking manner the relationships of domination and subordination assigned outside the dance-halls on racial lines. Of course, away from the shared spaces in which blacks and whites could interact and overlap, a further layer of exclusively black cultural institutions, clubs and dives was being created. Hiro estimates that during this period there were up to fifty black-owned and managed basement clubs in South London alone (1971). In the centre of London, the 59 Club, the Flamingo, the 77 Club and the Sunset, all in Soho, and the Contemporanean in Mayfair all catered to the needs of black workers. Dances organized by the British Council in its hostel at Hans Crescent in Knightsbridge kept the students occupied.

Sebastian Clarke (1980) has pointed out that 'Melodisc', a specialist label on which 'race' records from various sources could be issued, was operating successfully in this country from 1946 onwards (Cowley, 1985). Early releases on this label included material from the American Savoy catalogue. Melodisc first released calypso records here in 1951, having signed the celebrated troubadour, Lord Kitchener, who had been living in England since 1948.

Daddy Peckings, the proprietor of Peckings's Studio One record shop in West London, was the first person to sell reggae and its antecedents – bluebeat, ska and rocksteady – in this country. He has described the gradual transformation of American musical forms, particularly jazz and jump blues, and their junction with traditional Jamaican musics. This cross-fertilization would eventually lead to modern reggae, the evolution of which can be traced through the development of 'sound systems' (Bradshaw, 1981) – large mobile discos – and their surrounding culture in Jamaica and Britain. According to Peckings, the sound systems playing in the dance-halls of Kingston in the late 1940s and early 1950s – Waldron, Tom 'The Great' Sebastian and Nick – offered a mixture of bepop and swing. The big-band sounds of Duke Ellington and Count Basie were reworked by local musicians: Milton McPherson, Redva Cooke, Steve Dick and Jack Brown. Travelling to England in May 1960, Peckings set up a UK outlet for the product of legendary Jamaican producer and entrepreneur Coxsone Dodd, boss of the legendary Studio One label and the man credited not only with the discovery of modern Jamaica's greatest musical talents – The Heptones, Freddie McGregor, Jackie Mittoo, The Wailers – but with the creation of reggae itself.[5] The fledgling sound system culture of urban Jamaica was transplanted into Britain during the 1950s and, on his arrival, Peckings began to supply records to Duke Vin of Ladbroke Grove, the first sound system in this country.

The basic description of a sound system as a large mobile hi-fi or disco does little justice to the specificities of the form. They are, of course, many thousands of times more powerful than a domestic record player but are significantly different from the amplified discos through which other styles of music have been circulated and consumed. The sound that they generate has its own characteristics, particularly an emphasis on the reproduction of bass frequencies, its own aesthetics and a unique mode of consumption. The form of sound systems and the patterns of consumption with which they have become associated will be discussed in detail below. The mark of African elements can be identified on different aspects of sound system culture.

Regardless of their forms and characteristic content, it is necessary to comprehend the importance of the sound systems for both the Jamaican reggae music industry which grew directly out of their activities and for the expressive culture of black Britain in which they remain a core institution. Perhaps the most important effect of the sound systems on the contemporary musical culture of black Britain is revealed in the way that it is centred not on live performances by musicians and singers, though these are certainly appreciated, but on records. Public performance of recorded music is primary in both reggae and soul variants of the culture. In both, records become raw material for spontaneous performances of cultural creation in which the DJ and the MC or toaster who introduces each disc or sequence of discs, emerge as the principal agents in dialogic rituals of active and celebratory consumption. It is above all in these performances that black Britain has expressed the improvization, spontaneity and intimacy which are key characteristics of all new world black musics, providing a living bridge between them and African traditions of music-making which dissolve the distinctions between art and life, artefact and expression which typify the contrasting traditions of Europe (Hoare, 1975; Keil, 1972; Sithole, 1972). As Keil points out, 'outside the West, musical traditions are almost exclusively performance traditions' (1972, p. 85). Sound system culture redefines the meaning of the team performance by separating the input of the artists who originally made the recording from the equally important work of those who adapt and rework it so that it directly expresses the moment in which it is being consumed, however remote this may be from the original context of production. The key to this process is the orality of the artistic forms involved.

The shifting, specialized vocabularies of sound system culture have changed and developed within contradictions generated by wider political and cultural processes – changing patterns of 'race' and class formation in the Caribbean, the US and Britain. The reliance on recorded music takes on even greater significance when it is appreciated that for much of the post-war period, Britain, unlike the US and the Caribbean, lacked both a domestic capacity to produce black musics and any independent means for their distribution. At this stage, the BBC was not interested in including African and Caribbean music in their programmes. When 'pop' charts began to be compiled, black shops and products were structurally excluded from the operations which generated them. This situation contrasts sharply with the position in the US where a well-developed market for 'race records' had grown up (Gillett, 1972), with its own distributors, charts and above all radio stations as a crucial means to spread and reproduce the culture.

Black Britain prized records as the primary resource for its emergent culture and the discs were overwhelmingly imported or licensed from abroad. The dependency of the British music scene on musics produced elsewhere has progressed through several phases. But even as self-consciously British black forms have been constructed, the basic fact of dependency has remained constant. The cultural syncretism that has taken place across the national boundaries that divide the African diaspora has involved relations of unequal exchange in which Britain, for demographic and historical reasons, has until recently had a strictly subordinate place. The importing of music, often in small quantities, encouraged the underground aspects of a scene in which outlets into the dominant culture were already rare. Competition between sound system operators had been an early feature of the Jamaican dance-halls, and was entrenched over here as sound systems jostled for the most up-to-date and exclusive tunes imported from the US as well as the Caribbean. In a major survey of London's black music scene of the early 1970s, Carl Gayle explored the appeal of imported 'pre-release' records on the dance-hall circuit:

> The youngsters today spend more than they can afford on records, but they want the best and the rarest . . . 'We import our records three times a week from Jamaica' said a young guy called Michael . . . 'Pre-release music to me and many people like Sound System men and their followers, is like underground music. As soon as it's released it's commercial music. So you find the youth of today, the ghetto youth like myself, pre-release music is like medicine. They'll go anywhere to hear it'.[6]

The identification of imported music as free from the commercialization which characterized the British music industry is an important expression of the politics which infused the roots music scene. The supposedly non-commercial status of imported records added directly to their appeal and demonstrated the difference between black culture and the pop-world against which it was defined.

The rivalry between 'sounds' over records was paralleled on the dance-floors by intense competition between their followers. The ritual expressions of both were dance competitions and the occasional fight. In the early 1970s reggae and soul scenes, the formal competitions centred on 'shuffling' and the rivalry between different sound systems was particularly intense where operators from north and south of the river clashed, each operator and toaster striving to match the other tune for tune, rhythm for rhythm, until the system with the best tunes and the weightiest sound emerged as the victor. Carl Gayle identified the level of violence in these encounters as one factor in the decomposition of the scene into sharply differentiated soul and reggae sub-scenes during the 1970s.

> The rivalry which developed between North and South . . . was the foundation for much of the violence of the Ram Jam and other clubs and was perpetrated by the supporters of the Sound Systems – Coxon and Duke Reid in the South and Count Shelly in the North especially. This rivalry, which often erupted into violence, was responsible for the division of the black music scene as a whole. . . . The clubs lost their respectability. Consequently many black youngsters dropped out of the once peaceful reggae-oriented sub-culture, opting for the more tranquil soul scene. Soul had always been popular with West Indians anyway and a lot of people just got scared of the hooliganism.

Gayle tentatively suggests that this violence was something which made reggae attractive to white youth and that it was a significant element in the forging of links between reggae and the skinheads around common conceptions of masculinity and machismo.

At its height, the late 1960s and early 1970s club scene involved alcohol-free daytime sessions completely dominated by dance at some of the best venues. For example, the Sunday afternoon 2–6 p.m. sessions at the Ram Jam in Brixton provided an antecedent for the equally drinkless Saturday lunchtime events organized by DJ Tim Westwood, which were instrumental in the spread of hip-hop in London during the 1980s. Like the hip-hop mixers of the later era, the sound system DJs often removed the labels from the records which they used. This gesture combined the obvious desire to keep the information contained on the labels secret, with a comment on the distance which these subcultures had travelled from their commercialized, overground equivalents. The removal of labels subverted the emphasis on acquisition and individual ownership which the makers of black music cultures identified as an unacceptable feature of pop culture. This simple act suggested alternative collective modes of consumption in which the information essential to purchase was separated from the pleasure which the music created. The record could be enjoyed without knowing who it was by or where it was in a chart. Its origins were rendered secondary to the use made of it in the creative rituals of the dance-hall.

Deprived of access to the official charts, the black record sellers began to produce their own alternative indices of roots popularity in specialist publications devoted to black music and in the community's own news and political weeklies. The specialist monthly *Black Music* was launched in December 1973, at exactly the same time as minority programming of black musics was beginning to be introduced into the newly expanded local radio network. The size and distribution of Britain's black populations imposed severe limits on the amount of money which could be made from catering to their leisure needs. The communities remained diverse, small and scattered. These characteristics were important factors in the expansion of black leisure institutions and their partial adaptation to the demands of white Britons. The involvement of whites, particularly young people, in the consumption of black cultures was noted by commentators in the early 1960s. It has been discussed by other authors and by myself elsewhere (Gilroy and Lawrence, 1982; Hebdige, 1979; Patterson, 1966). The centrality of distinctively black forms to white youth cultures was observed by Hamblett and Deverson in 1964:

> The Blue Beat is here to stay. . . . Around the dancehalls and discotheques the Blue Beat has been added to the youngsters' already overstepping dance crazes. . . . Many mods that I have spoken to say that the Mersey Sound is out and this new sound is the big thing at the moment. As one youngster put it to me 'The Beatles have been well and truly squashed and we don't dig their sound anymore'.[7]

This mod's use of black American slang, 'dig', and the Beatles' early reliance on cover versions of material from rhythm and blues artists like Barrett Strong and Larry Williams are probably as significant as the blue beat itself in the history of how popular culture has formed spaces in which the politics of 'race' could be lived out and transcended in the name of youth.

The development of Jamaican popular music in the encounter between folk forms and American R and B picked up from radio stations transmitting in the southern states is well known (Clarke, 1980; Kimberley, 1982). At each stage of its progress through blue beat, ska, rocksteady and reggae it is possible to indicate shifting patterns in the involvement of young whites. For example, a white reggae band 'Inner Mind' was formed in London during 1967 and was considered good enough to back such vintage Jamaican performers as Laurel Aitken, Alton Ellis and Owen Grey.[8] The band played at all the leading black venues of the period – Mr B's, the Q and Colombo's in London, the Santa Rosa in Birmingham and Wolverhampton's Club '67. In *The empire strikes back* (1982) I have indicated some of the elements by means of which this substantial history of white involvement can be periodized [CCCS, 1982]. The mass marketing of Caribbean music as a pop form can be traced from Millie Small's 'My Boy Lollipop' through the reggae festival at Wembley Stadium in 1969 and into the selling of Bob Marley as a 'rebel superstar'. Simon Jones (1986) has pointed out that there were seventeen top-twenty hits based on Jamaican music during the period 1969–72. The attempts of white companies to sell the music to whites also relied on the growth of minority programming within the newly established local radio network. The local stations which proliferated between 1970 and

1972 were concentrated in urban areas and each of them featured two or three hours of black music per week. This development was more significant in the history of Caribbean forms, because the pirate radio stations and the American Forces station in Europe already carried a certain amount of soul music to British fans. Radio Luxembourg, a leading pirate, broadcast Dave Christian's 'Soul Bag' early (1.30 a.m.) on Monday mornings. The new local stations made black music available to anyone who was interested enough to tune in to the unpopular slots – usually Sunday lunchtime – in which the minority shows were programmed. In the south-east, Steve Barnard's 'Reggae Time' on Radio London became particularly influential. Having experimented with several presenters for their reggae programme, Capital Radio launched David Rodigan's 'Roots Rockers' in October 1979. This show became the most important in reggae broadcasting, extending its running time from one and a half to three hours. The power of the show and the extent to which the reggae industry depended on it were revealed in 1985 when Rodigan announced that he had been threatened and intimidated by a small minority of record producers who sought to use the show to push their own product and ensure its commercial success regardless of artistic considerations. Rodigan did not name the producers responsible for his harassment, but told his listeners over the air:

> I've reached the point of no return with these hustlers. I'm tired of the threats and I'm standing up to them from now on. I'm going to entertain the public, not the reggae producers. I'm not going to bow down any more. All they can do is kill me now – that's all they can do.[9]

The gradual involvement of large corporations with a broad base in the leisure industries in the selling of reggae stimulated important changes reflecting a conscious attempt to separate the product from its producers and from its roots in black life. Whatever the effect of the reggae film *The Harder They Come* in the Caribbean (Braithwaite, 1984), in Britain, it marked the beginning of a new strategy for white consumption. The film was presented as little more than visual support for the sound-track recording made available by Island Records, an Anglo-Jamaican company. Cinemas showing the film became artificially insulated spaces in which images of black life, in this case as backward, violent, sexist and fratricidal, could be consumed without having to face the difficulties associated with sharing leisure space with real live black people. Island Records, the company who pioneered this ploy, elaborated it further in subsequent films of reggae artists in live performance and in the 'adventure fantasy', *Countryman*, in 1982. This last film, a tale of Obeah and adventure, was based on a simple inversion of the Robinson Crusoe myth. 'Friday', recast in the form of a Rasta hermit-fisherman endowed with magical powers that originated in his total harmony with the natural world, saves and protects two young white Americans who fall into his Eden as the result of a plane crash. They are unwittingly involved in the drug business but with his help are reunited with their families and sent back to the US once the villains, the military wing of Michael Manley's socialist government, have been put in their place. This plot is less significant than the fact that the film was billed as 'A tribute to Bob Marley'. This time, the sound-track recording featured his songs.[10]

Island Records was also at the forefront of moves to sign black performers and, having adjusted their music and image to the expectations of white rock audiences, sell them as pop stars. The example of Bob Marley, an Island artist from 1972 until his death in 1981, provides the most acute illustration of a marketing process which was repeated by the company on a smaller, less successful scale with other lesser known (in rock terms) artists like the Heptones and Burning Spear. It was a strategy which was less productive for other rival British companies which lacked Island's roots in the Caribbean. Foremost among these was Virgin, who signed many leading Jamaican performers – the Gladiators, U Roy and the Mighty Diamonds – in the early 1970s. Marley's rise was also significant in that it facilitated the popularization of Rastafari ideology in Britain and throughout the world. The years between 1972 and 1981 saw him rise to outernational prominence and take reggae music forever into the lexicon of pop. There are good reasons to support the view that his foray into pop stardom was a calculated development in which he was intimately involved, having realized that the solidification of communicative networks across the African diaspora was a worthwhile prize. The minor adjustments in presentation and form that rendered his reggae assimilable across the cultural borders of the overdeveloped countries were thus a small price to pay. His incorporation of bluesy guitar playing and 'disco' rhythms can be interpreted not as obvious concessions to the demands of a white rock audience (Wallis and Malm, 1984), but as attempts to utilize the very elements most likely to appeal to the black audiences of North America.

Marley died at the very moment when he had steered reggae to the brink of an organic and overdue encounter with rhythm and blues. His work found considerable support in the new pop markets of Latin America and Africa, where he had performed at the independence ceremonies for Zimbabwe, symbolizing the recovery of Africa for the black peoples of the new world and the recovery of the new world diaspora for Africa. Whatever the ambiguities in Marley's music and mode of presentation, he provided a heroic personality around which the international mass-marketing of reggae could pivot. His 'Exodus' album remained on the British pop chart for fifty-six consecutive weeks in the period 1977–8. Marley acknowledged his newfound white listeners with the release of 'Punky Reggae Party' also in 1977. It signified not so much the confluence of two oppositional impulses – Rasta and punk – as the durability of pop and its capacity to absorb diverse and contradictory elements. The Caribbean was becoming an increasingly important subcultural resource once white British youth began to break free of their own dependency on American images and meanings (Hebdige, 1983). By consolidating reggae's position on the charts outside novelty categories and becoming a star, Marley created a new space in pop. In the period leading up to his death, it was a space filled primarily by the 'two-tone' cult. In this movement, earlier Caribbean forms, particularly ska, which had been exposed by the serious reggae fans' search for musical authenticity behind Marley's obvious compromises, were captured and rearticulated into distinctively British styles and concerns. This fusion took several contrasting paths. The assertively 'white' reggae of London bands like Madness and Bad Manners attracted the support of young racists, whose patriotic nativism had been reborn in the revival of the skinhead style. It contrasted sharply with the work of racially mixed groups from the Midlands. Where Madness simply hijacked ska and declared it white, the Beat, the Specials and other similar outfits sought to display the contradictory politics of 'race' openly in their work. Their best efforts acknowledged the destructive power of racism and simultaneously invited their audience to share in its overcoming, a possibility that was made concrete in the co-operation of blacks and whites in producing the music.

If Marley's excursions into pop had seeded the ground for this two-tone harvest, this era suggests that the lasting significance of his rise to prominence lies not at the flamboyant extremities of youth subculture where punks had reworked the themes and preoccupations of Rastafari around their dissent from and critique of Britishness, but in the youth-cultural mainstream. Here, the posters of Bob, locks flying, which had been inserted into his crossover product by Island, became icons in the bedroom shrines of thousands of young whites. In his egalitarianism, Ethiopianism and anti-imperialism, his critique of law and of the types of work which were on offer, these young people found meanings with which to make sense of their lives in post-imperial Britain. The two-tone bands appreciated this and isolated the elements in Marley's appeal that were most appropriate to the experiences of young, urban Britons on the threshold of the 1980s. They pushed the inner logic of his project to its conclusion by fusing pop forms rooted in the Caribbean with a populist politics. Marley's populism had been focussed by the imperatives of black liberation and overdetermined by the language of Rastafarian eschatology. Theirs was centred instead on pointing to the possibility that black and white young people might discover common or parallel meanings in their blighted, post-industrial predicament. The experience of living side by side in a 'ghost town' had begun to raise this question. The Specials' song, which topped the chart as the rioting of 1981 was at its peak, asked, 'Why must the youth fight against themselves?' and cleverly entangled its pleas against both racism and youth–cultural sectarianism. The two-tone operation depended on being seen to transcend the various prescriptive definitions of 'race' which faced each other across the hinterland of youth culture. With Marley's death equilibrium was lost. One pole of the cultural field in which two-tone had formed ceased functioning. Marley's position was usurped eagerly not by the next generation of Jamaican and British artists who had been groomed by their record companies to succeed him, but by a new wave of post-punk white reggae musicians. The best known of these inverted the preconceptions of Rasta by calling themselves The Police and armed with 'Aryan' good looks and dedication to 'Regatta de Blanc' served, within pop culture at least, to detach reggae from its historic association with the Africans of the Caribbean and their British descendants.

Notes

1 Hiro (1971) periodizes the early settlement and argues that skilled and semi-skilled settlers were in the majority between 1948 and 1955. In the later period

between 1955 and 1962 'the "typical" migrant was unskilled or semi-skilled with a rural or semi-rural background' (p. 10).

   Peach, (1968, pp. 41–2) has the figures on the gender difference among the black settler population. According to his tables, women were only an overall majority of immigrants in 1958 and 1959 though the percentage of men and women varied quite widely between the different West Indian territories. In 1958 for example, 60.6 per cent of Guyanese and 48.3 per cent of Jamaican emigrants were male.

2 *Caribbean Times*, 241, 25 October 1985. I spoke to Mr Stennett in October 1985.
3 See Leslie Thompson's *An autobiography* (1985).
4 *Caribbean Times*, 242, 1 November 1985.
5 The Cables' 'Baby Why' (Studio One) is one of the first discernably 'reggae' recordings, and typifies the Coxsone approach of the period.
6 *Black Music*, 1, no. 8, July 1974.
7 Charles Hamblett and Jane Deverson, 1964: *Generation X*, London: Tandem Books.
8 *Black Music*, March 1976.
9 *Time Out*, 16–22 May 1985.
10 The growth of reggae as a form of pop or rock music during the 1970s resulted in a proliferation of pictorial 'coffee table' books about Rastafari, reggae and Jamaica. Soft core porn photographs of black bodies, male and female, were interspersed by journalistic commentary about the brutishness and the hedonism of this Caribbean idyll. Typical manifestations of this genre include Michael Thomas and Adrian Boot's *Jah Revenge*, Eel Pie/Hutchinson, 1982; and Adrian Boot and Vivien Goldman's *Bob Marley Soul Rebel–Natural Mystic*. Eel Pie/Hutchinson, 1981.

References

Bradshaw, P. 1981: A big sound system splashdown. *New Musical Express* 21 February.
Braithwaite, E.K. 1984: *History of the voice: the development of nation language in anglophone Caribbean poetry*. London: New Beacon Press.
CCCS 1982: *The empire strikes back*, Centre for Contemporary Cultural Studies, University of Birmingham. London: Hutchinson.
Clarke, S. 1980: *Jah Music*. London: Heinemann.
Cowley, J. 1985: *West Indian gramophone records in Britain: 1927–1950*, ESRC Occasional Papers in Ethnic Relations 1.
Gillett, C. 1972: The black market roots of rock. In Denisoff and Peterson (eds), *The sounds of social change studies in popular culture*. Chicago, IL: Rand McNally.
Gilroy, P. and Lawrence, E. 1982: Two-tone Britain, black youth, white youth and the politics of anti-racism. In Bains and Cohen (eds), *Youth in multi-racist Britain*. London: Macmillan.
Hebdige, D. 1979: *Subculture: the meaning of style*. London: Methuen.
Hebdige, D. 1983: Ska tissue: the rise and fall of two tone. In Simon and Davis (eds) *Reggae international*. London: Thames & Hudson.
Hiro, D. 1971: *Black British white British*. London: Eyre & Spottiswoode.
Hoare, I. *et al.* 1975: *The south book*. London: Methuen.
Jones, S. 1986: *White youth and Jamaican culture*. Unpublished PhD thesis, Centre for Contemporary Cultural Studies, University of Birmingham.
Keil, C. 1972: Motion and feeling through music. In Kochman (ed.), *Rappin' and stylin' out*.
Kimberley, N. 1982: Ska: how Jamaica found a sound of its own. *The encyclopaedia of rock* 5(49).

Makonnen, R. [George Griffith] 1973: *Pan Africanism from within*. Nairobi: Oxford University Press.

Patterson, O. 1966: The dance invasion. *New Society*, reprinted in *Pressure Drop*, no. 2, undated.

Sithole, E. 1972: Black folk music. In Kochman (ed.), *Rappin' and stylin' out*.

Thompson, L. 1985: *An autobiography*. Crawley: Rabbit Press.

Wallis, R. and Malm, K. 1984: *Big sounds from small peoples*. London: Constable.

12

Minimal selves

Stuart Hall

From *The real me – postmodernism and the question of identity* (ICA Documents, 1987).

A few adjectival thoughts only . . .

Thinking about my own sense of identity, I realize that it has always depended on the fact of being a *migrant*, on the *difference* from the rest of you. So one of the fascinating things about this discussion is to find myself centred at last. Now that, in the postmodern age, you all feel so dispersed, I become centred. What I've thought of as dispersed and fragmented comes, paradoxically, to be *the* representative modern experience! This is 'coming home' with a vengeance! Most of it I much enjoy – welcome to migranthood. It also makes me understand something about identity which has been puzzling me in the last three years.

I've been puzzled by the fact that young black people in London today are marginalized, fragmented, unenfranchized, disadvantaged and dispersed. And yet, they look as if they own the territory. Somehow, they, too, in spite of everything, are centred, in place: without much material support, it's true, but nevertheless, they occupy a new kind of space at the centre. And I've wondered again and again: what it is about that long discovery–rediscovery of identity among blacks in this migrant situation, which allows them to lay a kind of claim to certain parts of the earth which aren't theirs, with quite that certainty? I do feel a sense of – dare I say – envy surrounding them. Envy is a very funny thing for the British to feel at this moment in time – to want to be black! Yet I feel some of you surreptitiously moving towards that marginal identity. I welcome you to that, too.

Now the question is: is this centring of marginality really *the* representative postmodern experience? I was given the title 'the minimal self'. I know the discourses which have theoretically produced that concept of 'minimal self'. But my experience now is that what the discourse of the postmodern has produced is not something new but a kind of recognition of where identity always was at. It is in that sense that I want to redefine the general feeling which more and more people seem to have about themselves – that they are all, in some way, *recently migrated*, if I can coin that phrase.

The classic questions which every migrant faces are twofold: 'Why are you here?' and 'When are you going back home?' No migrant ever knows the answer to the second question until asked. Only then does she or he know that really, in the deep sense, she/he's never going back. Migration is a one way trip. There is no 'home' to go back to. There never was. But 'why are you here?' is also a really interesting question, which I've never been able to find a proper answer to either. I know the reasons one is supposed to give: 'for education', 'for the children's sake', 'for a better life, more opportunities', 'to enlarge the mind', etc. The truth is, I am here because it's where my family is not. I really came here to get away from my mother. Isn't that the universal story of life? One is where one is to try and get away from somewhere else. That was the story which I could never tell anybody about myself. So I had to find other stories, other fictions, which were more authentic or, at any rate, more acceptable, in place of the Big Story of the endless evasion of patriarchal family life. Who I am – the 'real' me – was formed in relation to a whole set of other narratives. I was aware of the fact that identity is an invention from the very beginning, long before I understood any of this theoretically. Identity is formed at the unstable point where the 'unspeakable' stories of subjectivity meet the narratives of history, of a culture. And since he/she is positioned in relation to cultured narratives which have been profoundly expropriated, the colonized subject is always 'somewhere else': doubly marginalized, displaced always *other* than where he or she is, or is able to speak from.

It wasn't a joke when I said that I migrated in order to get away from my family. I did. The problem, one discovers, is that since one's family is always already 'in here', there is no way in which you can actually leave them. Of course, sooner or later, they recede in memory, or even in life. But these are not the 'burials' that really matter. I wish they were still around, so that I didn't have to carry them around, locked up somewhere in my head, from which there is no migration. So from the first, in relation to them, and then to all the other symbolic 'others', I certainly was always aware of the self as only constituted in that kind of absent–present contestation with something else, with some other 'real me', which is and isn't there.

If you live, as I've lived, in Jamaica, in a lower-middle-class family that was trying to be a middle-class Jamaican family trying to be an upper-middle-class Jamaican family trying to be an English Victorian family . . . I mean the notion of displacement as a place of 'identity' is a concept you learn to live with, long before you are able to spell it. Living with, living through difference. I remember the occasion when I returned to Jamaica on a visit sometime in the early 1960s, after the first wave of migration to England, my mother said to me: 'Hope they don't think you are one of those immigrants over there!' And of course, at that point I knew for the first time I was an immigrant. Suddenly in relation to that narrative of migration, one version of the 'real me' came into view. I said: 'Of course, I'm an immigrant. What do you think I am?' And she said in that classic Jamaican middle-class way, 'Well, I hope the people over there will shove all the immigrants off the long end of a short pier'. (They've been shoving ever since.)

The trouble is that the instant one learns to be 'an immigrant', one recognizes one can't be an immigrant any longer: it isn't a tenable place to be. I, then, went through the long, important, political education of discovering that I am 'black'. Constituting oneself as 'black' is another recognition of self through difference: certain clear polarities and extremities against which one tries to define oneself. We constantly underestimate the importance, to certain crucial political things that have happened in the world, of this ability of people to constitute themselves, psychically, in the black identity. It has long been thought that this is really a simple process: a recognition – a resolution of irresolutions, a coming to rest in some place which was always there waiting for one. The 'real me' at last!

The fact is 'black' has never been just there either. It has always been an unstable identity, psychically, culturally and politically. It, too, is a narrative, a story, a history. Something constructed, told, spoken, not simply found. People now speak of the society I come from in totally unrecognizable ways. Of course Jamaica is a black society, they say. In reality it is a society of black and brown people who lived for three or four hundred years without ever being able to speak of themselves as 'black'. Black is an identity which had to be learned and could only be learned in a certain moment. In Jamaica that moment is the 1970s. So the notion that identity is a simple – if I can use the metaphor – black or white question, has never been the experience of black people, at least in the diaspora. These are 'imaginary communities' – and not a bit the less real because they are also symbolic. Where else could the dialogue of identity between subjectivity and culture take place?

Despite its fragmentations and displacements, then, 'the self' does relate to a real set of histories. But what are the 'real histories' to which so many at this conference have 'owned up'? How new is this new condition? It does seem that more and more people now recognize themselves in the narratives of displacement. But the narratives of displacement have certain conditions of existence, real histories in the contemporary world, which are not only or exclusively psychical, not simply 'journeys of the mind'. What is that special moment? Is it simply the recognition of a general condition of fragmentation at the end of the twentieth century?

It may be true that the self is always, in a sense, a fiction, just as the kinds of 'closures' which are required to create communities of identification – nation, ethnic group, families, sexualities, etc. – are arbitrary closures; and the forms of political action, whether movements, or parties, or classes, those, too, are temporary, partial, arbitrary. I believe it is an immensely important gain when one recognizes that all identity is constructed across difference and begins to live with the politics of difference. But doesn't the acceptance of the fictional or narrative status of identity in relation to the world also require as a necessity, its opposite – the moment of arbitrary closure? Is it possible for there to be action or identity in the world without arbitrary closure – what one might call the necessity to meaning of the end of the sentence? Potentially, discourse is endless: the infinite semiosis of meaning. But to say anything at all in particular, you do have to stop talking. Of course, every full stop is provisional. The next sentence will take nearly all of it back. So what is this 'ending'? It's a kind of stake, a kind of wager. It says: 'I need to say something, something . . . just now'. It is not forever, not totally universally true. It is not underpinned by any infinite guarantees. But just now, this is what I mean; this is who I am. At a certain point, in a certain discourse, we call these unfinished closures, 'the self', 'society', 'politics', etc. Full stop. OK. There really (as they say) is no full stop of that kind. Politics, without the arbitrary interposition of power in language, the cut of ideology, the positioning, the crossing of lines, the rupture, is impossible. I don't understand political action without that moment. I don't see where it comes from. I don't see how it is possible. All the social movements which have tried to transform society and have required the constitution of new subjectivities, have had to accept the necessarily fictional, but also the fictional necessity, of the arbitrary closure which is not the end, but which makes both politics and identity possible.

Now I perfectly recognize that this recognition of difference, of the impossibility of 'identity' in its fully unified meaning, does, of course, transform our sense of what politics is about. It transforms the nature of political commitment. Hundred-and-one per cent commitment is no longer possible. But the politics of infinitely advancing while looking over the shoulder is a very dangerous exercise. You tend to fall into a hole. Is it possible, acknowledging the discourse of self-reflexivity, to constitute a *politics* in the recognition of the necessarily fictional nature of the modern self, and the necessary arbitrariness of the closure around the imaginary communities in relation to which we are constantly in the process of becoming 'selves'?

Looking at new conceptions of identity requires us also to look at re-definitions of the forms of politics which follow from that: the politics of difference, the politics of self-reflexivity, a politics that is open to contingency but still able to act. The politics of infinite dispersal is the politics of no action at all; and one can get into that from the best of all possible motives (i.e., from the highest of all possible intellectual abstractions). So one has to reckon with the consequences of where that absolutist discourse of postmodernism is pushing one. Now, it seems to me that it is possible to think about the nature of new political identities, which isn't founded on the notion of some absolute, integral self and which clearly can't arise from some fully closed narrative of the self. A politics which accepts the 'no necessary or essential correspondence' of anything with anything, and there has to be *a politics of articulation* – politics as a hegemonic project.

I also believe that out there other identities *do* matter. They're not the same as my inner space, but I'm in some relationship, some dialogue, with them. They are points of resistance to the solipsism of much postmodernist discourse. I have to deal with them, somehow. And all of that constitutes, yes, a politics, in the general sense, a politics of constituting 'unities'-in-difference. I think that is a new conception of politics, rooted in a new conception of the self, of identity. But I do think, theoretically and intellectually, it requires us to begin, not only to speak the language of dispersal, but also the language of, as it were, contingent closures of articulation.

You see, I don't think it's true that we've been driven back to a definition of identity as the 'minimal self'. Yes, it's true that the 'grand narratives' which constituted the language of the self as an integral entity don't hold. But actually, you know, it isn't just the 'minimal selves' stalking out there with absolutely no relation to one another. Let's think about the question of nation and nationalism. One is aware of the degree to which nationalism was/is constituted as one of those major poles or terrains of articulation of the self. I think it is very important the way in which some people now (and I think particularly of the colonized subject) begin to reach for a new conception of ethnicity as a kind of counter to the old discourses of nationalism or national identity.

Now one knows these are dangerously overlapping terrains. All the same they are not identical. Ethnicity *can* be a constitutive element in the most viciously regressive kind of nationalism or national identity. But in our times, as an imaginary community, it is also beginning to carry some other meanings, and to define a new space for identity. It insists on difference – on the fact that every identity is placed, positioned, in a culture, a language, a history. Every statement comes from somewhere, from somebody in particular. It insists on specificity, on conjuncture. But it is not necessarily armour-plated against other identities. It is not tied to fixed, permanent, unalterable oppositions. It is not wholly defined by exclusion.

I don't want to present this new ethnicity as a powerless, perfect universe. Like all terrains of identification, it has dimensions of power in it. But it isn't quite so framed by those extremities of power and aggression, violence and mobilization, as the older forms of nationalism. The slow contradictory movement from 'nationalism' to 'ethnicity' as a source of identities is part of a new politics. It is also part of the 'decline of the west' – that immense process of historical relativization which is just beginning to make the British, at least, feel just marginally 'marginal'.

13

Between holy text and moral void

Bhikhu Parekh

Originally published in *New Statesman and Society* on 24 March 1989, five weeks after the Ayatollah Khomeini issued his *fatwa* against Salman Rushdie and *The satanic verses*.

Salman Rushdie's *The satanic verses* has become a terrain for many different and interrelated battles. Strange alliances have been formed across different battle lines, and the British cultural, educational and political scene has undergone transformations hardly anyone could have predicted a few weeks ago. *The satanic verses* is a dense and highly complex book, articulated at a variety of levels held together by a range of common concerns. It is, therefore, hardly surprising that most of the protesting Muslims haven't read it all, or have not read it with the care it deserves, and throw around passages taken out of context as polemical hand grenades. I wonder how many of the journalists, and even the high-minded literary critics, have understood it either. The book has a distinctly Bombayite ambience, ethos and style of writing, and many of its nuances, allusions and literary mannerisms are likely to be lost upon those who have not lived in that great metropolitan melting pot.

It is also full of colloquial and evocative Hindi words which are not just thrown in as street talk but made to serve strategic literary purposes. A professor of English was surprised when I told him that the word *chamcha* in the name of one of the central characters means a stooge or a hatchet-man, that it is widely used to question a man's integrity and that Rushdie's use of it was highly suggestive. He was surprised, too, when I told him that *chod* was the Hindi equivalent of an English four-letter word, and that *behanchod* meant (but did not have the same emotional force as) 'sister-fucker'.

Again, the chapters dealing with 'Mahound' (Muhammad) and his new religion are suffused with subtle allusions and insinuations likely to be lost on or misunderstood by those who are not well-versed in the history of Islam and have not grown up in a Muslim household. If the much-maligned illiterate peasants of Bradford protest in ignorance of the book, many of those who arrogantly lecture them could also do with a little humility.

Though I am a Bombayite and know something of that city's culture, my knowledge of Islam is limited and distorted by the usual prejudices of a Hindu. Having read the book on my own, I decided to read the relevant chapters again with two Muslim friends. If we are to make sense of the

Muslims' fierce and apparently uncompromising protest, we owe them a basic moral obligation to read it with their eyes. What follows is my own construction of the book, based on critical reflections on its different readings, including the Muslim.

Much confusion is created by the view that *The satanic verses* is a work of fiction. It is a story of migration and exile, and represents, among other things, an attempt to see the world from the perspective of an immigrant. As such, it deals with contemporary social reality in a highly imaginative manner. Imaginative exploration of reality can take many forms depending on the level of abstraction adopted by the author. Rushdie adopts a relatively low level of abstraction. He fantasises and redefines real, recognizable men and women and does not create wholly new characters and images. His characters are not products of what Kant called 'pure' or 'transcendental' imagination, but real people subjected to the free play of fantasy. *The satanic verses* is thus a work of fantasy, not of pure fiction, of an imaginatively reinterpreted but not a radically reconstituted reality.

Many of Rushdie's major 'characters' resemble men and women we know, and some are even given the names they bear in real life. This is also true of his discussion of Islam in the controversial chapters. 'Mahound' is none other than a poorly abstracted and richly fantasized Muhammad. Muhammad *was* called Mahound by the nervous and bewildered Christians in the Middle Ages. Two of the verses in the Koran *were* suspected to be products of Satanic intervention. Pre-Islamic Mecca *was* called the land of *Jahil*, or ignorance. Muhammad did have twelve wives and they were called Ayesha, Khadija and all the other names Rushdie gives them in the book. The first man who answered 'the call of prayer' *was* called Bilal, an emancipated black slave. The promiscuous wife of Abu Suplian, the most powerful chief of Mecca and custodian of the temple, *was* called Hind. Ayesha *did* disappear for two days and that became a subject of much gossip. And so on.

Chapters two and six in *The satanic verses* are fantasized history; that is, they are *fantasies*, but fantasies relating to, deeply embedded in and severely hedged in by, *history*.

The frequent use of dreams does not alter its status. They are at best literary stratagems, at worst useful defences against possible attack and even perhaps litigation. Had its author totally abstracted from history and created characters, episodes, symbols and images that applied to all religions and hence to none in particular, the case would have been different.

This approach enables Rushdie to enter into and tease out with great clarity and vividness the structure and inner dynamics of the immigrant's everyday life, including racism, self-alienation, the joys and tortures of harbouring several selves, and the fantasized reality in which he is forced to live. It also helps him to reconstruct the dead world of historical individuals and to offer incisive insights into their dilemmas, struggles and states of mind.

Rushdie's approach, however, has its dangers. If a writer is not careful, he or she can end up treating recognizable men and women as *mere* objects of fantasies, as people whom he knows better than they do themselves, as *manipulable* material for the free play of his imagination. The writer may then become not just disrespectful and irreverent, but supercilious and dismissive, a shade crude, even perhaps exhibitionist, scoring cheap points off half-real characters. Rushdie's approach yields a splendid harvest when applied to politics, business, middle-class social life and other areas which are amenable to it, but it can come to grief when used to explore areas, experiences, activities, relationships and individuals considered holy or at least sacred.

By sacred, I mean that which is beyond utilitarian considerations and has an intrinsic or non-instrumental significance, which transcends and links up individuals with something greater than themselves and gives their lives depth and meaning. The holy represents sacredness anchored in, and defined in, terms of a divine principle. Religion is the realm of the holy *par excellence*, but it does not exhaust sacredness. Even the atheist regards certain relationships, activities, experiences, life and fellow-humans as sacred. Broadly speaking, holiness is a religious category, sacredness a spiritual category, and respect a moral category.

The central life experiences of immigrants cast them in a highly ambiguous relationship with the sacred. Lacking roots in an ongoing way of life, unable to feel in their bones the deepest joys and agonies of their adopted home, cut off from the social well-springs of meaning and value, their lives lack depth and richness, the commonest source of the experiences of sacredness. Their dignity as human beings is constantly mocked by the hostile 'host' society; their sacred family ties are brutally snapped by evil immigration laws; their children leave home every morning and return speaking a language increasingly unintelligible and even hurtful to them. Thanks to all this, their predominant mood is one of doubt and suspicion, a subdued rage at the hypocrisy of a society that says one thing but does the opposite.

Different immigrants respond to these experiences and moods differently and evolve different strategies of physical and moral survival. Of these, two are relevant to our discussion. At one extreme, there is total cynicism. All people stink, are imposters, ruthless, cheats, predators, manipulators. None can be trusted, not even or rather especially not fellow-immigrants. Everything in this world is superficial and crude, and can be mocked, deflated, perverted, turned upside down. At the other extreme, there is a retreat to the familiar certainties of the past.

The meaning of life is deemed to be permanently and incorrigibly revealed in a sacred text, a body of rituals, or a pool of inherited and inviolable traditions. Even if these are perceived to be irrelevant or inapplicable in the new environment, they are uniquely the immigrant's own in a society that has stripped him or her of all else, the only thing that *distinguishes* them, gives them a past, roots in the present and the confidence to face the future. The holy text or traditions give certainty in a world of moral void; they are a sure protection against the dehumanizing impact of cynicism. At one extreme, then, a deep and self-destructive doubt, at the other, an impenetrable and intolerant certainty. One has lost a sense of sacredness, the other has a surfeit of it.

All immigrants, however reflective and introspective they may be, harbour bits of both tendencies (and many others), nervously holding them in a precarious balance, turning to one when the other fails or becomes unbearable. Rushdie is no exception. He writes about the tension between these tendencies without fully appreciating that it lies at the very centre of his being and both enriches and distorts his perception of his subject matter.

This is evident in *The satanic verses*. An immensely daring and persistently probing exploration of the human condition, which only a rootless immigrant can undertake, lies ill at ease with timid obeisance to the latest literary and political fashions; profound seriousness lapses suddenly and without warning into pointless playfulness. The sacred is interlaced with flippancy, the holy with the profane. Intensely delicate explorations of human relationships and emotions are shadowed by an almost childlike urge to shock, hurt and offend.

As an immigrant, Rushdie sometimes seems to resent that everyone around him is not an immigrant; on other occasions, he is profoundly pleased that the natives have their roots intact and showers benediction. At a different level, he is both drawn towards and repelled by his fellow-immigrants. He both fights them and fights for them; both resents them and delights in their world of certainties; cares for them but also tramples on their dearest memories and sentiments. He loves them as real human beings, yet he also turns them into an abstract cause; and his holy anti-racism goes hand-in-hand with touches of contempt for them.

It is this that at least partly explains the current tension between him and the Muslims. The tension is a result of the conflict between two very different approaches to the predicament of an exile. Unlike the white onlookers who understand neither, the contestants know that nothing less than their fundamental existential choices, and even sanity, are at stake. The vast majority of Muslims have chosen one way of coping with their predicament; Rushdie another. They give meaning to their poor and empty lives by holding on to the holy and its rocklike certainties; he doubts almost everything, including the very search for meaning. Their approach has little room for doubt; Rushdie's has only a limited space for the holy, or even the sacred, and he is deeply nervous in its presence. They solace each other within a common fellowship and lead individually heterogeneous lives within an autonomous group; Rushdie's quest for personal autonomy leads to an ambiguous relationship with the white society and especially its literary establishment. The inescapable conflict between the two exploded the moment he produced a full-scale exploration of the sacred in *The satanic verses*.

In chapters two and six, as well as elsewhere in the book, Rushdie does not explore religion *per se* but Islam, not *a* prophet but Muhammad; and he remains too close to Islamic history to be justified in claiming, or to succeed in persuading his adversaries, that his account is fictional.

Rushdie's imaginative explorations of the birth of Islam, Muhammad's 'terrifying singularity', the way his new religion came to terms with the constraints of the contemporary world, and the logic of total submission are bold and penetrating. Though they might and do offend some of the faithful, they form part of a legitimate inquiry. To have called Muhammad Mahound rather than by any other historically less evocative name was unwise, and comes close to a deliberate attempt to offend and provoke. Since only two out of several hundred verses were suspected of being inspired by Satan, the title of the book, too, was unnecessarily provocative. Muhammad is often described as a businessman, constantly bargaining and doing 'deals' with the archangel. He is sometimes referred to as 'the Businessman'; his is a 'revelation of convenience'; 'his God is really a businessman'; the archangel was 'businesslike' and 'obliging', and even reduced the initial quota of forty prayers a day to five.

Here, as elsewhere, Rushdie's approach is not only irreverent but mocking, dismissive, angry. It is designed to put Muhammad in his place. Not surprisingly, it has deeply offended Muslim sensibilities. However, this is all part of a legitimate literary inquiry. And if a creative writer were to be hamstrung by the feelings and sentiments of over-sensitive readers, the writer's search for truth would be hampered and humankind would suffer a loss. The offence caused to Muslims could therefore be ignored in the larger interests of truth.

Doubts begin to arise with respect to other parts of *The satanic verses*. Muhammad is called a 'smart bastard', a debauchee who, after his wife's death, slept with so many women that his beard turned 'half-white' in a year. Muslims deeply respect Bilal, the emancipated black slave who was the first convert to Islam. Here, he is an 'enormous black monster . . . with a voice to match his size.' Muhammad's three revered colleagues, including Bilal, are 'those goons – those fucking clowns', the 'trinity of scum'. Like any great religious text, the Koran is full of rules and injunctions about forms of worship, helping the poor, concern for those in need, moral purity, self-discipline and surrender to the will of God. *The satanic verses* mockingly reduces it to a book 'spouting' rules about how to 'fart', 'fuck' and 'clean one's behind', and why only two sexual positions are legitimate, one of them being sodomy (that tired anti-Muslim canard yet again).

These remarks lack artistic justification. For Muslims, these and other such remarks are not only offensive and distressing; they also take on the character of what lawyers call 'fighting words'. Fighting words are verbal equivalents of the first shoves and pushes in a fight. They insult and provoke the devout; they challenge Muslim men to stand up and fight back if they have any self-respect and a sense of honour. They amount to a declaration of hostility. Even as we all feel not just hurt, but *provoked*, when we, our parents and loved ones or ethnic group are insulted and called obscene names, a Muslim man rightly feels challenged to a fight when those whose venerated memories he holds in sacred trust are ridiculed and abused.

Another passage, which rather surprisingly, Muslim leaders have not highlighted, relates to Mahound's twelve wives. When Ayesha, his young and favourite wife, protested against his taking on so many wives, the novel goes on: '*Who* can blame her? *Finally*, he went into – what else? One of his *trances*, and *out he came* with a message from the archangel. Gibreel had recited verses giving him full divine support. *God's own permission to fuck as many women as he liked*. So there: What could poor Ayesha say against the *verses of God*? *You know* what she did say? This: *Your God* certainly *jumps* to it when you need him to *fix things* up for you.'

Each of the words I have italicized reflects a supercilious and dismissive attitude. The reference to God's permission to fuck is cheap and vulgar.

Even if one rejected the Muslim criticism that Muhammad should not have been presented as an imposter and a devious manipulator, they are certainly right to insist that a man whom millions consider holy and who has for centuries given meaning and depth to their lives, deserves to be discussed in a less aggressive manner.

There is also a brothel scene in which twelve whores take the names of Muhammad's wives. Rushdie has argued that it was intended to provide a profane antithesis to (and thus to highlight and accentuate) the holy. But since the holy has been mocked the brothel scene cannot be its antithesis; rather it is a further expression of the same approach.

Unlike Jesus, a divine figure for Christians, Muhammad is a human being chosen as the vehicle of Allah's will. His family is *ahl-al-baith*, the first family, and his wives are invariably referred to as *alwaj-e-mutahire*, the sacred wives of the prophet. The brothel scene represents a gross assault on the tradition. In pretending to be the wives of Muhammad, the prostitutes do not acquire an aura of sacredness; rather the sacred wives are dragged down to the level of prostitutes. They are symbolically violated. Every customer who plays at being a Muhammad vulgarizes and reduces him to the status of an indiscriminate debauchee.

It is not difficult to see why the Muslims feel lacerated. Though they have sometimes called the book blasphemous, the term does not at all convey their basic criticisms. They seem to have adopted it largely because of the British law of blasphemy. Barring a few fundamentalists, most Muslims do not seem terribly worried by the irreverent tone, the questioning of the authenticity of the Koran, and the satirical treatment of Allah and the Archangel Gibreel. Nor are they worried that the book will shake their *faith*. They are *distressed* and *outraged* by what, with some exaggeration, their spokesmen have called the 'obscene', 'indecent', 'most filthy' and 'abominably foul language' in reference to the men whose memories they consider sacred and whose persons they consider holy. They also feel belittled and demeaned in their own and others' eyes, provoked and challenged to a fight by both the language and the 'outrageous liberties' taken with their sacred collective heritage.

These feelings are particularly strong among immigrants who cope with their predicament by holding on to traditionally inherited notions of sacredness. That is why the most uncompromising and tenacious reaction against *The satanic verses* came from British Muslims, representing the largest Muslim community in the west. This may also explain why the first generation of Muslims who turned to religion to give some meaning and hope to their empty lives (such as those in Bradford) responded more angrily to the book and more enthusiastically to Ayatollah Khomeini's *fatwa* than the others.

Religion represents the realm of the sacred *par excellence* and calls for an extremely delicate and sensitive handling. Otherwise one not only risks outraging people and provoking them to fight back, but also fails to comprehend the integrity of religion as a distinct form of consciousness. We have taken centuries to learn how to explore sexuality in literature without becoming either puritanical or pornographic. Religion requires a greater degree of sensitivity. While for the most part *The satanic verses* meets this requirement and the Muslims are wrong to deny that, it does from time to time become offensive and provocative.

Talking about our fellow human beings in a manner that insults, demeans, distresses or holds them up to contempt in their own or others' eyes betrays a lack of elementary respect for them and is rightly deplored. We do not generally prohibit it by law because of the obvious difficulties, but we do strongly disapprove of it morally.

Recently Sir James Miskin, the recorder of London, was rightly pulled up by the Lord Chancellor and the media for using the words 'nig-nogs'. Even when he apologized, many including the *Sun* (3 March) thought that he should 'hang up his wig; for good'. Several American courts have considered the use of such words as 'black bastards' and 'bloodsucking Jews' unacceptable and condoned their use in literary works *only when* that was shown to serve a literary purpose or to help explore or express literary truths.

This is a persuasive and sensible doctrine and applies to religious communities as well. When a prophet is treated in a supercilious, dismissive or crude manner, what is at stake is not his honour – for he is dead and too big a person to be affected by insults. What is really at stake is the sense of self-respect and integrity of those living men and women who define their identity in terms of their allegiance to the prophet. Their pride, good opinion of themselves, dignity and self-esteem deserve to be protected and nurtured, especially when these are subjected to daily assaults by a hostile society. It is self-contradictory to fight for their future and to undermine their past, to promote their political aspirations and to mock their cultural memories.

Some of the passages in *The satanic verses* do demean Muslims in their own and others' eyes. The passages perpetuate prejudices about them and give grounds for a few more into the bargain.

When such lapses occur, it is tempting to turn to the law, to press for a ban, to demand that the offending passages be expunged, and so on. The temptation must be resisted. Once a literary work is published, it is permanently in the public realm. No expedients can prevent its circulation or diminish its impact. Anyway, the law is too blunt an instrument to deal with creative literature, and bans and censorship have always done more harm than good.

The answer lies at the moral and social level. When a creative writer, conducting imaginative experiments and daring to think the unthinkable, outrages, hurts or provokes others, he should be challenged, criticized, asked to explain himself and made to suffer his peers' criticism and the anger of hurt sensibilities. It was a pity that for months Rushdie contemptuously dismissed the protests of the Muslims. However misguided, they were *his* people, or at least fellow-immigrants desperately struggling like him to cope with their predicament. His book was about them, and he owed them an obligation to understand their feelings, to explain his position, to argue with them, to do all in his power to mollify and hopefully win them over to his point of view.

But he treated them the way he had treaded Mahound and his companions and added to their hurt. He enjoyed the uncritical support of a literary establishment obsessed with 'terrifying singularity'. Until the book-burning in Bradford (predictably but inaccurately compared to the Nazi book-burning), no national newspaper published the offending passages, invited Muslim spokesmen to write about the book, or made a sympathetic attempt to read it with their eyes. Liberal opinion came down on Muslims like a ton of bricks, ridiculing them, and asking if such barbarians deserved to be citizens of a 'civilized' society. Liberals rightly remembered the principle of liberty but forgot the equally important principles of fairness, compassion and humanity.

The Muslims had no friends. They felt intensely lonely and helpless. Hence they felt compelled to step up their protest, to seek a place for their grievances on the national agenda and demand a long-denied dialogue.

It is only from such a painful ordeal that new truths, including new tools of exploring them, are born. A dialogue is only possible in a climate of mutual tolerance, free from intimidation and threats. Muslims have made their point, albeit with unacceptable threats of violence. They have highlighted the crucial question about a writer's moral responsibility to his or her fellow human beings as well as to their craft. They should now leave Rushdie alone to ponder over it in peace and security, and hope that he will one day provide an answer that reconciles a creative writer's right to freedom of thought and expression with other people's right to respect and dignity. If any harm were to come to him now, or fifty years hence, they would rightly be condemned for behaving as 'barbarians' and betraying the religion they use to defend such a ghastly deed. The prophet they revere has much to say about good manners and charity of spirit.

14

Technology and tradition – audio-visual culture among south Asian families in west London

Marie Gillespie

From *Cultural Studies*, vol. 3, no. 2 (Methuen, 1989).

This ethnographic account is based on research among south Asian families in Southall, Middlesex.[1] Southall is a 'town', formerly an autonomous London borough, with a population of some 65000. Its demographic majority is of south Asian origin, predominantly of Sikh religion, but divided along cross-cutting cleavages of national, regional, religious, and caste heritage.

The study evolved over seven years of teaching in two Southall high schools where the popularity of 'Indian' films was evident; and yet various manifestations of resistance to their pleasures seemed to signify a great deal more than mere expressions of taste or preference.

The extensive use of the VCR at home to view 'Indian'[2] films represents a powerful means for grandparents and parents to maintain links with their country of origin. Second-generation children, however, born and educated in Britain, position themselves and are positioned rather differently in relation to notions of 'Asian' and 'British' culture. The legitimation of state racism in postwar Britain has been secured in an important way around particular ideological constructions of south Asian cultures, especially their marriage and family systems. For long, these have been seen to be based on archaic and traditional customs and practices and are presented as an 'alien threat' to the 'British way of life'. But in much of the literature produced by the 'Race Relations Industry' it is 'culture-clash' and inter-generational conflict, low self-esteem and negative self-image, rather than racism, that, paradoxically, have been identified as both 'the problem' and 'the cause'.[3]

Such dominant assumptions went unchallenged as young Asian voices were usually excluded or marginalized from debates which concerned them. This paper therefore is an attempt to re-present 'their voices', concentrating on their interpretations of popular Indian films and the themes and issues arising from their viewing experiences and which they find salient.

The ethnographic data are based on interviews carried out with young people predominantly of Panjabi origin and aged 15–18. A set of basic questions was used to spark off each interview. When do you watch? What do you watch? With whom do you watch? Who chooses what you watch in which situations? The wide range of methodological issues which the study raises will not be dealt with here, and this account will be structured around four main concerns.

First, it will contextualize the shift by briefly outlining the history of Indian cinema in Southall, and the shift from public exhibition to private viewing in the home. Secondly, it will examine the implications of this shift by focussing on the family-viewing context. It will explore questions of choice and preference alongside issues of family power and control. The third part will examine the responses of young people to Indian films and the factors mediating their various interpretations. Finally, it will bring together the diverse strands of the study in order to highlight the different ways in which viewing experiences are used.

Indian cinema in Southall: from public pleasure to private leisure

The first 'Indian' films were shown in Southall in 1953 in hired halls and then in three local cinemas. During the 1960s and 1970s the cinema provided the principal weekend leisure activity in Southall and represented an occasion for families and friends to get together; the social event of the week.

In 1978, when VCRs came on the market, many families were quick to seize the opportunity to extend their choice and control over viewing in the home. Many Asian communities obtained them as early as 1978–9 before most other households in Britain. It is estimated that between 40 and 50 per cent of households in Britain now own or rent a VCR but in Southall the figure is held to be 80 per cent.[4]

Most shops rent popular Hindi (also known as 'Bombay') films and although films in Panjabi and Urdu are also available from shops they lack the broad-based appeal of the popular Hindi movie. In fact the Bombay film has gained something of a cultural hegemony in south Asia and among many 'Asian' settlers across the world. To understand this one has to look to the specific evolution of the popular Hindi genre which, in order to appeal to a mass audience, had to produce films which would cross the linguistic, religious, and regional differences that exist within India, as indeed within Southall.

Many of the films combine a catholicity or universality of appeal with a careful handling of regional and religious differences. A distinctive form of Bombay Hindi, characterized by a certain 'linguistic openness' has evolved which makes most films accessible also to speakers of other south Asian languages. The distinctive visual style, often foregrounded over dialogue, combines with successive modes of spectacle, action and emotion which facilitates cross-cultural understanding.[5] In the light of this we can understand the huge uptake of Hindi films on cassette among the diverse linguistic groups in Southall.

With the arrival of video, the adventure, romance, and drama of the Bombay film was to be enjoyed in domestic privacy. A small piece of home technology brought the cinema hall into the home, or so it appeared. A lot was gained but much was lost. The weekly outing became a thing of the past as the cinemas closed and the big screen image shrunk into the TV box and entered the flow of everyday life in the living room.

In Southall the rapid expansion of the home video market needs to be considered not only as providing an extension to an already important and dynamic film culture but also very much a response on the part of a black community to life in Britain. Southall, like many other black communities, has come into existence in the first instance as a result of racist immigration and housing policies. Such communities have developed as 'sanctuaries' against the racism they experience.[6] The exclusion and marginalization of many people in Southall from mainstream British society, coupled with the failure to provide adequate leisure/culture facilities, has (like among the *Gastarbeiter* (guest worker) Turkish community in West Germany) contributed to the development of an important home video culture.

But the consequences of a decade of video use are perceived in contradictory ways by the youth of Southall. Many young people feel that the VCR has served further to isolate the community from mainstream British society. It is also seen to have specific effects on the lives of women: 'The video has isolated the community even more. They might as well be in India, especially the women'. Others see it as a liberating pleasure, especially for females: 'Some girls can't get out of the house that much so they can get a film and keep themselves occupied within the four walls of the house. It's an advantage for them'.

Such contradictory evaluations need to be seen in the contexts in which they originate.

Domestic viewing contexts

During the course of the study it became possible to construct a broad typology of contexts and associated texts. For the purpose of this account I shall concentrate on weekend family viewing because this situation was so frequently and consistently discussed by all interviewees, and due to the importance given to it within this cultural context.[7]

The VCR is used predominantly at the weekend in most families. Viewing 'Indian' films on video is the principal, regular family leisure activity. Weekend family gatherings around the TV set are a social ritual repeated in many families. The VCR and TV screen become the focus and locus of interaction. Notions of togetherness and communality are stressed: 'It's probably the only time in the week that we are all together so when we're watching a film at least we're all together'.

This togetherness is by no means that of passive viewers: 'No one is silent, we're all talking through the film about what's happening here and there and generally having a chat . . . it sort of brings you closer together'.

The weaving of conversation through the narrative is facilitated by an impressive familiarity with films brought about by repeated viewings. The episodic structure of films which moves the spectator through the different modes of spectacle, song and dance, drama, action, and affect also provides natural breaks for talk, emotion and reflection.

With such large family gatherings the question of power and control over viewing becomes important. The interviews highlight the way in which parents actively set and maintain viewing rules which govern viewing patterns and modes of parent–child interaction.

While the father is usually seen to determine when children are allowed access to the screen by his absence or presence in the home, the mother is perceived as exercising a greater degree of power and control over the choice of what is watched. This was a significant pattern across the interviews, emphasizing the important role mothers play in socializing their children in the domestic context. It also makes clear that the relationship between family power structures and family viewing patterns is not one of simple correspondence.

There are also clear differences in the attentiveness and in the degree of salience of Indian films to various family members, which are obscured by the simple observation that the family all watched the same programme.[8] Many young people say they sit with parents and view parts of the films just to please them, or say that their parents encourage or even 'force' them to watch.

As gender differences are important to understand parental control over viewing they are also a significant factor in understanding young people's viewing preferences and behaviour. Boys tend to experience greater freedom in deciding how they use their leisure time and spend more time engaged in activities outside the home. In contrast, girls are usually socialized to remain within the domestic realm and often participate in strong and supportive female cultures in the home where the viewing of Indian films on video frequently plays an important role. This explains to some extent the generally greater engagement with popular Hindi videos on the part of most girls interviewed. In one interview two boys rather begrudgingly claim: 'It doesn't hurt to watch an Indian film with the parents'. 'No, it kills you'.

In spite of this repeatedly expressed reluctance the way in which the screen can serve social interaction in the family tends to override individual preferences and return young people to the family situation. One boy commented to the general agreement of the group: 'Well we don't usually stay in another room while they're watching, if you've got something to yourself, you isolate yourself, don't you?' It is clear that what might be seen on the one hand as 'enforced' or 'reluctant' viewing can take on pleasurable connotations where the emphasis is on 'being together'. Parents do not have much time for leisure due to long working hours and shift work, so the time when the family is together around the TV set is often much appreciated by all concerned.

Conversely, the family audience is frequently fragmented by English and American films: 'When it's Indian films it's all of us together but when it's English films it's just me and my brother'. This fragmentation is partly due to the texts of English and American films themselves. Given parental reservations about the language, sensuality, and references to sexuality, young people may often prefer to view them on their own to escape parental censure or vigilance.

You may now have the impression that the avid consumption of VCR films falls into two neat categories. While Hindi films tend to be viewed in large family gatherings and to be celebrated by intense social interaction, British and American films tend to be consumed on their own in a more or less assertive circumvention of parental control and preferences. While viewing patterns tend indeed to correspond to this dichotomy, young people's viewing of Hindi films raises further ethnographic questions about perceptions of 'Indianness' and Britain or India and 'Britishness'.

Representations of India

For young people in Southall who have little or no direct experience outside the UK, perceptions of India will be founded on a complex combination of factors. But invariably they will also be influenced by 'Indian' films. Even for those who have lived or spent long periods in India the films provide a counterpoint to their own personal experiences.

Throughout the interviews a series of related binary oppositions frame and structure accounts of how India is perceived through the films:

$$
\begin{array}{rcl}
\text{Village} & - & \text{City} \\
\text{Poverty} & - & \text{Wealth} \\
\text{Communality} & - & \text{Individualism} \\
\text{Tradition} & - & \text{Modernity} \\
\text{Morality} & - & \text{Vice}
\end{array}
$$

The interviewees' accounts are in some measure reconstructions of and responses to patterned social and moral discourses prevalent in popular Hindi films, where a pristine and moral rural India is often constructed by opposing it to an exotic and decadent 'other' – usually signified by symbols of the West and city life.

Thus, across the interviews, village life is frequently contrasted with city life. The village community is seen as one of extended kin where co-operation and communality prevail, notions of individualism are absent. Village life is seen as 'pure' because 'people are so honest there, they never look with the "evil eye", they help each other even though they're poor, they never "skank" [betray] one another'.

Such interpretations contrast with those of city life which, through the films, is perceived as decadent, immoral, and polluted – a place 'where prostitutes hang out and where even pundits [priests] try to rape girls'.

There was considerable criticism of the 'unrealistic' portrayal of village life and an often acute awareness is shown of the selective and ideological nature of representations: 'There's not so much about the landless labourers and the position of women, you know, who spend hours and hours looking for water and fuel . . . in the scorching heat'.

Exploitation of the poor by the rich is another common theme and the plight of the illiterate landless labourers was referred to on several occasions: 'The films show how rich treat poor, how they don't go to school and have to work from when very young, they can't read and so rich people trick them and take their lands and crops'.

Striking gender differences emerge in the framing of accounts. Girls often express their perceptions of India through an exploration of the social and moral values inherent in the films via a 'retelling' of the narratives. In contrast boys seem to be much more concerned with representational issues, particularly 'negative images' and, in many cases, reject Hindi films *per se* on that basis.

Several male respondents see Indian films as offensive in their emphasis on poverty and corruption: 'They should not portray India as if it's really poor and backward even though they're Indians themselves, it's degrading; that's a lot of the reason I don't like Indian films'.

Others ridicule the 'backward image' of 'Indians' in the films because of the different norms associated with fashion and style but they also remark upon the selective nature of images: 'they follow up too late in India, they still wear flares, though I must admit they're not backward in everything they're very advanced in technology but they don't show you those aspects of India'. One boy vehemently rejected the films and wished to dissociate himself from both films and India but not without some irony: 'I didn't learn anything from the films apart from the fact that India is one of the most corrupt countries in the world', and later, 'that country has nothing to do with me any more'.

Such discussions often provoke comments on representations of India in British media more generally which is seen on the whole to reinforce an 'uncivilized', poverty-stricken image of India: 'Documentaries shown in this country degrade India badly as well'. Strong resentment is expressed at the way India is 'degraded' in the West by the circulation of images of poverty, underdevelopment, death, and disease. Such images are linked to the 'degradation' of Indians in Britain where they 'get racist harassment'.

In identifying 'salient' themes and making selective interpretations, a range of 'meanings' are projected onto the films which undoubtedly derive from experiences of racism in Britain. Such experiences underpin and sensitize responses to constructions of Indian society in Hindi films and in the media generally. Boys, in particular, show an understanding of how Indian films may be rebuked and ridiculed as 'backward', 'foreign' and 'ludicrous' by 'outsiders' (for example, their white peers) but they also, clearly, feel somewhat estranged from the sense of 'Indianness' and from the 'India' represented in the films. At the same time, there is a tacit acknowledgement that the films may be used to confirm what constitute dominant discourses on India in British society, and an underlying awareness of how they function as racist discourses. As a result the boys would appear to occupy shifting and often contradictory positions from which they view and interpret the films – positions which vary according to context.

It would appear that experiences of racism as well as the reading of films are gender specific. A similar connection may be detected between gender and genre.

Genre

For nearly a century Hindi films have been either rebuked or ignored in the West by critics, academics, and film enthusiasts alike. Such institutionalized disdain and ignorance is not only a symptom of racism but feeds directly into it. The fierce rejection of the popular Hindi film, seen as a genre in itself, especially among the boys interviewed, echoes Western critical discourses about the genre. Films are consistently criticized for being 'all the same', based on 'ideas got from Westerns ... just a mixture of everything ... commercial ... full of songs and running round trees and rose gardens'.

An eighteen-year-old male interviewee in a rather eloquent condemnation of Indian films claims: 'With the standards of media appreciation in the West it's hard to understand the sort of psyche that would appreciate these kinds of film again and again and again. . . . If you've been exposed to a film culture based on plots and detailed cinematography then you'd expect the same from the other culture and if it doesn't match up to that standard you don't want to see it anymore ... it's like driving a Morris Minor after you've driven a Porsche'.

The widespread condemnation of popular Indian films and the coincidence of views held by both film critics and many of the boys interviewed does not confirm a 'truth' about Hindi cinema but, rather, exposes a common frame of reference which is based on dominant Hollywood and Western film-making practices. Clearly, a cultural experience dominated by Western film-genres will initially militate against an engagement with popular Hindi films, which are likely to disorientate the spectator by subverting generic conventions even where language presents no barrier.

The focus of this study on south Asian families should not exclude consideration of the context of power relations in which this community lives and between Western and 'Third World' countries and cultures. It should, rather, lead us further to consider the nature of white norms and white cultural practices, especially when they entail the abrogation of measures for culturally distinct genres which are clearly incommensurate. Otherwise such a study becomes merely a descriptive exercise, devoid of political responsibility, intent, or analysis.

What becomes clear from the interviews is that for those who do find pleasure in popular Hindi films, the skilful blending of certain generic ingredients is crucial: the screenplay, the music and songs, the emotional appeal, spectacle, production values, and, of course, the stars. But it is above all when narrative is discussed in the interviews that one becomes aware of a deeper engagement with the films. The pleasures involved become apparent but we can also begin to unravel some further causes of resistance to films.

Narrative

According to many writers, the popular Hindi film has evolved from village traditions of epic narration, and the dramas and characters, as well as the structure of the mythological epics, are regularly and openly drawn upon. Film-makers and theorists claim that there are only two stories or 'metatexts', the *Mahabharata* and the *Ramayana*, and that every film can be traced back to these stories.

Vijay Mishra (1985) sees Bombay films as transformations of the narrative structures that may be discovered in these epics. According to him their influence is not limited to narrative form alone since 'these epics were also ideological tools for the expansion of beliefs endorsed by the ruling classes'. In his view the Bombay film legitimates its own existence through a reinscription of its values into those of the *Mahabharata* and the *Ramayana*.

But what seems to distinguish the Hindi film most from its Western counterparts is the form and movement of the narrative. The balance between narrative development, spectacle and emotion is rather different from that in Western films. Spectacle alone risks losing an audience. Skilled narration involves the swift transition between well-balanced modes of spectacle and an emotional involvement invited by the reassuring familiarity of many narratives, structured by discourses, deeply rooted in Indian social, moral, and psychic life (Thomas, 1985).

One of the most common assertions across the interviews is that the films all have the same type of stories. Usually this means that the films are 'totally predictable' and therefore not worth watching: 'who wants to sit and watch a film where you can work out the whole plot in the first five minutes?'

Three basic narrative themes of Hindi cinema particularly popular in the late 1970s and 1980s are repeatedly identified and referred to by interviewees: (1) 'Dostana', where the bond of male friendship overcomes the desire for a woman; (2) 'lost and found' parents and children are separated and reunited years later following the revelation of mistaken identities; and (3) 'revenge', villains get their just deserts at the hands of the heroes they wronged.

Interviewees frame their accounts with references to the discourses which commonly structure these narratives, which are those of kinship duty, social obligation, solidarity, respect or 'izzat', and trust. A sense of social 'order' and 'ideal social relations' is related to living in harmony with fate and respecting social obligations and ties of friendship and family.

Hindi film aesthetics, it is argued, are based not on cognition, as in the West, but in re-cognition. Like Hindu epics whose familiar stories form part of the fundamental myths of Indian society, the Hindi film is said to have evolved a broad framework of its own. Anil Saari (1985) claims: 'thus one film is like another, each film confirms once again the world as it is and has been and is likely to remain. The very hopelessness created by poverty and social immobility demands that the world and distractions from it remain as they are. That is indeed how the world is for the average Indian who is not a member of the ruling elite'.

Many interviewees analyse the narrative closure of contemporary Hindi films and compare them with the older, black and white, social-realist films prevalent in the 1950s and 1960s, in which there is an upsurge of renewed interest among young and old alike: 'They all have happy endings by the way . . . unlike the older films, tragedies are being solved by lucky, fortunate events that turn everything upside down, if a heroine's about to die these days she's saved by a handsome doctor at the last moment . . . everything turns out all right and people have nothing to think about, nothing to cry about, unlike the older films'.

Certain fundamental differences in the narrative structures of 'Hindi' and

'Western' films are highlighted in the interviews. English films are seen as 'continuous all the way . . . they just continue, no songs, no dances . . . that's why I find them boring'. Pleasure is taken in the non-linear narratives. The intricate and convoluted nature of story-telling becomes apparent through attempts at narrative reconstructions. Hindi films are not tightly linear but build in more or less circular fashion through a number of climaxes which are counterposed with scenes of humour, spectacle, and 'pure' emotional import. It is not so much a question of *what* will happen next that drives the narrative but of *how* it will be framed, not so much an enigma to be solved as a moral disordering to be resolved.

Affective involvement is a crucial component of films and is ensured not only by cinematic techniques which encourage identification and involvement, e.g. the use of close-ups, subjective points of view shots, shot reverse shots, but also through the songs: 'The songs back up everything . . . they have real feeling in them and it's not just any old songs, they relate to the actual situations of the films, they get you emotionally involved and influence you'. As in melodrama, undischarged emotion which cannot be accommodated within the action is expressed in song and music: 'Whenever that song comes on, I cry, I can't control myself . . . it's the father of a girl singing to her before she leaves the family to get married, he sings about how you are leaving us now and saying how when you were young I used to hold you in my arms, how I used to play with you. . . . I can't listen to that song without tears pouring out . . . and I think of my sister when she will be leaving us'.

This passage highlights the way in which the Hindi film tends to address and move its spectator by way of affect. This positioning depends for its full effect on certain kinds of cultural competence, most notably a knowledge of the 'ideal moral universe' of the Hindi film. Such cultural knowledge is acquired by young people to very varying degrees and while clearly lending enormous spectator power to some, disallows others from any deep engagement with the films. Conventions of verisimilitude also affect the relationship between text and viewer.

Fantasy and realism

When I did watch an Indian film after that I'm in heaven but I don't relate to the real world like I did . . . they're in rose gardens and the music just springs up from nowhere . . . that's why people like watching them to get away from their own lives. What do drugs do? They take you to another world . . . so do Indian films but they are a safer way out of your problems.

For those who enjoy Hindi films fantasy is a chief source of pleasure. The songs and dances as well as their settings often provide discrete dream-like sequences and 'a moment of escape from reality' for the spectator. In comparing drug-induced euphoria with the sensations provoked by the fantasy sequences in films this young girl gives us some insight into the desire provoked by the fantasy films: 'I wouldn't mind sitting around in rose gardens or deserts being loved and things like that'.

Such anti-realism is seen by some as escapist: 'They're fantasies for the poor, they show them what they cannot afford . . . they're satisfied with the songs . . . they create the dream sequences for them'. They are also seen as exploitative and politically reactionary: 'Most of them are just sheer escapism. . . . I think that this has quite a negative effect because it allows people to ignore the reality of their situation, the political realities of India, the exploitation and oppression of the masses'. Several interviewees compared Hindi films of the 1970s and 1980s to the 'social realist' films of the 1950s: 'I think people could identify their immediate lives with them, they were true to life, if they showed a farmer losing his crops after years of hard labour that was a reflection of life and that used to happen to people and they would sit in the cinema and say "well that's true!" There was nothing magical about it as it is now. After this period, people didn't want tragedies, they wanted fantasies, they wanted a means of escape, they wanted to break out of reality and that's when the "masala" films started coming out'.

However, in spite of such criticisms, many of the interviewees do not ignore the cathartic and therapeutic aspects of films. Indeed they are seen to enable a temporary release from the tensions of everyday life and to help discharge distressful emotions: 'I must admit I'm scared of my parents (finding out I have a boyfriend) but after I've watched a film, and listened to a few songs and calmed myself down, I'm not scared of my parents anymore so they give you courage in a way'.

Selective but contradictory judgements about conventions of realism in films are frequent across the interviews as with this girl who on the one hand claims: 'Indian films don't really relate to reality, they're really sheltered . . . it's just fantasy they make it out so perfect'. And yet later, the film's realistic portrayal of love is endorsed: 'Sometimes we'll just sit there and wonder if there's a thing called love . . . whereas in an Indian film you're so convinced that love is real . . . that it's true, that it's really there'.

It is clear that an exposure to Western conventions of realism influence responses considerably. Attention is paid to *mise-en-scène* and anachronism is not easily tolerated. A determined fidelity to details of period representation and dress is adhered to by young male respondents: 'They'll show a man fighting for Independence and you'll see a man on a motorbike with sunglasses and jeans; they should at least have the clothes of the period'.

'They'll be showing a scene in the eighteenth century with horse-drawn carriage and at the back you'll see 1980s taxis, scooters, and high-rise buildings. It spoils everything. If only they [the directors] thought more about what they were doing, it looks as though they hadn't planned it'. Western conventions of realism also provide expectations about the way characters should behave, dress, and act. The reality status of stunt sequences is rebuked where production values are low: 'It's stupid motorbikes crossing lakes when you know it's a cartoon'.

There is in Hindi films an acceptable realism and logic beyond the material which is unbelievable. In fact the criteria of verisimilitude in Hindi cinema appears to refer primarily to the skill demonstrated in manipulating the rules of the film's moral universe. Among regular viewers one is more likely to hear accusations of unbelievability if the codes of ideal kinship are flouted than if the hero performs some outrageously unrealistic feat as is the case with disaffected viewers. In order to acquire a better understanding of the conventions of realism/anti-realism in Hindi cinema one would need to consider much wider issues including concepts and conventions of realism in Indian culture generally. Furthermore, a more detailed study of the important influence of the mythological film genre, essentially moral tales, might shed light on the anti-realist strategies of Bombay cinema.

Social and cultural uses of viewing experiences

The final part of this account concerns the social and cultural uses of viewing experiences, broadening the scope beyond that of contemporary popular Hindi films to include the full range of films viewed.

For the older members of the community, nostalgia is a key element in the pleasure experienced through film. In one particularly moving account by a man in his seventies, tears welled in his eyes as he recounted: 'When we see black-and-white films it reminds us of our childhood, our school days, our school mates, of what we were thinking, of what we did do, of our heroes . . . and I tell you this gives us great pleasure': The films would appear to act as a form of collective popular memory and some parents are able to convey a sense of their past in India to their children.

With the emergence of second-generation children parents and grandparents have found new uses for films. These uses are primarily defined in terms of linguistic, religious, and socio-cultural learning. In viewing Indian films together, many families are enabled to come together on a 'shared' linguistic basis. Both parents and children see this as a major advantage of watching films: 'They help children get a hold of the language'.

For many children the films provide one of the rare opportunities, outside communication in the family and community, to hear that language used and legitimated: 'They can hear and see how the language is used and should be used'. One boy put it more directly: 'They teach not only the language but how "to be" in an Indian environment'. The notion of language as transmitter of culture is prevalent among parents: 'If the children don't speak the language they lose their culture'. Language is a potent symbol of collective identity and often the site of fierce loyalties and emotional power. In the context of a society which constructs linguistic difference as a problem rather than as a tool, the desire to defend and maintain one's linguistic heritage becomes strong.

In a community faced with religious distinctiveness and at times division, it is not surprising that cultural identity is often construed as being based not only on linguistic but also on religious continuity. 'Religious' or mythological films are also watched for devotional purposes, particularly by Hindu families, and often integrated with daily acts of worship: 'When we start fasting we always watch these films, sometimes five times a day . . . you kind of pray to God at the same time you know'.

The films are also used as a form of religious education: 'They help parents teach their children about the Holy Books like the *Ramayana*, the *Mahabharat*, and the *Bhaghavat Gita*. It's the tradition in families to tell the young children the stories but some families don't have the time and so there are children who don't know who is Rama'. In some families viewing devotional films has come to replace reading the holy books. Certainly, the video is seen as a great advantage in familiarizing children with parables and religious stories, largely due to the widespread illiteracy of second- and third-generation children in their mother tongue. Not only are the religious and moral values inherent in the films an important aspect of viewing but the visual representation of the deity plays an extremely important symbolic role in the devotional and ritual acts of worship. This relates to the importance of popular forms of religious iconography in Indian society.

Parents use the films to talk about religious festivals: 'Here we can never really celebrate festivals like Holi which involves the whole village and people smearing each other's faces with colour. No one does that here but when you watch you can really appreciate what it's like in India. Here the kids just know about the fireworks but they don't know the real basic thing about why, they don't know about the religious aspects of the festivals'.

Young people and their parents use the films to negotiate, argue, and agree about a wider range of customs, traditions, values, and beliefs. Together, they often enjoy films which encourage discussion: 'films which bring out the contradictions in families, the arranged marriage system, the caste or class system'. The films function as tools for eliciting attitudes and views on salient themes; family affairs and problems, romance, courtship, and marriage were often discussed. There is a recurrent recognition of the 'influence' and value of the films in the lives of girls in particular. There are frequent references to the 'meanings, the really deep meanings, which reflect the way we think, it's just so . . . so . . . so I don't know, so influential'.

It would appear that Hindi films can serve to legitimate a particular view of the world and at the same time to open up contradictions within it. So while young people sometimes use films to deconstruct 'traditional culture' many parents use them to foster certain 'traditional' attitudes, values and beliefs in their children. Films are expected to have both an entertainment and a didactic function and are seen by parents as useful agents of cultural continuity and as contributing to the (re)-formation of cultural identity.

Various degrees of scepticism are registered among the boys about parents' attempts to 'artificially maintain a culture' through film: 'Parents want their children to maintain certain religious values, beliefs and customs but that doesn't mean that Indian films are necessarily going to educate them in that way. They may well do the opposite . . . I think the moral standards in most recent films is pretty appalling'. But clear distinctions are made between religion and a sense of cultural identity and whilst firmly upholding the Sikh faith one boy claims: 'Parents use the films to represent their culture to their children but that will not work because those are not my roots, that place [India] has nothing to do with me anymore'.

Many parents lament what they see as a process of progressive 'cultural loss' in each generation of children. Looking to the past they attempt to re-create 'traditional culture'. Meanwhile young people, with eyes to the future, are busy re-creating something 'new'. The striving after cultural continuity and the negotiation of cultural identity are thus inescapably dialectical processes and they must, moreover, be seen in the widest possible context. The notion of viewing as a social activity which takes place in families needs to be extended to include more detailed explorations of the wider social, cultural, and ideological contexts and uses of the VCR.

What is clear is that for the young people interviewed a sense of ethnic, national, and cultural identity does not displace or dominate the equally lived and formed identities based on age, gender, peer group, and neighbourhood. Static notions of culture are extremely disabling as are absolutist views of black-and-white cultures as fixed, mutually impermeable expressions of 'racial' or national identity. Notions of national culture with unique customs and practices understood as 'pure' homogeneous nationality need to be challenged.

One is reminded in this context of the arguments put forward by Benedict Anderson (1983) about the use of cultural artefacts in constructing 'imagined communities' based on notions of nation and nationness. The 'imagined communities', constructed and created through the viewing of films on VCR, may link Asian communities across the world. However, these communities, with their origins in history and experience, are not fixed but change, develop and combine, and are in turn redispersed in historic processes.

If cultural practices are detached from their origins they can be used to found and extend new patterns of communication which can give rise to new common identities. Perhaps most of all this study provides a contemporary example of how 'traditional' ties are created and recreated out of present rather than past conditions.

Notes

1 This paper is based on a dissertation submitted for MA Film and Television Studies for Education, University of London Institute of Education, 1987.
2 The term 'Indian' film is used most commonly by interviewees but distinctions between films are also drawn according to language (i.e. Hindi, Panjabi, and Urdu) as well as genre.
3 See, for example, Ballard (1979) and Community Relations Commission (1979), and for a critique of such perspectives see Parmar (1981).
4 This estimated figure is based on surveys carried out in three Southall schools.
5 Lutze (1985).
6 Gundara (1986).
7 Other contexts documented in the research included siblings viewing together in the home, viewing with friends/peers, women/girls-only groups, women solo viewing and male-only viewing.
8 For further accounts of family contexts of viewing see, for example, Morley (1986); Simpson (1987).
9 For a more detailed exploration of narration in the popular Hindi film see Thomas (1985).

References

Anderson, B. 1983: *Imagined communities*. London: Verso.
Ballard, C. 1979: Conflict, continuity and change: second generation Asians. In

Saifullah Khan, V. (ed.), *Minority families in Britain*. London: Macmillan.

Community Relations Commission 1979: *Between two cultures: a study of the relationship between generations in the Asian community*. London: Community Relations Commission.

Gundara, J. 1986: Education in a multicultural society. In Gundara *et al.* (eds), *Racism, diversity and education*. London: Hodder & Stoughton.

Lutze 1985: From Bharata to Bombay: change and continuity in Hindi film aesthetics. In Pfleiderer, B. (ed.), *The Hindi film: agent and re-agent of cultural change*. Manohar: 7.

Mishra, V. 1985: Towards a theoretical critique of Bombay Cinema. *Screen* **26**(3–4).

Morley, D. 1986: Family television. *Cultural power and domestic leisure*. London: Comedia.

Palmer, P. 1986: *The lively audience*. London: Allen & Unwin.

Parmar, P. 1981: Young Asian women: a critique of the pathological approach. *Multi-Racial Education* **10**(1).

Saari, A. 1985: In Pfleiderer, B. (ed.), *The Hindi film: agent and re-agent of cultural change*. Manohar: 23.

Simpson, P. (ed.) 1987: *Parents talking*. London: Comedia.

Thomas, R. 1985: Indian cinema: pleasures and popularity. *Screen* **26**(3–4), 123–35.

15

Just looking for trouble – Robert Mapplethorpe and fantasies of race

Kobena Mercer

From Lynne Segal and Mary McIntosh (eds), *Sex exposed – sexuality and the pornography debate* (Virago, 1992).

How does 'race' feature in the politics of anti-pornography? Well, it does and it doesn't. 'Race' is present as an emotive figure of speech in the rhetoric of certain feminist anti-pornography arguments; yet 'race' is also markedly absent, since there appears to be no distinctly black perspective on the contentious issue of sexuality, censorship and representation that underpin the volatile nature of the anti-porn debate. Although Audre Lorde and Alice Walker made important contributions early on in the debate in the United States over a decade ago, the question of pornography has hardly been a top priority on the agenda of black feminist politics in Britain in the 1980s and early 1990s.[1] If it is indeed the case that white and black women have not been equally involved in the anti-porn movement, or have not made it a shared political priority, then we have to ask: What role does 'race' play in the discourse of anti-pornography which has come mainly from white women?

'Race' as an issue in anti-pornography feminism

When 'race' is invoked to mobilize moral support for anti-pornography positions it tends to function as a rhetorical trope enabling a race and gender analogy between violence against women and incitement to racial hatred. In their recent campaigns, Labour MPs Clare Short and Dawn Primarolo have frequently used this analogy to argue that just as black people are degraded by racist speech and hurt by racial violence, so women are harmed and victimized by sexist and misogynist representations which portray, and thus promote, the hatred and fear of women that erupt in all acts of male violence. It follows, so the argument goes, that just as the law is supposedly empowered to prohibit and punish incitement to racial hatred, new regulative legislation is needed to 'protect' women from the harm and danger of male violence that pornography represents. Yet the 1965 Race Relations Act, which sought to prohibit racist speech, has never been

161

particularly beneficial to black people – more often than not it has been used against black people to curtail our civil rights to representation, and was proved to be notoriously useless and ineffective by the rise of new racist and fascist movements in the 1970s. Just as most black people know not to entrust our survival and protection to the state, one ought to question any argument, feminist or otherwise, that seeks to extend the intervention of the state in the form of prohibitionary legislation.

Indeed from a black perspective, the problem lies with the very analogy between racial hatred and male violence because it is based on a prior equation between those sexually explicit words and images labelled 'pornographic' and those acts of violence, brutality and homicide that do indeed take place against women in 'real life'. This equation – that 'pornography is the theory, rape is the practice' – is central to the radical feminist anti-pornography argument that gained considerable influence in the USA during the 1980s and is gaining ground in Britain now. One of the most worrying aspects of these developments is the strange alliance that has evolved between radical feminists demanding censorship in the name of women's freedom, and the anti-obscenity lobby of the New Right whose demands for the prohibition of sexual representations have always been part of the moral agenda of mainstream conservatism. For entirely different reasons, these two groups seek further state regulation of pornography, yet their convergence on this objective has created a wider constituency of support for a policy of cultural censorship. Where do black people stand in relation to this unhappy alliance?

While anti-porn feminists are more likely than their neo-conservative counterparts to observe that pornography itself is violently racist, one has to question the highly emotive way in which 'race' is used only to simplify complex issues and polarize opinion, as if everything were a matter of black and white, as if everything depended on whether you are simply for or against pornography and, by implication, male violence. In a theoretical defence of the radical feminist view that pornography does not merely reflect male violence but is itself a form of violence even as representation, Susanne Kappeler uses 'race' precisely in this way – not only to justify the unproven equation between images of sexual violence and actual violence experienced by women, but to elicit a moral response of horror and outrage that lends further credence to the anti-porn argument. At the beginning of her book *The pornography of representation*, by means of a graphic description of photographs depicting a black African man – one Thomas Kasire of Namibia – shown mutilated, tortured, and obliterated for the gratification of his white male European captors, Kappeler hopes to persuade us that, essentially, all pornography entails that women experience the same kind of actual violence as the brutal, sadistic and murderous violence of the colonial racism that resulted in the death of this black man.[2] Not only does this analogy reduce 'race' to rhetoric – whereby the black/white polarity serves to symbolize an absolute morality based on an either/or choice between good and evil – but it offers no analysis of racial representation in pornography, nor of black people's experiences of it, as Kappeler nowhere acknowledges the relative absence of black women in defining the feminist anti-porn agenda or the fact that black feminism, in all its varieties, has certainly not prioritized the issue as a touchstone of revolutionary morality.

Each of these issues concerning race, representation and sexual politics has arisen in the very different context of Robert Mapplethorpe's avowedly homoerotic photography, which was at the centre of a major controversy in the United States during 1989 and 1990. Paradoxically, as a result of the campaign led by Senator Jesse Helms to prevent the National Endowment for the Arts [NEA] from funding exhibitions of so-called 'indecent and obscene materials', Mapplethorpe's photographs have come to the attention of a far wider audience than at any point in his career before his death, from AIDS, in 1989. Although Helms's proposed amendment to NEA funding criteria was eventually defeated, the virulent homophobia that characterized his campaign against Mapplethorpe's 'immoral trash' has helped to create a climate of popular opinion favourable to cultural repression. Just as self-censorship has become routine among art-world decision-makers, so the policing and prosecution of cultural practitioners – from feminist performance artist Karen Finley to the black rap group 2 Live Crew – has also become commonplace. What is truly disturbing about these trends is both the way in which the New Right has successfully hijacked and appropriated elements of the feminist anti-pornography argument, and the way in which some feminists have themselves joined ranks with the law-and-order state. An instance of this occurred in Cincinnati in 1990 when feminist campaigners aligned themselves with the city police department to close down the touring Mapplethorpe retrospective and prosecute the museum director responsible for the exhibition, Dennis Barrie, for the violation of 'community standards'.

Mapplethorpe's black male nudes

In this context, I would like to offer a contribution to the debate on pornography that is based on my reading of Mapplethorpe's troublesome images of nude black men. Although the attack on Mapplethorpe focussed mainly on his depictions of gay male sadomasochism and portraits of naked children, his black male nudes are equally, if not more, problematic – not only because they explicitly resemble aspects of pornography, but because his highly erotic treatment of the black male body seems to be supported by a whole range of racist myths about black sexuality.

To shock was always the key verb in the modernist vocabulary. Like other audiences and spectators confronted by the potent eroticism of Mapplethorpe's most shocking images, black audiences are not somehow exempt from the shock effect that Mapplethorpe's images so clearly intend to provoke. Indeed, it was this sense of outrage – not at the homoeroticism, but at the potential racism – that motivated my initial critique of the work, from a black gay male perspective. I was shocked by what I saw: the profile of a black man whose head was cropped – or 'decapitated', so to speak – holding his semi-tumescent penis through the Y-fronts of his underpants, which is the first image that confronts you in Mapplethorpe's 1982 publication *Black males*. Given the relative silence of black voices at the time of Mapplethorpe's 1983 retrospective at the Institute of Contemporary Arts in London, when the art world celebrated his 'transgressive' reputation, it was important to draw critical attention to the almost pornographic flamboyance with which Mapplethorpe, whose trademark is cool irony, seemed to perpetuate the racist stereotype that, essentially, the black man is nothing more than his penis.

Yet, as the context for the reception and interpretation of Mapplethorpe's work has changed, I have almost changed my mind about these photographs, primarily because I am much more aware of the danger of simply hurling the accusation of 'racism' about. It leads only to the closure of debate. Precisely because of the hitherto unthinkable alliance between the New Right and radical feminism on the issue of pornography, there is now every possibility that a critique which stops only with this kind of moralistic closure inevitably plays into an anti-democratic politics of censorship and cultural closure sought by the ascendant forces of the New Right. In what follows, I explain how and why I changed my mind.[3]

Picture this: two reasonably intelligent black gay men pore over Mapplethorpe's 1986 publication *The black book*. When a friend lent me his copy, this was exactly how it circulated between us: as an illicit and highly troublesome object of desire. We were fascinated by the beautiful bodies and seduced by the pleasure in looking as we perused the repertoire of images. We wanted to look, but we didn't always find what we wanted to see. This was because we were immediately disturbed by the racial dimension of the imagery and, above all, angered by the aesthetic objectification that reduced these individual black men to purely abstract visual 'things', silenced in their own right as subjects and serving mainly as aesthetic trophies to enhance Mapplethorpe's privileged position as a white gay male artist in the New York avant-garde. In short, we were stuck in a deeply ambivalent structure of feeling. In an attempt to make sense of this experience, I drew on elements of feminist cultural theory.

The first thing to notice about Mapplethorpe's black males – so obvious that it goes without saying – is that all the men are nude. Framed within the generic conventions of the fine-art nude, their bodies are aestheticized and eroticized as 'objects' to be looked at. As such, they offer an erotic source of pleasure in the art of looking. But whose pleasure is being served? Regarding the depiction of women in dominant forms of visual representation, from painting to advertising or pornography, feminist cultural theory has shown that the female image functions predominantly as a mirror-image of what men want to see. As a figment of heterosexual wish-fulfilment, the female nude serves primarily to guarantee the stability of a phallocentric fantasy in which the omnipotent male gaze sees but is itself never seen. The binary opposition of seeing/being seen which informs visual representations of the female nude reveals that looking is never an innocent or neutral activity, but is always powerfully loaded by the gendered character of the subject/object dichotomy in which, to put it crudely, men look and women are there to be looked at.

In Mapplethorpe's case, however, the fact that both artist and model are male sets up a tension of sameness which thereby transfers the *frisson* of 'difference' from gender to racial polarity. In terms of the conventional dichotomy between masculinity as the active control of the gaze, and femininity as its passive visual object, what we see in Mapplethorpe's case is the way in which the black/white duality of 'race' overdetermines the power relations implicit in the gendered dichotomy between subject and object of representation.

In this sense, what is represented in Mapplethorpe's photographs is a 'look', or a certain 'way of looking', in which the pictures reveal more about the absent and invisible white male photographer who actively controls the gaze than they do about the black men whose beautiful bodies we see depicted in his photographs. Insofar as the pictorial space excludes any reference to a social, historical, cultural or political context that might tell us something about the lives of the black models who posed for the camera, Mapplethorpe facilitates the projection of certain racial and sexual fantasies about the 'difference' that black masculinity is assumed to embody. In this way, the photographs are very much about sexual investment in looking, because they disclose the tracing of desire on the part of the I/eye placed at the centre of representation by the male gaze.

Through a combination of formal codes and conventions – the posing and posture of the body in the studio enclosure; the use of strong chiaroscuro lighting; the cropping, framing and fragmentation of the whole body into parts – the 'look' constructed not only structures the viewer's affective disposition towards the image but reveals something of the *mise en scène* of power, as well as desire, in the racial and sexual fantasies that inform Mapplethorpe's representation of black masculinity. Whereas the white gay male sadomasochist pictures portray a subcultural sexuality that consists of 'doing' something, the black men are defined and confined to 'being' purely sexual and nothing but sexual – hence hypersexual. We look through a sequence of individually named African-American men, but we see only sexuality as the sum-total meaning of their black male identity. In pictures like 'Man in a Polyester Suit' (1980), apart from the model's hands, it is the penis, and the penis alone, that identifies him as a black man.

Mapplethorpe's obsessive focus on this one little thing, the black man's genitals, and the way in which the glossy allure of the quality monochrome print becomes almost consubstantial with the shiny, sexy texture of black skin, led me to argue that a certain racial fetishism is an important element in the pleasures (and displeasures) which the photographs bring into play. Such racial fetishism not only eroticizes the most visible aspect of racial difference – skin colour – but also lubricates the ideological reproduction of 'colonial fantasy', in which the white male subject is positioned at the centre of representation by a desire for mastery, power and control over the racialized and inferiorized black Other. Hence, alongside the codes of the fine-art nude, Mapplethorpe seems to make use of the regulative function of the commonplace racist stereotype – the black man as athlete, mugger or savage – in order to stabilize the invisible and all-seeing white subject at the centre of the gaze, and thereby 'fix' the black subject in its place not simply as the Other, but as the object in the field of vision that holds a mirror to the fears and fantasies of the supposedly omnipotent white male subject.

According to literary critic Homi Bhabha, 'an important feature of colonial discourse is its dependence on the concept of "fixity" in the ideological construction of otherness'.[4] Just as Mapplethorpe's photographs of female body-builder Lady Lisa Lyon seem obsessively to pin her down by processing the image of her body through a thousand cultural stereotypes of femininity, so the obsessive undercurrent in his black male nudes would appear to confirm this emphasis on fixity as a sign that betrays anxiety as well as pleasure in the desire for mastery. Mapplethorpe's scopic fixation on the luxurious beauty of black skin thus implies a kind of 'negrophilia', an aesthetic idealization of racial difference that merely inverts and reverses the binary axis of colonial discourse, in which all things black are equated with darkness, dirt and danger, as manifest in the psychic representations of 'negrophobia'. Both positions, whether they overvalue or devalue the visible signs of racial difference, inhabit the shared space of colonial fantasy. These elements for a psychoanalytic reading of fetishism, as it is enacted in the theatre of Mapplethorpe's sex–race fantasy, are forcefully brought together in a photograph such as 'Man in a Polyester Suit'.

The use of framing and scale emphasizes the sheer size of the big black penis revealed through the unzipped trouser fly. As Fanon said, when diagnosing the terrifying figure of 'the Negro' in the fantasies of his white psychiatric patients, 'One is no longer aware of the Negro, but only of a penis: the Negro is eclipsed. He is turned into a penis. He *is* a penis'.[5] By virtue of the purely formal device of scale, Mapplethorpe summons up one of the deepest mythological fears in the supremacist imagination: namely, the belief that all black men have monstrously large willies. In the phantasmic space of the white male imagery, the big black phallus is perceived as a threat not only to hegemonic white masculinity but to Western civilization itself, since the 'bad object' represents a danger to white womanhood and therefore the threat of miscegenation, eugenic pollution and racial degeneration. Historically, in nineteenth-century societies structured by race, white males eliminated the anxiety that their own fantastic images of black male sexuality excited through rituals of aggression in which the lynching of black men routinely involved the literal castration of the Other's strange fruit.

The historical myth of penis size amounts to a 'primal fantasy' in Western culture in that it is shared and collective in nature – and, moreover, a myth that is so pervasive and firmly held as a folk belief that modern sexology repeatedly embarked on the empirical task of actually measuring pricks to demonstrate its untruth. Now that the consensual management of liberal race relations no longer provides available legitimation for this popular belief, it is as if Mapplethorpe's picture performs a disavowal of the wish-fulfilment inscribed in the myth: *I know* (it's not true that all black guys have big willies), *but* (nevertheless, in my photographs they do).

Within the picture, the binary character of everyday racial discourse is underlined by the jokey irony of the contrast between the black man's exposed private parts and the public display of social respectability signified by the three-piece business suit. The oppositions hidden and exposed, denuded and clothed, play upon the Manichaean dualism of nature and culture, savage and civilized, body and mind, inferior and superior, that informs the logic of dominant racial discourse. In this way, the construction of racial difference in the image suggests that sexuality, and nothing but sexuality, is the essential 'nature' of the black man, because the cheap and tacky quality of the polyester suit confirms his failure to gain access to 'culture'. The camouflage of bourgeois respectability fails to conceal the fact that the black man, as the white man's Other, originates, like his dick, from somewhere anterior to civilization.

Conflicting readings of Mapplethorpe

Notwithstanding the problematic nature of Freud's pathologizing clinical vocabulary, his concept of fetishism can usefully be adapted, via feminist cultural theory, to help conceptualize issues of subjectivity and spectatorship in representations of race and ethnicity. Its account of the splitting of levels of belief may illuminate the prevalence of certain sexual fantasies and their role in the reproduction of racism in contemporary culture. The sexual fetish represents a substitute for something that was never there in the first place: the mother's penis, which the little boy expected to see. Despite conscious acknowledgement of sexual difference, the boy's castration anxiety forces the repression of his initial belief, such that it coexists on an unconscious level and finds manifestation, in adult sexuality, in the form of the erotic fetish.[6] One might say that, despite anatomical evidence, the belief symbolized in the fantasy of the big black willy – that black male sexuality is not only 'different' but somehow 'more' – is one many men and women, black and white, straight or gay, cling on to, because it retains currency and force as an element in the psychic reality of the social fantasies in which our racial and gendered identities have been historically constructed.

Yet because Freud's concept of fetishism is embedded in the patriarchal system of sexual difference that it describes, treating sexual perversion or deviation as a symptom which reveals the unconscious logic of the heterosexual norm, it is less useful as a tool for examining the perverse aestheticism of the modern homoerotic imagination which Mapplethorpe self-consciously employs. Moreover, there are limits to the race and gender analogy drawn from feminist cultural theory in the preceding analysis of visual fetishism: it ignores the obvious homoerotic specificity of the work. As a gay male artist whose sexual identity locates him in a subordinate relation to heterosexual masculinity, Mapplethorpe is hardly representative of the hegemonic model of straight, white, bourgeois male identity traditionally privileged in art history as the centred subject and agent of representation. Above all, as the recent exhibition history of his work attests, far from demonstrating the stability of this supposedly centred white male subject, the vitriol and anxiety expressed in hostile attacks on Mapplethorpe's *oeuvre* (such as those of radical neo-conservative art critic Hilton Kramer) would suggest that there is something profoundly troubling and disturbing about the emotional ambivalence experienced by different audiences through the salient shock effect of Mapplethorpe's work.

In the light of the changed context of reception, the foremost question is how different audiences and readers produce different and conflicting readings of the same cultural text. The variety of conflicting interpretations of the value of Mapplethorpe's work would imply that the text does not bear one, singular and unequivocal meaning, but is open to a number of competing readings. Thus Mapplethorpe's photographic text has become the site for a range of antagonistic interpretations. Once we adopt this view, we need to reconsider the relationship between artist and audience, or author and reader, because although we habitually attempt to resolve the question of the ultimate 'meaning' of a text by appealing to authorial intentions, poststructuralist theory has shown, by way of the 'death of the author' argument, that individual intentions never have the last word in determining the meaning or value of a text. This is because readers themselves play an active role in interpreting a multivalent and open-ended modernist cultural text.

One might say, therefore, that the difficult and troublesome question raised by Mapplethorpe's black male nudes – do they reinforce or undermine racist myths about black sexuality? – is strictly unanswerable, since his aesthetic strategy makes an unequivocal yes/no response impossible. The question is left open by the author and is thus thrown back to the spectator. Our recognition of the unconscious sex–race fantasies which Mapplethorpe's images arouse with such perverse precision does not confirm a stable or centred subject position, but is experienced precisely as an emotional disturbance which troubles the viewer's sense of secure identity.

The recent actual death of the author entails a reconsideration of the issue of authorship and intentionality, and the reciprocal role of the reader, because the articulation of race and homosexuality in Mapplethorpe's art can also be seen as a subversive move that begins to unravel the violent ambiguity at the interface of the social and the emotional. To clarify my suggestion that his black male nudes are open to an alternative evaluation from that of my initial reading, I should come clean with regard to the specific character of my own subject position as a black gay male reader.

My angry emphasis on racial fetishism as a potentially exploitative process of objectification was based on the way in which I felt identified with the black men depicted in the photographs, simply by virtue of sharing the same 'categorical' identity as a black man. As the source of this anger, the emotional identification can be best described again in Fanon's words as a feeling that 'I am laid bare. I am overdetermined from without. I am the slave not of the "idea" that others have of me but of my own appearance. I am being dissected under white eyes. I am fixed ... Look, it's a Negro'.[7] It was my anger at the aestheticizing effect of Mapplethorpe's coolly 'ironic' appropriation of racist stereotypes that informed the description of visual fetishism as a process of reduction, or dehumanization. This argument has many similarities with the early feminist critique of images of women in pornography.[8] But the problem with this view is that it moralizes images in terms of a reductive dichotomy between good and bad, 'positive' and 'negative', and thus fails to recognize the ambivalence of the text. If, on the other hand, we recognize that there is an important difference between saying that an image is racist and saying that it is 'about' racism, then we need a more reflexive approach to the ambiguities set into motion in the destabilizing moment of Mapplethorpe's shock effect.

On this view, the strategic use of visual fetishism is not necessarily a bad thing, as it encourages the viewer to examine his or her own implication in the fantasies which the images arouse. Once I acknowledge my own location in the image reservoir as a gay subject – a desiring subject not only in terms of sharing a desire to look, but in terms of an identical object-choice already there in my own fantasies and wishes – then the articulation of meanings about eroticism, race and homosexuality become a lot more complicated. Indeed, I am forced to confront the rather unwelcome fact that as a spectator I actually occupy the very position in the fantasy of mastery previously ascribed to the centred position of the white male subject! In other words, there was another axis of identification – between white gay male author and black gay male reader – that cut across the identification with the black men in the pictures. Could it not be the case that my anger was also mingled with feelings of jealousy, rivalry or envy? If I shared the same desire to look, which would place me in the position of mastery attributed to the author, the anger in the initial critique might also have arisen from a shared, homosexual identification, and thus a rivalry over the same unobtainable object of desire. Insofar as the anger and envy were effects of my identification with both object and subject of the look, I would say that my specific identity as a black gay reader placed me in two contradictory positions at one and the same time. I am sure that emotions such as these are at issue in the rivalry of interpretations around Mapplethorpe's most contentious work. Black gay male readers certainly do not have a monopoly on the conflicted and ambivalent structures of feeling they create. My point here is not confessional, but to use my own experience as a source of data about the complex operations of identification and desire that position us in antagonistic and contradictory relations of race, gender and power, which are themselves partly constituted in representations. In revising my views, I have sought to reopen the question of ambivalence, because rather than simply project it on the author (by asking whether he either perpetuates or challenges racism) one needs to take into account how different readers derive different meanings not only about race, but about sexuality and desire, in Mapplethorpe's work.

The perverse aesthetic

The whole point about the use of textual ambivalence in the modernist tradition is to foreground the uncertainty of any one, singular meaning – which, in the case of Mapplethorpe's double transgressions across race and homosexuality, is a risky business indeed. This is because the open-ended character of the images can provoke a racist reading as much as an anti-racist one, elicit a homophobic reading as much as arouse a homoerotic one. A great deal depends on the reader and the social identity she or he brings to the text. The same statement – the black man is beautiful, say – retains the same denotative meaning, but acquires different connotational values when enunciated by different groups of subjects: the same sentence, uttered by a white man, a black woman, a black man or a white woman, would inevitably take on a qualitatively different 'sound'. Similarly, once we situate the network of relations between author, text and reader, in the contingent, context-bound circumstances in which Mapplethorpe's work currently stands, then we can examine the way in which the open-ended structure of the text gives rise to antagonistic readings that are informed by the social identity of the audience.

Without returning to a naive belief in the author as a godlike figure of authority, it is necessary to argue that it really does matter who is speaking whenever artists, because of their sexual, gender or racial identity, are assigned 'minority' status in the arts and culture at large. Once we take the biographical dimension of Mapplethorpe's work as a gay artist into account it is possible to reinterpret the black male nudes as the beginning of an inquiry into the archive of 'race' in Western culture and history, which has rendered black men into 'invisible men', in Ralph Ellison's phrase. As Mapplethorpe put it in an interview shortly before his death, 'At some point I started photographing black men. It was an area that hadn't been explored intensively. If you went through the history of nude male photography, there were very few black subjects. I found that I could take pictures of black men that were so subtle, and the form was so photographical'. An awareness of the exclusion of the black subject from one of the most valued canonical genres of Western art – the nude – suggests that it is both possible and necessary to reread Mapplethorpe's work as part of an artistic inquiry into the hegemonic force of a Eurocentric aesthetic which historically rendered invisible not only black people but women, lesbians and gays and others before the radical social transformations of the modern and postmodern period.

By virtue of a perverse aesthetic of promiscuous intertextuality, whereby the overvalued aura of the fine-art nude is contaminated by the filthy and degraded form of the commonplace stereotype, Mapplethorpe transgresses on several fronts to make visible that which is repressed and made invisible in the dominant, and dominating, tradition of the West against the rest. In the contemporary United States, for example, black males constitute one of the 'lowest' social identities in the late-capitalist underclass: disenfranchised, disadvantaged, disempowered. Yet in Mapplethorpe's studio, some of the men who in all probability came from this class are elevated on to the pedestal of the transcendental aesthetic ideal of the male nude in Western culture, which had always excluded the black subject from such aesthetic idealization on account of its otherness. Mapplethorpe's achievement as a postmodern 'society photographer' lies in the way he renders invisible men visible in a cultural system – art photography – that always historically denied or marginalized their existence. One can see in Mapplethorpe's use of homoeroticism a subversive strategy of perversion in which the liberal humanist values inscribed in the idealized fine-art nude are led away from the higher aims of 'civilization' and brought face to face with that part of itself repressed and devalued as 'other' in the form of the banal, commonplace stereotype in everyday culture. What is experienced in the salient shock effect is the disruption of our normative expectations about distinctions that imply a rigid separation between fine art and popular culture, or between art and pornography. Mapplethorpe's transgressive crossing of such boundaries has the effect of calling into question our psychic and social investment in these cultural separations.

Changing political climates

If I am now more prepared to offer a defence rather than a critique of Mapplethorpe's representations of race, because of the changed ideological context, it is because the stakes have also changed. I am convinced that it was not the death of the author so much as the cause of his death that was a major factor in the timing of the Helms campaign against the NEA. Almost all the discourse surrounding the furore noted that Mapplethorpe died of AIDS. The new-found legitimacy of political homophobia and the creation of new folk devils through the mismanagement of the AIDS crisis has proved fertile ground for the spread of popular authoritarian tendencies across the left/right spectrum. Yet the Mapplethorpe/NEA crisis in the USA was often perceived, like the Rushdie crisis in Britain, simply in terms of a straightforward opposition between censorship and freedom of artistic expression. This model of a crude binary frontier is unfeasible because what was at stake in the conflicting readings of Mapplethorpe was not a neat dichotomy between bigoted Philistines and enlightened cultured liberals but a new configuration of social actors, some of whom have engaged in unexpected alliances which have transformed the terrain of contestation.

In many ways the Right's success in organizing a popular bloc of public opinion on issues like pornography derives from these new alliances. Just like the alliance formed between radical feminist anti-porn activists and the local state legislature in the form of the Dworkin–MacKinnon-drafted Minneapolis Ordinance in 1984, or the appropriation of the feminist argument that pornography itself is violence in the official discourse of the Meese Commission in 1986, the Helms campaign has highlighted some significant developments in popular right-wing politics. In his original proposal to regulate public funding of art deemed 'obscene and indecent', Jesse Helms went beyond the traditional remit of moral fundamentalism to add new grounds for legal intervention on the basis of discrimination against minorities. Helms wanted the state to intervene in instances where artistic and cultural materials' denigrate, debase or revile a person, group or class of citizens on the basis of race, creed, sex, handicap or national origin'. By means of this rhetorical move, he sought to appropriate the language of liberal anti-discrimination legislation to promote a climate of opinion favourable to new forms of coercive intervention. In making such a move, the strategy is not simply to win support from black people and ethnic minorities, nor simply to modernize the traditional 'moral' discourse against obscenity, but to broaden and extend the threshold of illegitimacy to a wider range of cultural texts. As the moral panic unfolds, more and more cultural forms transgress or come up against the symbolic boundary that such prohibitionary legislation seeks to impose. Consider the way in which parental warning labels on rap and rock albums have become commonplace: the Parents' Music Resource Centre that helped to initiate this trend in the 1980s has also inspired prosecutions of rock musicians on the grounds that their cultural texts do not simply 'deprave and corrupt', as it were, but have actually caused violence, in the form of suicides.

Under these conditions – when, despite its initial emancipatory intentions, elements of the radical feminist anti-porn movement of the 1980s have entered into alliance with neo-conservative forces – it is not inconceivable that a reading of Robert Mapplethorpe's work as racist, however well intended, could serve the ends of the authoritarian trend supported by this new alliance of social actors. The AIDS crisis has also visibly brought to light the way in which homophobia can be used to draw upon conservative forces within minority cultures. In black British communities, the anti-lesbian and gay hostility expressed in the belief that homosexuality is a 'white man's thing', and hence, because of the scapegoating of gay men, that AIDS is a 'white man's disease', has not only helped to cement alliances between black people and the New Right (for example, in the local campaign on 'Positive Images' in Haringey, London, in 1987) but has had tragically self-defeating consequences in the black community itself. Men and women have been dying, but the psychic mechanism of denial and disavowal in such fear of homosexuality has been particularly apparent in many black responses to AIDS.

Yet these contradictory conditions have also shaped the emergence of a new generation of black lesbian and gay cultural activists in Britain and the United States. Their presence is seriously important not only because they contest the repressive precepts of authoritarian politics in both white society and in black communities, but because their creativity points to new ways of making sense of the contemporary situation. Black lesbian and gay artists such as Isaac Julien, Pratibha Parmar, Michelle Parkerson and Marlon Riggs in film and video; or Essex Hemphill, Cheryl Clarke, Barbara Smith and Joseph Beam in writing and critique, or Sunil Gupta, Rotimi Fani-Kayode or Lyle Harris in the medium of photography, have widened and pluralized the political and theoretical debates about eroticism, prohibition, transgression and representation. In films such as Isaac Julien's *Looking for Langston* (1989) some of the difficult and troublesome questions about race and homosexuality that Mapplethorpe raised are taken on in a multifaceted dialogue on the lived experience of black gay desire. In his photographs, Rotimi Fani-Kayode also enters into this dialogue, not through a confrontational strategy but through an invitational mode of address which operates in and against the visual codes and conventions his work shares with Mapplethorpe's. But in this hybrid, Afrocentric, homoerotic image world, significant differences unfold as such artists critically 'signify upon' the textual sources they draw from. In the hands of this new generation of black diaspora intellectuals rethinking sex, such 'signifying' activity simultaneously critiques the exclusions and absences which previously rendered black lesbian and gay identities invisible, and reconstructs new pluralistic forms of collective belonging and imagined community that broaden the public sphere of multicultural society.

Such radical changes in black queer visibility were unthinkable ten or fifteen years ago, and one would hope that their emergence now suggests new possibilities for an alternative set of popular alliances that seek to open up and democratize the politics of desire. In the event that the legislation sought by those opposed to whatever can be called 'pornographic' is ever successful in Britain, it is far more likely that it will first be brought to bear on independent artists such as these rather than on the corporations and businessmen who own the porn industry, edit the tabloids or sell advertising. To propose to outlaw something the definition of which no one seems to agree upon is hardly in the interests of anyone seeking not just the protection of our existing civil rights and liberties (few as they are in Britain) but the necessary changes that would further democratize and deepen new practices of freedom.

Notes

1 Audre Lorde, 'Uses of the erotic: the erotic as power' (1978) and Alice Walker, 'Coming apart' (1979), both reprinted in Laura Lederer, (ed.), *Take back the night: women on pornography*. New York: William Morrow, 1980.
2 Susanne Kappeler, *The pornography of representation*, Cambridge: Polity Press, 1986, 5–10.
   One important alternative to the race and gender analogy is to open the debate to include racism in both pornography and in the women's movement. This is an important point, raised in the context of a historical overview of the mutual articulation of gender and sexuality in racial oppression, discussed by Tracey Gardner, 'Racism in pornography and the women's movement', in Lederer (ed.), *Take back the night: women on pornography*, New York: William Morrow, 1978.
3 See Kobena Mercer, 'Imaging the black man's sex', in Patricia Holland, Jo Spence and Simon Watney (eds), *Photography/Politics: two*, London: Comedia, 1986; and, for the revision of the initial analysis, 'Skin head sex thing: racial difference and the homoerotic imaginary', in Bad Object Choices (ed.), *How do I look? Lesbian and gay film and video*, Seattle, DC: Bay Press, 1991. Related work on the cultural politics of black masculinity may be found in Isaac Julien and Kobena Mercer, 'Race, sexual politics and black masculinity: a dossier', in Rowena Chapman and Jonathan Rutherford (eds), *Male order: unwrapping masculinity*, London: Lawrence & Wishart, 1988.
   The black male nude photographs referred to may be found in Robert Mapplethorpe, *Black males*, Amsterdam: Gallerie Jurka, 1982; *The black book*, Munich: Schirme-Mosel, 1986; and Richard Marshall (ed.), *Robert Mapplethorpe*, New York: Bullfinch Press, 1990.
4 Homi Bhabha, 'The other question: colonial discourse and the stereotype', *Screen* **24**, 4 (1983), p. 18.
5 Frantz Fanon, *Black skin/white masks*, London: Pluto Press, 1986 (first published 1952), p. 120.
6 Sigmund Freud, 'Fetishism' (1923), in *The Pelican Freud Library*, vol. 7, *On Sexuality*, Harmondsworth: Penguin, 1977.
7 Fanon, *Black skin/white masks*, London: Pluto Press, 1986 , p. 82.
8 The humanist critique of objectification is taken up by Essex Hemphill, 'Introduction', in Essex Hemphill (ed.), *Brother to brother: new writings by black gay men*, Boston, MA: Alyson Press, 1991.

Section 3

Meaning and power

This section comprises a diverse selection of writings broadly on the theme of meaning and power, representing the critical development of cultural studies, some of its constituencies of interest and various responses to 'the postmodern condition' as lived in socially and spatially situated environments rather than as merely theorized.

Liz Curtis's article, a precursor to her book, *Nothing but the same old story* (1984a), focuses upon meaning and power by reminding us of the painful history of British imperialism in the nearby colony of Ireland. Victorian newspapers blamed the victim and dehumanized the other – colonialist tropes that are still familiar in spite of the decline of empires. Contemporary political cartoons depicted the Irish as not yet human, images consistent with the Social Darwinist ideology of racial difference. Writing in the 1970s, when 'the Irish question' had once again exploded onto the domestic political agenda, Curtis illustrates very sharply how racism and the frequently unconscious ruses of collective guilt are connected together by referring, in addition, to the spate of Irish jokes told in Britain at the time. [For British media coverage of the Anglo/Irish conflict during this period, see Curtis's (1984b) book which provides extensively documented criticisms; for the history of what the early-twentieth-century Irish historian Alice Stopford Green called 'the English extirpation of Irish society', see Curtis (1993).]

The inclusion of **Judith Williamson**'s introduction to her *Decoding advertisements* is intended to whet the reader's appetite for one of the widely acknowledged and still illuminating classics of cultural studies. Williamson applies structuralist theories of ideology, signification and subjectivity that have been central to the development of textual analysis. Through a series of practical case studies, making up the bulk of the book, she seeks to explore how advertisements produce meaning and offer ideal selves with which to identify, in effect drawing attention to the mediation of psychic and economic processes by ideologies of consumption.

Fredric Jameson's piece is a synthesis of two earlier articles: his original

175

'Postmodernism and consumer society', published in Hal Foster's *The anti-aesthetic* (1983), supplemented by material from Jameson's subsequent formulations in the seminal 'Postmodernism; the cultural logic of late capitalism' (*New Left Review*, no. 146, 1984), the same title as his recent monumental book on the topic (Jameson, 1991). The version included here provides the most accessible entry to Jameson's controversial thinking on the articulation of culture and economics under postmodern conditions (see Harvey, 1989; Kellner, 1989; Lyotard, 1984). Jameson links current intellectual, social and spatial disorientations to the technological reinvigoration of capitalism and its globalization. Unlike Jean Baudrillard (1988), the guru of postmodernism and prophet of hyperreality (see Norris, 1992), Jameson views present arrangements with a critical rationality and calls for a demystifying political aesthetic of 'cognitive mapping'. Most importantly, he questions intensified commodification and the rebirth of consumer culture (see Lee, 1993).

The extract from **Paul Willis**'s *Common culture* reiterates some of the formative themes of British cultural studies: the political project of creating a 'common culture', enunciated by Raymond Williams (1958) after R.H. Tawney, and the Birmingham Centre for Contemporary Cultural Studies' thesis that cultural commodities are appropriated and rearticulated meaningfully by ordinary people, especially the young (Jefferson, 1975). Willis's unconcealed populism concerning the symbolic creativity of market-based cultural consumption runs counter to the social democratic tradition of public arts patronage which either sought to disseminate 'elite' culture to the masses or, in community arts, to engage ordinary people in primary cultural production.

Mike Davis, writing in a personalized mode about the region where he grew up, opens *City of quartz* by recalling the lost history of socialist utopianism in Southern California. This is where affluent community developments, turning the desert into a garden for the few, serve commuters in flight from the socially polarized and politically tense Los Angeles. However, these places are not entirely secure and safe havens for ex-city dwellers with the money to settle elsewhere. From the vantage point provided by Davis, an urban sociologist, the triumph of a displaced postmodern consumerism over local class and race wars seems far from complete. While there are signs that the critical edge of British cultural studies has been blunted, American writing like that of Mike Davis may remind students of cultural studies of its origins in social critique (see Clarke, 1991).

Writing in a similarly critical vein, **Jan Nederveen Pieterse** challenges the complacent rhetoric of European integration, associated with the introduction of a 'single market' at the end of 1992, by raising questions about the suppression of racial and cultural differences. Rather than the civilizing heritage and economic renewal of a greater Europe, Pieterse stresses the actual inequalities and exclusions of this post-imperial solution, the marginalization of peoples and regions, the construction of a 'European Mexico syndrome' in the wake of fallen communism and resurgent Islam.

Both Davis and Pieterse display a heightened sense of what **Doreen Massey** calls the 'power-geometry' of place This sensibility is consistent with 'postmodern geography' (Soja, 1989), which is to some extent reconstructing the preoccupations of cultural studies (see Jackson, 1989/1992). Appropriating and refining David Harvey's concept of 'time-space compression', Massey here connects a holistic concern with spatial dynamics to everyday lived experience. The transition from a predominantly Fordist system of mass production and consumption to a regime of 'flexible accumulation' brings about a certain 'annihilation of space by time' (Marx) whereby distance no longer delays communication (Harvey, 1989). A sense of 'place', both physical and social, is disconcerted in such a rapidly changing and communicating world. Massey draws our attention to the potential meanings of such obscure forces for ordinary people in their homes and on the street, and she stresses how time-space compression is differentially experienced in terms of class, gender and race. These issues were debated at the 1990 'Futures' conference in London's Tate Gallery (see Bird *et al.*, 1993), from which Massey's incisive piece derives.

Like many other subjects in the humanities and social sciences, cultural studies has in the past tended to neglect spatial dynamics, with some notable exceptions (see Cohen, 1972, in Section 2), in favour of temporal dynamics. Historical knowledge is, of course, essential to understanding cultural change. Yet, it is now becoming increasingly evident that the logics of meaning and power operate across socio-cultural space as well as through time, thus creating complex and globalizing interrelations between separate places, mediated by cultural, economic and political power.

References

Baudrillard, J. 1988: *Selected writings.* Cambridge: Polity Press.

Bird, J., Curtis, B., Putnam, T., Robertson, G. and Teichner, L. (eds) 1993: *Mapping the futures.* London/New York: Routledge.

Clarke, J. 1991: *New times and old enemies – essays on cultural studies and America.* London: HarperCollins.

Cohen, P. 1972: Subcultural conflict and working-class community. *Working Papers in Cultural Studies* 2, Centre for Contemporary Cultural Studies, University of Birmingham.

Curtis, L. 1984a: *Nothing but the same old story – the roots of anti-Irish racism.* London: Information on Ireland.

Curtis, L. 1984b: *Ireland – the propaganda war.* London: Pluto Press.

Curtis, L. 1993: *The cause of Ireland – from United Irishmen to partition.* Belfast: Beyond the Pale.

Harvey, D. 1989: *The condition of postmodernity.* Oxford: Basil Blackwell.

Jackson, P. 1989: *Maps of meaning – an introduction to cultural geography.* London/New York: Unwyn Hyman/Routledge.

Jameson, F. 1983: Postmodernism and consumer society. In Foster, H. (ed.), *The anti-aesthetic.* Port Townsend, WA: Bay Press.

Jameson, F. 1984: Postmodernism: the cultural logic of late capitalism. *New Left Review* no. 145 (July–August).

Jameson, F. 1991: *Postmodernism or, the cultural logic of late capitalism.* London: Verso.

Jefferson, T. (ed.) 1975: *Resistance through rituals.* Centre for Contemporary Cultural Studies, University of Birmingham.

Kellner, D. (ed.) 1989: *Postmodernism/Jameson/critique.* Washington, DC: Maisonneuve Press.

Lee, M. 1993: *Consumer culture reborn*. London/New York: Routledge.

Lyotard, J. 1984: *The postmodern condition*. Minneapolis, MN: University of Minnesota Press; Manchester: Manchester University Press.

Norris, C. 1992: *Uncritical theory – postmodernism, intellectuals and the Gulf War*. London: Lawrence & Wishart.

Soja, E. 1989: *Postmodern geographies*. London: Verso.

Williams, R. 1958: *Culture and society*. London: Chatto and Windus.

16

Echoes of the present – the Victorian press and Ireland

Liz Curtis

From *Truth: the first casualty* (Information on Ireland, 1978).

> The cry is now for strong measures. Such is the language which is now held by the English journals, which, in their habitual ignorance and presumption, undertake to supply remedies for a social condition, with whose disturbing elements they are utterly unaquainted. They argue from facts of their own creation, and presuppose a state of things to give colour to their absurdities.
>
> *Freeman's Journal*, 30 January 1843

England's largest newspapers, wrote Belgian essayist Gustave de Molinari in 1880, 'allow no occasion to escape them of treating the Irish as an inferior race – as a kind of white negroes – and a glance at *Punch* is sufficient to show the difference they establish between the plump and robust personification of John Bull and the wretched figure of lean and bony Pat.'[1]

By the nineteenth century the native Irish had long since been dispossessed of their land by English and Scottish settlers. Their religious and civil rights had been denied. They were racked by repeated famines and evicted from their holdings by rapacious landlords. They were not surprisingly rebellious.

But the major British papers of the period saw no connection between British rule and Irish poverty and violence. Instead they argued that the Irish condition was the fault of the Irish themselves and resulted from moral failings inherent in the Celtic character.

A contributor to *Fraser's Magazine*, popular with the English middle classes, declared in March 1847,

> The English people are naturally industrious – they prefer a life of honest labour to one of idleness. . . . Now of all the Celtic tribes, famous everywhere for their indolence and fickleness as the Celts everywhere are, the Irish are admitted to be the most idle and the most fickle. They will not work if they can exist without it.

The *Times* asked in the same year, 'What is an Englishman made for but for work? What is an Irishman made for but to sit at his cabin door, read O'Connell's speeches and abuse the English?' (*Times*, 26 January 1847).

Supposed criminal tendencies in the Celtic character were used to explain away successive Irish rebellions – the rising of the United Irishmen in 1798, the peasant unrest in the first part of the nineteenth century, the Fenian rising of 1867 and the Land War of 1879–81.

A small minority of English people, including some working-class radicals in the Midlands and a few prominent intellectuals such as the economists George Poulett Scrope and John Stuart Mill, put forward a different view.

John Stuart Mill pointed out that under the existing system of land tenure the peasant had nothing to gain from hard work. 'If he were industrious or prudent, nobody but his landlord would gain; if he is lazy or intemperate, it is at his landlord's expense.'[2]

And in 1834 Scrope urged the government to limit landlords' powers, arguing,

> It is impossible ... to have any doubt as to the real cause of the insurrectionary spirit and agrarian outrages of the Irish peasantry. They are the struggles of an oppressed, starving people for existence![3]

But in the 1840s only three major newspapers – the *Morning Chronicle*, the *Westminster Review* and the radical *Northern Star* – shared this perspective. The rest all argued that Irish violence was due to the natural criminality of the Celt.

On 13 October 1846 the *Times* put forward this analysis:

> An Irishman commits a murder as a Malay runs a-muck. In certain circumstances it is expected of him, and he would be thought a mean and spiritless wretch if he demurred at it. It is only unfortunate that these circumstances are so indefinite. The conditions under which a Malay draws his krise for the last rush ... are pretty well known by those conversant with the native character, ... But it is impossible to catalogue the offences which amongst Irishmen entail sudden murder or secret assassination.

The press discovered yet another side to the Irish character in order to denigrate the non-violent movement for the Repeal of the Union between Britain and Ireland. This movement was highly popular, attracting as many as half a million people to its meetings.

The Repeal leader Daniel O'Connell was described in one *Times* article in 1836 as 'scum condensed of Irish bog' and 'a greedy self-serving Satan' (*Times*, 16 June 1836). And on 24 January 1843 the *Times* had this to say about the Irish people and their support for Repeal,

> A people of acute sensibilities and lively passions, more quick in feeling wrongs than rational in explaining or temperate in addressing them ... such is the people whose virtues and whose vices ... O'Connell has so fiendishly exploited.

Coercion, it was widely argued, was the answer to repeal: establish 'tranquillity' first, then reform could follow. The press greeted Government's repressive measures against the Repealers with delight.

The British presupposed that the Irish were inferior in a number of ways to themselves. This inferiority was manifested in Irish poverty and violence. The cure was a further dose of colonial methods. This is how the *Times* argued in 1846 for a coercive response to the Repealers:

The great obstacle to tranquillity in Ireland is the national character – the character of the masses, of the middle classes of the senators of Ireland ... When Ireland acts according to the principles of civilised man, then she can be ruled by the laws of civilised man (*Times*, 30 March 1846).

So the destitution and rebelliousness of the Irish, which British rule had brought about, were used to justify the continuation of British rule. Colonialism produced its own justification. Jean-Paul Sartre described the process thus, 'Terror and exploitation dehumanise, and the exploiter authorises himself with that dehumanisation to carry his exploitation further'.[4]

The Irish were not the only people to be regarded by Victorian Britons as inferior. All the imperial subjects were seen in this light: as, in Kipling's words, 'half devil and half child'. Richard Ned Lebow, who studied colonial attitudes in his book *White Britain and black Ireland*, points out,

with almost monotonous regularity colonial natives have been described as indolent and complacent, cowardly but brazenly rash, violent, uncivilised and incapable of hard work. On the more complimentary side, they have been characterised as hospitable, good-natured, possessing a natural talent for song and dance and frequently as curious but incapable of a prolonged span of attention. In short, the image of simple creatures in need of paternal domination emerged very clearly.[5]

Following Sartre and Albert Memmi, Lebow suggests that the stereotype of the inferior native allows the colonizing nation to apply harsher standards of justice than would be applied at home with a clear conscience. It provides a way out of the liberal dilemma: how to reconcile principles with what you see as political necessity.

In earlier days the subject peoples were not even regarded as inferior humans – instead they were seen as animals or as races born to be slaves. In the sixteenth century a great debate took place in Spain over whether American Indians were in fact human beings. Most conquistadors argued that despite their human form, the Indians were really animals – a view which justified treating them as beasts of burden. A similar outlook enabled Cromwell and the Pilgrim Fathers to retain a clear conscience as they exterminated, respectively, the indigenous Irish and American peoples.

Victorian cartoonists appropriated the image of the 'inferior and uncivilised' Irish and translated it into powerfully propagandistic images.

At the time of the French Revolution in 1789, rioters, radicals and rebels of all nationalities were drawn with sub-human features, and often with pig-like noses, to suggest that they were part of the primitive 'swinish' mob. And when the United Irishmen rose in 1798 they were immediately caricatured as brutish peasants with snub noses and bulging jaws.

In the 1840s brutish caricatures became increasingly identified with Irish people. The Irish were by now a favourite butt for cartoonists. Thousands of destitute Irish immigrants were pouring into England and Scotland. The Repeal movement had started, and the end of the decade was to see the Young Ireland movement attempt to launch an armed uprising.

Daniel O'Connell was portrayed as Frankenstein – a theme that was to

PUNCH, OR THE LONDON CHARIVARI.—March 3, 1866.

THE FENIAN-PEST.

Hibernia. "O MY DEAR SISTER, WHAT *ARE* WE TO DO WITH THESE TROUBLESOME PEOPLE!"
Britannia. "TRY ISOLATION FIRST, MY DEAR, AND THEN———."

'The Fenian Pest'. In this cartoon by Tenniel Brittania stamps on rebellion and protects Hibernia from the Fenians (*Punch*, 3 March 1866).

recur – conjuring up a monstrous Irish peasant with horns like the Devil. In 1848 *Punch* repeatedly caricatured John Mitchel, the outstanding Young Ireland leader, as a vicious monkey.

The rise of the revolutionary Fenian movement in the 1860s, dedicated to liberating Ireland through force of arms and to returning the land to the

PUNCH, OR THE LONDON CHARIVARI.—December 31, 1881.

TIME'S WAXWORKS.

(1881 *JUST ADDED TO THE COLLECTION.*)

Mr. P. "HA! YOU'LL HAVE TO PUT HIM INTO THE CHAMBER OF HORRORS!"

'Time's Waxworks'. In 1881 the rebellious Irish join other British 'Imperial problems' in Father Time's waxworks collection (Tenniel, *Punch*, 31 December 1881).

people, sparked off anti-Irish hysteria in England and Scotland. The *Glasgow Herald* even produced a special report entitled, 'A night among the Fenians and other wild animals'.[6]

The Fenian campaign of raids on police stations in Ireland and bombings in Britain coincided with a major debate among British scientists about the origins of mankind: are humans descended from Adam and Eve, or do they share an ancestor with the ape?

Many Victorians took comfort from the idea that other races, such as blacks and Irish, were lower on the evolutionary ladder than themselves. Apes were then believed to be vicious creatures – so it was easy to explain away Irish violence as resulting from Irish affinity with apes. Cartoonists and satirists were not slow to utilize the scientists' ideas, and when the first gorilla arrived in London Zoo in 1860 they had the material to hand.

They were quick to caricature the Fenians as ape-like monsters threatening British civilization. As Lewis P. Curtis puts it in his study of Victorian caricature, *Apes and Angels*, famous illustrators like John Tenniel who drew for *Punch* 'leaned heavily on the traditional theme of Beauty (Hibernia or Erin) being rescued from the clutches of the Beast (Fenianism) by a handsome Prince or St. George (Law and Order).'[7]

On 18 March 1862 *Punch* published this barbed satire:

'Setting Down in Malice'. An Irish cartoonist, possibly John O'Hea, mocks the efforts of English artists to depict the Irish as monsters (*Pat*, 22 January 1881).

A creature manifestly between the gorilla and the negro is to be met with in some of the lowest districts of London and Liverpool by adventurous explorers. It comes from Ireland, whence it has contrived to migrate; it belongs in fact to a tribe of Irish savages: the lowest species of Irish Yahoo. When conversing with its kind it talks a sort of gibberish. It is, moreover, a climbing animal, and may sometimes be seen ascending a ladder laden with a hod of bricks. The Irish Yahoo generally confines itself within the limits of its own colony, except when it goes out of them to get its living. Sometimes, however, it sallies forth in states of excitement, and attacks civilised human beings that have provoked its fury.

When the Land War started in 1879 cartoonists made the Irish even more monstrous and brutish than before. A spate of evictions – 2100 families were evicted in the year 1880 alone – led to increasingly bitter agrarian warfare. The cartoonists responded by portraying the Land League's supporters with ape-like faces, huge mouths and sharp fangs to convey that they had not a shred of humanity.

And as the constitutional agitation of the Irish Home Rule Party in Parliament became more militant, Parnell and his supporters too were depicted as ape-like creatures.

As the debate about the origin of species became less controversial, so did the gorilla-Celt begin to fade from the cartoons. The Irish, however, did not. And when the War of Independence started in 1919 the cartoonists displayed their feelings for the rebels by returning to the image of the pig.

Needless to say, the Irish did not see themselves as their British masters saw them. In the satirical magazines read by Ireland's middle and upper classes from 1870 to 1914 it was the Irish – and especially the Home Rulers – who appeared as handsome, honest and even angelic.

Irish cartoonists did not systematically set out to portray the British as apes. But they knew how to make John Bull and his minions – Orangemen, policemen and officials – look cruel. Serious political cartoonists such as John O'Hea, an advocate of Home Rule, contrasted the honest Irishman Pat with unscrupulous British politicians and showed how cruelly Irish landlords – supported by the Tory government – oppressed their tenants. Irish cartoonists also delighted in mocking British stereotypes of the Irish, and poked fun at their efforts to turn Paddy into a monster.

Today

Today the press still fosters the belief that the current conflict in Ireland is due to the inherent irrationality of the Irish – their illogical religious passions, their proneness to violence. It follows from this view that only the presence of the more 'rational' Briton prevents the situation degenerating even further. In an article in The *Times* on 23 September 1977 – later the subject of a complaint to the Commission for Racial Equality – Bernard Levin invoked the Victorian image of the Irish. 'There they go still', he wrote, 'the Irish "patriots" (*sic*), with minds locked and barred, mouths gaping wide to extrude the very last morsel of folly, and consumed with a wild terror that sense may one day prevail'. Levin was reacting to widespread calls in Ireland for British withdrawal and he was backing up Conor Cruise O'Brien – who had lost his seat in the June election. Levin considered that O'Brien, who supports the link with Britain, was the only sane Irishman. If Ireland were towed into the sea and sunk, said Levin, the British Government would 'send a helicopter to take Senator O'Brien off at the last minute'.

There are echoes of Victorian days, too, in the view that coercion is a legitimate response to Irish 'irrationality'.

'The Irish Frankenstein', by Matt Morgan (*The Tomahawk*, 18 December 1869).

'What do we want at Christmas?' asked the *Daily Express* on Christmas Eve in 1977:

> What do we want for Northern Ireland, that wretched, God-stricken back alley of Europe where they shoot people's kneecaps. As a matter of fact, yes – there *are* prospects for Ulster. She has easily the best, toughest, least tractable and most effective Secretary of State ever in Roy Mason.

Such attitudes are reflected – and reinforced – at a popular level by the prevalent anti-Irish joke, which plays a comparable role to the Victorian cartoons. Such jokes, which portray the target group as 'thick', are common wherever there is tension – or a relationship perceived as one of superiority and inferiority – between two groups of people. Indeed the same stories reappear in Australian anti-Pom jokes, American anti-Polish jokes, Glaswegian jokes about 'teuchters' (country bumpkins) and Dublin jokes about Kerrymen.

The rash of anti-Irish jokes has developed since the upsurge in the conflict in 1969 and has had enormous assistance from television. Virtually no TV comedy show is complete without them. Mike Yarwood, the Two Ronnies, Marti Caine, Dick Emery, Jim Davidson, Spike Milligan, Galton and Speight's Tea Ladies and so on all have their quota.

Irish people in Britain fail to find the jokes funny. Indeed, they are so angered by them that for some time the *Irish Post*, 'The Voice of the Irish Community in Britain', has carried a heated correspondence on the subject. And in 1977 Terry Wogan won the *Post*'s 'Irish Person of the Year' award largely on the strength of his public opposition to anti-Irish jokes.

When English people suggest that Irish people are lacking in a sense of humour if they fail to laugh at the jokes – 'everyone should be able to laugh at themselves' – Irish people respond with jokes that English people are reluctant to try out on their friends, and which TV comics ignore.

> Heard the one about the two Englishmen who were trying to have a go at an Irishman in a pub? One of them goes up to the Irishman and says, 'Did you know the Pope's a bastard?' The Irishman takes no notice, just goes on drinking. Then the other Englishman goes up to him and says, 'Hey Paddy! The Pope's an Englishman!' 'I know', says the Irishman, 'your mate just told me'.

Irish people recognize that anti-Irish jokes inflame popular prejudice against them and feed on the concept – carefully nurtured by the government and the media – that the current war is due to Irish bloody-mindedness.

For their part Irish people see the war as caused by history not psychology. If anything they see the British as stupid, with their chauvinist narrow-mindedness. 'Heard the one about the Englishman with the inferiority complex? He thought he was the same as everybody else.'

For English people, ill-informed or misinformed about the continuing war in Ireland, anti-Irish jokes provide a way of laughing off a situation which they find frustrating and fail to understand. And anti-Irish jokes also provide a kind of misplaced reassurance that John Bull, after all, knows best.

Notes

This article is particularly indebted to two books: *White Britain and black Ireland* by Richard Ned Lebow (Institute for the Study of Human Issues, Philadelphia, 1976) and *Apes and angels* by Lewis P. Curtis Jr (David and Charles, 1971).

1 Quoted in Curtis 1971: *Apes and angels*, p. 1.
2 John Stuart Mill, *Principles of political economy with some of their applications to social philosophy*, Boston, 1848, vol. II, p. 283.
3 George Poulett Thomason Scrope, *How is Ireland to be governed?*, London, 1834, 20–1.
4 Jean-Paul Sartre, Introduction to Albert Memmi's *The colonizer and the colonized*, Souvenir Press, London, 1974, p. xxvi.
5 Lebow 1976: *White Britain and black Ireland*, p. 104.
6 Quoted in Curtis (1971) *Apes and angels*, p. 98.
7 Curtis 1971: *Apes and angels*, p. 37.

17

Meaning and ideology

Judith Williamson

Introduction to her *Decoding advertisements* (Marion Boyars, 1978).

> The process, then, is simply this: The product becomes a commodity, i.e. a mere moment of exchange. The commodity is transformed into exchange value. In order to equate it with itself as an exchange value, it is exchanged for a symbol which represents it as exchange value as such. As such a symbolized exchange value, it can then in turn be exchanged in definite relations for every other commodity. Because the product becomes a commodity, and the commodity becomes an exchange value, it obtains, at first only in the head, a double existence. This doubling in the idea proceeds (and must proceed) to the point where the commodity appears double in real exchange: as a natural product on one side, as exchange value on the other.
>
> Karl Marx, *Grundrisse*

Advertisements are one of the most important cultural factors moulding and reflecting our life today. They are ubiquitous, an inevitable part of everyone's lives: even if you do not read a newspaper or watch television, the images posted over our urban surroundings are inescapable. Pervading all the media, but limited to none, advertising forms a vast superstructure with an apparently autonomous existence and an immense influence. It is not my purpose here to *measure* its influence. To do so would require sociological research and consumer data drawing on a far wider range of material than the advertisements themselves. I am simply analysing what can be *seen* in advertisements. Their very existence in more than one medium gives them a sort of independent reality that links them to our own lives; since both share a continuity they constitute a world constantly experienced as real. The ad 'world' becomes seemingly separate from the material medium – whether screen, page, etc. – which carries it. Analysing ads in their *material form* helps to avoid endowing them with a *false* materiality and letting the 'ad world' distort the real world around the screen and page.

It is this ubiquitous quality and its tenacity as a recognizable 'form' despite the fact that it functions within different technical media and despite different 'content' (that is, different messages about different products) that indicates the significance of advertising. Obviously it has a function, which is to sell things to us. But it has another function, which I believe in many ways replaces that traditionally fulfilled by art or religion. It creates structures of meaning.

For even the 'obvious' functions of advertising – the definition above, 'to sell things to us' – involves a meaning process. Advertisements must take into account not only the inherent qualities and attributes of the products they are trying to sell, but also the way in which they can make those properties *mean something to us*.

In other words, advertisements have to translate statements from the world of things, for example, that a car will do so many miles per gallon [mpg], into a form that means something in terms of people. Suppose that the car did a high mpg: this could be translated into terms of thriftiness, the user being a 'clever' saver, in other words, *being a certain kind of person*. Or, if the mpg was low, the ad could appeal to the 'above money pettiness', daredevil kind of person who is too 'trendy' to be economizing. Both the statements in question could be made on the purely factual level of a 'use-value' by the simple figures of '50 mpg' and '20 mpg'. The advertisement translates these 'thing' statements to us as human statements; they are given a humanly symbolic 'exchange-value'.

Thus advertising is not, as might superficially be supposed, a single 'language' in the sense that a language has particular identifiable constituent parts and its words are predetermined. The components of advertisements are variable [. . .] and *not* necessarily all part of one 'language' or social discourse. Advertisements rather provide a structure which is capable of transforming the language of objects to that of people, and vice versa. The first part of this book attempts to analyse the way that structure functions. The second part looks at some of the actual systems and things that it transforms.

But it is too simple to say that advertising reduces people to the status of things, though clearly this is what happens when both are used symbolically. Certainly advertising sets up connections between certain types of consumers and certain products (as in the example above); and having made these links and created symbols of exchange it can use them as 'given', and so can we. For example: diamonds may be marketed by likening them to eternal love, creating a symbolism where the mineral means something not in its own terms, as a rock, but in human terms, as a sign. Thus a diamond comes to 'mean' love and endurance for us. Once the connection has been made, we begin to translate the other way and in fact to skip translating altogether: taking the sign for what it signifies, the thing for the feeling.

So in the connection of people and objects, the two do become interchangeable, as can be seen very clearly in ads of two categories. There are those where objects are made to speak – like people: 'say it with flowers'; 'a little gold says it all', etc. Conversely there are the ads where people become identified with objects: 'the *Pepsi People*' and such like. [. . .] This aspect of advertising's system of meaning is shown in Mick Jagger's lines[1] [. . .]. The classifications of advertisements rebound like a boomerang, as we receive them and come to use them. When 'the man' comes on in one advertisement, the TV watcher (who, it is interesting to note, sees all advertisements as one, or rather, sees their rules as applicable to one another and thus part of an interchangeable system) *uses* the classificatory speech from *another* advertisement and directs this speech back at the screen. 'Well he can't be a man 'cause he doesn't smoke/the same cigarettes as me'. Advertisements are selling us something else besides consumer goods: in providing us with a structure in which we, and those goods, are interchangeable, they are selling us ourselves.

And we need those selves. It is the materiality and historical context of this need which must be given as much attention as that equation of people with things. An attempt to differentiate amongst both people and products is part of the desire to classify, order, and understand the world, including one's own identity. But in our society, while the real distinctions between people are created by their role in the *process* of production, as workers, it is the *products* of their own work that are used, in the false categories invoked by advertising, to obscure the real structure of society by replacing class with the distinctions made by the consumption of particular goods. Thus instead of being identified by what they produce, people are made to identify themselves with what they consume. From this arises the false assumption that workers 'with two cars and a colour TV' are not part of the working class. We are made to feel that we can rise or fall in society through what we are able to buy, and this obscures the actual class basis which still underlies social position. The fundamental differences in our society are still class differences, but use of manufactured goods as means of *creating* classes or groups forms an overlay on them.

This overlay is ideology. Ideology is the meaning *made necessary* by the conditions of society while helping to *perpetuate* those conditions. We feel a need to belong, to have a social 'place'; it can be hard to find. Instead we may be given an imaginary one. All of us have a genuine need for a social being, a common culture. The mass media provide this to some extent and can (potentially) fulfil a positive function in our lives.

But advertising seems to have a life of its own; it exists in and out of other media, and speaks to us in a language we can recognize but a voice we can never identify. This is because advertising has no 'subject'. Obviously people invent and produce adverts, but apart from the fact that they are unknown and faceless, the ad in any case does not claim to speak from them, it is not their speech. Thus there is a space, a gap left where the speaker should be; and one of the peculiar features of advertising is that we are drawn in to fill that gap, so that we become both listener and speaker, subject and object. This works in practice as an anonymous speech, involving a set of connections and symbols directed at us; then on receiving it, we *use* this speech, as shown in the 'diamond' example, or in the use of 'a little gold' to 'say it all'. Ultimately advertising works in a circular movement which once set in motion is self-perpetuating. It 'works' because it feeds off a genuine 'use-value'; besides needing social meaning we obviously *do need* material goods. Advertising gives those goods a social meaning so that two needs are crossed, and neither is adequately filled. Material things that we need are made to represent other, non-material things we need; the point of exchange between the two is where 'meaning' is created.

This outlines and necessarily anticipates ground covered step by step below. By examining the *ideological function* of advertisements' *way of meaning*, Part I, 'Advertising Work', seeks to understand the meaning process: this is where structuralism has been influential and helpful. Part II,

'Ideological Castles', examines the ideological context in which things and people are re-used in that process to create new symbolic systems. These systems are an ideological bric-à-brac of things, people, and people's need for things.

The need for relationship and human meaning appropriated by advertising is one that, if only it was not diverted, could radically change the society we live in.

Note

1 From 'Satisfaction'.

18

Postmodernism and consumer society[1]

Fredric Jameson

From E. Ann Kaplan (ed.) *Postmodernism and its discontents* (Verso, 1988).

The concept of postmodernism is not widely accepted or even understood today. Some of the resistance to it may come from the unfamiliarity of the work it covers, which can be found in all the arts: the poetry of John Ashbery, for instance, but also the much simpler talk poetry that came out of the reaction against complex, ironic, academic modernist poetry in the 1960s; the reaction against modern architecture and in particular against the monumental buildings of the International Style, the pop buildings and decorated sheds celebrated by Robert Venturi in his manifesto, *Learning from Las Vegas*; Andy Warhol and Pop art, but also the more recent Photorealism; in music, the moment of John Cage but also the later synthesis of classical and 'popular' styles found in composers like Philip Glass and Terry Riley, and also punk and new-wave rock with such groups as the Clash, Talking Heads and the Gang of Four; in film, everything that comes out of Godard – contemporary vanguard film and video – but also a whole new style of commercial or fiction films, which has its equivalent in contemporary novels as well, where the works of William Burroughs, Thomas Pynchon and Ishmael Reed on the one hand, and the French new novel on the other, are also to be numbered among the varieties of what can be called postmodernism.

This list would seem to make two things clear at once: first, most of the postmodernisms mentioned above emerge as specific reactions against the established forms of high modernism, against this or that dominant high modernism which conquered the university, the museum, the art gallery network, and the foundations. Those formerly subversive and embattled styles – Abstract Expressionism; the great modernist poetry of Pound, Eliot or Wallace Stevens; the International Style (Le Corbusier, Frank Lloyd Wright, Mies); Stravinsky; Joyce, Proust and Mann – felt to be scandalous or shocking by our grandparents are, for the generation which arrives at the gate in the 1960s, felt to be the establishment and the enemy – dead, stifling, canonical, the reified monuments one has to destroy to do anything new. This means that there will be as many different forms of postmodernism as there were high modernisms in place, since the former are at least initially specific and local reactions *against* those models. That obviously does not make the job of describing postmodernism as a coherent thing any easier, since the unity of this new impulse – if it has one – is given not in itself but in the very modernism it seeks to displace.

The second feature of this list of postmodernisms is the effacement in it of some key boundaries or separations, most notably the erosion of the older distinction between high culture and so-called mass or popular culture. This is perhaps the most distressing development of all from an academic standpoint, which has traditionally had a vested interest in preserving a realm of high or elite culture against the surrounding environment of philistinism, of schlock and kitsch, of TV series and *Reader's Digest* culture, and in transmitting difficult and complex skills of reading, listening and seeing to its initiates. But many of the newer postmodernisms have been fascinated precisely by that whole landscape of advertising and motels, of the Las Vegas strip, of the late show and Grade-B Hollywood film, of so-called paraliterature with its airport paperback categories of the gothic and the romance, the popular biography, the murder mystery and the science fiction or fantasy novel. They no longer 'quote' such 'texts' as a Joyce might have done, or a Mahler; they incorporate them, to the point where the line between high art and commercial forms seems increasingly difficult to draw.

A rather different indication of this effacement of the older categories of genre and discourse can be found in what is sometimes called contemporary theory. A generation ago there was still a technical discourse of professional philosophy – the great systems of Sartre or the phenomenologists, the work of Wittgenstein or analytical or common language philosophy – alongside which one could still distinguish that quite different discourse of the other academic disciplines – of political science, for example, or sociology or literary criticism. Today, increasingly, we have a kind of writing simply called 'theory' which is all or none of those things at once. This new kind of discourse, generally associated with France and so-called French theory, is becoming widespread and marks the end of philosophy as such. Is the work of Michel Foucault, for example, to be called philosophy, history, social theory or political science? It's undecidable, as they say nowadays; and I will suggest that such 'theoretical discourse' is also to be numbered among the manifestations of postmodernism.

Now I must say a word about the proper use of this concept: it is not just another word for the description of a particular style. It is also, at least in my use, a periodizing concept whose function is to correlate the emergence of new formal features in culture with the emergence of a new type of social life and a new economic order – what is often euphemistically called modernization, postindustrial or consumer society, the society of the media or the spectacle, or multinational capitalism. This new moment of capitalism can be dated from the post-war boom in the United States in the late 1940s and early 1950s or, in France, from the establishment of the Fifth Republic in 1958. The 1960s are in many ways the key transitional period, a period in which the new international order (neocolonialism, the Green Revolution, computerization and electronic information) is at one and the same time set in place and is swept and shaken by its own internal contradictions and by external resistance. I want here to sketch a few of the ways in which the new postmodernism expresses the inner truth of that newly emergent social order of late capitalism, but will have to limit the description to only two of its significant features, which I will call pastiche and schizophrenia; they will give us a chance to sense the specificity of the postmodernist experience of space and time respectively.

Pastiche eclipses parody

One of the most significant features or practices in postmodernism today is pastiche. I must first explain this term, which people generally tend to confuse with or assimilate to that related verbal phenomenon called parody. Both pastiche and parody involve the imitation or, better still, the mimicry of other styles and particularly of the mannerisms and stylistic twitches of other styles. It is obvious that modern literature in general offers a very rich field for parody, since the great modern writers have all been defined by the invention or production of rather unique styles: think of the Faulknerian long sentence or of D.H. Lawrence's characteristic nature imagery; think of Wallace Stevens's peculiar way of using abstractions; think also of the mannerisms of the philosophers, of Heidegger for example, or Sartre; think of the musical styles of Mahler or Prokofiev. All of these styles, however different from each other, are comparable in this: each is quite unmistakable; once one is learned, it is not likely to be confused with something else.

Now parody capitalizes on the uniqueness of these styles and seizes on their idiosyncrasies and eccentricities to produce an imitation which mocks the original. I won't say that the satiric impulse is conscious in all forms of parody. In any case, a good or great parodist has to have some secret sympathy for the original, just as a great mimic has to have the capacity to put himself/herself in the place of the person imitated. Still, the general effect of parody is – whether in sympathy or with malice – to cast ridicule on the private nature of these stylistic mannerisms and their excessiveness and eccentricity with respect to the way people normally speak or write. So there remains somewhere behind all parody the feeling that there is a linguistic norm in contrast to which the·styles of the great modernists can be mocked.

But what would happen if one no longer believed in the existence of normal language, of ordinary speech, of the linguistic norm (the kind of clarity and communicative power celebrated by Orwell in his famous essay, say)? One could think of it in this way; perhaps the immense fragmentation and privatization of modern literature – its explosion into a host of distinct private styles and mannerisms – foreshadows deeper and more general tendencies in social life as a whole. Supposing that modern art and modernism – far from being a kind of specialized aesthetic curiosity – actually anticipated social developments along these lines; supposing that in the decades since the emergence of the great modern styles society has itself begun to fragment in this way, each group coming to speak a curious private language of its own, each profession developing its private code or idiolect, and finally each individual coming to be a kind of linguistic island, separated from everyone else? But then in that case, the very possibility of any linguistic norm in terms of which one could ridicule private languages and idiosyncratic styles would vanish, and we would have nothing but stylistic diversity and heterogeneity.

That is the moment at which pastiche appears and parody has become impossible. Pastiche is, like parody, the imitation of a peculiar or unique style, the wearing of a stylistic mask, speech in a dead language: but it is a neutral practice of such mimicry, without parody's ulterior motive, without the satirical impulse, without laughter, without that still latent feeling that there exists something *normal* compared to which what is being imitated is rather comic. Pastiche is blank parody, parody that has lost its sense of humour: pastiche is to parody what that curious thing, the modern practice of a kind of blank irony, is to what Wayne Booth calls the stable and comic ironies of, say, the eighteenth century.

The death of the subject

But now we need to introduce a new piece into this puzzle, which may help to explain why classical modernism is a thing of the past and why postmodernism should have taken its place. This new component is what is generally called the 'death of the subject' or, to say it in more conventional language, the end of individualism as such. The great modernisms were, as we have said, predicated on the invention of a personal, private style, as unmistakable as your fingerprints, as incomparable as your own body. But this means that the modernist aesthetic is in some way organically linked to the conception of a unique self and private identity, a unique personality and individuality, which can be expected to generate its own unique vision of the world and to forge its own unique, unmistakable style.

Yet today, from any number of distinct perspectives, the social theorists, the psychoanalysts, even the linguists, not to speak of those of us who work in the area of culture and cultural and formal change, are all exploring the notion that that kind of individualism and personal identity is a thing of the past; that the old individual or individualist subject is 'dead'; and that one might even describe the concept of the unique individual and the theoretical basis of individualism as ideological. There are in fact two positions on all this, one of which is more radical than the other. The first one is content to say: yes, once upon a time, in the classic age of competitive capitalism, in the heyday of the nuclear family and the emergence of the bourgeoisie as the hegemonic social class, there was such a thing as individualism, as individual subjects. But today, in the age of corporate capitalism, of the so-called organization man, of bureaucracies in business as well as in the state, of demographic explosion – today, that older bourgeois individual subject no longer exists.

Then there is a second position, the more radical of the two, what one might call the poststructuralist position. It adds: not only is the bourgeois individual subject a thing of the past, it is also a myth; it *never* really existed in the first place; there have never been autonomous subjects of that type. Rather, this construct is merely a philosophical and cultural mystification which sought to persuade people that they 'had' individual subjects and possessed this unique personal identity.

For our purposes, it is not particularly important to decide which of these positions is correct (or rather, which is more interesting and productive).

What we have to retain from all this is rather an aesthetic dilemma: because if the experience and the ideology of the unique self, an experience and ideology which informed the stylistic practice of classical modernism, is over and done with, then it is no longer clear what the artists and writers of the present period are supposed to be doing. What is clear is merely that the older models – Picasso, Proust, T.S. Eliot – do not work any more (or are positively harmful), since nobody has that kind of unique private world and style to express any longer. And this is perhaps not merely a 'psychological' matter: we also have to take into account the immense weight of seventy or eighty years of classical modernism itself. There is another sense in which the writers and artists of the present day will no longer be able to invent new styles and worlds – they've already been invented; only a limited number of combinations are possible; the unique ones have been thought of already. So the weight of the whole modernist aesthetic tradition – now dead – also 'weighs like a nightmare on the brains of the living', as Marx said in another context.

Hence, once again, pastiche: in a world in which stylistic innovation is no longer possible, all that is left is to imitate dead styles, to speak through the masks and with the voices of the styles in the imaginary museum. But this means that contemporary or postmodernist art is going to be about art itself in a new kind of way; even more, it means that one of its essential messages will involve the necessary failure of art and the aesthetic, the failure of the new, the imprisonment in the past.

The nostalgia mode

As this may seem very abstract, I want to give a few examples, one of which is so omnipresent that we rarely link it with the kinds of developments in high art discussed here. This particular practice of pastiche is not high-cultural but very much within mass culture, and it is generally known as the 'nostalgia film' (what the French neatly call *la mode rétro* – retrospective styling). We must conceive of this category in the broadest way: narrowly, no doubt, it consists merely of films about the past and about specific generational moments of that past. Thus, one of the inaugural films in this new 'genre' (if that's what it is) was Lucas's *American Graffiti*, which in 1973 set out to recapture all the atmosphere and stylistic peculiarities of the 1950s United States, the United States of the Eisenhower era. Polanski's great film *Chinatown* does something similar for the 1930s, as does Bertolucci's *The Conformist* for the Italian and European context of the same period, the fascist era in Italy; and so forth. We could go on listing these films for some time: why call them pastiche? Are they not rather work in the more traditional genre known as the historical film – work which can more simply be theorized by extrapolating that other well-known form which is the historical novel?

I have my reasons for thinking that we need new categories for such films. But let me first add some anomalies: supposing I suggested that *Star Wars* is also a nostalgia film. What could that mean? I presume we can agree that this is not a historical film about our own intergalactic past. Let me put it somewhat differently: one of the most important cultural experiences of the generations that grew up from the 1930s to the 1950s was the Saturday afternoon serial of the Buck Rogers type – alien villains, true American heroes, heroines in distress, the death ray or the doomsday box, and the cliffhanger at the end whose miraculous resolution was to be witnessed next Saturday afternoon. *Star Wars* reinvents this experience in the form of a pastiche: that is, there is no longer any point to a parody of such serials since they are long extinct. *Star Wars*, far from being a pointless satire of such now dead forms, satisfies a deep (might I even say repressed?) longing to experience them again: it is a complex object in which on some first level children and adolescents can take the adventures straight, while the adult public is able to gratify a deeper and more properly nostalgic desire to return to that older period and to live its strange old aesthetic artifacts through once again. This film is thus *metonymically* a historical or nostalgia film: unlike *American Graffiti*, it does not reinvent a picture of the past in its lived totality; rather, by reinventing the feel and shape of characteristic art objects of an older period (the serials), it seeks to reawaken a sense of the past associated with those objects. *Raiders of the Lost Ark*, meanwhile, occupies an intermediary position here: on some level it is *about* the 1930s and 1940s, but in reality it too conveys that period metonymically through its own characteristic adventure stories (which are no longer ours).

Now let me discuss another interesting anomaly which may take us further towards understanding nostalgia film in particular and pastiche generally. This one involves a recent film called *Body Heat*, which, as has abundantly been pointed out by the critics, is a kind of distant remake of *The Postman Always Rings Twice* or *Double Indemnity*. (The allusive and elusive plagiarism of older plots is, of course, also a feature of pastiche.) Now *Body Heat* is technically not a nostalgia film, since it takes place in a contemporary setting, in a little Florida village near Miami. On the other hand, this technical contemporaneity is most ambiguous indeed: the credits – always our first cue – are lettered and scripted in a 1930s Art-Deco style which cannot but trigger nostalgic reactions (first to *Chinatown*, no doubt, and then beyond it to some more historical referent). Then the very style of the hero himself is ambiguous: William Hurt is a new star but has nothing of the distinctive style of the preceding generation of male superstars like Steve McQueen or even Jack Nicholson, or rather, his persona here is a kind of mix of their characteristics with an older role of the type generally associated with Clark Gable. So here too there is a faintly archaic feel to all this. The spectator begins to wonder why this story, which could have been situated anywhere, is set in a small Florida town, in spite of its contemporary reference. One begins to realize after a while that the small town setting has a crucial strategic function: it allows the film to do without most of the signals and references which we might associate with the contemporary world, with consumer society – the appliances and artifacts, the high rises, the object world of late capitalism. Technically, then, its objects (its cars, for instance) are 1980s products, but everything in the film conspires to blur that immediate contemporary reference and to make it possible to receive this too as nostalgia work – as a narrative set in some indefinable nostalgic past, an eternal 1930s, say, beyond history. It seems to me exceedingly symptomatic to find the very style of nostalgia films invading and colonizing even those movies today which have contemporary settings: as though, for some reason, we were unable today to focus our own present, as though we have become incapable of achieving aesthetic representations of our own current experience. But if that is so, then it is a terrible indictment of consumer capitalism itself – or, at the very least, an alarming and pathological symptom of a society that has become incapable of dealing with time and history.

So now we come back to the question of why nostalgia film or pastiche is to be considered different from the older historical novel or film. (I should also include in this discussion the major literary example of all this, to my mind: the novels of E.L. Doctorow – *Ragtime*, with its turn-of-the-century atmosphere, and *Loon Lake*, for the most part about our 1930s. But these are, in my opinion, historical novels in appearance only. Doctorow is a serious artist and one of the few genuinely left or radical novelists at work today. It is no disservice to him, however, to suggest that his narratives do not represent our historical past so much as they represent our ideas or cultural stereotypes about that past.) Cultural production has been driven back inside the mind, within the monadic subject: it can no longer look directly out of its eyes at the real world for the referent but must, as in Plato's cave, trace its mental images of the world on its confining walls. If there is any realism left here, it is a 'realism' which springs from the shock of grasping that confinement and of realizing that, for whatever peculiar reasons, we seem condemned to seek the historical past through our own pop images and stereotypes about that past, which itself remains forever out of reach.

Postmodernism and the city

Now, before I try to offer a somewhat more positive conclusion, I want to sketch the analysis of a full-blown postmodern building – a work which is in many ways uncharacteristic of that postmodern architecture whose principal names are Robert Venturi, Charles Moore, Michael Graves, and more recently Frank Gehry, but which to my mind offers some very striking lessons about the originality of postmodernist space. Let me amplify the figure which has run through the preceding remarks, and make it even more explicit: I am proposing the notion that we are here in the presence of something like a mutation in built space itself. My implication is that we ourselves, the human subjects who happen into this new space, have not kept pace with that evolution; there has been a mutation in the object, unaccompanied as yet by any equivalent mutation in the subject; we do not yet possess the perceptual equipment to match this new hyperspace, as I will call it, in part because our perceptual habits were formed in that older kind of space I have called the space of high modernism. The newer architecture therefore – like many of the other cultural products I have evoked in the preceding remarks – stands as something like an imperative to grow new organs to expand our sensorium and our body to some new, as yet unimaginable, perhaps ultimately impossible, dimensions.

The Bonaventure Hotel

The building whose features I will very rapidly enumerate in the next few moments is the Bonaventure Hotel, built in the new Los Angeles downtown by the architect and developer John Portman, whose other works include the various Hyatt Regencies, the Peachtree Center in Atlanta, and the Renaissance Center in Detroit. I have mentioned the populist aspect of the rhetorical defence of postmodernism against the elite (and utopian) austerities of the great architectural modernisms: it is gently affirmed, in other words, that these newer buildings are popular works on the one hand; and that they respect the vernacular of the American city fabric on the other, that is to say, that they no longer attempt, as did the masterworks and monuments of high modernism, to insert a different, a distinct, an elevated, a new utopian language into the tawdry and commercial sign-system of the surrounding city, but rather, on the contrary, seek to speak that very language, using its lexicon and syntax as that has been emblematically 'learned from Las Vegas'.

On the first of these counts, Portman's Bonaventure fully confirms the claim: it is a popular building, visited with enthusiasm by locals and tourists alike (although Portman's other buildings are even more successful in this respect). The populist insertion into the city fabric is, however, another matter, and it is with this that we will begin. There are three entrances to the Bonaventure, one from Figueroa, and the other two by way of elevated gardens on the other side of the hotel, which is built into the remaining slope of the former Beacon Hill. None of these is anything like the old hotel marquee, or the monumental *porte-cochère* with which the sumptuous buildings of yesteryear were wont to stage your passage from city street to the older interior. The entryways of the Bonaventure are as it were lateral and rather backdoor affairs: the gardens in the back admit you to the sixth floor of the towers, and even there you must walk down one flight to find the elevator by which you gain access to the lobby. Meanwhile, what one is still tempted to think of as the front entry, on Figueroa, admits you, baggage and all, onto the second-storey balcony, from which you must take an escalator down to the main registration desk. More about these elevators and escalators in a moment. What I first want to suggest about these curiously unmarked ways-in is that they seem to have been imposed by some new category of closure governing the inner space of the hotel itself (and this over and above the material constraints under which Portman had to work). I believe that, with a certain number of other characteristic postmodern buildings, such as the Beaubourg in Paris, or the Eaton Centre in Toronto, the Bonaventure aspires to being a total space, a complete world, a kind of miniature city (and I would want to add that to this new total space corresponds a new collective practice, a new mode in which individuals move and congregate, something like the practice of a new and historically original kind of hyper-crowd). In this sense, then, ideally the mini-city of Portman's Bonaventure ought not to have entrances at all, since the entryway is always the seam that links the building to the rest of the city that surrounds it: for it does not wish to be a part of the city, but rather its equivalent and its replacement or substitute. That is, however, obviously not possible or practical, whence the deliberate downplaying and reduction of the entrance function to its bare minimum. But this disjunction from the surrounding city is very different from that of the great monuments of the International Style: there, the act of disjunction was violent, visible, and had a very real symbolic significance – as in Le Corbusier's great *pilotis* whose gesture radically separates the new utopian space of the modern from the degraded and fallen city fabric which it thereby explicitly repudiates (although the gamble of the modern was that this new utopian space, in the virulence of its Novum, would fan out and transform that eventually by the power of its new spatial language). The Bonaventure, however, is content to 'let the fallen city fabric continue to be in its being' (to parody Heidegger); no further effects, no larger protopolitical utopian transformation, is either expected or desired.

This diagnosis is to my mind confirmed by the great reflective glass skin of the Bonaventure, whose function I will now interpret rather differently than I did a moment ago when I saw the phenomenon of reflexion generally as developing a thematics of reproductive technology (the two readings are, however, not incompatible). Now one would want rather to stress the way in which the glass skin repels the city outside; a repulsion for which we have analogies in those reflector sunglasses which make it impossible for your interlocutor to see your own eyes and thereby achieve a certain aggressivity towards and power over the Other. In a similar way, the glass skin achieves a peculiar and placeless dissociation of the Bonaventure from its neighbourhood: it is not even an exterior, inasmuch as when you seek to look at the hotel's outer walls you cannot see the hotel itself, but only the distorted images of everything that surrounds it.

Now I want to say a few words about escalators and elevators: given their very real pleasures in Portman, particularly these last, which the artist has termed 'gigantic kinetic sculptures' and which certainly account for much of the spectacle and the excitement of the hotel interior, particularly in the Hyatts, where like great Japanese lanterns or gondolas they ceaselessly rise and fall – given such a deliberate marking and foregrounding in their own right, I believe one has to see such 'people movers' (Portman's own term, adapted from Disney) as something a little more than mere functions and engineering components. We know in any case that recent architectural theory has begun to borrow from narrative analysis in other fields, and to attempt to see our physical trajectories through such buildings as virtual narratives or stories, as dynamic paths and narrative paradigms which we as visitors are asked to fulfil and to complete with our own bodies and movements. In the Bonaventure, however, we find a dialectical heightening of this process: it seems to me that the escalators and elevators here henceforth replace movement but also and above all designate themselves as new reflexive signs and emblems of movement proper (something which will become evident when we come to the whole question of what remains of older forms of movement in this building, most notably walking itself). Here the narrative stroll has been underscored, symbolized, reified and replaced by a transportation machine which becomes the allegorical signifier of that older promenade we are no longer allowed to conduct on our own: and this is a dialectical intensification of the autoreferentiality of all modern culture, which tends to turn upon itself and designate its own cultural production as its content.

I am more at a loss when it comes to conveying the thing itself, the experience of space you undergo when you step off such allegorical devices into the lobby or atrium, with its great central column, surrounded by a miniature lake, the whole positioned between the four symmetrical residential towers with their elevators, and surrounded by rising balconies capped by a kind of greenhouse roof at the sixth level. I am tempted to say that such space makes it impossible for us to use the language of volume or volumes any longer, since these last are impossible to seize. Hanging streamers indeed suffuse this empty space in such a way as to distract systematically and deliberately from whatever form it might be supposed to have; while a constant busyness gives the feeling that emptiness is here absolutely packed, that it is an element within which you yourself are immersed, without any of that distance that formerly enabled the perception of perspective or volume. You are in this hyperspace up to your eyes and your body; and if it seemed to you before that that suppression of depth I spoke of in postmodern painting or literature would necessarily be difficult to achieve in architecture itself, perhaps you may now be willing to see this bewildering immersion as the formal equivalent in the new medium.

Yet escalator and elevator are also in this context dialectical opposites; and we may suggest that the glorious movement of the elevator gondolas is also a dialectical compensation for this filled space of the atrium – it gives us the chance at a radically different, but complementary, spatial experience, that of rapidly shooting up through the ceiling and outside, along one of the four symmetrical towers, with the referent, Los Angeles itself, spread out breathtakingly and even alarmingly before us. But even this vertical movement is contained: the elevator lifts you to one of those revolving cocktail lounges, in which you, seated, are again passively rotated about and offered a contemplative spectacle of the city itself, now transformed into its own images by the glass windows through which you view it.

Let me quickly conclude all this by returning to the central space of the lobby itself (with the passing observation that the hotel rooms are visibly marginalized: the corridors in the residential sections are low-ceilinged and dark, most depressingly functional indeed: while one understands that the rooms are in the worst of taste). The descent is dramatic enough, plummeting back down through the roof to splash down in the lake; what happens when you get there is something else, which I can only try to characterize as milling confusion, something like the vengeance this space takes on those who still seek to walk through it. Given the absolute symmetry of the four towers, it is quite impossible to get your bearings in this lobby; recently, colour coding and directional signals have been added in a pitiful and revealing, rather desperate attempt to restore the coordinates of an older space. I will take as the most dramatic practical result of this spatial mutation the notorious dilemma of the shopkeepers on the various balconies: it has been obvious, since the very opening of the hotel in 1977, that nobody could ever find any of these stores, and even if you located the appropriate boutique, you would be most unlikely to be as fortunate a second time; as a consequence, the commercial tenants are in despair and all the merchandise is marked down to bargain prices. When you recall that Portman is a businessman as well as an architect, and a millionaire developer, an artist who is at one and the same time a capitalist in his own right, you cannot but feel that here too something of a 'return of the repressed' is involved.

So I come finally to my principal point here, that this latest mutation in space – postmodern hyperspace – has finally succeeded in transcending the capacities of the individual human body to locate itself, to organize its immediate surroundings perceptually, and cognitively to map its position in a mappable external world. And I have already suggested that this alarming disjunction point between the body and its built environment – which is to the initial bewilderment of the older modernism as the velocities of spacecraft are to those of the automobile – can itself stand as the symbol and analog of that even sharper dilemma which is the incapacity of our minds, at least at present, to map the great global multinational and decentred communicational network in which we find ourselves caught as individual subjects.

The new machine

But I am anxious that Portman's space not be perceived as something either exceptional or seemingly marginalized and leisure-specialized on the order of Disneyland. I would like in passing to juxtapose this complacent and entertaining (although bewildering) leisure-time space with its analog in a very different area, namely the space of postmodern warfare, in particular as Michael Herr evokes it in his great book on the experience of Vietnam, called *Dispatches*. The extraordinary linguistic innovations of this work may still be considered postmodernism, in the eclectic way in which its language impersonally fuses a whole range of contemporary collective idiolects, most notably rock language and black language: but the fusion is dictated by problems of content. This first terrible postmodernist war cannot be told in any of the traditional paradigms of the war novel or movie – indeed that breakdown of all previous narrative paradigms is, along with the breakdown of any shared language through which a veteran might convey such experience, among the principal subjects of the book and may be said to open up the place of a whole new reflexivity. Benjamin's account of Baudelaire, and of the emergence of modernism from a new experience of city technology which transcends all the older habits of bodily perception, is both singularly relevant here, and singularly antiquated, in the light of this new and virtually unimaginable quantum leap in technological alienation:

> He was a moving-target-survivor subscriber, a true child of the war, because except for the rare times when you were pinned or stranded the system was geared to keep you mobile, if that was what you thought you wanted. As a technique for staying alive it seemed to make as much sense as anything, given naturally that you were there to begin with and wanted to see it close; it started out sound and straight but it formed a cone as it progressed, because the more you moved the more you saw, the more you saw the more besides death and mutilation you risked, and the more you risked of that the more you would have to let go of one day as a 'survivor'. Some of us moved around the war like crazy people until we couldn't see which way the run was taking us anymore,

only the war all over its surface with occasional, unexpected penetration. As long as we could have choppers like taxis it took real exhaustion or depression near shock or a dozen pipes of opium to keep us even apparently quiet, we'd still be running around inside our skins like something was after us, ha, ha, La Vida Loca. In the months after I got back the hundreds of helicopters I'd flown in begin to draw together until they'd formed a collective meta-chopper, and in my mind it was the sexiest thing going: saver–destroyer, provider–waster, right hand–left hand, nimble, fluent, canny and human; hot steel, grease, jungle-saturated canvas webbing, sweat cooling and warming up again, cassette rock and roll in one ear and door-gun fire in the other, fuel, heat, vitality and death, death itself, hardly an intruder.[2]

In this new machine, which does not, like the older modernist machinery of the locomotive or the airplane, represent motion, but which can only be represented *in motion*, something of the mystery of the new postmodernist space is concentrated.

The aesthetic of consumer society

Now I must try very rapidly in conclusion to characterize the relationship of cultural production of this kind to social life in this country today. This will also be the moment to address the principal objection to concepts of postmodernism of the type I have sketched here: namely that all the features we have enumerated are not new at all but abundantly characterized modernism proper or what I call high modernism. Was not Thomas Mann, after all, interested in the idea of pastiche, and are not certain chapters of *Ulysses* its most obvious realization? Can Flaubert, Mallarmé and Gertrude Stein not be included in an account of postmodernist temporality? What is so new about all of this? Do we really need the concept of *post*modernism?

One kind of answer to this question would raise the whole issue of periodization and of how a historian (literary or other) posits a radical break between two henceforth distinct periods. I must limit myself to the suggestion that radical breaks between periods do not generally involve complete changes of content but rather the restructuring of a certain number of elements already given: features that in an earlier period or system were subordinate now become dominant, and features that had been dominant again become secondary. In this sense, everything we have described here can be found in earlier periods and most notably within modernism proper: my point is that until the present day those things have been secondary or minor features of modernist art, marginal rather than central, and that we have something new when they become the central features of cultural production.

But I can argue this more concretely by turning to the relationship between cultural production and social life generally. The older or classical modernism was an opposition art; it emerged within the business society of the gilded age as scandalous and offensive to the middle-class public – ugly, dissonant, bohemian, sexually shocking. It was something to make fun of (when the police were not called in to seize the books or close the exhibitions): an offence to good taste and to common sense, or, as Freud and

Marcuse would have put it, a provocative challenge to the reigning reality-
and performance-principles of early twentieth-century middle-class society.
Modernism in general did not go well with over-stuffed Victorian furniture,
with Victorian moral taboos, or with the conventions of polite society. This
is to say that whatever the explicit political content of the great high
modernisms, the latter were always in some mostly implicit ways dangerous
and explosive, subversive within the established order.

   If then we suddenly return to the present day, we can measure the
immensity of the cultural changes that have taken place. Not only are Joyce
and Picasso no longer weird and repulsive, they have become classics and
now look rather realistic to us. Meanwhile, there is very little in either the
form or the content of contemporary art that contemporary society finds
intolerable and scandalous. The most offensive forms of this art – punk rock,
say, or what is called sexually explicit material – are all taken in stride by
society, and they are commercially successful, unlike the productions of the
older high modernism. But this means that even if contemporary art has all
the same formal features as the older modernism, it has still shifted its
position fundamentally within our culture. For one thing, commodity
production and in particular our clothing, furniture, buildings and other
artifacts are now intimately tied in with styling changes which derive from
artistic experimentation; our advertising, for example, is fed by
postmodernism in all the arts and inconceivable without it. For another, the
classics of high modernism are now part of the so-called canon and are
taught in schools and universities – which at once empties them of any of
their older subversive power. Indeed, one way of marking the break
between the periods and of dating the emergence of postmodernism is
precisely to be found there: in the moment (the early 1960s, one would think)
in which the position of high modernism and its dominant aesthetics
become established in the academy and are henceforth felt to be academic by
a whole new generation of poets, painters and musicians.

   But one can also come at the break from the other side, and describe it in
terms of periods of recent social life. As I have suggested, non-Marxists and
Marxists alike have come around to the general feeling that at some point
following World War II a new kind of society began to emerge (variously
described as postindustrial society, multinational capitalism, consumer
society, media society and so forth). New types of consumption; planned
obsolescence; an ever more rapid rhythm of fashion and styling changes; the
penetration of advertising, television and the media generally to a hitherto
unparalleled degree throughout society; the replacement of the old tension
between city and country, centre and province, by the suburb and by
universal standardization; the growth of the great networks of super-
highways and the arrival of automobile culture – these are some of the
features which would seem to mark a radical break with that older prewar
society in which high modernism was still an underground force.

   I believe that the emergence of postmodernism is closely related to the
emergence of this new moment of late, consumer or multinational
capitalism. I believe also that its formal features in many ways express the
deeper logic of that particular social system. I will only be able, however, to
show this for one major theme: namely the disappearance of a sense of

history, the way in which our entire contemporary social system has little by little begun to lose its capacity to retain its own past, has begun to live in a perpetual present and in a perpetual change that obliterates traditions of the kind which all earlier social formations have had in one way or another to preserve. Think only of the media exhaustion of news: of how Nixon and, even more so, Kennedy are figures from a now distant past. One is tempted to say that the very function of the news media is to relegate such recent historical experiences as rapidly as possible into the past. The informational function of the media would thus be to help us forget, to serve as the very agents and mechanisms for our historical amnesia.

But in that case the two features of postmodernism on which I have dwelt here – the transformation of reality into images, the fragmentation of time into a series of perpetual presents – are both extraordinarily consonant with this process. My own conclusion here must take the form of a question about the critical value of the newer art. There is some agreement that the older mechanism functioned against its society in ways which are variously described as critical, negative, contestatory, subversive, oppositional and the like. Can anything of the sort be affirmed about postmodernism and its social moment? We have seen that there is a way in which postmodernism replicates or reproduces – reinforces – the logic of consumer capitalism; the more significant question is whether there is also a way in which it resists that logic. But that is a question we must leave open.

Notes

1   The present text combines elements of two previously published essays: 'Postmodernism and consumer society', in *The anti-aesthetic*, Port Townsend, WA: Bay Press, 1983; and 'Postmodernism: the cultural logic of late capitalism', *New Left Review* no. 146 (July–August, 1984).
2   Michael Herr, *Dispatches*, New York: Knopf, 1977, 8–9.

19

Symbolic creativity

Paul Willis

From his *Common culture* (Open University Press, 1990).

The institutions and practices, genres and terms of high art are currently categories of exclusion more than of inclusion. They have no real connection with most young people or their lives. They may encourage some artistic specializations but they certainly discourage much wider and more general symbolic creativity. The official existence of the 'arts' in institutions seems to exhaust everything else of its artistic contents. If some things count as 'art', the rest must be 'non-art'. Because 'art' is in the 'art gallery', it can't therefore be anywhere else. It is that which is special and heightened, not ordinary and everyday.

The arts establishment, by and large, has done little to dispel these assumptions. It prefers instead to utilize or even promote fears of cultural decline and debasement in order to strengthen its own claims for subsidy, institutional protection and privilege. In general the arts establishment connives to keep alive the myth of the special, creative individual artist holding out against passive mass consumerism, so helping to maintain a self-interested view of elite creativity.

Against this we insist that there is a vibrant symbolic life and symbolic creativity in everyday life, everyday activity and expression – even if it is sometimes invisible, looked down on or spurned. We don't want to invent it or propose it. We want to recognize it – literally recognize it. Most young people's lives are not involved with the arts and yet are actually full of expressions, signs and symbols through which individuals and groups seek creatively to establish their presence, identity and meaning. Young people are all the time expressing or attempting to express something about their actual or potential *cultural significance*. This is the realm of living common culture. Vulgar sometimes, perhaps. But also 'common' in being everywhere, resistant, hardy. Also 'common' in being shared, having things 'in common'. Where 'arts' exclude, 'culture' includes. 'Art' has been cut short of meanings, where 'culture' has not.

As Raymond Williams always insisted, culture is ordinary.[1] It is the extraordinary in the ordinary, which is extraordinary, which makes both into culture, common culture. We are thinking of the extraordinary symbolic creativity of the multitude of ways in which young people use, humanize, decorate and invest with meanings their common and immediate life spaces and social practices – personal styles and choice of clothes; selective and active use of music, TV, magazines; decoration of bedrooms; the rituals of romance and subcultural styles; the style, banter and drama of friendship groups; music-making and dance. Nor are these pursuits and activities trivial or inconsequential. In conditions of late modernization and the widespread crisis of cultural values they can be crucial to the creation and sustenance of individual and group identities, even to cultural survival of identity itself. There is work, even desperate work, in their play. [. . .]

Our project is to uncover, explore and present symbolic creativity in everyday life. Apart from merely asserting its importance and, we hope, demonstrating its existence, why do we insist on the visceral connection of symbolic creativity to the everyday? At bottom, what anchors it?

We argue that symbolic creativity is not only part of everyday human activity, but also a necessary part. This is because it is an integral part of *necessary work* – that which has to be done every day, that which is not extra but essential to ensure the daily production and reproduction of human existence. It is this which actually guarantees and locks in the relevance of symbolic creativity. It is this which underlies claims that the real roots of art lie in the everyday. But of what kind of necessary work do we speak? What is the basis for including symbolic creativity in it?

Necessary work is taken usually to designate the application of human capacities through the action of tools on raw materials to produce goods and services, usually through wage labour, to satisfy physical human needs. [. . .]

But there is another kind of humanly necessary work – often unrecognized but equally necessary – *symbolic work*. This is the application of human capacities to and through, on and with symbolic resources and raw materials (collections of signs and symbols – for instance, the language as we inherit it as well as texts, songs, films, images and artefacts of all kinds) to produce meanings. This is broader than, logically prior to and a condition of material production, but its 'necessariness' has been forgotten.

Necessary symbolic work is necessary simply because humans are communicating as well as producing beings. Perhaps they are communicative before they are productive. Whilst all may not be productive, all are communicative. *All*. This is our species distinction. Nor is this a merely formal or physiological property that might lie unused in some. Only through its exercise does communication exist and all of us communicate. This is how we manifest and produce the social and dynamic nature of our humanity.

We argue that necessary symbolic work is spread across the whole of life. It is a condition of it, and of our daily humanity. Those who stress the separateness, the sublime and quintessential in 'art' have actually assumed and encouraged a mindlessly vulgar, materialist view of everyday life. They counterpose this to their view of 'the imaginative'. They thereby view daily life as a cultural desert. The imagined symbolic deficit of everyday life is then, in its turn, to be repaired by recourse to a free-floating 'imaginative realm', to 'useless things', to 'art for art's sake', to the 'socially redundant'. But this is not only circular, it's incoherent. It's like trying to make time go faster by speeding up clocks. 'Art' is taken as the *only* field of qualitative symbolic activity, the one-per-cent transcendental value that preserves humanity. As daily life is drained of its symbolic work, 'art' is grotesquely bloated till its pores leak pure imagination. And only from 'art' can come a cultural mission into the humdrum, a doomed attempt to save the masses. Again 'art' produces culture. Symbolic work starts, not ends, in separate artefacts. The imaginative is self-validating!

We insist, against this, that imagination is not extra to daily life, something to be supplied from disembodied 'art'. It is part of the necessariness of everyday symbolic and communicative work. If declared redundant here, it will certainly not be welcomed back in the finer robes of 'art'.

This point cannot be overstated: where we can't now realistically acknowledge and promote the prospect of symbolic creativity in the sinews of necessary work as material production, we can and must recognize symbolic creativity in the sinews of necessary work as symbolic production.

What are some of the basic elements of necessary symbolic work?

First, language as a practice and symbolic resource. Language is the primary instrument that we use to communicate. It is the highest ordering of our sensuous impressions of the world, and the ultimate basis of our hope and capacity to control it. It enables interaction and solidarity with others and allows us to assess our impact on others and theirs on us. It therefore allows us to see ourselves as others.

Second, the active body as a practice and symbolic resource. The body is a site of somatic knowledge as well as a set of signs and symbols. It is the source of productive and communicative activity – signing, symbolizing, feeling.

Third, drama as a practice and symbolic resource. Communicative interaction with others is not automatic. We do not communicate from head to head through wires drilled into our skulls. Communication is achieved through roles, rituals and performances that we produce with others. Dramaturgical components of the symbolic include a variety of non-verbal communications, as well as sensuous cultural practices and communal solidarities. These include dancing, singing, joke-making, story-telling in dynamic settings and through performance.

Fourth and most importantly, symbolic creativity. Language, the body, dramatic forms are, in a way, both raw material and tools. Symbolic creativity is more fully the practice, the making – or their essence, what all practices have in common, what drives them. This is the production of *new* (however small the shift) meanings intrinsically attached to feeling, to energy, to excitement and psychic movement. This is the basis of confidence in dynamic human capacities as realities rather than as potentials – to be made conscious, through some concrete practice or active mediation, of the quality of human consciousness and how it can further be developed through the exercise and application of vital powers. Symbolic creativity can be seen as roughly equivalent to what an all-embracing and inclusive notion of the living arts might include (counterposed, of course, to the current exclusions of 'art'). Symbolic creativity may be individual and/or collective. It transforms what is provided and helps to produce specific forms of human identity and capacity. Being human – human be-ing-ness – means to be creative in the sense of remaking the world for ourselves as we make and find our own place and identity.

What exactly is produced by symbolic work and symbolic creativity?

First, and perhaps most important, they produce and reproduce individual identities – who and what 'I am' and could become. These may be diffuse, contradictory or decentred but they are produced through symbolic work including struggles to make meaning. Sensuous human communicative activities are also intersubjective. It is through knowing 'the other', including recognizing the self as an other for some others, that a self or selves can be known at all.

Second, symbolic work and creativity place identities in larger wholes. Identities do not stand alone above history, beyond history. They are related in time, place and things. It is symbolic work and creativity which realize the structured collectivity of individuals as well as their differences, which realize the materiality of context as well as the symbolism of self. This reminds us that locations and situations are not only *determinations* – they're also relations and resources to be discovered, explored and experienced. Memberships of race, class, gender, age and region are not only learned, they're lived and experimented with. This is so even if only by pushing up against the oppressive limits of established order and power.

Third and finally, symbolic work and especially creativity develop and affirm our active senses of our own vital capacities, the powers of the self and how they might be applied to the cultural world. This is what makes activity and identity *transitive* and specifically human. It is the dynamic and, therefore, clinching part of identity. It is the expectation of being able to apply power to the world to change it – however minutely. It is how, in the future, there is some human confidence that unities may be formed out of confusion, patterns out of irregularity. This is to be able to make judgements on who's a friend, who's an enemy, when to talk, when to hold silence, when to go, when to stop. But it's also associated with, and helps to form, overall styles of thinking which promise to make most sense of the world for you. It's also a cultural sense of what symbolic forms – languages, images, musics, haircuts, styles, clothes – 'work' most economically and creatively for the self. A culturally learned sense of the powers of the self is what makes the self in connecting it to others and to the world.

In many ways this is directly a question of cultural survival for many young people. Processes of symbolic work and symbolic creativity are very open, contested and unstable under conditions of late modernization. All young people experience one aspect or another of the contemporary 'social condition' of youth: unwilling economic dependence on parents and parental homes; uncertainty regarding future planning; powerlessness and lack of control over immediate circumstances of life; feelings of symbolic as well as material marginality to the main society; imposed institutional and ideological constructions of 'youth' which privilege certain readings and definitions of what young people should do, feel or be.[2]

Many of the traditional resources of, and inherited bases for, social meaning, membership, security and psychic certainty have lost their legitimacy for a good proportion of young people. There is no longer a sense of a 'whole culture' with allocated places and a shared, universal value system. Organized religion, the monarchy, trade unions, schools, public broadcasting, high culture and its intertwinings with public culture no longer supply ready values and models of duty and meaning to help structure the passage into settled adulthood. This is certainly partly a result of much commented-upon wider processes related to late modernization: secularization; consumerism; individualization; decollectivization; weakening respect for authority; new technologies of production and distribution. But it is also the case that these inherited traditions owe their still continuing and considerable power to the stakes they offer and seem to offer to the individual: some graspable identity within a set of relationships to other identities; some notion of citizenship within a larger whole which offers rights, satisfactions and loyalties as well as duty and submission. However, for many young people, made to feel marginal to this society, and without their own material stake in it, these merely symbolic stakes can seem very remote. These public traditions and meanings cannot make good what they offer, because they are undercut at another more basic level by unfulfilled expectations. These things are for parents and adults, for those who have an interest in and make up the civil body. For the young black British they're even more remote – they are for other people's parents. No longer can we be blind to the 'whiteness' of our major traditional public sources of identity.

Young working-class women may experience this youth condition in a special way. On the one hand, they are a target consumption group for many home commodities as well as for feminine-style-and-identity products. On the other hand, and with no money recompense and no real power in the consumer market, they may be making partial, early and exploited 'transitions' (often in an imperceptible extension of childhood domestic chores 'naturally' expected of girls but not of boys) into domestic roles of care and maintenance. This may seem to be a destination of sorts and a meaningful, useful activity when labour-market opportunities are scarce or difficult, but it can often be a specific unofficial training and subjective preparation for a lifetime's future of domestic drudgery coupled with job 'opportunities' only in part-time, low-paid, insecure, usually dead-end 'female' service work.

In general the arrival of a new and extended youth stage announces itself through the arrival of new institutional forms, and the adaption of old ones, aimed at its regulation. [In Britain,] the Youth Training Scheme, Employment Training, recent developments in youth work practice and drop-in centres for the unemployed, 'civil disorder' and community policing, changes in benefit rules for the under-25s, are all aimed in some way at controlling and filling the time of youth or at maintaining some promise (and discipline) for future transitions or at preventing and pre-empting alternative uses of time and capacity not devoted to preparation for future transitions.

There is a set of meanings and identities on offer here, highly restricted, applied and focussed. They are unlikely to replace the collapsing traditional ones. Indeed the tasks of symbolic work and creativity may include not only the attempt to retain identity in the face of the erosion of traditional value systems but also to forge new resistant, resilient and independent ones to survive in and find alternatives to the impoverished roles proffered by modern state bureaucracies and rationalized industry. [. . .]

As we have used the term so far, 'symbolic creativity' is an abstract concept designating a human capacity almost in general. It only exists, however, in contexts and, in particular, sensuous living processes. To identify the particular dynamic of symbolic activity and transformation in concrete named situations we propose the term 'grounded aesthetic'. This is the creative element in a process whereby meanings are attributed to symbols and practices and where symbols and practices are selected, reselected, highlighted and recomposed to resonate further appropriated and particularized meanings. Such dynamics are emotional as well as cognitive. There are as many aesthetics as there are grounds for them to operate in. Grounded aesthetics are the yeast of common culture.

We have deliberately used the term 'aesthetic' to show both the differences and the continuities of what we are trying to say with respect to the culture and arts debate. We are certainly concerned with what might be called principles of beauty, but as qualities of living symbolic activities rather than as qualities of things; as ordinary aspects of common culture, rather than as extraordinary aspects of uncommon culture. This is the sense of our clumsy but strictly accurate use of 'grounded'.

Our 'groundedness' for some will seem simply no more than the reckless destruction of flight, potting birds of paradise with sociological lead. For others the strange search for archaic aesthetics in grounded, everyday social relations will seem perverse, un-material and even mystical. We're happy to work on the assumption that 'the truth' lies somewhere, always provisionally, in between, that human be-ing-ness needs both air and earth and, in turn, makes possible our very idea of both.

Within the process of creating meanings from and within the use of symbols there may be a privileged role for texts and artefacts, but a grounded aesthetic can also be an element and a quality of everyday social relations. For instance, there is a dramaturgy and poetics of everyday life, of social presence, encounter and event. It may have become invisible in the routinized roles of adult life, but the young have much more time and they face each other with fewer or more fragile masks. They are the practical existentialists. They sometimes have no choice but to be, often too, absorbed in the moment and to ransack immediate experience for grounded aesthetics. For them some features of social life may not be about the regulation and containment of tension, but about its creation and increase. The 'aimless' life of groups and gangs may be about producing something from nothing, from 'doing nothing'. It may be about building tensions, shaping grounded aesthetics, orchestrating and shaping their release and further build-ups, so that a final 'catharsis' takes with it or changes other tensions and stresses inherent in the difficulties of their condition. Making a pattern in an induced swirl of events can produce strangely still centres of heightened awareness where time is held and unusual control and insight are possible. Grounded aesthetics are what lift and mark such moments.

Grounded aesthetics are the specifically creative and dynamic moments of a whole process of cultural life, of cultural birth and rebirth. To know the cultural world, our relationship to it, and ultimately to know ourselves, it is necessary not merely to be in it but to change – however minutely – that cultural world. This is a making specific – in relation to the social group or individual and its conditions of life – of the ways in which the received natural and social world is made human *to them* and made, to however small a degree (even if finally symbolic), controllable by them.

The possibility of such control is, of course, a collective principle for the possibility of political action on the largest scale. But it also has importance in the individual and collective awareness of the ability to control symbols and their cultural work. Grounded aesthetics produce an edge of meaning which not only reflects or repeats what exists, but transforms what exists – received expressions and appropriated symbols as well as what they represent or are made to represent in some identifiable way.

In so-called 'primitive art' and culture, for instance, a central theme is the naming of fundamental forces as gods and demons, thereby to reveal them, make them somehow knowable and therefore subject to human persuasion or placation. Of course, the urban industrial world is much more complex in its organization than are 'primitive' societies, and our apparent technical control over the threatening forces of nature seems greater and different in kind from theirs. What we seek to control, persuade or humanize through grounded aesthetics may be, in part, the force and expression of other human beings rather than forces emanating directly from nature – if you like the work of culture on culture.

A sense of or desire for timelessness and universality may be part of the impulse of a grounded aesthetic. The natural, obvious and immutable become particular historical constructions capable of variation. Subjectivity, taken to some degree out of the particular, is the force which can change it. But we may equally focus on the particular extracted from its context to make sense of the universal (Blake's grain of sand). Such psychic separation may be part of and/or a condition for some grounded aesthetics.

This is not to say that 'universals' really exist, certainly not internally in 'art-objects'. It is extraordinary how many universals – and contradictory ones – are claimed. Nevertheless, experienced universalism, as a movement out of or reperception of the particular, may well be a universal feature of heightened human awareness. This universalism is also a kind of awareness of the future in terms of what it is possible to become. This is part of heightened aspiration and the quest for wider significance and expanded identity. Universalism also gives some vision of the kind of socialness and human mutuality which might locate better and more expanded identities. Grounded aesthetics provide a motivation towards realizing different futures, and for being in touch with the self as a dynamic and creative force for bringing them about.

The received sense of the 'aesthetic' emphasizes the cerebral, abstract or sublimated quality of beauty. At times it seems to verge on the 'an-aesthetic' – the suppression of all senses. By contrast we see grounded aesthetics as working through the senses, through sensual heightening, through joy, pleasure and desire, through 'fun' and the 'festive'.

Concrete skills, concretely acquired rather than given through natural distinction or gift, are involved in the exercise of grounded aesthetics. 'Economy', and 'skill', for instance, enter into the grounded aesthetics of how the body is used as a medium of expression. A bodily grounded aesthetic enters into personal style and presence, dance and large areas of music and performance.

Although they are not things, grounded aesthetics certainly have uses. Such uses concern the energizing, developing and focussing of vital human powers on to the world in concrete and practical ways, but also in lived connected cognitive ways. This is in producing meanings, explanations and pay-offs in relation to concrete conditions and situations which seem more efficient or adequate than other proffered official or conventional meanings. Such 'useful' meanings may well have moral dimensions in providing collective and personal principles of action, co-operation, solidarity, distinction or resistance.

But 'useful' meanings can also be very private. There are perhaps especially private, symbolic and expressive therapies for the injuries of life. They 'work', not through their direct musical, literary or philosophical forms, but through the ways in which a grounded aesthetic produces meanings and understandings which were not there before. This may involve internal, imaginative and spiritual life. It may be in the realm of dream and fantasy, in the realm of heightened awareness of the constructedness and constructiveness of the self: alienation from obvious givens and values; the sense of a future made in the present changing the present; the fear of and fascination for the 'terra incognita' of the self. The usefulness of grounded aesthetics here may be in the holding and repairing, through some meaning creation and human control even in desperate seas, of the precariousness and fragmentedness of identity whose source of disturbance is outside, structural and beyond the practical scope of individuals to influence.

The crucial failure and danger of most cultural analysis are that dynamic, living grounded aesthetics are transformed and transferred into ontological properties of things, objects and artefacts which may represent and sustain aesthetics but which are, in fact, separate. The aesthetic effect is not *in* the text or artefact. It is part of the sensuous/emotive/cognitive creativities of human receivers, especially as they produce a stronger sense of emotional and cognitive identity as expanded capacity and power – even if only in the possibility of *future* recognitions of a similar kind. These creativities are not dependent on texts, but might be enabled by them.[3]

Surprising meanings and creativities can be generated from unpromising materials through grounded aesthetics. But texts and artefacts can also fail to mediate symbolic meanings for many reasons. Many supply only a narrow or inappropriate (for particular audiences) range of symbolic resources. Others encourage *reification* (literally, making into a thing) rather than the *mediation* and enablement of the possibility of grounded aesthetics. They move too quickly to supply a putative aesthetic. The receivers are simply sent a 'message', the meaning of which is pre-formed and pre-given. Signs are pinned succinctly and securely to their meanings. Human receivers are allowed no creative life of their own. The attempt to encapsulate directly an aesthetic militates against the possibility of its realization through a grounded aesthetic because the space for symbolic work of reception has been written out.

There are many ways in which the 'official arts' are removed from the possibility of a living symbolic *mediation*, even despite their possible symbolic richness and range. Most of them are out of their time and, even though this should enforce no veto on current *mediation*, the possibilities of a relevant structuring of symbolic interest are obviously limited. The institutions and practices which support 'art', however, seem designed to break any living links or possibilities of inducing a grounded aesthetic appropriation. 'Official' art equates aesthetics with artefacts. [. . .] The past as museum, Art as objects! The reverence and distance encouraged by formality, by institutions, and by the rites of liberal–humanist education as 'learning the code', kill dead, for the vast majority, what the internal life of signs might offer through grounded aesthetics to current sensibility and social practice. It is as hard for the 'official arts' to offer themselves to grounded aesthetics, as it is for grounded aesthetics to find recognition in the formal canons.

Commercial cultural commodities, conversely, offer no such impediments. At least cultural commodities – for their own bad reasons – are aimed at exchange and therefore at the possibility of use. In responding to, and attempting to exploit, current desires and needs, they are virtually guaranteed to offer some relevance to the tasks of current socially necessary symbolic work. In crucial senses, too, the modern media precisely 'mediate' in passing back to audiences, at least in the first instance, symbolic wholes they've taken from the streets, dance-halls and everyday life. Along with this they may also take, however imperfectly and crudely, a field of aesthetic tensions from daily life and from the play of grounded aesthetics there.

Of course, part of the same restless process is that cultural commodities, especially style and fashion 'top end down', may become subject overwhelmingly to reification, symbolic rationalization and the drastic reduction of the symbolic resources on offer. But consumers move too. When cultural commodities no longer offer symbolic mediation to grounded aesthetics, they fall 'out of fashion'. And in the cumulative symbolic landscape of consumer capitalism, dead packaged, reified grounded aesthetics are turned back into primary raw material for other processes of inevitable necessary symbolic work, with only the cultural theorists paranoiacally labouring back along their 'meta-symbolic' routes to 'golden age' symbolic homologies. This commercial process may, to say the least, be flawed, but it offers much more to grounded aesthetics than do the dead 'official arts'.

There may well be a better way, a better way to cultural emancipation than through this continuous instability and trust in the hidden – selfish, blind, grabbing – hand of the market. But 'official art' has not shown it yet. Commercial cultural commodities are all most people have. History may be progressing through its bad side. But it progresses. For all its manifest absurdities, the cultural market may open up the way *to* a better way. We have to make our conditions of life before we can dominate and use them. Cultural pessimism offers us only road-blocks.

Against postmodernist pessimism

The much commented upon incandescence – instability, changeability, luminosity – of cultural commodities ('all that is solid melts into air'[4]) is not some form of spontaneous combustion in commodities or another 'wonder' of capitalist production. It is not without or against meaning. This very incandescence passes through *necessary symbolic work*, changes and enables it. The incandescence is not simply a surface market quality. It produces, is driven by, and reproduces further forms and varieties for everyday symbolic work and creativity, some of which remain in the everyday and in common culture far longer than they do on the market.

The market is the source of a permanent and contradictory revolution in everyday culture which sweeps away old limits and dependencies. The markets' restless search to find and make new appetites raises, wholesale, the popular currency of symbolic aspiration. The currency may be debased and inflationary, but aspirations now circulate, just as do commodities. That circulation irrevocably makes or finds its own new worlds.

The style and media theorists – and terrorists – of the left and right see only market incandescence. They warn us of an immanent semiotic implosion of all that is real. They call us to a strange rejection of all that glitters and shimmers over the dark landscape, as if it *were* the landscape. But this usually metropolitan neurosis is nothing more than a bad case of idealist theorists' becoming the victims of their own nightmares. Mistaking their own metaphors for reality, they are hoist by their own semiotic petards. They are caught by – defined in professionally charting – the symbolic life on the surface of things without seeing, because not implicated in, the *necessary* everyday role of symbolic work, of how sense is made of structure and contradiction. They then coolly announce that modern culture is all surface in danger of collapse.

We must catch up with the movement of the real world. We must not be satisfied with a phantom history and demonology of its surface movement. Above all, self-deluding and complacent beliefs in aesthetic self-sufficiency and separateness, as sanctuaries in and against an imaginary history, must be firmly rejected.

Commerce and consumerism have helped to release a profane explosion of everyday symbolic life and activity. The genie of common culture is out of the bottle – let out by commercial carelessness. Not stuffing it back in, but seeing what wishes may be granted, should be the stuff of our imagination.

Notes

1 Raymond Williams, 'Culture is ordinary' (1958), reprinted at the beginning of this book and in his *Resources of hope*, Verso, 1988.
2 For a full account of the 'new social condition of youth' in relation to youth unemployment, see P. Willis *et al.*, *The youth review*, Avebury, 1988.
3 It is possible to get into a fine and tautological argument about the distinctions and relationships between 'invisible' internal subjective meanings and external 'visible' signs, symbols and practices. Though we insist that grounded aesthetics are a quality of living processes of meaning-making, not of things, this is not necessarily a wholly invisible internal process, though it can be. Words, signs, symbols and practices as 'things' in the world can certainly be part of the operation of particular grounded aesthetics for particular people. They are also taken in by and made sense of in the meaning-making of others. Also we

recognize and, in what follows, give many examples of the possibility of grounded aesthetics becoming properly externalized: formalized, made concrete and public in some way. We argue for this as a process which decisively blurs and questions the conventional distinctions between consumption and production. What's crucial here, though, is not the 'thing-like' qualities of such externalizations, but their capacity both to reflect *and promote* the grounded aesthetics of their producers and of others, individuals and collectivities.

Our internal subjective meanings will never transcend or make redundant the 'given-ness' of textuality, of things, of forms, of symbols. Indeed, these latter are intrinsic to the possibility and creativity of human meanings, but they should always be seen transitively for their role in the mediation of human meaning. They're humble, malleable things, not the kings and queens of expression and experience. In particular, we should understand that processes of human meaning-making and creativity are stopped dead when aesthetics are attached to things instead of to human activities.

4   The title of a book by Marshall Berman (New York: Simon and Schuster, 1982) which helped to launch the many faceted and pervasive postmodern debate.

20

The view from futures past

Mike Davis

From his *City of quartz: excavating the future in Los Angeles* (Verso, 1990).

The best place to view Los Angeles of the next millennium is from the ruins of its alternative future. Standing on the sturdy cobblestone foundations of the General Assembly Hall of the Socialist city of Llano del Rio – Open Shop Los Angeles's utopian antipode – you can sometimes watch the Space Shuttle in its elegant final descent towards Rogers Dry Lake. Dimly on the horizon are the giant sheds of Air Force Plant 42 where Stealth Bombers (each costing the equivalent of 10 000 public housing units) and other, still top secret, hot rods of the apocalypse are assembled. Closer at hand, across a few miles of creosote and burro bush, and the occasional grove of that astonishing yucca, the Joshua tree, is the advance guard of approaching suburbia, tract homes on point.

The desert around Llano has been prepared like a virgin bride for its eventual union with the Metropolis: hundreds of square miles of vacant space engridded to accept the future millions, with strange, prophetic street signs marking phantom intersections like '250th Street and Avenue K'. Even the eerie trough of the San Andreas Fault, just south of Llano over a foreboding escarpment, is being gingerly surveyed for designer home sites. Nuptial music is provided by the daily commotion of ten thousand vehicles hurtling past Llano on 'Pearblossom Highway' – the deadliest stretch of two-lane blacktop in California.

When Llano's original colonists, eight youngsters from the Young Peoples' Socialist League (YPSL), first arrived at the 'Plymouth Rock of the Cooperative Commonwealth' in 1914, this part of the high Mojave Desert, misnamed the Antelope Valley,[1] had a population of a few thousand ranchers, borax miners and railroad workers as well as some armed guards to protect the newly-built aqueduct from sabotage. Los Angeles was then a city of 300 000 (the population of the Antelope Valley today), and its urban edge, now visible from Llano, was in the new suburb of Hollywood, where D.W. Griffith and his cast of thousands were just finishing an epic romance of the Ku Klux Klan, *Birth of a Nation*. In their day-long drive from the Labor Temple in Downtown Los Angeles to Llano over ninety miles of rutted wagon road, the YPSLs in their red Model-T trucks passed by scores of billboards, planted amid beet fields and walnut orchards, advertising the impending subdivision of the San Fernando Valley (owned by the city's

217

richest men and annexed the following year as the culmination of the famous 'water conspiracy' fictionally celebrated in Polanski's *Chinatown*).

Three-quarters of a century later, forty thousand Antelope Valley commuters slither bumper-to-bumper each morning through Soledad Pass on their way to long-distance jobs in the smog-shrouded and overdeveloped San Fernando Valley. Briefly a Red Desert in the heyday of Llano (1914–18), the high Mojave for the last fifty years has been pre-eminently the Pentagon's playground. Patton's army trained here to meet Rommel (the ancient tank tracks are still visible), while Chuck Yeager first broke the sound barrier over the Antelope Valley in his Bell X-1 rocket plane. Under the 18 000-square-mile, ineffable blue dome of R-2508 – 'the most important airspace in the world' – ninety thousand military training sorties are still flown every year.

But as developable land has disappeared throughout the coastal plains and inland basins, and soaring land inflation has reduced access to new housing to less than 15 per cent of the population, the militarized desert has suddenly become the last frontier of the Southern California Dream. With home prices $100 000 cheaper than in the San Fernando Valley, the archetypical suburban fringe of the 1950s, the Antelope Valley has nearly doubled in population over the last decade, with another quarter million new arrivals expected by 2010. Eleven thousand new homes were started in 1988 alone. But since the Valley's economic base, not counting real-estate agents, consists almost entirely of embattled Cold War complexes – Edwards Air Force Base and Plant 42 (altogether about eighteen thousand civilian jobs) – most of the new homebuyers will simply swell the morning commute on the Antelope Valley Freeway.

The pattern of urbanization here is what design critic Peter Plagens once called the 'ecology of evil'.[2] Developers don't grow homes in the desert – this isn't Marrakesh or even Tucson – they just clear, grade and pave, hook up some pipes to the local artificial river (the federally subsidized California Aqueduct), build a security wall and plug in the 'product'. With generations of experience in uprooting the citrus gardens of Orange County and the San Fernando Valley, the developers – ten or twelve major firms, headquartered in places like Newport Beach and Beverly Hills – regard the desert as simply another abstraction of dirt and dollar signs. The region's major natural wonder, a Joshua tree forest containing individual specimens often thirty feet high and older than the Domesday Book, is being bulldozed into oblivion. Developers regard the magnificent Joshuas, unique to this desert, as large noxious weeds unsuited to the illusion of verdant homesteads. As the head of Harris Homes explained: 'It is a very bizarre tree. It is not a beautiful tree like the pine or something. Most people don't care about the Joshuas'.[3]

With such malice toward the landscape, it is not surprising that developers also refuse any nomenclatural concession to the desert. In promotional literature intended for homebuyers or Asian investors, they have started referring to the region euphemistically as 'North Los Angeles County'. Meanwhile they christen their little pastel pods of Chardonnay lifestyle, air-conditioned and over-watered, with scented brand-names like Fox Run, Mardi Gras, Bravo, Cambridge, Sunburst, New Horizons, and so on. The most hallucinatory are the gated communities manufactured by Kaufman and Broad, the homebuilders who were famous in the 1970s for exporting Hollywood ramblers to the suburbs of Paris. Now they have brought back France (or, rather, California homes in French drag) to the desert in fortified mini-*banlieus*, with lush lawns, Old World shrubs, fake mansard roofs and *nouveaux riches* titles like 'Chateau'.

But Kaufman and Broad only expose the underlying method in the apparent madness of L.A.'s urban desert. The discarded Joshua trees, the profligate wastage of water, the claustrophobic walls, and the ridiculous names are as much a polemic against incipient urbanism as they are an assault on an endangered wilderness. The *eutopic* (literally no-place) logic of their subdivisions, in sterilized sites stripped bare of nature and history, masterplanned only for privatized family consumption, evokes much of the past evolution of tract-home Southern California. But the developers are not just repackaging myth (the good life in the suburbs) for the next generation; they are also pandering to a new, burgeoning fear of the city.

Social anxiety, as traditional urban sociology likes to remind us, is just maladjustment to change. But who has anticipated, or adjusted to, the scale of change in Southern California over the last fifteen years? Stretching now from the country-club homes of Santa Barbara to the shanty *colonias* of Ensenada, to the edge of Llano in the high desert and of the Coachella Valley in the low, with a built-up surface area nearly the size of Ireland and a GNP bigger than India's – the urban galaxy dominated by Los Angeles is the fastest growing metropolis in the advanced industrial world. Its current population of fifteen million, encompassing six counties and a corner of Baja California, and clustered around two super-cores (Los Angeles and San Diego–Tijuana) and a dozen major, expanding metro-centres, is predicted to increase by another seven or eight million over the next generation. The overwhelming majority of these new inhabitants will be non-Anglos, further tipping the ethnic balance away from WASP hegemony toward the polyethnic diversity of the next century. (Anglos became a minority in the city and county of Los Angeles during the 1980s, as they will become in the state before 2010.)[4]

Social polarization has increased almost as rapidly as population. A recent survey of Los Angeles household income trends in the 1980s suggests that affluence (incomes of $50 000 plus) has almost tripled (from 9 per cent to 26 per cent) while poverty ($15 000 and under) has increased by a third (from 30 per cent to 40 per cent); the middle range, as widely predicted, has collapsed by half (from 61 per cent to 32 per cent).[5] At the same time the worst popular fears of a generation ago about the consequences of market-driven overdevelopment have punctually come true. Decades of systematic underinvestment in housing and urban infrastructure, combined with grotesque subsidies for speculators, permissive zoning for commercial development, the absence of effective regional planning, and ludicrously low property taxes for the wealthy have ensured an erosion of the quality of life for the middle classes in older suburbs as well as for the inner-city poor.

Ironically the Antelope Valley is both a sanctuary from this maelstrom of growth and crisis, and one of its fastest growing epicentres. In the desperate reassurance of their gated subdivisions, the new commuter population attempts to recover the lost Eden of 1950s-style suburbia. Older Valley residents, on the other hand, are frantically trying to raise the gangplanks against this ex-urban exodus sponsored by their own pro-growth business and political elites. In their increasingly angry view, the landrush since 1984 has only brought traffic jams, smog, rising crime, job competition, noise, soil erosion, a water shortage and the attrition of a distinctively countrified lifestyle.

For the first time since the Socialists left the desert (in 1918 for their New Llano colony in Louisiana) there is wild talk of a 'total rural revolution'. The announcement of several new mega-projects – instant cities ranging from 8500 to 35 000 units, designed to be plugged into the Valley's waiting grid – have aroused unprecedented populist ire. On one recent occasion, the representative of the Ritter Ranch project in rustic Leone Valley was 'ambushed by an angry mob . . . screaming and bitching and threatening to kill [him]'. In the Valley's two incorporated municipalities of Lancaster (the international headquarters of the Flat Earth Society) and Palmdale (the fastest growing city in California for most of the 1980s), more than sixty different homeowners' associations have joined together to slow down urbanization, as well as to contest the state's plan for a new 2200-bed prison for Los Angeles drug and gang offenders in the Mira Loma area.[6]

Meanwhile the myth of a desert sanctuary was shattered shortly after New Year's Eve 1990 when a stray bullet from a gang member's gun killed a popular high-school athlete. Shortly afterwards, the trendy Quartz Hill area, advertised as the emergent 'Beverly Hills' of the desert, was wracked by a gun-battle between the local 5 Deuce Posse and some out-of-town Crips. The *grand peur* of L.A. street gangs suddenly swept the high desert. While sheriffs hunted fugitive teenagers with dogs – like escapees from a Georgia chain-gang – local businessmen formed the semi-vigilante Gangs Out Now (GON). Intimidated by official warnings that there were six hundred and fifty 'identified gang members' in the Valley, the local high school attempted to impose a draconian dress-code banning 'gang colours' (blue and red). Outraged students, in turn, protested in the streets.[7]

While the kids were 'doin' the right thing', the local NAACP was demanding an investigation of three suspicious killings of non-whites by sheriffs' deputies. In one case the deputies gunned down an unarmed Asian college student while in another a Black man accused of wielding a three-pronged garden tool was shot eight times. The most egregious incident, however, was the slaying of Betty Jean Aborn, a homeless middle-aged Black woman with a history of mental illness. Confronted by seven burly sheriffs after stealing an ice-cream from a convenience store, she supposedly brandished a butcher's knife. The response was an incredible volley of twenty-eight rounds, eighteen of which perforated her body.[8]

As the desert thus announced the arrival of the *fin de siècle* with a staggering overture of bulldozers and gunfire, some old-timers – contemplating the rapidly diminishing distance between the solitude of the Mojave and the gridlock of suburban life – began to wonder out loud whether there was any alternative to Los Angeles after all.

The May Pole

Class war and repression are said to have driven the Los Angeles Socialists into the desert. But they also came eagerly, wanting to taste the sweet fruit of cooperative labour in their own lifetime. As Job Harriman, who came within a hair's-breadth of being Los Angeles's first Socialist mayor in 1911, explained:

> It became apparent to me that a people would never abandon their means of livelihood, good or bad, capitalistic or otherwise, until other methods were developed which would promise advantages at least as good as those by which they were living.'

What Llano promised was a guaranteed $4 per day wage and a chance to 'show the world a trick they do not know, which is how to live without war or interest on money or rent on land or profiteering in any manner'.'

With the sponsorship not only of Harriman and the Socialist Party, but also of Chairman W.A. Engle of the Central Labor Council and Frank McMahon of the Bricklayers' Union, hundreds of landless farmers, unemployed labourers, blacklisted machinists, adventurous clerks, persecuted IWW soapbox orators, restless shopkeepers, and bright-eyed bohemians followed the YPSLs to where the snow-fed Rio del Llano (now Big Rock Creek) met the edge of the desert. Although they were 'democracy with the lid off . . . democracy rampant, belligerent, unrestricted', their enthusiastic labour transformed several thousand acres of the Mojave into a small Socialist civilization.[10] By 1916 their alfalfa fields and modern dairy, their pear orchards and vegetable gardens – all watered by a complex and efficient irrigation system – supplied the colony with 90 per cent of its own food (and fresh flowers as well). Meanwhile, dozens of small workshops cobbled shoes, canned fruit, laundered clothes, cut hair, repaired autos, and published the *Western Comrade*. There was even a Llano motion picture company and 'an ill-fated experiment in aviation (the homemade plane crashed).

In the spirit of Chautauqua as much as Marx, Llano was also one big Red School House. While babies (including Bella Lewitzky, the future modern dancer) played in the nursery, children (among them Gregory Ain, the future modern architect) attended Southern California's first Montessori school. The teenagers, meanwhile, had their own Kid Kolony (a model industrial school), and adults attended night classes or enjoyed the Mojave's largest library. One of the favourite evening pastimes, apart from dancing to the colony's notorious ragtime orchestra, was debating Alice Constance Austin's design for the Socialist City that Llano was to become.

Although influenced by contemporary City Beautiful and Garden City ideologies, Austin's drawings and models, as architectural historian Dolores Hayden has emphasized, were 'distinctively feminist and California'. Like Llano kid Gregory Ain's more modest 1940s plans for cooperative housing, Austin attempted to translate the specific cultural values and popular enthusiasms of Southern California into a planned and egalitarian social landscape. In the model that she presented to colonists on May Day 1916, Llano was depicted as a garden city of ten thousand people housed in graceful Craftsman apartments with private gardens but communal kitchens and laundries to liberate women from drudgery. The civic centre, as befitted a 'city of light', was composed of 'eight rectangular halls, like factories, with sides almost wholly of glass, leading to a glass-domed assembly hall'. She crowned this aesthetic of individual choice within a fabric of social solidarity with a quintessentially Southern California gesture: giving every household an automobile and constructing a ring road around the city that would double 'as a drag strip with stands for spectators on both sides'.[11]

If Austin's vision of thousands of patio apartments radiating from the Bonaventure Hotel-style Assembly Hall, surrounded by socially owned orchards, factories and a monumental drag strip sounds a bit far-fetched today, imagine what Llanoites would have made of a future composed of Kaufman and Broad *chateaux* ringed by mini-malls, prisons and Stealth Bomber plants. In any event, the nine hundred pioneers of the Socialist City would enjoy only one more triumphant May Day in the Mojave.

> The May Day festivities of 1917 commenced at nine o'clock in the morning with intra-community athletic events, including a Fat Women's Race. The entire group of colonists then formed a Grand Parade and marched to the hotel where the Liberty Program followed. The band played from a bunting-draped grandstand, the choral society sang appropriate revolutionary anthems like the 'Marseillaise', then moved into the Almond Grove for a barbecue dinner. After supper a group of young girls injected the English into the radical tradition by dancing about the May Pole. At 7:30 the dramatic club presented 'Mishaps of Minerva' with newly decorated scenery in the assembly hall. Dancing consumed the remainder of the evening.[12]

Despite an evident sense of humour, Llano began to fall apart in the later half of 1917. Plagued by internal feuding between the General Assembly and the so-called 'brush gang', the colony was assailed from the outside by creditors, draft boards, jealous neighbours, and the Los Angeles *Times*. After the loss of Llano's water rights in a lawsuit – a devastating blow to its irrigation infrastructure – Harriman and a minority of colonists relocated in 1918 to Louisiana, where a hard-scrabble New Llano (a pale shadow of the original) hung on until 1939. Within twenty-four hours of the colonists' departure, local ranchers ('who precariously represented capitalism in the wilderness') began to demolish its dormitories and workshops, evidently with the intention of erasing any trace of the red menace. But Llano's towering silo, cow byre, and the cobblestone foundation and twin fireplaces of its Assembly Hall, proved indestructible: as local patriotic fury subsided, they became romantic landmarks ascribed to increasingly mythic circumstances.

Now and then, a philosophical temperament, struggling with the huge paradox of Southern California, rediscovers Llano as the talisman of a future lost. Thus Aldous Huxley, who lived for a few years in the early 1940s in a former Llano ranch house overlooking the colony's cemetery, liked to meditate 'in the almost supernatural silence' on the fate of utopia. He ultimately came to the conclusion that the Socialist City was a 'pathetic little Ozymandias', doomed from the start by Harriman's 'Gladstone collar' and his 'Pickwickian' misunderstanding of human nature – whose history 'except in a purely negative way . . . is sadly uninstructive'.[13]

Llano's other occasional visitors, lacking Huxley's vedic cynicism, have generally been more charitable. After the debacle of 1960s–70s communitarianism (especially the deadly trail that led into the Guyanese jungle), the pear trees planted by this ragtime utopia seem a more impressive accomplishment. Moreover, as its most recent historians point out, Huxley grossly underestimated the negative impact of wartime xenophobia and the spleen of the Los Angeles *Times* upon Llano's viability. There but for fortune (and Harry Chandler), perhaps, would stand a brave red *kibbutz* in the Mojave today, canvassing votes for Jesse Jackson and protecting Joshuas from bulldozers.[14]

The developers' millennium?

But, then again, we do not stand at the gates of Socialism's New Jerusalem, but at the hard edge of the developers' millennium. Llano itself is owned by an absentee speculator in Chicago who awaits an offer he cannot refuse from Kaufman and Broad. Setting aside an apocalyptic awakening of the neighbouring San Andreas Fault, it is all too easy to envision Los Angeles reproducing itself endlessly across the desert with the assistance of pilfered water, cheap immigrant labour, Asian capital and desperate homebuyers willing to trade lifetimes on the freeway in exchange for $500 000 'dream homes' in the middle of Death Valley.

Is this the world-historic victory of Capitalism that everyone is talking about?

On May Day 1990 (the same day Gorbachev was booed by thousands of alienated Muscovites) I returned to the ruins of Llano del Rio to see if the walls would talk to me. Instead I found the Socialist City reinhabited by two twenty-year-old building labourers from El Salvador, camped out in the ruins of the old dairy and eager to talk with me in our mutually broken tongues. Like hobo heroes out of a Jack London novel, they had already tramped up and down California, but following a frontier of housing starts, not silver strikes or wheat harvests. Although they had yet to find work in Palmdale, they praised the clear desert sky, the easy hitchhiking and the relative scarcity of La Migra. When I observed that they were settled in the ruins of a *ciudad socialista*, one of them asked whether the 'rich people had come with planes and bombed them out'. No, I explained, the colony's credit had failed. They looked baffled and changed the subject.

We talked about the weather for a while, then I asked them what they thought about Los Angeles, a city without boundaries, which ate the desert, cut down the Joshua and the May Pole, and dreamt of becoming infinite. One of my new Llano *compañeros* said that L.A. already was everywhere. They had watched it every night in San Salvador, in endless dubbed reruns of *I Love Lucy* and *Starsky and Hutch*, a city where everyone was young and rich and drove new cars and saw themselves on television. After ten thousand daydreams like this, he had deserted the Salvadorean Army and hitchhiked two thousand five hundred miles to Tijuana. A year later he was standing at the corner of Alvarado and Seventh Streets in the MacArthur Park district near Downtown Los Angeles, along with all the rest of yearning, hardworking Central America. No one like him was rich or drove a new car – except for the coke dealers – and the police were as mean as back home. More importantly no one like him was on television; they were all invisible.

His friend laughed. 'If you were on TV you would just get deported anyway and have to pay some *coyote* in Tijuana $500 to sneak you back to L.A.'. He argued that it was better to stay out in the open whenever possible, preferably here in the desert, away from the centre. He compared L.A. and Mexico City (which he knew well) to volcanoes, spilling wreckage and desire in ever-widening circles over a denuded countryside. It is never wise, he averred, to live too near a volcano. 'The old gringo *socialistas* had the right idea.'

I agreed, even though I knew it was too late to move, or to refound Llano. Then, it was their turn to interrogate me. Why was I out here alone, among the ghosts of May Day? What did *I* think of Los Angeles? I tried to explain that I had just written a book. . . .

Notes

1 Despite the incautious claims of Lynne Foster in her recent Sierra Club guide · (*Adventuring in the California Desert*, San Francisco, 1987), there is absolutely no evidence that 'many thousands of pronghorn antelope roamed the area' in the nineteenth century. On the contrary, small numbers of pronghorn were introduced in the Space Age, partially to allow the Valley to live up to its name!

2 'Los Angeles: The ecology of evil'. *Artforum* December 1972.

3 Los Angeles *Times*, 3 January 1988; Antelope Valley *Press*, 29 October 1989.

4 For demographic projections, see Southern California Association of Governments (SCAG), *Growth Management Plan*, Los Angeles, February 1989. To the rather arbitrary five-country SCAG area I have added projections for San Diego and Tijuana.

5 County research quoted on KCET-TV's, 'A class by itself', May 1990.

6 Los Angeles *Business Journal*, 25 December 1989; *Press* 14 and 19 January 1990.

7 *Press* 17 and 19 January.

8 *Daily News* 4 June 1989. (It was months before the Los Angeles *Times* reported the Aborn murder in its main edition.)

9 Harriman quoted in Robert Hine, *California's utopian colonies*, San Marino, CA, 1953, p. 117; and Dolores Hayden, *Seven American utopias*, Cambridge, MA, 1976, 289–90.

10 Llano chronicler Ernest Wooster quoted in Nigey Lenon, Lionel Rolfe, and Paul Greenstein (eds), *Bread and hyacinths: Job Harriman and his political legacy*, unpublished manuscript, Los Angeles, 1988, p. 21.

11 Cf. Hayden, (1996) *Seven American utopias*, 300–1 (on Austin's design); and Sam Hall Kaplan, *L.A. lost and found*, New York, 1987, p. 137 (on Ain's attempts to design for cooperative living).

12 Hine (1953) *California's utopian colonies*, p. 127.

13 'Ozymandias, The utopia that failed', in *Tomorrow and tomorrow and tomorrow . . .*, New York, 1956, 84–102.

14 Of course I deliberately beg the question of the Joshuas ploughed away to build Llano (ominously they have never grown back), not to mention what would have come of Austin's car in every red garage or where the water for 10000 singing tomorrows would have been 'borrowed' from.

21

Fictions of Europe

Jan Nederveen Pieterse

From *Race and Class*, vol. 32, no. 3 (January–March 1991).

'European culture'

It is not difficult to find a definition of 'European culture'. For instance:

> What determines and characterises European culture? . . . Europe is formed by
> the . . . community of nations which are largely characterised by the inherited
> civilisation whose most important sources are: the Judaeo-Christian religion,
> the Greek-Hellenistic ideas in the fields of government, philosophy, arts and
> science, and finally, the Roman views concerning law.[1]

This is a definition so average that it is almost official. In fact, it is official,
because it is given by the Netherlands Ambassador for International
Cultural Cooperation, Mr M. Mourik. We are taken past the familiar stations
of Europe: Greece–Rome–Christianity. This is a well-known entity in the
United States also, where it is often referred to as 'Western civilisation',
which may be summed up as 'from Plato to Nato'.[2]

This is the usual façade of Europe, so familiar that it is boring. This is the Europe
that is now being resurrected in the discourses of the official magisters of culture.
The problem, however, is not just that it is boring. The problem is that, in addition to being chauvinistic, elitist, pernicious and alienating, it is wrong.

It is wrong as regards the origins of European culture; it is wrong in so
representing European culture that European regional cultures and
subcultures are overlooked; it is wrong in representing elite culture as
culture *tout court* and in denying popular culture; it is wrong in defining
European culture in terms of the past ('inherited civilization') and in totally
ignoring Europe's contemporary multicultural realities.

This old culture is presently being revived in the context of the 'new
Europe'. Many of the political and economic negotiations and virtually all of
the debate on culture focus on *Europe and the nations*. The usual questions are
whether the Europe of '1992' will be dominated by the largest national
European cultures, Germany and France. What about Britain? What about
the identities of the smaller European cultures? What about central Europe,
Mitteleuropa? Will European cultures be steamrollered into a continent-
wide pattern of uniformity, propelled by market forces and media magnates
and directives from a few Europe metropoles?

The continent that pioneered nationalism pioneers the transcendence of nationalism, and in this context these questions are very meaningful. Yet, this is essentially a discussion about 'Europe and Europe'. There is another question on the horizon which is both larger and potentially more incisive in its implications, and that is *Europe and the continents*. This is infrequently talked about, except in the context of decolonization and the critique of eurocentrism, topics which are not particularly high on the agenda.

We are living in a post-imperial Europe which still maintains an imperial culture. Official European culture, reproduced in declarations, textbooks, media programmes, continues to be the culture of imperial Europe.

Another issue is that Europe, from the point of view of the many migrants in Europe of non-European origin, is now a New World, yet its self-image, its dominant culture, is still that of an Old World – that is a world from which people emigrate.

Certain key experiences are missing from this new old European culture: the experience of decolonization, of migrations, post-imperial ('we are here because you were there') and otherwise, and of globalization.

Walk in any street of any European city and ask yourself – is this European culture'? Is this 'Greece–Rome and Judaeo-Christianity'? Ask contemporary citizens of Europe about their ancestors, their origins – how many of you hail from non-European worlds? Or, to use nineteenth-century racist language, how many of you are half-caste? How many of you were never represented in this elite European project in the first place – as members of the working class or living in the countryside, or in regional cultures such as the 'Celtic fringe'? What is being recycled as 'European culture' is nineteenth-century elite imperial myth-formation. Is it not high time then to open up the imperial fac[accent],ade of European culture, to place it under an X-ray and ask, what here is really Europe and what is not?

Fortress Europe

Europe 1992 means that, as internal borders become lower, the external borders become higher, both in terms of the 'Zollverein Europe' of the internal market and in terms of 'European identity'. Concretely, it refers to the plans for a 'European visum' and to the Schengen Accord, which is to regulate immigration and asylum on a European basis.

Each European country thereby assumes a double identity, national and as member of a United States of Europe, each a gateway towards, or a ramparts of, the European world. As the physical frontier with Africa and the Middle East, Mediterranean Europe occupies a special place in this constellation. There are writings on the wall.

Spain, Portugal and Greece have recently become immigration countries – now more people come from the south than leave for the north. Italy had already held this status for some time. Thus, the Italian and French patterns of racism and racial attacks on minorities of non-European origin, mainly from North and West Africa, may be becoming a Mediterranean pattern. Spanish sociologist Alberto Moncada speaks of 'Spain functioning as a southern European police over the human mass from the Maghreb and Latin America'.[3] In news reports, Greece and also Bulgaria are already talked about as 'frontline states with fundamentalist Islam'.

What is developing in these areas is a European Mexico syndrome – a border-zone where economic, political, cultural, religious and demographic differences accumulate to create a gap between worlds, a zone of confrontation. Like Hong Kong, Europe will, and indeed already does, face refugees, boat people, and police hunting for illegal foreigners.[4]

NATO is also shifting its sights towards the south.[5] With the Cold War past, this is where the 'new enemy' lurks. 'Islamic fundamentalism', poverty and high population growth are identified as the main problems in classified and not-so-classified documents. Over recent years, we have seen the enemy images shifting and new Hitlers paraded on the front pages – Arafat, Khadafi, Khomeini, Assad, and now Saddam Hussein.

Thus, Fortress Europe is becoming a reality. The situation is primarily identified as a security problem, although it is also, secondarily, acknowledged as an economic and humanitarian problem. Europe's historic frontier of confrontation with the world of Islam is being reactivated. The question of Europe and the south, Africa, Asia and Latin America, is acquiring new dimensions. We may sum up this set of problems as: *Europe and the continents*.

These problems also reflect on migrants of non-European origin within Europe, so they also run *through* Europe. We may sum up this question as: *Europe and the minorities*. Thus, the problems of Europe and the continents are reproduced locally throughout Europe, interacting with the problem of Europe and the minorities. Local frontiers, of status and neighbourhood, colour and education, intersect with global frontiers. How minorities of non-European origin are viewed is affected by how Europe views itself in relation to the continents.

The prospect is that of Europe as a fort, with the Straits of Gibraltar and the Bosphorus for moats, and parts of the Third World as hinterlands, optional labour reserves. Gradually, a discreet neo-Malthusianism is becoming a way of thinking about Africa in particular: famine and starvation as the means of re-establishing equilibrium between population and resources.

The inauguration of 'Europe 1992' will coincide with the 1992 Columbus celebrations in Spain and Portugal and the Americas – 500 years since the Old World spawned the New World, 500 years of modernization, 500 years to contemplate the paradoxes of progress. . . . In Spain and Portugal, this will be an occasion to erect monuments to commemorate the 'Discoveries' and to celebrate the Conquista, thereby reaffirming and reproducing in their claim to fâme the very dualism of the Americas, where Columbus Day is a day of celebration for Europeans and a day of mourning for native Americans.

European identity is no longer an imperial, expansionist identity in the old sense. The era of imperialism is past: the era of decolonization is past and Third Worldism is no longer *à la mode*. European chauvinism now is prosperous, complacent, aloof. Fortress Europe, in its cultural uniform, is not expansionist but critical.

Many 'progressives', intellectuals and left-wing people included, share this kind of definition of the situation. Europe is their castle. Europe is the fortress of their mind. And much as they identify with the Europe of the Enlightenment, they abhor 'Islamic fundamentalism', and, since 'Third Worldism' is out of fashion, they look down, if they look at all, on the poor in the Third World, and find shelter in a self-image of Europe as a world of modernity. The discourse of postmodernism, busy critiquing modernity, turns its back on the 'pre-modern' world.

This situation is an open door to the European Right, culture-baiting minorities as 'aliens'. This creates the danger of a new European consensus of exclusion, a right-to-centre political and cultural coalition that may turn Europe into a complacent shelter of conservatism – in the name of Enlightenment.

One of the European projects waiting in the wings is that of a Europe-wide coalition of right-wing parties, a continental chain of 'national fronts'. It is ironical to realize that, for all their 'national' posturing, several of these organizations are being funded and supported from foreign sources, ranging from American right-wing foundations to the Unification Church of Rev Moon.

The deconstruction of Europe

Rather than recycling the illusions of imperial Europe, we should address and welcome the multicultural realities and opportunities of post-imperial Europe. Recreating Europe in '1992' means to relocate Europe's place in world history, in terms of the real relationship between Europe and the continents and not according to the great walls of empire.

The familiar stations of Europe are: Greece–Rome–Christendom–Renaissance–Enlightenment–industrialization–colonialism. The two main definitions of European identity derived from this are, in shorthand, Christianity and the Enlightenment.

From Santiago de Compostella, Pope John Paul II calls out to a 'Christian Europe'. This historical field mattered to Catholic statesmen Schuman, Adenauer, de Gasperi, who came together for the Treaty of Rome in 1956. The notion of Christian Europe matters to Christian Democrats and to many on the Right, from Otto von Habsburg to Jean Marie le Pen.[6]

There is no question that the histories of Europe and Christianity are interwoven. Yet, indeed, there are many problems with defining European identity in terms of Christianity. What about the Renaissance, the humanists, the anticlericals, the Enlightenment? And what about the great schisms in Christianity – between Greek and Latin Christianity, between Constantinople and Rome, between Europe east and west, and between Roman Catholicism and Protestantism, between Europe south and north? Indeed, Christianity is Asian in origin, and on many medieval maps we find Jerusalem depicted as the centre of the world, an Asian site as the centre of the Christian world – this is the dominant depiction on *mappae mundi* from the seventh to the thirteenth centuries and occurs frequently on maps from 1200 to 1500.

Much more pervasive and more formidable as a definition of Europe is the legacy of the Renaissance/Enlightenment. The characteristic feature of the Europe of the Enlightenment, as Jack Lively has argued, is the Enlightenment itself: European identity was discovered 'in the modernity of Europe'.

> The European personality was distinct and its role was unique, not because its traditionally rooted society marked it out from other cultures, but because it had moved sufficiently far along a path of development to serve as an example for the rest of humanity. The emphasis was now on time rather than space, promise rather than achievement, the future rather than the past. . . . Moreover . . . the modernity of Europe consisted in the Enlightenment itself.[7]

Europe equals modernity, or the critical spirit, its attitude of self-criticism, its tolerance and openness to other views. From Kant to Raymond Aron, this is a recurrent theme.

It relates closely to another European topos: the 'autonomy of the spirit' as a European characteristic, the tension and friction between faith and reason, the aversion to dogma. This is Nietzsche's tradition of the free thinkers, the *libres penseurs*.

This, in turn, overlaps with a discourse which finds the specificity of Europe in the autonomy of its cities, hence the development of its burghers, its citizens and, over time, civil society.

Again we hear the echo of a classic theme: Europe as the land of liberty, as against Asia, the land of despotism and oppression – in a word, oriental despotism and occidental liberty. This is a thesis that harks back to the Greeks: to the east in Persia, despotism; to the north in Europe, the free barbarians; and in the middle, Greece, that is civilization.

These overtones – autonomy, liberty – still play a part in Europe's self-definition but drawn into the background since the experiences with Nazism, fascism, European totalitarianism. The keynote in the self-assessments of Europe remains that of modernity. That is essentially the Europe of the Enlightenment, also as the dapper antidote to totalitarian Europe.

This is the most prominent rhetoric of difference between Europe and non-European worlds, in particular, between Europe and the world of Islam – the common European interpretation of 'fundamentalist Islam' is as a revolt against modernity (that is, against Europe), a countermodernization and the International of '*Unvernunft*'.[8]

'Identity' implies a relationship to what is different and thus a statement of boundaries. Both these European identities – Christianity and the Enlightenment – are such statements of boundaries, border flags which serve as internal as much as external boundaries – protection from the 'barbarians' both within and outside the gates. They are projects rather than realities, mirrors of power and rhetorics of control.

European paradoxes

Why deconstruct Europe? It's not fair. It's hardly been constructed. Americans would say the same thing, why deconstruct Europe? We like Europe, it means a lot to us, it is the prototype of Disneyland.

It is true that European identity is weak. First, because Europeanism is recent. It dates, by and large, from after 1700. Before that, Christendom was the predominant identity. The humanists of the Renaissance looked towards Greece and Rome as the centres of culture. Moreover, until 1683 when the Turks stood before Vienna, Europe was still under threat from the east.

Second, European development has not known a single centre. There has been a continual shift of centres, and with the centre also the peripheries shifted. The Renaissance, the Enlightenment and French Revolution, industrialization and colonial expansion, unfolded in different parts of Europe and spread in different directions. There was never a centre which embodied European identity.

Third, from 1700, European development has taken place by means of single rival states. Already, from the sixteenth century, Europe existed in the form of a 'European balance of power', that is as a polycentric world. From 1700, the keynote of political development were the different monarchies, while from 1800, the keynote of development was *national* development.

Also, outward expansion was undertaken by single rival states. Europe's 'new imperialism' of the late nineteenth century and the scramble for Africa was a pre-emptive imperialism – both in concert with European competitors and aiming to outmanoeuvre them. This is one of the paradoxes of European imperialism: it implied and brought forth both European unity (as in the Berlin Conference on the division of Africa) and European divisions.

Another paradox. The backdrop to nineteenth-century European expansion in Asia and Africa was a concept of 'European civilization'. This was implied in the '*mission civilisatrice*', even if this was executed primarily by means of national missions. It correlated with racial thinking. 'European civilization' made for a certain affinity among Europeans of different countries even while they were rivals for overseas territory and influence. This European civilization, the bedrock of European superiority and arrogance, received a deadly blow with the First World War. The long conflict from 1914 to 1945 shook the foundations of Europe's overseas imperialism and ushered in the era of decolonization.

Then 'Europe' was born – born out of the contraction of empire: thrown back upon themselves the European nations began to discover each other. 'Europe' was born in the shadow of the superpowers, not as the world's Queen, as she had been in eurocentric iconography since the sixteenth century, but merely as a buffer zone between the superpowers. Now the superpowers themselves are waning and new centres are emerging.

Notes

1   M. Mourik, 'European cultural co-operation', in A. Rijksbaron, W.H. Roobol, M. Weisglas (eds.), *Europe from a cultural perspective: historiography and perceptions*, The Hague, 1987, p. 19.
2   Elissa McBride, 'Western civilisation: from Plato to Nato', *The Activist* no. 21 (summer 1988), p. 7.
3   Information Bulletin XIIth World Congress of Sociology, Madrid, July 1990, no. 1.
4   Plans are under way to 'manage' and control this problem zone. Spain, France, Italy and Portugal seek the establishment of a Conference for Security and

Cooperation in the Mediterraneañ, a 'Mediterranean Helsinki', modelled on the European Conference for Security and Cooperation. Already they have established a Forum for Regional Cooperation in the Mediterranean, together with Morocco, Algeria, Tunisia, Libya and Mauretania – five countries united in the Arab Maghreb Union (*Volksrant*, 4 August 1990).

5 Mariano Aguirre, 'Looking southwards', in Dan Smith (ed.), *European security in the 1990s*, London, 1989.
6 Although another section of the Right, notably GRECE in France, rather identifies with 'pagan Europe'.
7 Jack Lively, 'The Europe of the Enlightenment', *History of European ideas*, vol. I, no. 2, 1981, p. 93. 'Europe's distinction lay in its possessions of truths which, while applicable to all humanity, were not presently available to all humanity' (p. 98).
8 T. Meyer (ed.), *Fundamentalismus in der modernen Welt*, Frankfurt, 1989.

22

A global sense of place

Doreen Massey

From *Marxism Today* (June 1991).

This is an era – it is often said – when things are speeding up, and spreading out. Capital is going through a new phase of internationalization, especially in its financial parts. More people travel more frequently and for longer distances. Your clothes have probably been made in a range of countries from Latin America to South East Asia. Dinner consists of food shipped in from all over the world. And if you have a screen in your office, instead of opening a letter which – care of Her Majesty's Post Office – has taken some days to wend its way across the country, you now get interrupted by e-mail.

This view of the current age is one now frequently found in a wide range of books and journals. Much of what is written about space, place and postmodern times emphasizes a new phase in what Marx once called 'the annihilation of space by time'. The process is argued, or – more usually – asserted, to have gained a new momentum, to have reached a new stage. It is a phenomenon which has been called 'time-space-compression'. And the general acceptance that something of the sort is going on is marked by the almost obligatory use in the literature of terms and phrases such as speed-up, global village, overcoming spatial barriers, the disruption of horizons, and so forth.

One of the results of this is an increasing uncertainty about what we mean by 'places' and how we relate to them. How, in the face of all this movement and intermixing, can we retain any sense of a local place and its particularity? An (idealized) notion of an era when places were (supposedly) inhabited by coherent and homogeneous communities is set against the current fragmentation and disruption. The counterposition is anyway dubious, of course; 'place' and 'community' have only rarely been coterminous. But the occasional longing for such coherence is nonetheless a sign of the geographical fragmentation, the spatial disruption, of our times. And occasionally, too, it has been part of what has given rise to defensive and reactionary responses – certain forms of nationalism, sentimentalized recovering of sanitized 'heritages', and outright antagonism to newcomers and 'outsiders'. One of the effects of such responses is that place itself, the seeking after a sense of place, has come to be seen by some as necessarily reactionary.

But is that necessarily so? Can't we re-think our sense of place? Is it not possible for a sense of place to be progressive; not self-enclosing and defensive, but outward-looking? A sense of place which is adequate to this era of time-space-compression? To begin with, there are some questions to be asked about time-space-compression itself. Who is it that experiences it, and how? Do we all benefit and suffer from it in the same way?

For instance, to what extent does the currently popular characterization of time-space-compression represent very much a Western, colonizer's, view? The sense of dislocation which some feel at the sight of a once well-known local street now lined with a succession of cultural imports – the pizzeria, the kebab house, the branch of the Middle-Eastern bank – must have been felt for centuries, though from a very different point of view, by colonized peoples all over the world as they watched the importation, maybe even used the products, of, first, European colonization, maybe British (from new forms of transport to liver salts and custard powder), later US, as they learned to eat wheat instead of rice or corn, to drink Coca Cola, just as today we try out enchiladas.

Moreover, as well as querying the ethnocentricity of the idea of time-space-compression and its current acceleration, we also need to ask about its causes: what is it that determines our degrees of mobility, that influences the sense we have of space and place? Time-space-compression refers to movement and communication across space, to the geographical stretching-out of social relations, and to our experience of all this. The usual interpretation is that it results overwhelmingly from the actions of capital, and from its currently increasing internationalization. On this interpretation, then, it is time, space and money which make the world go round, and us go round (or not) the world. It is capitalism and its developments which are argued to determine our understanding and our experience of space.

But surely this is insufficient. Among the many other things which clearly influence that experience, there are, for instance, race and gender. The degree to which we can move between countries, or walk about the streets at night, or venture out of hotels in foreign cities, is not just influenced by 'capital'. Survey after survey has shown how women's mobility, for instance, is restricted – in a thousand different ways, from physical violence to being ogled at or made to feel quite simply 'out of place' – not by 'capital', but by men. Or, to take a more complicated example, Birkett, reviewing books on women adventurers and travellers in the nineteenth and twentieth centuries, suggests that 'it is far, far more demanding for a woman to wander now than ever before'.[1] The reasons she gives for this argument are a complex mix of colonialism, ex-colonialism, racism, changing gender-relations, and relative wealth. A simple resort to explanation in terms of 'money' or 'capital' alone could not begin to get to grips with the issue. The current speed-up may be strongly determined by economic forces, but it is not the economy alone which determines our experience of space and place. In other words, and put simply, there is a lot more determining how we experience space than what 'capital' gets up to.

What is more, of course, that last example indicated that 'time-space-compression' has not been happening for everyone in all spheres of activity. Birkett again, this time writing of the Pacific Ocean:

Jumbos have enabled Korean computer consultants to fly to Silicon Valley as if popping next door, and Singaporean entrepreneurs to reach Seattle in a day. The borders of the world's greatest ocean have been joined as never before. And Boeing has brought these people together. But what about those they fly over, on their islands five miles below? How has the mighty 747 brought them greater communion with those whose shores are washed by the same water? It hasn't, of course. Air travel might enable businessmen to buzz across the ocean, but the concurrent decline in shipping has only increased the isolation of many island communities. . . . Pitcairn, like many other Pacific islands, has never felt so far from its neighbours.[2]

In other words, and most broadly, time-space-compression needs differentiating socially. This is not just a moral or political point about inequality, although that would be sufficient reason to mention it; it is also a conceptual point.

Imagine for a moment that you are on a satellite, further out and beyond all actual satellites; you can see 'planet earth' from a distance and, rarely for someone with only peaceful intentions, you are equipped with the kind of technology which allows you to see the colours of people's eyes and the numbers on their numberplates. You can see all the movement and tune-in to all the communication that is going on. Furthest out are the satellites, then aeroplanes, the long haul between London and Tokyo and the hop from San Salvador to Guatemala City. Some of this is people moving, some of it is physical trade, some is media broadcasting. There are faxes, e-mail, film-distribution networks, financial flows and transactions. Look in closer and there are ships and trains, steam trains slogging laboriously up hills somewhere in Asia. Look in closer still and there are lorries and cars and buses, and on down further, somewhere in sub-Saharan Africa, there's a woman on foot who still spends hours a day collecting water.

Now, I want to make one simple point here, and that is about what one might call the *power-geometry* of it all; the power-geometry of time-space-compression. For different social groups, and different individuals, are placed in very distinct ways in relation to these flows and interconnections. This point concerns not merely the issue of who moves and who doesn't, although that is an important element of it; it is also about power in relation *to* the flows and the movement. Different social groups have distinct relationships to this anyway differentiated mobility: some people are more in charge of it than others; some initiate flows and movement, others don't; some are more on the receiving-end of it than others; some are effectively imprisoned by it.

In a sense at the end of all the spectra are those who are both doing the moving and the communicating and who are in some way in a position of control in relation to it – the jet-setters, the ones sending and receiving the faxes and the e-mail, holding the international conference calls, the ones distributing the films, controlling the news, organizing the investments and the international currency transactions. These are the groups who are really in a sense in charge of time-space-compression, who can really use it and turn it to advantage, whose power and influence it very definitely increases. On its more prosaic fringes this group probably includes a fair number of Western academics and journalists – those, in other words, who write most about it.

But there are also groups who are also doing a lot of physical moving, but who are not 'in charge' of the process in the same way at all. The refugees from El Salvador or Guatemala and the undocumented migrant workers from Michoacan in Mexico, crowding into Tijuana to make a perhaps fatal dash for it across the border into the US to grab a chance of a new life. Here the experience of movement, and indeed of a confusing plurality of cultures, is very different. And there are those from India, Pakistan, Bangladesh, the Caribbean, who come half way round the world only to get held up in an interrogation room at Heathrow.

Or – a different case again – there are those who are simply on the receiving end of time-space-compression. The pensioner in a bed-sit in any inner city in this country, eating British working-class-style fish and chips from a Chinese take-away, watching a US film on a Japanese television; and not daring to go out after dark. And anyway the public transport's been cut.

Or – one final example to illustrate a different kind of complexity – there are the people who live in the favelas of Rio, who know global football like the back of their hand, and have produced some of its players; who have contributed massively to global music, who gave us the samba and produced the lambada that everyone was dancing to last year in the clubs of Paris and London; and who have never, or hardly ever, been to downtown Rio. At one level they have been tremendous contributors to what we call time-space-compression; and at another level they are imprisoned in it.

This is, in other words, a highly complex social differentiation. There are differences in the degree of movement and communication, but also in the degree of control and of initiation. The ways in which people are placed within 'time-space-compression' are highly complicated and extremely varied.

But this in turn immediately raises questions of politics. If time-space-compression can be imagined in that more socially formed, socially evaluative and differentiated way, then there may be here the possibility of developing a politics of mobility and access. For it does seem that mobility and control over mobility both reflects and reinforces power. It is not simply a question of unequal distribution, that some people move more than others, and that some have more control than others. It is that the mobility and control of some groups can actively weaken other people. Differential mobility can weaken the leverage of the already weak. The time-space-compression of some groups can undermine the power of others.

This is well established and often noted in the relationship between capital and labour. Capital's ability to roam the world further strengthens it in relation to relatively immobile workers, enables it to play off the plant at Genk against the plant at Dagenham. It also strengthens its hand against struggling local economies the world over as they compete for the favour of some investment. The 747s that fly computer scientists across the Pacific are part of the reason for the greater isolation today of the island of Pitcairn. But also, every time someone uses a car, and thereby increases their personal mobility, they reduce both the social rationale and the financial viability of the public transport system – and thereby also potentially reduce the mobility of those who rely on that system. Every time you drive to that out-of-town shopping centre you contribute to the rising prices, even hasten the demise, of the corner shop. And the 'time-space-compression' which is involved in producing and reproducing the daily lives of the comfortably-off in First World societies – not just their own travel but the resources they draw on, from all over the world, to feed their lives – may entail environmental consequences, or hit constraints, which will limit the lives of others before their own. We need to ask, in other words, whether our relative mobility and power over mobility and communication entrenches the spatial imprisonment of other groups.

But this way of thinking about time-space-compression also returns us to the question of place and a sense of place. How, in the context of all these socially-varied time-space-changes do we think about 'places'? In an era when, it is argued, 'local communities' seem to be increasingly broken up, when you can go abroad and find the same shops, the same music as at home, or eat your favourite foreign-holiday food at a restaurant down the road – and when everyone has a different experience of all this – how then do we think about 'locality'?

Many of those who write about time-space-compression emphasize the insecurity and unsettling impact of its effects, the feelings of vulnerability which it can produce. Some therefore go on from this to argue that, in the middle of all this flux, people desperately need a bit of peace and quiet – and that a strong sense of place, of locality, can form one kind of refuge from the hubbub. So the search after the 'real' meanings of places, the unearthing of heritages and so forth, is interpreted as being, in part, a response to desire for fixity and for security of identity in the middle of all the movement and change. A 'sense of place', of rootedness, can provide – in this form and on this interpretation – stability and a source of unproblematical identity. In that guise, however, place and the spatially local are then rejected by many progressive people as almost necessarily reactionary. They are interpreted as an evasion; as a retreat from the (actually unavoidable) dynamic and change of 'real life', which is what we must seize if we are to change things for the better. On this reading, place and locality are foci for a form of romanticized escapism from the real business of the world. While 'time' is equated with movement and progress, 'space'/'place' is equated with stasis and reaction.

There are some serious inadequacies in this argument. There is the question of why it is assumed that time-space-compression will produce insecurity. There is the need to face up to – rather than simply deny – people's need for attachment of some sort, whether through place or anything else. Nonetheless, it is certainly the case that there is indeed at the moment a recrudescence of some very problematical senses of place, from reactionary nationalisms, to competitive localisms, to introverted obsessions with 'heritage'. We need, therefore, to think through what might be an adequately progressive sense of place, one which would fit in with the current global–local times and the feelings and relations they give rise to, *and* which would be useful in what are, after all, political struggles often inevitably based on place. The question is how to hold on to that notion of geographical difference, of uniqueness, even of rootedness if people want that, without it being reactionary.

There are a number of distinct ways in which the 'reactionary' notion of place described above is problematical. One is the idea that places have single, essential, identities. Another is the idea that identity of place – the sense of place – is constructed out of an introverted, inward-looking history based on delving into the past for internalized origins, translating the name from the Domesday Book. Thus Wright recounts the construction and appropriation of Stoke Newington and its past by the arriving middle class (the Domesday Book registers the place as 'Newtowne' . . . 'There is land for two ploughs and a half. . . . There are four villanes and thirty seven cottagers with ten acres', pp. 227 and 231), and contrasts this version with that of other groups – the white working class and the large number of important minority communities.[3] A particular problem with this conception of place is that it seems to require the drawing of boundaries. Geographers have long been exercised by the problem of defining regions, and this question of 'definition' has almost always been reduced to the issue of drawing lines around a place. I remember some of my most painful times as a geographer have been spent unwillingly struggling to think how one could draw a boundary around somewhere like the 'East Midlands'. But that kind of boundary around an area precisely distinguishes between an inside and an outside. It can so easily be yet another way of constructing a counterposition between 'us' and 'them'.

And yet, if one considers almost any real place, and certainly one not defined primarily by administrative or political boundaries, these supposed characteristics have little real purchase.

Take, for instance, a walk down Kilburn High Road, my local shopping centre. It is a pretty ordinary place, north-west of the centre of London. Under the railway bridge the newspaper stand sells papers from every county of what my neighbours, many of whom come from there, still often call the Irish Free State. The postboxes down the High Road, and many an empty space on a wall, are adorned with the letters IRA. Other available spaces are plastered this week with posters for a special meeting in remembrance: Ten Years after the Hunger Strike. At the local theatre Eamon Morrissey has a one-man show; the National Club has the Wolfe Tones on, and at the Black Lion there's Finnegan's Wake. In two shops I noted this week's lottery ticket winners: in one the name is Teresa Gleeson, in the other, Chouman Hassan.

Thread your way through the often almost stationary traffic diagonally across the road from the newsstand and there's a shop which as long as I can remember has displayed saris in the window. Four life-sized models of Indian women, and reams of cloth. On the door a notice announces a forthcoming concert at Wembley Arena: Anand Miland presents Rekha, live, with Aamir Khan, Salman Khan, Jahi Chawla and Raveena Tandon. On another ad, for the end of the month, is written 'All Hindus are cordially invited'. In another newsagents I chat with the man who keeps it, a Muslim unutterably depressed by events in the Gulf, silently chafing at having to sell *The Sun*. Overhead there is always at least one aeroplane – we seem to be on a flight-path to Heathrow and by the time they're over Kilburn you can see them clearly enough to tell the airline and wonder as you struggle with your shopping where they're coming from. Below, the reason the traffic is snarled up (another odd effect of time-space-compression!) is in part because this is one of the main entrances to and escape-routes from London, the road to Staples Corner and the beginning of the M1 to the North.

This is just the beginnings of a sketch from immediate impressions but a proper analysis could be done, of the links between Kilburn and the world. And so it could for almost any place.

Kilburn is a place for which I have a great affection; I have lived there many years. It certainly has 'a character of its own'. But it is possible to feel all this without subscribing to any of the static and defensive – and in that sense reactionary – notions of 'place' which were referred to above. First, while Kilburn may have a character of its own, it is absolutely not a seamless, coherent identity, a single sense of place which everyone shares. It could hardly be less so. People's routes through the place, their favourite haunts within it, the connections they make (physically, or by phone or post, or in memory and imagination) between here and the rest of the world vary enormously. If it is now recognized that people have multiple identities then the same point can be made in relation to places. Moreover, such multiple identities can either be a source of richness or a source of conflict, or both.

One of the problems here has been a persistent identification of place with 'community'. Yet this is a misidentification. On the one hand communities can exist without being in the same place – from networks of friends with like interests, to major religious, ethnic or political communities. On the other hand, the instances of places housing single 'communities' in the sense of coherent social groups are probably – and, I would argue, have for long been – quite rare. Moreover, even where they do exist this in no way implies a single sense of place. For people occupy different positions within any community. We could counterpose to the chaotic mix of Kilburn the relatively stable and homogeneous community (at least in popular imagery) of a small mining village. Homogeneous? 'Communities' too have internal structures. To take the most obvious example. I'm sure a woman's sense of place in a mining village – the spaces through which she normally moves, the meeting places, the connections outside – are different from a man's. Their 'senses of the place' will be different.

Moreover, not only does 'Kilburn', then, have many identities (or its full identity is a complex mix of all these) it is also, looked at in this way, absolutely *not* introverted. It is (or ought to be) impossible even to begin thinking about Kilburn High Road without bringing into play half the world and a considerable amount of British imperialist history (and this certainly goes for mining villages too). Imagining it this way provokes in you (or at least in me) a really global sense of place.

And finally, in contrasting this way of looking at places with the defensive reactionary view, I certainly could not begin to, nor would I want to, define 'Kilburn' by drawing its enclosing boundaries.

So, at this point in the argument, get back in your mind's eye on a satellite; go right out again and look back at the globe. This time, however, imagine not just all the physical movement, nor even all the often invisible communications, but also and especially all the social relations, all the links between people. Fill it in with all those different experiences of time-space-compression. For what is happening is that the geography of social relations is changing. In many cases such relations are increasingly stretched out over space. Economic, political and cultural social relations, each full of power and with internal structures of domination and subordination, stretched out over the planet at every different level, from the household to the local area to the international.

It is from this perspective that it is possible to envisage an alternative interpretation of place. In this interpretation, what gives a place its specificity is not some long internalized history but the fact that it is constructed out of a particular constellation of social relations, meeting and weaving together at a particular locus. If one moves in from the satellite towards the globe, holding all those networks of social relations and movements and communications in one's head, then each 'place' can be seen as a particular, unique, point of their intersection. It is, indeed, a *meeting* place. Instead then, of thinking of places as areas with boundaries around, they can be imagined as articulated movements in networks of social relations and understandings, but where a large proportion of those relations, experiences and understandings are constructed on a far larger scale than what we happen to define for that moment as the place itself, whether that be a street, or a region or even a continent. And this in turn allows a sense of place which is extroverted, which includes a consciousness of its links with the wider world, which integrates in a positive way the global and the local.

This is not a question of making the ritualistic connections to 'the wider system' – the people in the local meeting who bring up international capitalism every time you try to have a discussion about rubbish-collection – the point is that there are real relations with real content – economic, political, cultural – between any local place and the wider world in which it is set. In economic geography the argument has long been accepted that it is not possible to understand the 'inner city', for instance its loss of jobs, the decline of manufacturing employment there, by looking only at the inner city. Any adequate explanation has to set the inner city in its wider geographical context. Perhaps it is appropriate to think how that kind of understanding could be extended to the notion of a sense of place.

These arguments, then, highlight a number of ways in which a progressive concept of place might be developed. First of all, it is absolutely not static. If places can be conceptualized in terms of the social interactions which they tie together, then it is also the case that these interactions themselves are not motionless things, frozen in time. They are processes. One of the great one-liners in Marxist exchanges has for long been 'ah, but capital is not a thing, it's a process'. Perhaps this should be said also about places; that places are processes, too.

Second, places do not have to have boundaries in the sense of divisions which frame simple enclosures. 'Boundaries' may of course be necessary, for the purposes of certain types of studies for instance, but they are not necessary for the conceptualization of a place itself. Definition in this sense does not have to be through simple counterposition to the outside; it can come, in part, precisely through the particularity of linkage to that 'outside' which is therefore itself part of what constitutes the place. This helps get away from the common association between penetrability and vulnerability. For it is this kind of association which makes invasion by newcomers so threatening.

Third, clearly places do not have single, unique 'identities'; they are full of internal conflicts. Just think, for instance, about London's Docklands, a place which is at the moment quite clearly *defined* by conflict: a conflict over what its past has been (the nature of its 'heritage'), conflict over what should be its present development, conflict over what could be its future.

Fourth, and finally, none of this denies place nor the importance of the uniqueness of place. The specificity of place is continually reproduced, but it is not a specificity which results from some long, internalized history. There are a number of sources of this specificity – the uniqueness of place.[4] There is the fact that the wider social relations in which places are set are themselves geographically differentiated. Globalization (in the economy, or in culture, or in anything else) does not entail simply homogenization. On the contrary, the globalization of social relations is yet another source of (the reproduction of) geographical uneven development, and thus of the uniqueness of place. There is the specificity of place which derives from the fact that each place is the focus of a distinct *mixture* of wider and more local social relations. There is the fact that this very mixture together in one place may produce effects which would not have happened otherwise. And finally, all these relations interact with and take a further element of specificity from the accumulated history of a place, with that history itself imagined as the product of layer upon layer of different sets of linkages, both local and to the wider world.

In her portrait of Corsica, *Granite Island*, Dorothy Carrington travels the island seeking out the roots of its character.[5] All the different layers of peoples and cultures are explored; the long and tumultuous relationship with France, with Genoa and Aragon in the thirteenth, fourteenth and fifteenth centuries, back through the much earlier incorporation into the Byzantine Empire, and before that domination by the Vandals, before that being part of the Roman Empire, before that the colonization and settlements of the Carthaginians and the Greeks . . . until we find . . . that even the megalith builders had come to Corsica from somewhere else.

It is a sense of place, an understanding of 'its character', which can only be constructed by linking that place to places beyond. A progressive sense of place would recognize that, without being threatened by it. What we need, it seems to me, is a global sense of the local, a global sense of place.

Notes

1   D. Birkett, *New Statesman and Society*, 13 June 1990, 41–2.
2   D. Birkett, *New Statesman and Society*, 15 March 1991, p. 38.
3   P. Wright, *On living in an old country*, Verso, 1985.
4   D. Massey, *Spatial divisions of labour: social structures and the geography of production*, Macmillan, 1984.
5   D. Carrington, *Granite Island: a portrait of Corsica*, Penguin.

Section 4

Social selves and public policy

When we were putting together the first edition of this book in 1992 it was already very difficult to talk of cultural studies as a unified field with a consensually agreed set of theoretical traditions and analytical pre-occupations. We spoke then also of 'the globalization of cultural studies'. Ioan Davies (1995) has since traced the historical fragmentation and multiple routes of cultural studies in a manner which demonstrates the diversification of concerns and the sheer international variability and complexity of the field. Cultural studies is clearly implicated in one way or another with legacies of empire, post-colonialism and reconfigurations of cultural, economic and political power on a world scale. The call for a 'transnationalist perspective' in cultural studies (Ang and Stratton, 1996), for instance, is appealing but rhetorically vague, however, and, in practice, it has a very specific and localized provenance in the political and economic 'Asianization' of Australia. Moreover, as Kuan-Hsing Chen (1996, p. 37) has commented, 'Cultural studies as an internationalist project will run the risk of losing its critical edges and even reproducing the existing power structure of the nation-states and global capital'.

It is not by any means our intention to propose a definitive map of the field as a whole or to advocate any overarching way of studying culture on a global scale. What is clear, though, is that the literature that makes up something like a community of scholarship in cultural studies and the preferred objects of study in the field are indeed becoming more international than it seemed to us only four years ago, and this is to an extent represented in the final section of this book. We have, nevertheless, sought to maintain a sense of continuity with the earlier material, which largely represents the tradition of cultural studies that was developed in Britain, while including American contributions and contributions from France and Australia. In the spirit of the magpie, the bird best suited to adoption as the symbol for cultural studies, the texts here are drawn from several different disciplines and begin to reflect a growing diversity of national and international contexts for cultural studies.

241

The texts are selected according to two major themes, which at first sight may appear to be at opposite corners of the field: first, the social construction of the self; second, the role of public policy in the cultural field. Quite apart from any connections that can be drawn between these two themes, they are themes that are of particular interest to the editors of this book: they represent our intellectual preferences, and we believe they signal important directions for the development of cultural studies in any case. One of the distinctive features of cultural studies, in our experience, is its personal appeal, its promise of illuminating one's own situation in the world and in relation to others. That is the subjective pole of cultural studies, what at one level brings about passionate involvement and a sense of agency. One might also feel passionate about the politics of culture in public debate, the policy pole which necessarily entails a certain objectification in the sense of an attention to structural determinations.

To begin with the work of **Pierre Bourdieu** in this section, then, makes sense. His major study *La distinction*, originally published in France in 1979, made the scandalous claim that aesthetic taste is socially produced rather than a matter of individual cultivation or some extra-social standards of value. For Bourdieu, taste is a marker of class and, to an extent, represents class struggle on the plane of the cultural. In the passages selected here, Bourdieu is concerned with comparative indeterminacy of position in the class structure, the position of the new petite bourgeoisie and especially those of its members employed in occupations of 'presentation and representation'. According to Bourdieu, this is the social basis for postmodern sensibility and its taste-making power, an insight which has been taken up and developed further by Fred Pfeil (1991) in his discussion of the culture of the North American professional-managerial class.

With **Susan Christopherson** and **Michael Storper**'s classic essay, 'The city as studio; the world as back lot', we move onto an analytical terrain, in this case informed by economic geography, essential to a policy orientation in cultural studies. They analyse the 'vertical disintegration' of the US movie business, illustrated by the emergence of 'independent' film production in the 1950s, which superseded the assembly-line system of studio production that was characteristic of Hollywood in its classic period and which exemplified economic and cultural Fordism during the mid-twentieth century. As Christopherson and Storper point out, however, vertical disintegration is accompanied by horizontal reintegration and agglom-eration around Los Angeles. The Hollywood majors and their successors retain their power at the nodal point of distribution. And, as critics of Christopherson and Storper (Aksoy and Robins, 1992; Wasko, 1994) have noted, this has in effect facilitated a process of vertical *re-integration*, incorporating the 'flexibility' of 'outsourcing' for product, while restoring and extending the command of US entertainment corporations in global markets.

Staying in the USA for a little longer, we move on to an essay by **Cornel West**, who compares 'liberal structuralist' and 'conservative behaviourist' explanations of the plight of the black urban poor. Neither, in his opinion, produce a satisfactory account of the corrosive nihilism which is endemic in the abandoned inner cities of what is still the biggest national economy in the world, nor do they offer viable solutions. West is preoccupied by the African-American relationship to corporate America and he advocates a 'politics of conversion' which will enable blacks to participate more successfully in a system that has denied opportunity to many (see West, 1993). West's contribution represents an essentially culturalist perspective on the problems of the black 'underclass'. It might usefully be contrasted with William Julius Wilson's (1994, p. 59) alternative case for 'race-neutral programmes to address the plight of the disadvantaged sections of the minority population'.

Citizenship has risen up the agendas of social criticism and cultural studies, partly in response to the decline of Marxism and very largely because of the inequalities associated with the erosion of welfare state provisions and the all-pervasive power of 'the free market'. This is so in the United States and it is also a dominant feature of the post-communist states of Eastern Europe. **Barbara Einhorn** considers the position of women after the fall of European communism and the fate of the citizenship movements that contributed to this defining historical moment of the final decade of the twentieth century (see Hobsbawn, 1994). Whereas under state socialism women's rights at work had been formally guaranteed whilst general citizenship rights were minimal, liberalization of the economy has not actually improved and may even have worsened the situation of women. Einhorn calls for a revival of civil society in relation to the feminist project, a demand which is not solely confined to feminism (for example, see Gellner, 1996).

Elspeth Probyn is also concerned with the representation of women in addition to the articulation of different sexualities but, in her case, more specifically from the point of view of the politics of cultural studies. She is interested in how 'experience' functions as an ontological and epistemological category and, in this respect, calls into question the structuralist and post-structuralist view that experience can be conceived of only as a discursive construction and not as a source of meaning. Probyn produces a reading of Raymond Williams's essay, 'Culture is ordinary', the first reading in this book, and in so doing stresses 'the centrality of experience of and in the material world'.

Stuart Cunningham offers the most direct discussion concerning the relationship between cultural studies and cultural policy of all the pieces in this section. Along with Tony Bennett (1992), Cunningham is one of the major proponents of a turn towards policy in cultural studies, a position which was particularly emphasized under the socio-democratic regime in Australia which came to an abrupt electoral termination in 1996. The key question here is: what does it mean to reframe questions of cultural studies according to considerations of public policy? Cunningham presents a coherent yet contestable case that is rooted in the values of social democracy (for a further discussion of cultural policy studies, see McGuigan, 1996).

The turn towards policy is not just a methodological problem for cultural studies: it requires a close attention to transformations in 'the real world'. Such a transformation is the development of what **Manuel Castells** calls 'the informational society' and the emergence of a truly global economy in the sense of an economy that operates across the earth in a single time frame.

This is obviously facilitated by the application of computing and telematics to business as well as to entertainment. According to Castells, 'the space of flows' thus gains pre-eminence over 'the space of places', with enormous consequences for urban policy. He identifies the problematical formation of 'the dual city' which is socially split between an information-rich and mobile elite, on the one hand, and large sections of the population, on the other hand, who are trapped in parochialism and tribalism.

Many of the older models of social explanation and cultural interpretation have ceased to work in a world where the imbrications of knowledge and power have become increasingly complex and apparently opaque. One traditional way of making sense, which survives the decline of positivistic and modernist thought, is narrativization (for example, see Seidman, 1994). Human beings have always told each other stories in order to make sense of themselves and their worlds. **Ken Plummer**, in his discussion of 'a sociology of stories', explores the methodological implications of narrative in social and cultural analysis, particularly with regard to accounts of sexual identity.

Finally, **Julian Stallabrass** presents a devastating critique of cyberculture, which is immensely significant both for grasping the potential of democratic communications and for a critical understanding of how transnational capital commands the international cultural field. Most interestingly he argues that the cybernetic imagination has been driven by literary and artistic forms, far ahead of actual technical application. Like Castells, Stallabrass stresses complex issues of communicational and cultural inequality that are often neglected by technological enthusiasts. Around the ongoing debates concerning information technologies and the Internet, there are major questions of public policy. However, as Stallabrass points out, there are also questions concerning the self and identity in the kind of technologically-mediated cultures that are emerging with greater intensity towards the close of the twentieth century and which we may speculate about from our present vantage points and begin to analyse critically.

References

Aksoy, A. and Robins, K. 1992: Hollywood for the 21st century – global competition for critical mass in image markets. *Cambridge Journal of Economics*, 16(1).

Ang, I. and Stratton, J. 1996: Asianing Australia – notes towards a critical transnationalism in cultural studies. *Cultural Studies*, 10(1).

Bennett, T. 1992: Putting policy into cultural studies. In Grossberg, L., Nelson, C. and Treichler, P. (eds), *Cultural studies*, London/New York: Routledge.

Chen, K.-H. 1996: Not yet the postcolonial era – the (super) nation-state and transnationalism of cultural studies – response to Ang and Stratton. *Cultural Studies*, 10(1).

Davies, I. 1995: *Cultural studies and beyond – fragments of empire*. London/New York: Routledge.

Gellner, E. 1996: *Conditions of liberty – civil society and its rivals*. London: Penguin Books.

Hobsbawm, E. 1994: *Age of extremes – the short twentieth-century 1914–1991*. London: Michael Joseph.

McGuigan, J. 1996: *Culture and the public sphere*. London/New York: Routledge.

Pfeil, F. 1991: *Another tale to tell – politics and narrative in postmodern culture*. London: Verso.

Seidman, S. (ed.) 1994: *The postmodern turn – new perspectives on social theory*. Cambridge/New York: Cambridge University Press.

Wasko, J. 1994: *Hollywood in the information age*. Cambridge: Polity Press.

West, C. 1993: The new cultural politics of difference. In During, S. (ed.), *The cultural studies reader*. London/New York, Routledge.

Wilson, W.J. 1994: Citizenship and the inner-city ghetto poor. In Van Steenbergen, B. (ed.), *The condition of citizenship*. London/Newbury Park, CA: Sage.

23

The new petite bourgeoisie

Pierre Bourdieu

From his *Distinction* (Routledge, 1984).

[. . .] The new petite bourgeoisie comes into its own in all the occupations involving presentation and representation (sales, marketing, advertising, public relations, fashion, decoration and so forth) and in all the institutions providing symbolic goods and services. These include the various jobs in medical and social assistance (marriage guidance, sex therapy, dietetics, vocational guidance, paediatric advice etc.) and in cultural production and organization (youth leaders, play leaders, tutors and monitors, radio and TV producers and presenters, magazine journalists), which have expanded considerably in recent years; but also some established occupations, such as art craftsmen or nurses. Thus, the art craftsmen in the old sense – upholsterers, wrought-iron workers, cabinetmakers, picture-framers, goldsmiths, jewellers, gilders or engravers, trained in technical schools and very close to small craftsmen and their values – have been joined in the last fifteen years or so by makers of jewellery, printed fabrics, ceramics or hand-woven clothes, with a higher level of general education, often Parisian and of bourgeois origin, who are closer in life-style to the cultural intermediaries. Similarly, among the secretaries and nurses, some, originating from the lower or middle classes, are very close to the junior administrative executives, while others, younger, often Parisian and of bourgeois origin, present all the features of the new occupations. In general, the indeterminacy of the new or renovated occupations means that the heterogeneity of the agents' trajectories is particularly marked. One can almost always distinguish two groups separated by social origin and all the associated dispositions, who disagree more or less overtly over the definition of the job and the competences or virtues necessary in order to fill it. [. . .]

Those members of the new petite bourgeoisie who originate from the upper classes and who, for lack (most often) of educational capital, have had to reconvert into the new occupations such as cultural intermediary or art craftsman have had fewer years of schooling than the average for their class of origin but more than the average for the middle classes; they therefore possess a very great cultural capital of familiarity and a social capital of 'connections'. They manifest the highest competence within the middle classes and incline towards a system of choices very similar to that of the bourgeoisie: the *Art of Fugue*, the *Concerto for the Left Hand*, the *Firebird Suite*, the *Four Seasons*, Goya, Braque, Breughel, Jacques Douai, the Modern Art Museum, antique shops and the Flea Market, a 'harmonious', 'discreet', 'studied' interior, 'refined', 'artistic', 'stylish' friends, 'intellectual' films, *Salvatore Giuliano*, *Exterminating Angel*, *The Trial*, or, among the comedies, *The Suitor* [. . .]. Their ambivalent relationship with the educational system, inducing a sense of complicity with every form of symbolic defiance, inclines them to welcome all the forms of culture which are, provisionally at least, on the (lower) boundaries of legitimate culture – jazz, cinema, strip cartoons, science fiction – and to flaunt (for example) American fashions and models – jazz, jeans, rock or the avant-garde underground, which is their monopoly – as a challenge to legitimate culture; but they often bring into these regions disdained by the educational establishment an erudite, even 'academic' disposition which is inspired by a clear intention of rehabilitation, the cultural equivalent of the restoration strategies which define their occupational project. [. . .]

The fact that a large proportion of these new positions are occupied by women no doubt contributes to the realization of their potentialities, which express themselves precisely in this recruitment. It would clearly be naive to look to the sex-ratio of the category, which is one of the properties of the category, for the explanation of this or that other property of the category. The socially inculcated dispositions (in particular, the inclination towards the things of taste) which lead especially the women of these fractions towards the adjectives they see as most distinguished ('stylish', 'refined' etc.) are also the basis of the 'vocation' which brings them to the new occupations and of the entirely functional aptitudes they apply in them. Not the least of these are the aesthetic dispositions required both in the production or sale of goods and services and in the self-presentation which is often an essential condition for successful symbolic imposition.

The key to the whole system of preferences of these déclassé petite bourgeois aspiring to recover their lost class is found in the frequency with which they choose adjectives which unambiguously declare an attraction for the most naively aristocratic qualities ('stylish', 'distinguished', 'refined', 'recherché'). This systematic pretension to distinction, this quasi-methodical concern to stand aloof from the tastes and values most clearly associated with the established petite bourgeoisie and the working classes, which give to all their practices an air of tension even in relaxation, constraint in the pursuit of a 'liberated' life-style, affectation in simplicity, are indeed the most significant manifestations of this new variant of the petit-bourgeois ethos.

This well-armed pretension, based on a familiarity with culture combined with high social origin, is quite distinct in its means and its modality from the anxious pretension of the promoted petite bourgeoisie. It functions as a sort of social 'flair', allowing its owner to steer through difficult situations when the usual landmarks are missing. Thus, although the members of the new petite bourgeoisie are no more inclined than the others to concede (especially in practice) that photography can transfigure objects such as a pregnant woman, a scrap-yard, a butcher's stall or a car crash, they are more skilful at identifying the 'soppy' objects of popular taste or petit-bourgeois aestheticism – the sunset, the landscape, the little girl playing with a cat, the folk dance (all of which they much more rarely say would make a beautiful photograph). In general, the cultural 'bluff' which relies on this flair – measured by the gap between the tendency to select the rarest painters, composers or works (*L'Enfant et les sortilèges*, the *Firebird Suite*, Kandinsky, Dali, Braque) and the frequency of visits to museums, especially the Modern Art Museum – varies with the proportion of inheritors and parvenus in each category. It is particularly frequent among the cultural intermediaries and commercial executives, very rare among the promoted petit bourgeois (as it is among the public-sector executives and secondary teachers), and is reduced to an empty intention of distinction in the rising fraction of the new occupations (situated on the negative-value side of the second axis).

The dispositions of which the new petite bourgeoisie is the bearer find the conditions for their full development only in Paris. [. . .] Cultural pretension – together with education, of which it reinforces the effects – is no doubt one of the factors conducive to appropriation of the advantages associated with proximity to the centre of cultural values, such as a more intense supply of cultural goods, the sense of belonging and the incentives given by contact with groups who are also culturally favoured. Consequently there is no other category in which the systematic differences between Parisians and provincials are more marked: differences in the intensity of the legitimate practices (museum visits etc.) and the range of competence (in music, for example); differences in the relationship to legitimate culture, with the sense of being an outsider to the world of painting or music ('not my strong point', 'I don't know much about it') always being more marked among provincials, other things being equal; differences, above all, in the ability to recognize – often without knowing them – smart opinions, the Parisians always being more inclined, at all levels of competence, to opt for the most legitimate judgements ('All music of quality interests me') as soon as they are formulated, whereas the provincials more often concur with the judgements expressing a recognition of legitimacy combined with a confession of ignorance ('I don't know much about it') or incompetence ('It's complicated'); differences in the indices of cultural pretension, with, for example, the choice of an 'imaginative' or 'studied' interior, clothes that are 'chic' and 'stylish' (*racé*), two expressions typical of the new art of living promulgated by the mass-circulation women's magazines, and above all the declared preference for the rarest works of music, the *Firebird Suite*, the *Art of Fugue*, the *Well-Tempered Clavier* (instead of the provincials' *Rhapsody in Blue*), through which the new petite bourgeoisie distinguishes itself from the promoted petite bourgeoisie much more decisively in Paris than in the provinces; and differences in all the indices of life-style, in the choice of clothes, in tastes in cooking or ethical preferences, in which the provincials are always more prudent, less audaciously 'liberated'.

Together with the opposition between the Parisians and the provincials, the opposition (strongly marked in cultural competence) between the occupants of the new positions who originate from the dominant class and those who originate from the other classes underlines the conditions of success of the social bluff which always plays a part in the definition of the new occupations. Having acquired only the most visible and least prestigious aspects of the new life-style, the upwardly mobile individuals who seek in marginal, less strictly defined positions a way of escaping destinies incompatible with the promises implied in their scholastic careers, without possessing the cultural competences, the ethical dispositions and, above all, the social capital and investment sense from which individuals originating from the dominant class expect a recovery of their former position, have every likelihood of being expelled from positions to which they have been led by educationally induced allodoxia, as those positions are progressively revalued (partly through their own elimination) by the activity of the sole legitimate occupants.

One can see how inherited dispositions predispose individuals to occupy the positions towards which they orient them. With these 'need merchants', sellers of symbolic goods and services who always sell themselves as models and as guarantors of the value of their products, and who sell so well because they believe in what they sell, the symbolic authority of the honest, trustworthy vendor takes the form of an imposition that is both more violent and more gentle, since the vendor deceives the customer only insofar as he deceives himself and is sincerely 'sold' on the value of what he sells. Because the new 'substitution' industry, which sells fine words instead of things to those who cannot afford the things but are willing to settle for words, finds its ideal clientele in the new petite bourgeoisie, this group is predisposed to collaborate with total conviction in imposing the life-style handed down by the new bourgeoisie, the probable destination of its trajectory and the real goal of its aspirations. In short, this petite bourgeoisie of consumers, which means to acquire on credit, i.e., before its due time, the attributes of the legitimate life-style – 'residences' with 'olde-worlde' names and holiday flats at Merlin-Plage, mock luxury cars and mock luxury holidays – is perfectly adapted to act as a transmission belt and pull into the race for consumption and competition those from whom it means to distinguish itself. In fact, one of its distinguishing features is precisely its sense of legitimacy in teaching others the legitimate life-style by a symbolic action which not only produces the need for its own product, and therefore, in the long run, legitimates itself and those who exercise it, but also legitimates the life-style put forward as a model, that is, that of the dominant class, or, more precisely, of the fractions which constitute its ethical avant-garde.

A very different image of themselves and their activity is, of course, held by all those who, in industry or in the great bureaucracies of cultural production – radio, television, research organizations, the major daily or weekly newspapers – and especially in the occupations of 'social work' and 'cultural facilitation', perform the tasks of gentle manipulation assigned to them by the new division of labour. Occupying a dominated position within the hierarchy of the institutions of cultural production and circulation and experiencing a quasi alienation which sometimes provides the basis for an intellectual solidarity with the dominated classes, the new cultural intermediaries are inclined to sympathize with discourses aimed at challenging the cultural order and the hierarchies which the cultural 'hierarchy' aims to maintain, and to return to the themes of all heresies – denunciation of the (technocratic) pretension to the monopoly of competence, hostility to hierarchies and 'the' hierarchy, the ideology of universal creativity. But in fact these occupations condemn their occupants to the essential ambiguity resulting from the discrepancy between the (symbolically) subversive dispositions linked to their position in the division of labour and the manipulative or conservative functions attached to the position, between the subjective image of the occupational project and the objective function of the occupation. The very performance of the function may presuppose this discrepancy, a principle of dissimulation and misrecognition, as in the case of some veteran revolutionaries of May 1968 who have become industrial psychologists: to accept their ambiguous position and to accept themselves doing so, they are forced to invent the skilfully ambiguous discourses and practices that were, so to speak, inscribed in advance in the very definition of the position. Obliged to live out the contradiction between their messianic aspirations and the reality of their practice, to cultivate uncertainty as to their social identity in order to be able to accept it, and therefore condemned to a questioning of the world which masks an anxious self-questioning, these 'intellectual lackeys' are predisposed to experience with particular intensity the existential mood of a whole intellectual generation, which, weary of desperately hoping for a collective hope, seeks in a narcissistic self-absorption the substitute for the hope of changing the social world or even of understanding it.

Thus, in the struggle it wages, within the dominant fractions of the dominant class, to replace old-style conservatism based on an overtly authoritarian image of the hierarchical relations between the classes, generations or sexes with a reconverted conservatism corresponding to the enlightened self-interest of those for whom a rational use of the educational system has provided the means of reconverting themselves in accordance with the new logic of the economy, the new or renovated bourgeoisie finds a natural ally, both economically and politically, in the new petite bourgeoisie. The latter recognizes in the new bourgeoisie the embodiment of its human ideal (the 'dynamic' executive) and, having abandoned the somewhat morose asceticism of the rising petite bourgeoisie, collaborates enthusiastically in imposing the new ethical norms (especially as regards consumption) and the corresponding needs.

Seeking its occupational and personal salvation in the imposition of new doctrines of ethical salvation, the new petite bourgeoisie is predisposed to play a vanguard role in the struggles over everything concerned with the art of living, in particular, domestic life and consumption, relations between the sexes and the generations, the reproduction of the family and its values. It is opposed on almost every point to the repressive morality of the declining petite bourgeoisie whose religious or political conservatism often centres on moral indignation at moral disorder, and especially the disorder of sexual mores – as witness the theme of 'pornocracy' and the anti-feminism which run through a whole current of predominantly petit-bourgeois right-wing thought, from Proudhon to Pareto. But it is equally opposed, by the aristocratic pretension of its fundamental choices and by its subversive representation of the relations between the sexes, to the asceticism of the promoted petite bourgeoisie, whose austere optimism, rigorous but not without a sort of heroism, is opposed to the repressive pessimism of the declining petite bourgeoisie.

Thus, whereas the old morality of duty, based on the opposition between pleasure and good, induces a generalized suspicion of the 'charming and attractive', a fear of pleasure and a relation to the body made up of 'reserve', 'modesty' and 'restraint', and associates every satisfaction of the forbidden impulses with guilt, the new ethical avant-garde urges a morality of pleasure as a duty. This doctrine makes it a failure, a threat to self-esteem, not to 'have fun', or, as Parisians like to say with a little shudder of audacity, [. . .] pleasure is not only permitted but demanded, on ethical as much as on scientific grounds. The fear of not getting enough pleasure, the logical outcome of the effort to overcome the fear of pleasure, is combined with the search for self-expression and 'bodily expression' and for communication with others [. . .], even immersion in others (considered not as a group but as subjectivities in search of their identity); and the old personal ethic is thus rejected for a cult of personal health and psychological therapy. At the opposite pole from the 'politicization' which depersonalizes personal experiences by presenting them as particular cases of generic experiences common to a class, 'moralization' and 'psychologization' personalize experiences, and are thus perfectly consistent with the more or less secularized forms of the search for religious salvation. As is shown by the use it makes of psychoanalytic jargon, the modernist morality is a psychological vulgate which moralizes under the guise of analysis; and as is shown by the emphasis it places on Erikson's 'utopia of full orgasmic reciprocity', it transmutes a spuriously positive definition of the 'normal' into an imperative of normality and bases the orgasm-duty of its theoretical morality on the findings of a bogus science of mores à la Kinsey, thus introducing the deadly, rational accountancy of equivalences into the area of sexual exchanges, which for most societies is one of the last refuges of collective misrecognition. Invoking the prestige of a false science of sexual behaviour to naturalize a conception and an experience of 'sexuality' – a very recent historical invention which depends on social conditions of possibility that are very unequally distributed – it consigns to the pathology of 'sexual poverty', i.e., to·the attentions of the psychoanalyst or the sexologist, sole arbiters of legitimate sexual competence, all those whom the old morality would have consigned to the inferno of 'natural' sexuality. These 'barbarians' who have not caught up with the 'sexual revolution' are once again the victims of a universalization of the definition of competence not accompanied by a universalization of the conditions of acquisition.

Closer in this respect to religious prophecy than to science, whose truths are always partial and provisional, this would-be scientific morality provides a systematic answer to the problems of daily existence. It proposes, for example, a conception of bodily exercise and a representation of childhood and child-rearing which are in perfect harmony with its vision of sexuality. Out goes the asceticism of traditional gymnastics, which measures the value of an exercise by its cost in effort, and even suffering [. . .], which sees physical effort as 'character-building' and may even find a form of pleasure in the experience of tension; in its place comes the 'new gymnastics', a self-styled 'anti-gymnastics', with a system of equally imperative and exactly opposite precepts. Aiming to substitute relaxation for tension, pleasure for effort, 'creativity' and 'freedom' for discipline, communication for solitude, it treats the body as the psychoanalyst treats the soul, bending its ear to 'listen' to a body which has to be 'unknotted', liberated or, more simply, rediscovered and accepted ('feeling at home'). This psychologization of the relation to the body is inseparable from an exaltation of the self, but a self which truly fulfils itself ('growth', 'awareness', 'responsiveness') only when 'relating' to others ('sharing experiences') through the intermediary of the body treated as a sign and not as an instrument (which opens the door to a whole politics of the 'alienated body'). Such are the intentions which lie behind exercises of 'bodily expression', a sort of painless delivery of one's own body.

The same oppositions are found in the area of child-rearing. The puritanical view of the child's nature as a site of dangerous, powerful (essentially auto-erotic) desires leads upbringing to be seen as a 'training', a straightening, and pedagogy as a set of techniques for controlling the child while taming his bad instincts; it gives adults the power to define needs, i.e., legitimate desires, to distinguish, for example, between legitimate cries (of hunger or pain) and illegitimate ones, or between 'good' and 'bad' habits. By contrast, the therapeutic ethic, with its psychobabble of 'liberationist' commonplaces ('father figure', 'Peter Pan complex' etc.), credits the child with a good nature which must be accepted as such, with its legitimate pleasure needs (for attention, affection, maternal care). Child-rearing, which is also a source of legitimate pleasures (so that procreation, which produces this consumer object bringing joy, youth and union to both parents, is also a psychotherapeutic duty), treats the child as a sort of apprentice who must discover his body and the world through exploration; and, blurring the boundaries between work and play, duty and pleasure, it defines play as muscular and mental learning and therefore a necessary pleasure, subjectively agreeable and objectively indispensable, thus making pleasure a duty for children and parents alike.

Psychoanalysis, the rationalizing mystique of the age of science, is freely interpreted to supply the legitimating discourse which gives the appearances of a rational foundation to the arbitrary (but socially necessary) presuppositions of an ethos. And the slide from ethics to therapy produces the need for the therapist of which it is the product; there is no doubt that the search for psychological health through recourse to specialists in the rational cure of souls (psychoanalysts, psychotherapists, marriage guidance counsellors and so on) stands in a dialectical relation to the development of a body of professionals capable of producing the need for their own product, i.e., a market for the goods and services they are equipped to supply.

It would no doubt be a mistake to attribute to this single factor all the changes in domestic ethics which result from the combined impact of a number of (relatively) independent causal series, including the appearance of new psychological theories (psychoanalysis, genetic psychology etc.); the vastly increased number of girls from the bourgeoisie entering higher education and adapting to the associated life-style; the transformation of the mode of social reproduction, which means that scholastic errors tend to count more than moral errors, with academic anxiety, previously more a male concern, replacing ethical anxiety, which used to affect mainly girls; women's increased access to the labour market; and the changes in economic production itself, which, having to place ever greater emphasis on the production of needs and the artificial creation of scarcities, helps in many indirect ways to encourage a consumer morality. The fact remains that the rise of the therapeutic morality is unquestionably linked to the constitution of a corps of professionals (psychoanalysts, sexologists, counsellors, psychologists, specialized journalists and so forth) claiming a monopoly of the legitimate definition of legitimate pedagogic or sexual competence; and that the constitution of a field of production of goods and services called for by the disparity between the competence now demanded in such matters and real competence cannot be understood independently of the whole set of reconversion strategies through which agents, whose domestic or educational training predisposed them to play the role of an ethical vanguard, have been able to find the substitute for the prestigious positions the labour market refused them, in the interstices between the teaching profession and the medical profession. Thus the exemplary history of all those who started by professing a faith and ended up making it a profession, especially of all those associations which, in the areas of social work, adult education, cultural organization or advice on child-rearing and sexuality, have moved, in the space of a generation, from the enthusiastic uncertainties of voluntary evangelism to the security of quasi-civil-servant status, unfolds in time the ambiguous nature of all those professions which are bureaucratized forms of 'exemplary prophecy' and which involve offering (or selling) one's own art of living as an example to others.

If the ethical proselytism of these ethical prophets of bureaucratic societies systematically reverses the ascetic morality of the established petite bourgeoisie, this is because, like the choice, by which they are defined, of making their profession rather than entering ready-made professions, their life-style and ethical and political positions are based on a rejection of everything in themselves that is finite, definite, final, in a word, petit bourgeois, that is, a refusal to be pinned down in a particular site in social space, a practical utopianism which was until then the privilege of intellectuals and which predisposes them to welcome every form of utopia. Classified, déclassé, aspiring to a higher class, they see themselves as unclassifiable, 'excluded', 'dropped out', 'marginal', anything rather than categorized, assigned to a class, a determinate place in social space. And yet all their practices, cultural, sporting, educational, sexual, speak of classification – but in the mode of denial, as one sees from a few headings taken from the index of a 'resource' guide to adolescent counter-culture: aikido, agit-prop, alternative press, anthroposophy, anti-gymnastics, anti-nuclear, anti-psychiatry, anti-radiation, anti-scientism, anti-vaccination, astrology, basket-making, biodynamics, bio-energy, biological farming, body, Charlie Hebdo, childhood, communes, creativity, dance, diet, drugs, ecology, encounters, esoterica, extra-terrestrial, folk, freedom, free flight, futuristics, gays, Gestalt therapy, gliding, go, green, hallucinogens, hiking, grass, homeopathy, imagination, immigrants, independent cinema, invention, judo, kendo, kyudo, Larzac, life, macrobiotics, madness, magnetism, nomads, non-verbal communication, non-violence, one-night stands, ongoing education, oriental medicine, parallel, parapsychology, parascientific popularization, physiotherapy, plants, pottery, prisons, psi-phenomena, regionalism, repression, science fiction, struggles, telepathy, therapy, trailers, transcendental meditation, travel, trekking, vegetarianism, weaving, yoga, Zen. An inventory of thinly disguised expressions of a sort of dream of social flying, a desperate effort to defy the gravity of the social field.

Guided by their anti-institutional temperament and the concern to escape everything redolent of competitions, hierarchies and classifications and, above all, of scholastic classifications, hierarchies of knowledge, theoretical abstractions or technical competences, these new intellectuals are inventing an art of living which provides them with the gratifications and prestige of the intellectual at the least cost; in the name of the fight against 'taboos' and the liquidation of 'complexes' they adopt the most external and most easily borrowed aspects of the intellectual life-style, liberated manners, cosmetic or sartorial outrages, emancipated poses and postures, and systematically apply the cultivated disposition to not-yet-legitimate culture (cinema, strip cartoons, the underground), to everyday life (street art), the personal sphere (sexuality, cosmetics, child-rearing, leisure) and the existential (the relation to nature, love, death). The perfect audience for a new intellectual popularization which is also a popularization of the intellectual life-style, they spontaneously 'relate' to the new spontaneist ideology culled from Freud and Freinet, Rogers and Reich, Fourier and Bakunin. It is scarcely necessary to point out the 'cultivated', even scholastic aspects of this romantic flight from the social world, which, because it exalts the body and nature, sometimes sees itself as a return to the 'wild' and the 'natural': like legitimate culture, the counter-culture leaves its principles implicit (which is understandable since it is rooted in the dispositions of an ethos) and so is still able to fulfil functions of distinction by making available to *almost* everyone the distinctive poses, the distinctive games and other external signs of inner riches previously reserved for intellectuals.

The convergences between the routine themes of advertising – which has long been versed in the language of desire – and the most typical topics of high philosophical popularization, the parallels between the 'social policy' of a dominant class which concedes the better to conserve, and the new child-rearing – specifically bourgeois in its diffusion – which opts for liberalism and indulgence, would be sufficient to show that the new ethic espoused by the vanguard of the bourgeoisie and petite bourgeoisie is perfectly compatible with a form of enlightened conservatism. It may even be wondered if the ethic of liberation is not in the process of supplying the economy with the perfect consumer whom economic theory has always dreamed of, and not only by inducing him to consume and to consume the latest thing. The most important contribution of the new ethic may well be that it produces consumers who are isolated (despite all their associations, which are purely statistical groupings) and therefore free (or forced) to confront in extended order the separate markets ('juniors', 'teenagers', 'senior citizens' etc.) of the new economic order and untrammelled by the constraints and brakes imposed by collective memories and expectations – in short, freed from the temporal structures imposed by domestic units, with their own life-cycle, their long-term 'planning', sometimes over several generations, and their collective defences against the immediate impact of the market.

24

The city as studio; the world as back lot: the impact of vertical disintegration on the location of the motion picture industry

Susan Christopherson and Michael Storper

From *Environment and Planning D: Society and Space*, vol. 4, no. 3 (Pion, 1986).

Abstract. Motion picture production is currently carried out by small firms under contract to an independent producer rather than in large integrated firms, the major studios. In this paper the emergence of this vertically disintegrated industry is traced and its impact on the location of the motion picture industry is analyzed. Vertical disintegration has led to a reagglomeration of motion picture employment and establishments in Los Angeles, despite the dispersal of film shooting throughout the world. The processes that are shaping the present-day organization of motion pictures can be observed across a range of industries. An examination of these processes in motion pictures suggests that their association with reagglomeration in urban centers could have an important impact on patterns of urbanization.

Introduction

Over the past three decades, the motion picture industry has undergone a dramatic transformation. Until the 1950s, the industry was dominated by large vertically integrated firms which produced films via a routinized factory-like production process. In the contemporary motion picture industry, by contrast, production is carried out primarily by independent production companies which subcontract direct production activity to small specialized firms. The industry is vertically disintegrated and its production process is nonroutinized and designed to maximize variability of outputs and flexibility with respect to inputs. The numerous transactions required to produce the film product now take place on the market rather than within a firm. As vertical disintegration has proceeded, those firms providing services to producers have become smaller and more specialized. These specialized subcontractors reduce their own risks by marketing their services to other entertainment industries, including recording and television. As a result of these combined processes of vertical disintegration and cross-industry subcontracting, an entertainment industry complex has developed.

The processes that are shaping the present-day organization of motion picture production can be observed across a range of industries, in which organizational regimes of 'flexible specialization' are emerging. In these industries, firms produce specialty goods with relatively short production runs. They are capable of responding quickly to changing market conditions. They are connected to the market via contractual relationships with other firms. These trends can be observed in the textile industries of the 'Third Italy', the·mini-steel mills in the USA, and machine-tool and electronics industries in Japan and the USA (Bagnasco, 1977; Brusco and Sabel, 1983; Ikeda, 1979; Piore and Sabel, 1984).

In concert with other recent studies of industrial production via subcontracting linkages (Holmes, 1986; Piore and Sabel, 1984; Sayer, 1985; Scott, 1985) our examination of the evolution of motion picture production suggests that mass production is not necessarily the culmination of industrial development. Instead, the process of competition creates strategic junctures at which an industry can go in several organizational directions. In the case of the motion picture industry, firms responded to historical possibilities presented by changing technology, markets, and labor conditions, thus creating a vertically disintegrated production organization.

An analysis of these processes in the motion picture industry suggests that they are associated with reagglomeration in urban centers. Over the past two decades motion picture employment and establishments have reconcentrated in Los Angeles, even as a major proportion of motion pictures are filmed on location outside California. If the locational trends observed in the motion picture industry are indicative of a general relationship between vertical disintegration and industrial location, then industrial restructuring in the form of flexible specialization could have profound impacts on patterns of urbanization in the coming decades.

The historical trajectory of the industry

From craft to mass production
The history of the motion picture industry is similar to that of many other industries as they developed in the United States of America after the turn of the century. It began as a craft, but when the production process was rationalized it imitated modern manufacturing.

The motion picture industry developed in New York shortly after the turn of the century, closely replicating the craft-production techniques of the theater. Firms such as Lumiere were small-scale technological innovators. Production was carried out by small firm crews, whose members worked together to produce an individualized product. In spite of their artisanal production technique, motion pictures were very early defined as an entertainment product rather than as an art form. The speculative capital to produce films came out of the entertainment industry, nickelodeons, and vaudeville. The intended market was a mass market, the new urban immigrants. This broadening of markets led to the establishment of industrialized production methods by the time the studios were established in California in the 1920s. The giants of the industry – Cecil B De Mille, D W

Griffiths, Adolph Zukor – shaped the production process in the image of the assembly line, as in the auto and machinery industries.

Although we classify motion pictures as a service industry, one of the earliest studios was named the Universal Film *Manufacturing* Company. Its artificially lighted stage was dedicated by the mass production capitalist of the age, Henry Ford. Within a year of its establishment in 1918, this plant had produced 250 films. The other early studios in California, such as Griffiths's Arts Studio, were established as full-service film-production facilities intended to produce a standardized film product, not as craft shops. The film product was sold by the foot rather than on the basis of content.

Two major figures involved in establishing the industry, Adolph Zukor and Thomas Ince, were responsible for rationalizing the production process. Zukor, founder of Paramount Pictures, integrated production and distribution through the use of contracted exhibitors nationwide. 6000 theaters contracted with Paramount to receive three to four films per week. The Zukor empire was directed from his office on Times Square in New York City.

Parallel to Zukor's innovations in corporate structure were the production innovations of Thomas Ince. With an assured and stable theatrical market, the entire range of filmmaking activities could be integrated into one large firm, the studio. Ince set up the studio as an assembly line for large-scale production of a standardized film product, the 'formula' picture. Unlike on the stage, film production crews carried out discrete, well-defined, repetitive tasks. Ince was the master of standardization in the film production process. He made a conscious choice of the mass production model in shaping the organization of the motion picture industry. He had been a stage actor and could have chosen a production process based on the theater. Alternatively, he could have chosen the improvisational model used by Griffiths and others in the very first films. Instead, he developed a management-oriented model that strictly separated conception from execution. The vehicle for this efficiency-based production process was the 'continuity script'. Scenes were shot not chronologically, in story order, but sequenced to maximize production efficiency. This production-management process was honed in Inceville, as it was known, under a schedule of two film productions per week.

Another Ince contribution was the prominence given to the producer as the organizer, owner, and initiator of the filmmaking process, placing the director – who had originally been responsible for improvising much of the content of the film and was considered to be a creative agent – in the role of executor. Ince and his peers established the 'star system' as the initial source of film product differentiation. Under the star system, potential stars, or 'starlets', were trained under contract to the studio. If they appealed to the public, the studio reaped the benefits of a long-term contract whose terms had been established prior to stardom.

Through the efforts of Zukor, Ince, and other film entrepreneurs, the management-oriented Hollywood model for motion picture production was well established by the mid-1920s. This factory-like organization, popularly known as the 'studio system', prevailed until the late 1940s. This period is viewed by many as the golden age of the industry, but also because of the volume of production, but also because the studios constituted a regional craft community. In this system, workers expected stable work over a fairly long period of time. Skills were handed down, father-to-son, and apprenticeships represented admission to a social world as well as to a livelihood. Entry barriers to someone not already in 'the industry' were enormous. Crafts were small, and, with the exception of a few occupations, exclusively open to white men. Thus, along with a stable market and production process came a rigid social and economic hierarchy. The craft community was only one element in that hierarchy. In describing this period, old-timers frequently refer to the family feeling that characterized the industry. Studio heads were paternalistic figures who exercised arbitrary power. As in other oligopolistic industries of this era, the studios provided very large and visible targets against which unionization drives were waged. Virtually all major unions and guilds in the industry were established in the 1930s.

The studios reduced risk by vertically integrating the industry from production through distribution and exhibition. In 1944, for example, the five major studios earned 73% of domestic theatrical rentals and owned or had interests in 4424 theaters – 24% of the US total. These theaters included 70% of all the first-run theaters in the ninety-two cities with populations over 100 000, and they accounted for over 50% of total US box-office receipts. If one examines market shares at smaller geographical scales, the extent of concentration increases: RKO owned 100% of first-run capacity in Minneapolis and Cincinnati, Warner's had 90% of Philadelphia, and so on. In 46% of US markets, one distributor owned all theaters (Waterman, 1978; 1982). The size of the studios' production apparatus, the scale of their output, the stability of their markets, the cost efficiencies of which they were capable, and their monopolization of resources and skilled personnel, created barriers to entry by potential rivals. It was the destruction of these assured market outlets that spelled the end of the studio system[1].

The decline of the studio system

Two shocks to the studio system dramatically changed competitive conditions. The 'Paramount Decision' (*US v Paramount Pictures*, 1948) forced the studios to divest their ownership in theater chains. This decision eliminated an assured market for films and increased the risks associated with production. Each film became a potential source of loss as well as of profit because it no longer had a relatively assured market. Returns per picture could vary greatly. The studios responded by reducing the number of pictures produced. As a result, a production organization based on economies of scale could no longer be justified. The diminished volume of production could not support large studio overhead costs.

In addition to the Paramount decision, demographic and technological developments significantly altered market size and growth prospects. probably the most important of these was the emergence of television as an alternative entertainment medium. The success of television is closely tied to demographic changes, such as the high rate of family formation, and, spatially, to the process of suburbanization. The young people who had faithfully attended downtown cinemas had moved to the suburbs and could not find a babysitter. In the 1950s the drive-in arose as the first suburban alternative to downtown neighborhood theaters.

Television was a technological innovation from outside the motion picture industry and was perceived within the motion picture industry as an inferior product. But it was also correctly understood to be a major potential source of competition in the market for visual electronic entertainment. The advent of television marked the first stage of the segmentation of the market for film entertainment. What had been essentially one market dominated by one medium became a segmented market in which different products competed for the consumer's entertainment expenditures.

The feature film audience declined by 50% between 1946 and 1956. The gross revenues of the ten leading companies fell by 26% during this same period, from $968 million to $717 million. Profits of the leading eight studios declined more than 50%, and the size of the box office as a whole declined by almost 40% between 1945 and 1955. In 1960, box office was only 39% of its level at the end of World War 2 (all in constant dollars).

The initial industry response to the threat of television was to modify the motion picture product, differentiating it to appeal to more specific market segments. One whole category of filmmaking, short subjects, including newsreels, was virtually eliminated from the major studios' product range. Moreover, the number of US-produced features declined by 28% between 1946 and 1956, while the number of imported features in distribution rose by 233%. The average number of films made per year in the USA during the 1950s was only 80% of the 1940s level and by the end of the decade less than half the number of films were made than in the peak year of 1941. In Los Angeles, there was a sharp and persistent decline in employment in the industry. By 1953, employment in the industry in Los Angeles County had dropped to 20000 from a top figure of 33000 in 1944.

With respect to the remaining theatricals, product differentiation became a key strategy to draw people back to the theaters. The 'spectacular', in particular, represented the filmmaker's attempt to recast the feature as a form of entertainment significantly different from television. Technical innovations were aimed at the 'look' of the film, in an effort to differentiate motion pictures from television. Cinerama, technicolor, and three-dimension all aimed at constituting the image of the film as an event, rather than an everyday experience. The increased attention to the individual film project meant increased film budgets for talent, marketing, and advertising. The average cost per picture made by MGM in 1952/53 was $1307000. This increased to $1815000 in 1954/55. For Paramount, the comparable figures are $1777000 in 1952/53 and $2540000 in 1954/55.

To achieve product differentiation, the studios increasingly turned to independent producers to develop film projects. This strategy maximized the studios' possibilities for finding the differentiated film projects they required for success in the market. Thus, the studios first began to disintegrate the preproduction phase of the production process. Warner Brothers, for example, made advances to outside producers of $6426000 in 1951 and $26000000 in 1956. As the decade progressed, additional aspects of the filmmaking process began to be split off from the studios' routine operations. Activities that had been within the studio framework gradually moved to the external market. Eventually, this meant the complete end of the 'term contract', under which writers, actors, and skilled production people worked exclusively for one studio for a specified period of time. It was replaced by a film-to-film contract.

Even though the principal reason for this early disintegration was the studios' deliberate strategy of reducing their overhead, the greater role of the market in allocating resources in the production process also created a series of complex economic tensions in the industry. As noted above, the studio system had functioned as a 'star creation machine'. With the end of the star apprenticeship system in the studio, the stars who were already established became valuable commodities. Released into the open market, they turned their market power back on the studios.

The reduction in industry output also led to changes in the composition of industry employment and to reductions in the amount of work available and in wage levels. Production workers suffered more than other workers from the end of the studio system. Without the apprentice system to bring in new recruits, the industry 'aged'. Older workers, already established in the industry, were able to maintain employment at the expense of younger workers. This was partially the result of the establishment of the roster system which protected workers on the basis of their seniority in the industry (Storper and Christopherson, 1985). An analysis of Motion Picture Health and Welfare Fund recipients in 1957 shows that 91% were men and that only 6.4% were under 30; 50% were over 50 years of age. New people were simply not able to move into the industry (Bernstein, 1957).

Last, both as part of the product-differentiation strategy, and in an attempt to recoup some of the losses suffered in domestic markets, the studios began to diversify motion picture production and distribution internationally. Film production moved outside the USA for several reasons: (1) in response to the growing theatrical market, (2) because the studios owned facilities outside the USA, and (3) because some spectaculars required a look unavailable in US locations. The goal was to produce more films with universal appeal. The reasoning behind these new product decisions was clear. Foreign markets were an important source of income, providing 50% of total film rentals, primarily through presales.

The 1960s: failed attempts at building stable markets
The major studios continued to dominate finance and distribution throughout this period. From 1960 to 1972, for example, the eight major studios accounted for 83% of distributors' grosses in the USA and Canada. At the same time the studios' position in production was becoming less prominent. During the 1960s, independent production became more important to the industry than it had been in the previous decade. Moreover, the 1960s were the nadir of filming in Los Angeles, the time when the future of Los Angeles as a shooting location seemed least assured. There were several reasons for this, all related to the uncertainty that prevailed in the industry as to the future role of the major studios.

The major studios made two major attempts to shore up their position in production. First, they continued the process of internationalization, both to use foreign markets to compensate for increasing uncertainty in the domestic market, and to exploit the cost advantages of foreign locations. Foreign rentals continued to rise as a portion of total rentals. The same was true of foreign production. Only 60% of the total number of production starts by US companies between 1950 and 1973 were located in the USA. This trend accelerated during the 1960s until in 1968 only 47% of film starts were filming in the USA. Second, they changed their relationship to television. In 1965, television networks spent $115 million to rent made-for-television (MFT) films. The average cost per film increased from $169 000 in 1961 to $290 000 in 1966 because of the depletion of film libraries. As a result, producers increased the output of motion pictures for television consumption. Clearly, the studios had hoped that the market for MFT pictures, combined with their European strategy, would enable them to increase the scale of their operations. But the rising costs of MFT films caused the networks to put significant cost-cutting pressures on the studios. The networks (as oligopsonistic consumers of MFTs) began to contract with mini-majors and independents in order to force the majors into price competition. Moreover, foreign producers began to invade US theatrical feature markets for the first time since the War.

This was a critical turning point in the organization of the motion picture industry. The studios had not succeeded in reestablishing stable markets or in enlarging the market as a whole. Since the studios had only partially disintegrated their operations, they still carried a large overhead. In 1970, the major studios suffered their worst year ever, all suffering large losses. The crisis revealed the difficulty of holding vast amounts of property in studios and film libraries. With low profits but large assets, their stocks were undervalued and they became vulnerable to take-overs. Some studios responded by allowing friendly takeovers to occur, becoming divisions of large diversified corporations. Most, however, began to divest themselves of significant proportions of their studio properties. This necessitated that a majority of the output of the industry be produced with vertically disintegrated production methods. The trend toward vertical disintegration – begun in the 1950s – was finally realized.

The studios redefined the studio facilities as 'profit centers', required to support themselves through rentals to independent producers making films with studio financing. In a number of cases, the major studios sold back-lot facilities to reduce overhead and to take advantage of the enormous increases in Southern California real estate prices in recent years. Twentieth Century-Fox sold the land that is now Century City in Los Angeles – a major office, hotel, entertainment, and residential development. Others developed their landholdings in an effort to spread the overhead across additional revenue bases. Universal, for example, has built offices, a major theater, and a studio tour on their land.

There were, therefore, several stages in vertical disintegration. In the 1950s, the studios began to use independent subcontractors to absorb the unstable part of their output and to differentiate the product. In the 1960s, low-budget theatrical films and MFT films were carried out largely by independent companies. Up to this point, subcontracting and independent production companies resembled the familiar case of industrial dualism. By the mid-1970s, however, disintegration gave rise to a circular and cumulative process of further disintegration in the industry that now affects all types of production, not merely low-budget efforts and unstable market segments: the studios' strategy of specializing in high-budget productions is also falling prey to vertical disintegration.

The trend toward production by independent companies and away from the major studios is demonstrated by shifts over time in the proportion of motion pictures produced by different types of production organizations.[2] In 1960, 28% of the motion pictures were produced by independents or independents and others. 66% were produced by majors or majors along with another producer. Independent production as a proportion of the total number of motion pictures produced dropped even further to 21% in 1965 but by 1970 had begun a steady rise in proportion to the majors and mini-majors. Of the motion pictures produced in 1975, independents made up 60% of the total, while the share of productions undertaken exclusively by major studios declined to 33%. In 1980, the dominance of the independents continued even as the total number of films produced declined. Independents produced 58% of the total number of films whereas majors produced 31%. Mini-majors produced 11% of the total number of films for 1980.

To establish the nature and extent of the vertical disintegration of the industry, we examined the births and deaths of selected filmmaking services and facilities in the Los Angeles area.[3] One would expect these firms to increase in number, but to drop in size, as major studios externalize inputs they formerly provided from units within their own organizations. Our tabulations indicate that facilities and services all increase in absolute numbers during the period. Given that motion picture output was stable, the magnitude of these increases provides convincing evidence of a trend toward vertical disintegration. Certain production activities were spun off from the large integrated studios into increasingly specialized establishments, and are now purchased from those subcontractors.

The greatest gains in number of firms during the 1966–82 period were in those firms with functions directly related to the production process – production companies, rental studios, properties, editing, and lighting. Editing firms increased by 2725% during the 1966–82 period; lighting firms, 1050%; rental studios, 415%; properties, 178%; and production companies, the largest single category in absolute number of firms (1473 firms), increased by 162%. In every one of these cases, the major leap in the number of firms was in the 1974–82 period, after the cyclical downturn of the early 1970s.

We also examined the date of founding and employment in a sample of 231 Los Angeles production houses, including firms specializing in commercials, industrials, animation, and special effects, as well as theatrical and television production. The establishment dates of these firms replicate other data indicating industry cycles. Most of the firms were established after 1970. Out of a total of 200 firms reporting establishments dates, 140 were established between 1971 and 1982 and only 39 between 1961 and 1970. The largest surge in firm establishment was in the late 1970s (Nicolaides, 1984). All of these firms are characterized by variable employment depending on projects. They frequently qualify their employment figures with 'regular' or 'full-time'. Their stable employment base is small. Average firm size is 10, but employment for 120 out of the 159 firms reporting employment data is between 1 and 10. The remaining 39 are much larger.

Among firms providing postproduction services (recording; film effects; and film laboratories) the growth profile is more variable than for facilities and services as a whole. Film-processing laboratories increased in number from 1966 to 1974 but have declined since then by 27%. This is presumably attributable to the technological advances in film processing that occurred in this period and which are confirmed in occupational statistics that show a drop in the demand for technicians. Recording studios, in contrast, increased by 835% between 1966 and 1982. Firms specializing in film effects increased by 320% throughout the period.

Vertical disintegration, as we have noted, is generally associated with market differentiation. Thus, it is logical to expect a greater number of firms involved in marketing in a vertically disintegrated industry than in an integrated one, and for the number to increase with greater disintegration. The importance of marketing in this increasingly complex industry is suggested by trends in the group of services loosely categorized under public relations. These include market research and artists' representatives and publicists. Among these firms the big gainer has been in market research which increased from 5 to 24 firms between 1974 and 1982. Artists' representatives increased by 48% between 1966 and 1974 and then declined by 6% by 1982.

The findings with respect to specific types of firms confirm the organizational proliferation that is expected in a disintegrated industry and are confirmed by statistics on the total numbers of establishments in the Standard Industrial Classifications (SICs) related to motion picture production [see Table 24.1].

The emergence of a transactions-intensive entertainment industry
The motion picture industry and closely allied entertainment activities have become a horizontally integrated entertainment industry. The major studios, at the top of the hierarchy, and the production subcontractors, at the bottom, both spread the risk that comes with unstable markets and highly differentiated products, by diversifying into related industries. The studios

Table 24.1   Number of establishments related to motion picture production in the USA (source: US Department of Commerce, Annual County Business Patterns).

SIC*	Description	1968	1974	1981
7813	Motion pictures (MP) excluding television	666	1279	1023
7814	MP and tape production for television	490	978	1420
7819	Services allied to MP production	na	716	1077
	Totals	1156	2983	3520

*SIC Standard Industrial Classification.   na not available.

form financial alliances with other entertainment industries, playing the role of institutional investor. As major investors, they control the profit-expanding 'afterlife' of a film, in television, or book rights and video cassettes. This is made possible by the merging and overlapping of entertainment technologies, such as television, motion pictures, and recording. Partially as a result of this increasing financial scale, other industries have purchased motion picture companies (for example, Paramount by Gulf and Western), and motion picture studios are investing in other entertainment industries.

Production subcontractors spread risk by serving a variety of clients, with different final outputs. They specialize in certain generic functions (props and scenery, film editing, sound mixing, etc.) but are able to work on a broader range of product outputs. They are both flexible and specialized. All of these activities require constant access to new information, personal visibility, and the use of intermediaries, particularly entertainment lawyers and agents. Every actor, director and goods or service contractor is also a deal maker, negotiating his or her way through a maze of possibilities and potential or actual contractual agreements. This complex transactional process is not unlike that in financial services and, not coincidentally, has had the same agglomerative effect.

The drive, skill, and persistence required in this transactions-intensive industry contrasts strongly with the image of Los Angeles in the popular imagination. As Morris once wrote about Los Angeles, a spiritually anarchistic society can afford to be disorganized, a highly materialistic society (of which Los Angeles is the epitome), requires massive discipline (Morris, 1980).

The spatial consequences of vertical disintegration
Los Angeles was initially a shooting location for the independent producers of the first decade of film production. Silent filmmakers preferred exotic outdoor locations and had no need for studio sets which only became necessary with sound. So, the first productions in Los Angeles (between 1907 and 1920) were shot throughout the region. Westerns, the most popular genre of the time, were frequently filmed in the San Fernando Valley. *Birth of a Nation*, the D W Griffith masterpiece, was filmed in the Hollywood Hills.

In the first phase of industry production in Los Angeles some small operations were located in Hollywood, a citrus-growing area a trolley ride away from downtown. As the volume of production grew, studios were transformed into large vertically integrated motion picture factories. These facilities were located in what was then the metropolitan fringe where large blocks of land were available. MGM located in Culver City (1915), Universal in Universal City (1915), Warner Brothers in Burbank (1928), Republic in Studio City, Disney in Burbank, and Twentieth Century-Fox in Westwood (1928). The introduction of sound accelerated tendencies toward vertical integration and large-scale production. It increased the studio's need for back-lot properties, expanded the skilled labor force, and raised capital requirements. In its choice of suburban facilities, the locational behavior of the industry was consistent with that of other large vertically integrated industries in the middle of the 20th century.

Hollywood functioned as the 'downtown' of the industry rather than as its production center. Hollywood Boulevard theaters premiered films and its Roosevelt Hotel hosted the first Motion Picture Academy Awards. Sunset Boulevard and Vine Street were centers of business services and industry 'watering holes', such as the Brown Derby restaurant. The Hollywood Hills became the residence of executives and stars. These functions have since been displaced to Westwood, Beverly Hills, and Beverly Hills–Brentwood–Malibu, respectively. Hollywood was the center of the motion picture industry, but not in the way the myth has it.

The suburban location of the motion picture studios contributed to the development of Los Angeles as a polycentric metropolitan region. The motion picture industry was a major employer in Los Angeles in the 1920s, employing 12 000 people full-time with another 150 000 extras on call. These people worked in over fifty studios, concentrated in the region but not in a central-city industrial district. Business and residential districts developed around these studio centers. Much of the work force of the industry settled in the flatlands of West Los Angeles, and in the early suburban communities of North Hollywood and Burbank, and the executives and stars ultimately moved to the growing suburb of Beverly Hills.

As we have described, the vertical disintegration of the industry that commenced in the 1950s began to alter the location of various activities in the industry. Beginning in the 1960s, location shooting began to move away from Los Angeles. In that decade, there were some tendencies for business establishments and employment to decentralize away from the center of the industry in Southern California, as well. Indeed, in the mid-1960s, when the studios failed to reestablish their markets, the nadir of shooting activity in Los Angeles occurred. In retrospect, this was the point at which it was most probable that the studios would move their facilities outside Los Angeles and try to establish cost-conscious, but still integrated, production methods. But by the mid-1970s, with vertical disintegration, a powerful trend was established to reagglomerate industry establishments and employment in Los Angeles. This trend has continued through the early 1980s.

Motion picture employment concentrated in California between 1968 and 1981, with a temporary drop in the Californian state in 1974 [Table 24.2(a)]. In services allied to motion picture production (SIC 7819) employment has always been highly concentrated in New York and California. More recently, employment is further concentrating in California at the expense of New York [Table 24.2(b)].

In comparison with the trends in employment, establishments in the motion picture industry (SIC 7813) show a certain tendency to decentralize nationally – that is, the position of New York as secondary center is giving way to a more dispersed pattern – while the position of California as the principal national center is stable or slightly stronger [Table 24.2(c)]. In motion picture services (SIC 7819), by contrast, reagglomeration in California is very strongly in evidence. California shows gains of 9%–10% in its share between 1974 and 1981 [Table 24.2(d)].[1]

Establishments were more spatially concentrated in motion pictures services (SIC 7819) than in motion picture production (SIC 7813). This can be explained by the much larger establishment size in SIC 7813, where the

Table 24.2 State shares[a] of employment in and numbers of establishments in the USA, 1968–1981 (source: US Department of Commerce, County Business Patterns).

	CA	FL	TX	NY	IL	NJ	USA	Top states
(a) Employment in motion picture production (SIC 7813)[b]								
1968	10 252	193	202	2611	712		15 461	
	(66.3)	(1.3)	(1.3)	(16.9)	(4.6)			(85.5)
1974	8490	157	417	2173	500–999	88	14 318	
	(59.3)	(1.1)	(2.9)	(15.2)		(0.6)		(78.2)
1981	18 807	148	368	1879	1139	51	25 611	
	(73.4)	(0.6)	(1.4)	(7.3)	(4.4)	(0.2)		
(b) Employment in services ancillary to motion picture production (SIC 7819)[b]								
1974	9663	206	131	3110	382	90	15 274	
	(63.3)	(1.3)	(0.9)	(20.4)	(2.5)	(0.6)		(89.0)
1981	12 205	73	437	3135	426	85	18 169	
	(67.2)	(0.4)	(2.4)	(17.3)	(2.3)	(0.3)		(89.9)
(c) Motion picture establishments (SIC 7813)[b]								
1968	263	12	14	199	18		666	
	(39.5)	(1.8)	(2.1)	(29.9)	(2.7)			
1974	534	33	36	303	53	24	1279	
	(41.8)	(2.6)	(2.8)	(23.7)	(4.1)	(1.9)		(77.9)
1981	414	19	25	214	57	17	1023	
	(40.5)	(1.9)	(2.4)	(20.9)	(5.6)	(1.7)		(71.0)
(d) Services ancillary to motion picture production (SIC 7819)[b]								
1974	284	14	13	233	36	12	716	
	(39.7)	(1.9)	(1.8)	(32.5)	(5.0)	(1.7)		
1981	536	11	28	289	33	21	1077	
	(49.8)	(1.0)	(2.6)	(26.8)	(3.1)	(1.9)		

[a]These are given in parentheses, as percentages of the national figures.
[b]Standard Industrial Classification.

Key to US states

CA California
FL Florida
TX Texas
NY New York
IL Illinois
NJ New Jersey

lowest proportion of establishments is agglomerated in Los Angeles, but the highest proportion of employment (more than 73%). In other words, there are many motion picture production establishments spread across the country, but they do not appear to be responsible for a proportionately large share of the filming. We do not have specific information on the physical size of these establishments, but our analysis suggests that a much larger share of production capacity is concentrated in Los Angeles than our figures allow. Moreover, many of the facilities outside Los Angeles are, in effect, double counted, because they are really adjuncts to regional television facilities that can be pressed into service for the occasional motion picture project.

Although in our industrial analysis we have focused on motion picture production, the recent merger of motion picture and television production facilities suggested the need to compare locational trends in the two industries. Employment in television rapidly concentrated in California between 1968 and 1974, at which point some of the gain to California was lost. Only a portion of this was reestablished in New York, however. Over the long period, there was net concentration both of television employment and of establishments in California (Storper and Christopherson, 1985, chapter 2).

Motion picture production consists of three main phases, or bundles of tasks: preproduction, production (filming), and postproduction. Location of the production (filming) stage in features and MFT films is more widely dispersed than the location of employment and establishments. The peak year for filming in metropolitan Los Angeles was 1960 and the trough both in relative and in absolute terms was 1970. Since 1970, the shares of both Los Angeles and California as a whole have risen, but much more slowly than the concentration of employment and establishments, implying that Los Angeles is recovering from a devastating loss of filming activity in the 1960s, but is not on the way to reasserting its position as the undisputed center of filming activity in the USA [Table 24.3]. The motion picture industry of the 1980s thus has a split locational pattern: businesses and the work force have reconcentrated in the Los Angeles region, but shooting has taken on a widely dispersed pattern.

The restructured motion picture industry has not only recentralized in the Los Angeles region, it also has a different intraregional pattern than that of the major studios. Fully 65% of the subcontracting firms are located in Hollywood proper, which has only 13% of the sound stage capacity in the region. 20% of the subcontracting firms are located in the San Fernando Valley which has a 50% share of sound stages. 2% of subcontracting firms are located in Culver City which has 20% of regional sound stages.

Explaining the split locational pattern
Vertical disintegration is the principal cause both of the concentration of establishments and employment and of the dispersal of filming. Firms have concentrated in Los Angeles because the specialized nature of their services and the constant change in product output requires nonroutine, frequent market transactions with other firms, such as production companies and major studios. By concentrating in the center of the motion picture industry they maximize their opportunities for making the deals we described earlier.

Table 24.3 Location of production activity (source: *Daily Variety*, our calculations).

Year	Metro Los Angeles	California	Metro New York	Rest of USA	Europe	Rest of World	Totals[a]
1960	50	50	5	12.5	22.5	7.5	97.5
	(74)	(74)	(7)	(18)	(33)	(13)	(151)
1965	47.5	47.5	0	2.5	22.5	10.0	82.5
	(93)	(93)	(0)	(7)	(43)	(19)	(190)
1970	22.5	30	10	17.5	32.5	7.5	97.6
	(48)	(62)	(19)	(36)	(67)	(?)	(209)
1975	25	30.0	5	17.5	27.5	17.5	97.5
	(64)	(81)	(10)	(44)	(67)	(43)	(244)
1980	30	33.5	12.5	22.5	15	15	97.5
	(65)	(74)	(27)	(55)	(33)	(34)	(223)
1984	33	38	13	36.5	6	6	99.5
	(68)	(79)	(28)	(76)	(13)	(13)	(209)
Exclusive locations[b]							
1984	31	38	14	40.5	3	4.5	100.0
	(39)	(48)	(18)	(51)	(4)	(6)	(126)

Note: The entries are percentages; numbers in parentheses are actual number of films.
[a]Total percentages may be less than 100 where some films were not classified. Totals may be greater than the sum of classified films because many films are classified more than once, as they have several locations.
[b]Films made exclusively at one location.

Horizontal integration and industrial complex reformation strengthens the external economies that exist in the motion picture industry alone. Many of the subcontracting firms are specialized in a certain type of activity (recording, special effects, etc.) but not in a particular fixed output. They market not only to motion pictures, but to as many segments of the electronic entertainment industries as they can. Almost all work both in film and in video formats and produce commercials, industrial and educational films, as well as theatrical or MFT movies. Only a small minority concentrates exclusively on television and feature films. The formation of this flexible entertainment industrial complex implies very strong forces of agglomeration. As uncertainty has been transmitted down the subcontracting hierarchy within the motion picture industry, those firms on the receiving end have marketed services across what formerly were rigid boundaries among entertainment industries. Cross-industry markets offset some of the uncertainty created by disintegration. Simultaneously, the advantages of spatial agglomeration are increased.

Agglomeration also maintains and reproduces a highly skilled labor force. In many motion picture occupations, skill transmission within families is very important. Strong social and ethnic connections are also important to industry transactions and to skill transmission. These connections are ever more important in an industry in which 'the deal' and thus personal knowledge and credibility are central elements. Among above-the-line personnel, the creative and managerial portion of the industry, entrepreneurial skills are transmitted through social and family networks, localized on the Westside of Los Angeles and in the San Fernando Valley. Institutions, such as the University of Southern California and the University of California – Los Angeles play a role in transmitting industry-specific skills and are strongly supported by the industry community in this effort. In many respects, the strong social network of the motion picture industry resembles aspects of craft communities in cities in early industrial Europe and the 19th century United States. As such it cannot be analyzed strictly in terms evolved to explain mass production industries with stable long-term employment relations. It appears that the importance of social networks has been enhanced rather than diminished by the vertical disintegration of the industry.

The concentration of a large number of industry employers in Los Angeles is vital to the way work is distributed among the work force and to the job-search process of the individual worker. The larger the overall demand for labor, the greater the chance that as one job terminates, a worker will be able to search for and secure another job. Most workers in the entertainment industry, however, do not participate in an open labor market. They secure positions through well-established networks of contacts or through institutional means such as the roster system. Even these networks, however, can only channel the work that is available, so the higher the proportion of the work of the industry that is concentrated in the region, the greater chance there is to find work.

In addition, many of the skills demanded in motion picture production are required in the other entertainment industries, including television, recording and theater. To the extent that these industries concentrate in the same place as motion picture production, workers who possess skills applicable across industries will find an even larger pool of job opportunities. The presence of an entertainment industry complex in Los Angeles makes it easier for various industries to offset risks that unstable work creates for the labor force. They help each other to maintain the labor pool they all use in common (Storper and Christopherson, 1985).

The other side of the locational pattern is the increasing tendency for films to be shot outside the Los Angeles region. There are several reasons for this. First, once the script, crew, equipment, and locations have been chosen and financing has been secured, the level of specialized external transactions drops. During filming, transactions principally take the form of retail purchases. So, it becomes possible to relocate production during this phase. The decentralization of the relatively more routine filming process away from Los Angeles is further facilitated by technologies such as mobile vans and lighting and handheld lightweight cameras.

Initially, the independent production companies sought alternative locations because they were faced with greater production-cost constraints than the major studios and had no studio facilities to fill with productions. As a consequence, there are differences in the spatial patterns of filming on the part of different types of production companies. Of the films shot in

California, but outside Los Angeles, between 1965 and 1980, 68% were made by independents and 29% by major studios. Of those made in Los Angeles and Southern California, 34% were made by independents and 55% by the major studios alone or in partnership with another producer. Of the films made in New York, 41% were produced by independents and 50% by the majors. In Florida, 67% were made by independents; in Texas, 53% were made by independents. Of the 132 films shot in other places in the USA, 45% were made by independents and 45% by majors. The major studios clearly have produced the majority of pictures shot in Europe (53%) whereas of the films shot outside of North America and Europe, 59% were made by independents.

The practice of location shooting has been self-reinforcing. For example, production companies have used locations outside Los Angeles and New York to avoid the work rules in force in those areas. West Coast union work rules prevail within a radius of 300 miles from the corner of Beverly and La Cienega Boulevards in Hollywood. Since these rules limit the length of the working day, they can force a production to use more shooting than would be the case in another location. This is critical given the high fixed costs of the shooting day. Wage rates are more important with respect to screen extras and construction workers than the skilled crew members. However, skilled members often informally waive union work rules when they are on location outside the geographical limit.

Technological innovations, the avoidance of work rules, and the new standard of realism in motion pictures have made location shooting a basic part of every production company's locational calculus. This includes the major studios which have shed much of the overhead associated with their facilities and backlots, freeing them to carry out production on location. As a result, however, the studios have become victims of their own vertical disintegration strategy. Because it is difficult to attract productions to their high-priced back lots they suffer consistent shortfalls in capacity utilization. These shortfalls encourage them to continue shedding overhead, leading to more vertical disintegration. Location shooting results in continuous improvement in the technologies required for cost-competitive and high-quality output outside the studios, and it accustoms audiences to a realistic look. What began, then, as a strategy of using subcontractors to absorb uncertainty has, in circular and cumulative fashion, come to dictate the competitive standard for production in the industry, including the major studios.

Conclusions

Given the trends toward flexible organization in a variety of industries and in a wide range of modern industrial economies, this study of vertical disintegration in filmmaking has implications beyond those for the Los Angeles regional economy. In particular, our study is in concert with other recent work that shows that industries do not have a 'normal' development path. In the case examined here there were two critical junctures. The first came with the Paramount decision in 1948, which began the process of vertical disintegration by forcing the studios to divest themselves of their captive theater chains. The second came in the 1960s when the studios attempted to save mass production by moving into television. They failed to reestablish mass production and decisively turned the industry toward greater vertical disintegration. Oligopoly was broken down through a combination of political forces. and technological-cum-product competition, and the strategic responses of studios, independent production companies, and television networks to these forces. Flexible specialization followed. Our study thus supports the notion that an industry can have a number of organizational 'fates' including vertical integration but also including vertical disintegration.

The split locational pattern we have described has relevance for regional economies dominated by service industries organized around the production of a service product (that is, software, contracts, advertisements, films). Vertical disintegration in the motion picture industry created powerful agglomeration tendencies at the regional level by increasing the transactions intensity of production and the instability of employment relations. The instability and uncertainty it created for subcontractors and supplier firms encouraged the recomposition of the motion picture industry and the breakdown of interindustry barriers. This process may be occurring in other similarly situated industries, explaining the recentralization of service production activities with high value added in a relatively few metropolitan areas, particularly New York and Los Angeles.

Finally, the evolution of motion picture industry structure has important implications for the economic future and urban character of Los Angeles. The new motion picture industry has become relocalized in Los Angeles because its managerial process requires industry-specific knowledge and social interaction, because there are myriad deals to be made, and the input–output relations between firms are largely unstandardized and of small scale. Yet, much production work still occurs outside the metropolitan area. In effect, the reagglomeration of the industry means that Los Angeles is the headquarters and technological center for an industrial complex that has the whole world as its back lot.

Acknowledgements

The research on which this paper is based was carried out with a grant from the John Randolph Haynes and Dora Haynes Foundation. The conclusions are solely those of the authors. A more extensive discussion of the motion picture industry is contained in a report (Storper and Christopherson, 1985).

The authors would like to thank the following students in the UCLA Urban Planning Program for their research assistance: Larry Barth, Robin Bloch, Gillian Court, Rebecca Day, and Rehema Gray.

Notes

1   The studio system reached its apex during the World War 2 years, both in employment and in the number of pictures released. Employment peaked in 1944

at 33 000. The importance of the industry to Los Angeles is demonstrated by the fact that total salaries and wages paid to all employees in this industry in the post-peak year of 1947 exceeded those of any other manufacturing industry in the Los Angeles metropolitan area. US theater attendance reached its peak in 1946 with over 90 million admissions to movie theaters per week.

2   To measure this phenomenon, we constructed a file of all films whose production was reported in the 'film charts' of *Daily Variety* and *The Hollywood Reporter*, at five-year intervals between 1960 and 1980, with a supplement for 1984. This resulted in a sample of approximately 1200 films.

3   Information on filmmaking services and facilities in the Los Angeles region was obtained by using service directories for the industry, the *Hollywood Reporter Studio Blu-Book Directory* and the *International Motion Picture Industry Almanac*, as well as *The Production Company*. Although the firms listed in the *Blu-Book* and *Motion Picture Almanac* represent a selective sample of services and facilities, they provide the best historical source available.

In establishing the numbers of firms in each category, we assumed that a firm not listed in the previous period had been established in the interim. We were careful, also, to eliminate any duplication in directory listing, so as to minimize double counting. Listings in the following categories of facilities and services were tabulated: animation; artists' representatives and talent agencies; editing; film effects; film processing laboratories; rental studios; lighting; market research; production companies; properties; recording and sound studios.

4   California had a temporary drop in share of employment in SIC 7813 in 1974 because the industry was in a deep cyclical recession from 1971 to 1975. The Californian share of establishments remained stable during the period. Layoffs between 1968 and 1974 were more severe in California than the national average (1974 employment per establishment at only 40.7% of 1968 levels, as opposed to 48.2% for the USA and 54.3% for New York). Note, however, that in all periods, the gross size of establishment (measured in terms of employees) is much greater in California than elsewhere. Recession layoffs were proportionately greatest in California. Moreover, the ratio of supervisory or managerial personnel to total employment is probably lower in California than elsewhere (as a consequence of the greater proportion of the work force involved in production and the larger establishment size, permitting managerial economies of scale), leading to a greater proportionate loss of employment in the recession than in the other places (Storper and Christopherson, 1985). In other words, 1974 does not represent a structural tendency in the location of employment, only a cyclical effect.

References

Bagnasco, A. 1977: *Tre Italie: La Problematica dello Svillupo*; Bologna: Il Mulino.

Bernstein, I. 1957: The changing motion picture industry. Institute for Industrial Relations, University of California, Los Angeles.

Brusco, S. and Sabel, C. 1983: Artisanal production and economic growth. In Wilkinson, F. (ed.), *The dynamics of labor market segmentation*. London: Academic Press, 99–113.

Hollywood Reporter Studio Blu-Book Directory annual: Los Angeles, CA: Hollywood Reporter.

Holmes, J. 1986: The organization and locational structure of production subcontracting. In Scott, A.J. and Storper, M. (eds), *Production, work, territory: the geographical anatomy of industrial capitalism*. Winchester, MA: Allen and Unwin, 80–106.

Ikeda, M. 1979: The subcontracting system in the Japanese electronic industry. *Engineering industries of Japan* **19**, 43–71.

International Motion Picture Industry Almanac 1933–1985, annual: New York: Quigley Publications.

Morris, J. 1980: Los Angeles, the know-how city. In *Destinations*. New York: Oxford University Press, 42–57.

Nicolaides, L. (ed.) 1984: *The production company: the complete guide to commercial and industrial production companies in Los Angeles*, 1984 edn. Los Angeles, CA: Paramount Publications.

Piore, M. and Sabel, C. 1984: *The second industrial divide*. New York: Basic Books.

Sayer, A. 1985: New developments in manufacturing and their spatial implications: from flexible manufacturing systems to just-in time. Paper presented at conference on Spatial Structures and Social Processes, Lesbos, Greece; WP49, Urban and Regional Studies, University of Sussex, Brighton, Sussex.

Scott, A. 1985: Industrial organization and location: division of labor, the firm, and spatial process. Department of Geography, University of California – Los Angeles, CA.

Storper, M. and Christopherson, S. 1985: The changing location and organization of the motion picture industry: interregional shifts in the United States. School of Architecture and Urban Planning, University of California – Los Angeles, CA.

US v Paramount Pictures 1948: 334 US 131 (1948).

Waterman, D. 1978: *Economic essays on the theatrical motion picture industry*. PhD dissertation, Department of Economics, Stanford University, Stanford, CA.

Waterman, D. 1982: The structural development of the motion picture industry. *American Economist* **26**, 16–27.

25

Nihilism in black America

Cornel West

From Gina Dent (ed.), *Black popular culture* (Bay Press, 1992).

Recent discussions about the plight of African Americans – especially those at the bottom of the social ladder – tend to divide into two camps. On the one hand, there are those who highlight the *structural* constraints on the life chances of black people. This point of view involves a subtle historical and sociological analysis of slavery, Jim Crowism, job and residential discrimination, skewed unemployment rates, inadequate health care, and poor education. On the other hand, there are those who stress the *behavioral* impediments to black upward mobility. They focus on the waning of the Protestant ethic – hard work, deferred gratification, frugality, and responsibility – in much of black America.

Those in the first camp – the liberal structuralists – call for full employment, health, education and child-care programs, and broad affirmative action practices. In short, a new, more sober version of the best of the New Deal and the Great Society: more government money, better bureaucrats, and an active citizenry. Those in the second camp – the conservative behaviorists – promote self-help programs, black business expansion, and non-preferential job practices. They support vigorous 'free market' strategies that depend on fundamental changes in how black people act and live. To put it bluntly, their projects rest largely upon a cultural revival of the Protestant ethic in black America.

Unfortunately, these two camps have nearly suffocated the crucial debate that should be taking place about the prospects for black America. This debate must go far beyond the liberal and conservative positions in three fundamental ways. First, we must acknowledge that structures and behavior are inseparable, that institutions and values go hand in hand. How people act and live is shaped – though in no way dictated or determined – by the larger circumstances in which they find themselves. These circumstances can be changed, their limits attenuated, by positive actions to elevate living conditions.

Second, we should reject the idea that structures are primarily economic and political creatures – an idea that sees culture as an ephemeral set of behavioral attitudes and values. Culture is quite as structural as the economy or politics; it is rooted in institutions like families, schools, churches, synagogues, mosques, and communication industries (television, radio, video, music). Similarly, the economy and politics are not only influenced by values, they also promote particular cultural ideals of the good life and good society.

Third, and most important, we must delve into the depths where neither liberals nor conservatives dare to tread, namely, into the murky waters of despair and dread that now flood the streets of black America. To talk about the depressing statistics of unemployment, infant mortality, incarceration, teenage pregnancy, and violent crime is one thing. But to face up to the monumental eclipse of hope, the unprecedented collapse of meaning, the incredible disregard for human (especially black) life and property in much of black America is something else.

The liberal-conservative discussion conceals the most basic issue now facing black America: *the nihilistic threat to its very existence.* This threat is not simply a matter of relative economic deprivation and political powerlessness – though economic well-being and political clout are requisites for meaningful black progress. It is primarily a question of speaking to the profound sense of psychological depression, personal worthlessness, and social despair so widespread in black America.

The liberal structuralists fail to grapple with this threat for two reasons: First, their focus on structural constraints relates almost exclusively to the economy and politics. They show no understanding of the structural character of culture. Why? Because they tend to view people in egoistic and rationalist terms, according to which they are motivated primarily by self-interest and self-preservation. Needless to say, this is partly true about most of us. Yet, people, especially degraded and oppressed people, are also hungry for identity, meaning, and self-worth.

The second reason liberal structuralists overlook the nihilistic threat is a sheer failure of nerve. They hesitate to talk honestly about culture, the realm of meanings and values, because to do so may seem to lend itself too readily to conservative conclusions in the narrow way Americans discuss race. If there is a hidden taboo among liberals, it is to resist talking about values *too much* because it takes the focus away from structures, especially the positive role of government. But this failure leaves the existential and psychological realities of black people in the lurch. In this way, liberal structuralists neglect the battered identities rampant in black America.

As for the conservative behaviorists, they not only misconstrue the nihilistic threat, but inadvertently contribute to it. This is a serious charge, and it rests upon three claims. First, conservative behaviorists talk about values and attitudes as if political and economic structures hardly exist. They rarely, if ever, examine the innumerable cases in which black people do act on the Protestant ethic and still remain at the bottom of the social ladder. Instead, they highlight the few instances in which blacks ascend to the top, as if such success is available to all blacks, regardless of circumstances. Such a vulgar rendition of Horatio Alger in blackface may serve as a source of inspiration to some – a kind of model for those already on the right track. But it cannot serve as a substitute for serious historical and social analysis of the predicaments of and prospects for all black people, especially the grossly disadvantaged ones.

Second, conservative behaviorists discuss black culture as if acknowledging one's obvious victimization by white supremacist practices (compounded by sexism and class condition) is taboo. They tell black people to see themselves as agents, not victims. And on the surface, this is comforting advice, a nice cliché for downtrodden people. But inspirational slogans cannot substitute for substantive historical and social analysis. Although black people have never been simply victims, wallowing in self-pity and begging for white giveaways, they have been – and are – victimized. Therefore, to call on black people to be agents makes sense only if we also examine the dynamics of this victimization against which their agency will, in part, be exercised. What is particularly naive and peculiarly vicious about the conservative behavioral outlook is that it tends to deny the lingering effect of black history – a history inseparable from though not reducible to victimization. In this way, crucial and indispensable themes of self-help and personal responsibility are wrenched out of historical context and contemporary circumstances – as if it is all a matter of personal will.

This ahistorical perspective contributes to the nihilistic threat within black America in that it can be used to justify right-wing cutbacks for poor people struggling for decent housing, child care, health care, and education. And, as I pointed out earlier, although liberals are deficient in important ways, they are right on target in their critique of conservative government cutbacks for services to the poor. These ghastly cutbacks are one cause of the nihilistic threat to black America.

The proper starting point for the crucial debate about the prospects for black America is the nihilism that increasingly pervades black communities. *Nihilism is to be understood here not as a philosophic doctrine that there are no rational grounds for legitimate standards or authority; it is, far more, the lived experience of coping with a life of horrifying meaninglessness, hopelessness, and (most important) lovelessness.* This usually results in a numbing detachment from others and a self-destructive disposition toward the world. Life without meaning, hope, and love breeds a coldhearted, mean-spirited outlook that destroys both the individual and others.

Nihilism is not new in black America. The first African encounter with the New World was an encounter with a distinctive form of the Absurd. The initial black struggle against degradation and devaluation is the enslaved circumstances of the New World was, in part, a struggle against nihilism. In fact, the major enemy of black survival in America has been, and is, neither oppression nor exploitation but rather the nihilistic threat – that is, loss of hope and absence of meaning. For as long as hope remains and meaning is preserved, the possibility of overcoming oppression stays alive. The self-fulfilling prophecy of the nihilistic threat is that without hope there can be no struggle.

The genius of our black foremothers and forefathers was to create powerful buffers to ward off the nihilistic threat, to equip black folk with cultural armor to beat back the demons of hopelessness, meaninglessness, and lovelessness. These buffers consisted of cultural structures of meaning and feeling that created and sustained communities; this armor constituted ways of life and struggle that embodied values of service and sacrifice, love and care, discipline and excellence. In other words, traditions for black surviving and thriving under usually adverse New World conditions were major barriers against the nihilistic threat. These traditions consist primarily of black religious and civic institutions that sustained familial and communal networks of support. If cultures are, in part, what human beings create (out of antecedent fragments of other cultures) in order to convince themselves not to commit suicide, then black foremothers and forefathers are to be applauded. In fact, until the early seventies black Americans had the lowest suicide rate in the United States. But, now young black people lead the nation in suicides.

What has changed? What went wrong? The bitter irony of integration? The cumulative effects of a genocidal conspiracy? The virtual collapse of rising expectations after the optimistic sixties? None of us fully understands why the nihilistic threat is more powerful now than ever before. I believe that the commodification of black life and the crisis of black leadership are two basic reasons. The recent shattering of black civil society – black families, neighborhoods, schools, churches, mosques – leaves more and more black people vulnerable to the nihilistic threat. This shattering spawns a deracinated and denuded people with little sense of self and few existential moorings.

Black people have always been in America's wilderness in search of a promised land. Yet many black folk now reside in a jungle with a cutthroat morality devoid of any faith in deliverance or hope for freedom. Contrary to the superficial claims of conservative behaviorists, these jungles are not primarily the result of pathological behavior. Rather, this behavior is the tragic response of a people bereft of resources to confront the workings of US capitalist society. This does not mean that individual black people are not responsible for their actions – black murderers and rapists should go to jail. But it does mean that the nihilistic threat contributes to criminal behavior – a threat that feeds on poverty *and* shattered cultural institutions. The nihilistic threat is now more powerful than ever before because the armor to ward against it is weaker.

But why this shattering of black civil society, this weakening of black cultural institutions in asphalt jungles? Corporate market institutions have contributed greatly to this situation. By corporate market institutions I mean that complex set of interlocking enterprises that have a disproportionate amount of capital, power, and influence on how our society is shaped. Needless to say, the primary motivation of these institutions is to make profits, and their basic strategy is to convince the public to consume. These institutions have helped create a seductive way of life, a culture of consumption that capitalizes on every opportunity to make money. Market calculations and cost-benefit analyses hold sway in almost every sphere of US society.

The common denominator in these calculations and analyses is usually the provision, expansion, and intensification of pleasure. Pleasure is a multivalent term; it means different things to many people. In our way of life it involves comfort, convenience, and sexual stimulation. This mentality pays little heed to the past, and views the future as no more than a repetition of a hedonistically driven present. This market morality stigmatizes others as objects for personal pleasure or bodily stimulation. In this view, traditional morality is not undermined by radical feminists, cultural radicals in the sixties, or libertarians, as alleged by conservative behaviorists. Rather, corporate market institutions have greatly contributed to undermining traditional morality in order to stay in business and make a profit. This is especially evident in the culture industries – television, radio, video, music – in which gestures of foreplay and orgiastic pleasure flood the marketplace.

Like all Americans, African Americans are influenced greatly by the images of comfort, convenience, machismo, femininity, violence, and sexual stimulation that bombard consumers. These seductive images contribute to the predominance of the market-inspired way of life over all others – and thereby edge out nonmarket values – love, care, service to others – handed down by preceding generations. The predominance of this way of life among those living in poverty-ridden conditions, with a limited capacity to ward off self-contempt and self-hatred, results in the possible triumph of the nihilistic threat in black America.

A major contemporary strategy for holding the nihilistic threat at bay is to attack directly the sense of worthlessness and self-loathing in black America. The angst resembles a kind of collective clinical depression in significant pockets of black America. The eclipse of hope and collapse of meaning in much of black America is linked to the structural dynamics of corporate market institutions that affect all Americans. Under these circumstances, black existential angst derives from the lived experience of ontological wounds and emotional scars inflicted by white supremacist beliefs and images permeating US society and culture. These wounds and scars attack black intelligence, black ability, black beauty, and black character daily in subtle and not-so-subtle ways.

The accumulated effect of these wounds and scars produces a deep-seated anger, a boiling sense of rage, and a passionate pessimism regarding America's will to justice. Under conditions of slavery and Jim Crow segregation, this anger, rage, and pessimism remained relatively muted because of a well-justified fear of brutal white retaliation. The major breakthroughs of the sixties – more psychically then politically – swept this fear away. Sadly, the combination of the market way of life, poverty-ridden conditions, black existential angst, and the lessoning of fear toward white authorities has directed most of the anger, rage, and despair toward fellow black citizens, especially black women. Only recently has this nihilistic threat – and its ugly inhumane outlook and actions – surfaced in the larger American society. And it surely reveals one of the many instances of cultural decay in a declining empire.

What is to be done about this nihilistic threat? Is there really any hope, given our shattered civil society, market-driven corporate enterprises, and white supremacism? If one begins with the threat of concrete nihilism, then one must talk about some kind of *politics of conversion*. New models of collective black leadership must promote a version of this politics. Like alcoholism and drug addiction, nihilism is a disease of the soul. It can never be completely cured, and there is always the possibility of relapse. But there is always a chance for conversion – a chance for people to believe that there is hope for the future and a meaning to struggle. This chance rests neither on an agreement about what justice consists of nor on an analysis of how racism, sexism, or class subordination operate. Such arguments and analyses are indispensable, but a politics of conversion requires more. Nihilism is not overcome by arguments or analyses; it is tamed by love and care. Any disease of the soul must be conquered by a turning of one's soul. This turning is done by one's own affirmation of one's worth – an affirmation fueled by the concern of others. This is why a love ethic must be at the center of a politics of conversion.

This love ethic has nothing to do with sentimental feelings or tribal connections. Rather it is a last attempt at generating a sense of agency among a downtrodden people. The best exemplar of this love ethic is depicted on a number of levels in Toni Morrison's novel *Beloved*. Self-love and love of others are both modes toward increasing self-valuation and encouraging political resistance in one's community. These modes of valuation and resistance are rooted in a subversive memory – the best of one's past without romantic nostalgia – and guided by a universal love ethic. For my purposes here, *Beloved* can be construed as bringing together the loving yet critical affirmation of black humanity found in the best of black nationalist movements, the perennial hope against hope for transracial coalition in progressive movements, and the painful struggle for self-affirming sanity in a history in which the nihilistic threat *seems* insurmountable.

The politics of conversion proceed principally on the local level – in those institutions in civil society still vital enough to promote self-worth and self-affirmation. It surfaces on the state and national levels only when grass-roots democratic organizations put forward a collective leadership that has earned the love and respect of and, most important, that has proved itself *accountable* to these organizations. This collective leadership must exemplify moral integrity, character, and democratic statesmanship within itself and within its organizations.

Like liberal structuralists, the advocates of a politics of conversion never lose sight of the structural conditions that shape the sufferings and lives of people. Yet, unlike liberal structuralism, the politics of conversion meet the nihilistic threat head-on. Like conservative behaviorism, the politics of conversion openly confronts the self-destructive and inhumane actions of black people. Unlike conservative behaviorists, the politics of conversion situates (not exonerates) these actions within inhumane circumstances. The politics of conversion shuns the limelight – a limelight that solicits status seekers and ingratiates egomaniacs. Instead, it stays on the ground among the toiling everyday people, ushering forth humble freedom fighters – both followers and leaders – who have the audacity to take the nihilistic threat by the neck and turn back its deadly assaults.

The nihilistic threat to black America is inseparable from a crisis in black leadership. This crisis is threefold. First, at the national level, the courageous yet problematic example of Jesse Jackson looms large. On the one hand, his presidential campaigns based on a progressive multiracial coalition were *the* major left–liberal response to Reagan's conservative policies. For the first time since the last days of Martin Luther King, Jr – with the grand exception of Harold Washington – the nearly de facto segregation in US progressive politics was confronted and surmounted. On the other hand, Jackson's televisual style resists grass-roots organizing and, most important, democratic accountability. His brilliance, energy, and charisma sustain his public visibility – but at the expense of programmatic follow-through. We are approaching the moment in which this style exhausts its progressive potential.

Other national nonelectoral black leaders – like Benjamin Hooks of the NAACP and John Jacobs of the National Urban League – rightly highlight the traditional problems of racial discrimination, racial violence, and slow racial progress. Yet their preoccupation with race – the mandate from their organizations – downplays the crucial class, environmental, and patriarchal determinants of black life chances. Black politicians – especially new victors like Mayor David Dinkins of New York City and Governor Douglas Wilder of Virginia – are part of a larger, lethargic electoral system riddled with decreasing revenues, loss of public confidence, self-perpetuating mediocrity, and pervasive corruption. Like most American elected·officials, few black politicians can sidestep these seductive traps. So black leadership at the national level tends to lack a moral vision that can organize (not just periodically energize) subtle analyses that enlighten (not simply intermittently awaken), and exemplary practices that uplift (not merely convey status that awes), black people.

Second, this relative failure in leadership creates vacuums to be filled by bold and defiant black nationalist figures with even narrower visions, one-note racial analyses, and sensationalist practices. Louis Farrakhan, Al Sharpton, and others vigorously attempt to be protest leaders in this myopic mode – a mode often, though not always, reeking of immoral xenophobia. This kind of black leadership not only is symptomatic of black alienation and desperation in a country more and more indifferent or hostile to the quality of life among black working and poor people, it also reinforces the fragmentation of US progressive efforts that could reverse this deplorable plight. In this way, black nationalist leaders often inadvertently contribute to the very impasse they are trying to overcome: inadequate social attention and action to change the plight of America's 'invisible people', especially disadvantaged black people.

Third, this crisis of black leadership contributes to political cynicism among black people; it encourages the idea that we cannot really make a difference in changing our society. This cynicism – already promoted by the larger political culture – dampens the fire of engaged *local* activists who have made a difference, yet who also have little interest in being in the national limelight. Rather they engage in protracted grass-roots organizing in principled coalitions that bring power and pressure to bear on specific issues.

Without such activists there can be no progressive politics. Yet state, regional, and national networks are also required for an effective progressive politics. That is why local-based collective (and especially multigendered) models of black leadership are needed. These models must shun the idea of one black national leader; they also should put a premium on critical dialogue and democratic accountability in black organizations.

Work must get done. Decisions must be made. But charismatic presence is no legitimate substitute for collective responsibility. Only a charisma of humility and accountability is worthy of a leadership grounded in a genuine democratic struggle for greater freedom and equality. This indeed may be the best – and last – hope to hold back the nihilistic threat to black America.

26

Can Cinderella become a citizen?

Barbara Einhorn

From her *Cinderella goes to market – citizenship, gender and women's movements in East Central Europe* (Verso, 1993).

On the whole, women will probably come off losers in many respects: the 'revolution' of 1989 left the patriarchal system of power intact, transforming its more superficial manifestations from bad to worse.

What could be done? At least some of us, women who have been part of the Great Experiment, understand something which could be passed down to our daughters: that capitalist society is not the only option; that beyond it there can be another, more mutually concerned way of living. It may be very far away, especially now when the failure of 'Communism' is taken to mean the failure of each and every effort to transcend capitalism. So we can only try to keep the flame burning – the small flame of sympathy, of simple concern for the other. Sisterhood may play a powerful part in this commitment.

Dimitrina Petrova, Bulgaria[1]

Active citizenship and the revival of civil society was what the upheavals of 1989 seemed to promise for the former state socialist countries of East Central Europe. Yet since then, women's rights appear to have been eroded. Women have been made redundant on a mass scale, and currently constitute the majority of the unemployed in most of these countries. The levels of female political representation have fallen drastically. Laws guaranteeing the right to have one's job held open during maternity and extended childcare leave are being ignored. Reproductive rights are massively under attack, with moves in several countries to rescind the laws providing the right to free and legal abortions.

Gender issues are at the hub of potentially explosive processes of historical and social transformation. The family and the nation are being posited as central in the search for identity and for new ethical and moral values. Yet while market-oriented democratic theories stress individual autonomy, nationalist pressure subordinates women yet again to a collectivity which denies them participatory citizenship and democratic control. Nationalism appears, as for much of its history, to be constructing a definition of autonomy and citizenship which is male. Woman, even when represented as the Nation, is in fact the quintessential Other of nationalist discourse. This construes women as passive beings who are not viewed as mature political subjects, yet are in their reproductive role simultaneously

282

the crucible of the nation, for whose protection (male) citizens are prepared to lay down their lives. Indeed one might argue that in this too, there is more continuity with the state socialist period than at first meets the eye. The fact that the 'Woman Question' was posited by the socialist states of East Central Europe as a discrete issue, with gender relations a woman's problem rather than a subject of concern for society as a whole, suggests a similar inscription of woman as different, as Other.

Nationalism in the nineteenth century confined citizenship and suffrage to property-owning adult males. Women, confined to the private sphere, were excluded on the basis of gender. State socialism catapulted women into the public sphere of work and politics. But the fundamental contradiction for women in East Central Europe was that 'they did not get emancipation as citizens but as a right to work, together with certain advantages as members of the labour force (which can be manipulated to meet the demands of the economy), and as mothers (who can be made responsible for the nation's demographic situation)'.[2] Now, market pressures are retrenching women, sending them back to hearth and home, where nationalist ideology tells them that their primary responsibility is to 'produce babies for the nation'. This book contends that currently resurgent nationalist ideologies are building a concept of citizenship in East Central Europe which is both gendered and more generally exclusionary. Exclusion on grounds of sex, ethnic group, or language defines a national identity which is profoundly undemocratic, and inherently dangerous.

The reality of women's current and changing situation in East Central Europe remains paradoxical and contradictory. Neither state socialism nor the newly democratic societies seem able to provide the environment in which women could develop their full potential as equal citizens. In the past rights were given, from above, now they are taken away by market and 'new' ideological pressures.

The patriarchal socialist state expanded workplace rights at the expense of 'citizen rights'.[3] But there was no miraculous transformation after autumn 1989. Rather, there seems at one level to have been a simple reversal. Women now 'find themselves in the peculiar position of having gained a significant expansion of their civil rights at the expense of vital economic ones'.[4] Socialist patriarchy cramped and confined the exercise of individual initiative and autonomy; unemployment and the traumas of social upheaval and economic insecurity do not empower women to become active, participatory citizens.

Nor is the elevation of the market to an absolute good favourable to the flowering of a socially just society. T. H. Marshall's earlier prioritizing of 'the social rights of citizenship' has renewed relevance in the face of the growing social inequalities and poverty in East Central Europe. Yet it is also true, as Ursula Vogel and Michael Moran note, that Marshall's 'focus on class ... was bound ... to conceal or marginalize the continued existence of other divides, notably gender'.[5]

Theorists of nationalism and the nation-state have emphasized its conferral, at least in theory, of a unitary and egalitarian status as citizen. Citizenship was defined in terms of membership of the nation-state. In practice, as William Rogers Brubaker argues, in the model of the French

Revolution 'the principle of unitary citizenship ... far outstripped revolutionary practice, to which distinctions of class and gender were crucial'.[6] English history too provides ample illustration for the fact that women were excluded from citizenship status on the basis of their lack of majority in the eyes of the law, based on their inability to own property. Floya Anthias and Nira Yuval-Davis emphasize that in conceptualizing the more recent relationship between women and the state, it must be remembered that 'the very project of the welfare state itself has constructed the "state subject" in a gendered way'.[7]

Hence gender, while rarely encountered in works on nationalism and the nation-state, has in practice operated as an exclusionary mechanism, hindering female entitlement to citizenship rights, and to the duties of citizenship. Reviewing historical concepts of citizenship and past social practicè, Vogel and Moran conclude: 'It is not merely that citizenship is gender-specific, but that the very formulations of this concept in past and present have been *predicated* upon gender division'.[8] They also point out that concepts of citizenship and the nation-state are currently disputed and problematic, and that 'under pressure of economic and political crises, the frontiers óf membership may contract'. Tendencies in East Central as well as some of Western Europe to confine citizenship status to the members of one ethnic or linguistic community at the expense of another are examples of such a contraction. Relegating women to the private sphere in the name of the national interest, depriving them of the right to autonomy and self-determination through active participation as citizens in the public sphere, is another.

A culture of active citizenship necessitates both state legislation and social infrastructure, *and* for people to have the political space for articulating demands and exerting pressure. An independent women's movement *and* a political climate responsive to women's needs are crucial ingredients in implementing the kind of gender equality essential to democratic societies. Vogel emphasizes that both grassroots activism and the involvement of women at the level of state institutions are necessary to the implementation of gender equity and women's autonomy. And participatory citizenship needs to be non-gender specific, she suggests, to be meaningful and effective for both men and women in a democratic society.[9]

One of the current problems with realizing such a conception of citizenship is the general distaste felt across East Central Europe for any form of state intervention whatsoever. Hungarian sociologist Júlia Szalai writes:

> There is a strong and broad opposition in our countries to everything that has the slightest flavour of "statism". It is a long process to get rid of the idea and practice of the totalitarian state and to define a state that is "ours", that is created and controlled by the democratic processes of the civil society.... We shouldn't throw away, however, all the concepts of solidarity, public responsibility, less inequality and so on, those values that have been long associated with the concept and practice of the state.[10]

Indeed the reaction against state intervention is so violent as to render almost impossible any careful examination of the state socialist record on women's behalf. Nor is it easy, in the aftermath of state socialism, to hypothesize alternatives. As Slavenka Drakulić wrote in 1991:

> We may have survived communism, but we have not yet outlived it ... [because] what communism instilled in us was precisely this immobility, this absence of a future, the absence of a dream, of the possibility of imagining our lives differently. There was hardly a way to say to yourself: This is just temporary, it will pass, it must. On the contrary, we learned to think: This will go on forever, no matter what we do. We can't change it.[11]

Such a failure of imagination, overlaid with women's physical exhaustion, opens the way for an idealized vision which unites woman, family and nation.

It will be interesting to see how far, in the future, the loss of economic and social rights encourages the emergence of a women's movement devoted to the goal of gender equality. Of equal importance will be recognition by the new democratic states of the advantages to be gained in terms of social cohesion from fostering forms of active citizenship which encompass both women and men. Given the strength of exclusionary nationalist forms of self-definition, the prospects are not rosy. Current nationalist ideologies too often assert themselves, not in positive terms, expressing pride in the national traditions or cultural heritage, but rather in defensive or aggressive terms *against* the Other. Such self-identification in terms of what one is *not* make women the next to be excluded after ethnically different Others. Only time, the revival of civil society networks, and women's activism may change this.

One could conclude that the story has no happy ending. If socialism subordinated women to the macro needs of the economy and demographic demands, as some maintain, so now nationalism is instrumentalizing women by reducing them to their reproductive role. State socialism's commitment to women's 'emancipation' could be read as having become debased to a matter of form and externality rather than genuine concern. Nationalism is overtly dismissive of the notion that women have needs other than maternal ones which should be addressed during the transition period. Against the difficulties and short-term setbacks, however, must be set the positive potential. This emanates from women themselves, resourceful through years of 'improvisation'[12] and making do, buoyant despite the pressures of the past and uncertainties of the present.

Validating women's subjective experiences of contradiction, of continuity and change, may make a substantive contribution to addressing the problems of the environment, of intolerance, and of conflict in East Central Europe today. The very notions of participatory democracy, or of politics from below, reject the privileging of male-dominated institutionalized forms of experience gained in the public sphere and of politics as exclusively concerned with electoral questions or the affairs of government.

It is thus in the organizations of a revived civil society like the emerging women's movement that hope for future transformation lies. Transcending the difficulties in East–West communication and avoiding the 'colonialist gaze' of many Western institutions, East–West networking can contribute to the process of renewed understanding. The non-hierarchical and egalitarian approach of the women's, environmental and peace movements in Western and East Central Europe informs productive dialogue taking place between scholars and activists. Through such dialogue may come a mutual redefinition of the concept of citizenship itself, as a non-exclusionary category informed by the need for social justice as well as gender equity. [...]

Notes

1 Petrova, D. 1992: The farewell dance: women in the Bulgarian transition. Paper presented to the Conference on Mary Wollstonecraft and 200 Years of Feminism, Sussex University, 5–6 December 1992.

2 Adamik, M. 1991: Hungary: a loss of rights?. *Shifting territories: feminism in Europe*, special issue no. 39 of *Feminist Review* (winter) 169.

3 Chamberlayne, P. 1990: Neighbourhood and tenant participation in the GDR. In Bob Deacon and Júlia Szalai (eds), *Social policy in the new Eastern Europe: what future for socialist welfare?* Aldershot: Avebury, 155–6.

4 Rosenberg, D. 1991: Shock therapy: GDR women in transition from a socialist welfare state to a social market economy. *Signs*, **17** (1) 129.

5 Vogel, U. and Moran, M. (eds) 1973: *The frontiers of citizenship*. Basingstoke: Macmillan, p. xi. In the introduction to this volume, Vogel and Moran refer to Marshall's 'seminal essay on "Citizenship and Class"', which was originally prepared as a lecture in 1949 and appeared in Marshall, T. H. 1973: *Class, citizenship and social development*. Westport, CT: Greenwood Press, 65–122.

6 Brubaker, W.R. 1990: Immigration, citizenship and the nation-state in France and Germany: a comparative historical analysis. *International Sociology* **5** (4) 379–407.

7 Anthias, F. and Yuval-Davis, N. (eds) 1989: *Woman–nation–state*. Basingstoke: Macmillan, p. 6.

8 Vogel, U. and Moran, M. 1991: *The frontiers of citizenship*. Basingstoke: Macmillan, xii and xvi.

9 Vogel, U. 1991: Is citizenship gender-specific?. In Vogel, U. and Moran, M. (eds), *The frontiers of citizenship*. Basingstoke: Macmillan, p. 82.

10 Szalai, J. *et al.* 1990: Social policy and socialism: citizenship, the working class, women and welfare. In Deacon, D. and Szalai, J. (eds), *Social policy in the new Eastern Europe: what future for socialist welfare?* Aldershot: Avebury, 34–5.

11 Drakulić, S. 1992: *How we survived communism and even laughed*. London: Hutchinson, xvii, 7.

12 Similar terms are used both by Hana Navarová to describe family life in Czechoslovakia, and by Júlia Szalai in reference to the experience gained by women in Hungary's second economy.

27

A problematic – speaking the self

Elspeth Probyn

From her *Sexing the self – gendered positions in cultural studies* (Routledge, 1993).

One of the central problematics that has emerged from postmodernist debates is that of representation. From one side of the argument, Jean Baudrillard's denial of the possibility of representation deeply challenges many of cultural studies' assumptions, theoretical and commonsensical, about the stakes involved in speaking; of who speaks for whom, and why. As Baudrillard bluntly puts it, the death of a social to represent is, or should be, the death of sociological theory: 'The hypothesis of the death of the social is also that of theory' (1982, pp. 9–10). Alongside these deaths, the question of who is speaking within theoretical accounts of the social is increasingly rendered transparent. Recalling Marx's distinction between representation as *Vertretung* (the political project of standing in for another group) and *Darstellung* (depicting the social), Gayatri Spivak argues that the critic as 'proxy' should be dislodged. The critic's position as a privileged speaker for class interests is undermined by the absence, or the indifference, of any constituency: 'the choice of and the need for "heroes", paternal proxies, agents of power – Vertretung' (Spivak 1988, p. 279). In turn, the problematic nature of being a proxy deeply troubles practices of interpretation, or at least those which seek to interpret the social for someone, or some group.

Now, it would be comforting to be able to state that this injunction against proxies only applies to male theorists, to middle-aged lefty heroes. Unfortunately, this is not the case and at the expense of alienating myself immediately, it's been a while since anyone seriously considered some cultural theorists as the proxy for whomsoever. However, the project of representing women has been a condition of possibility for feminism and continues to provide the underlying epistemological basis for the articulation of feminisms. Quite simply, it continues to be the ground upon and from which many feminists and feminisms speak. Yet this ground, or rather, the representation of women as horizon, is not only undermined by theoretical decrees, it is increasingly attacked by the 'public' – men and women alike.

The ambivalence towards feminism could be clearly seen in the aftermath of the 1989 massacre of fourteen women engineering students at the Université de Montréal; in fact, feminists were doubly hit. On 6 December

1989, a lone man in hunting gear entered classrooms at the Engineering Faculty (L'Ecole Polytéchnique), separated the women from the men and then shot them. Marc Lépine, the killer, clearly stated both at the moment of the shooting and in a letter that he wanted to kill feminists, that feminists had ruined his life. Later it was reported that these poor young women had protested that they weren't feminists, and much was made of the fact that they were bright, articulate women who wanted good jobs as engineers – that they didn't hate men. Amid all the public agony over why or how this tragedy had happened, some of the media turned to what became known as 'la récuperation', as they criticized feminists for 'recuperating' this event for their cause. Without forgetting either the actual pain of the massacre or the fact that most women are murdered or beaten or raped in their own homes and at the hands of husbands or acquaintances, we can move from this overall situation, as it is called in Quebec, 'L'événement', and raise the very real problematics of feminist representation. Included in this event was the stated motive for the killing (that the women were feminists) and two denials of feminism (both in the reported words of the murdered women and then in the media's recriminations against those feminists who spoke their interpretations of the slaughter).

Feminist representations of the event fought against certain popular arguments which portrayed Lépine's actions as the isolated incident of a madman. Perhaps more importantly, many feminists took their own anguish as a discursive point of departure. (I should clarify here my use of the third person when I speak of feminist reactions. Although I teach at the university I was in London both during and after the event. Thus, I was informed from afar by the bloody bodies on the first page of the British tabloids, caught in the nightmare of trying to find what exactly had happened from the location of a geopolitical point not much moved by colonial happenings, however sensational they may be.) Back home, two of my colleagues, Danielle Juteau and Nicole Laurin, powerfully argued that in a racist and sexist society crimes against women and minorities make sense. As Québécoises watched the media search for motives, as the nomenclatures of 'un fou', 'un détraqué', 'un malade' piled up, a fairly common feminist response was: 'it's absurd, they are looking for a motive, but haven't they understood anything?' (Juteau and Laurin 1989, p. 206). The awful recognition of where we are as women, the terrible feeling as the very space of the university, of the streets, was rearranged in fear, brought forward another tone. There was no way of avoiding a sexed interpretation of the situation. As Juteau and Laurin wrote: 'This action was aimed at each one of us and at us all. ... Fear, anger, fear, pain, fear, sorrow invade us ... tearing us apart, piercing our hearts' [p. 206].

While there have since been many responses to the event at the Polytéchnique, ranging from feminist collections of articles (Malette and Chaloux, 1990) to pamphlets blaming feminists, the immediate feminist representation of the massacre turned on the *Vertretung*, the spontaneous move to speak of and to a collectivity of women; grounded in their own fear and anger, feminist academics and journalists spoke out and represented the anguish of all Québécois women. And at the same time, this movement of anger and sadness was portrayed as parasitic in some press accounts;

represented publicly and perhaps privately as a speaking position located upon the dead bodies of fourteen young women.

In many ways this is but a very brutal exemplar of the larger debates within cultural studies over identity and difference and who gets to speak, from where, and for whom. The tone of these debates is also bloody, if less immediately tragic. A recent British example of this is the collection of essays edited by Jonathan Rutherford, *Identity, community, culture, difference* (1990). While this book brings together many important interventions, the tenor is one of agonistics, if not downright antagonism. Among the many targets, the Left and white feminism are the most severely trounced for having erected a hierarchy of difference. Pratibha Parmar argues that white feminism's articulation of the politics of identity has 'given rise to a self-righteous assertion that if one inhabits a certain identity this gives one the legitimate and moral right to guilt-trip others into particular ways of behaving' (Parmar 1990, p. 107). According to Andrea Stuart, by the early 1980s, 'Being a feminist had come to say more about what you didn't do – eat meat, fuck men, wear make-up – than what you did do' (Stuart 1990, p. 32). Many of these writers are from a generation influenced by the writing and the political stance of Stuart Hall, and so it was not surprising that Hall's article was included at the end of the collection. There he argues for a theorization of identity that would be:

> constituted, not outside but within representation ... not as a second-hand mirror held up to reflect what already exists, but as that form of representation which is able to constitute us as new kinds of subjects, and thereby enable us to discover places from which to speak (Hall, 1990, pp. 236–7).

While most of the authors cite, refer and defer to Hall, it is strange to note the ways in which 'Identity' emerges as an articulation of a rather static and rhetorical use of difference; difference as a second-hand image of various theoretical battles among feminists and within the Left. It's as if in the late twentieth century, with the fragmentation of populist causes and political programmes as well as the commercial success of popular enterprises like 'The Environment', the project of *Vertretung* has given way to a rather vicious game of issues and individuals elbowing each other out of the way, each crying 'listen to *me*', 'hear *my* difference'.

At this point in the game, at this sociocultural and theoretical conjuncture, it might be beneficial to remember Jane Gallop's articulation of 'the necessarily double and ... urgent questions of feminism: not merely who am I? But who is the other woman?' (1988, p. 177). Now, of course, the first part of this equation, the question of who am I?, has already generated a small industry as, increasingly, theorists turn to their own difference, to the 'I', occasionally trying to explicate the world metonymically from their own situation, at times merely embroiled in the exigencies of their own locales. From Valerie Walkerdine's analysis of herself as Tinkerbell (1986) to John Fiske's semiotics of his living room (1990), the 'me' generation lives on. As Laura Marcus puts it: '"Enough about you, let's talk about me"' (1987).

In a charitable vein, one could ask, when faced with public indifference (be it manifested in the severe cutbacks in the educational systems or to the funding agencies for academic and artistic work, or just the widespread feeling that nobody really cares), where are intellectuals to turn to if not to themselves? It is, of course, easy to scoff at the idea of middle-aged tenured university professors, dressed in black leather jackets, cut loose from an ideal of the 'public' or 'organic' intellectual, desperately going through their personal crises of lost authority. However, individual crises sometimes meet up with a more general situation. In a sense, Dick Hebdige's theoretical statement can be understood as describing a fairly common sentiment: the '"we" is the imaginary community which remains unspeakable with the Post ... there is no space to struggle over, to struggle from (or ... to struggle towards)' (1986, pp. 86–95). For instance, I was just recently agonizing over whether to go on a demonstration celebrating Gay Pride in Montréal and denouncing the police brutality towards the gay and lesbian community. Here was a space that desperately needs struggling over; however, while I know that marching is a very necessary form of struggle, it is not my favourite form of contestation; the 'solidarity' of large crowds makes me feel slightly uncomfortable, if not claustrophobic. Eventually I did go because a visible presence of gays, lesbians and bisexuals peacefully walking along through the downtown centre is an effective way of combating homophobia and heterosexism. However, as we proceeded along our route, it became obvious that many of these marchers were of another generation – the ten years separating me from those proudly 'out' dykes in their early twenties meant that the 'we' somehow died in my throat along with the chant, 'We're here, we're queer, we're fabuuulous'.

While the creation of a 'we' is a pragmatic political question, it is also and always a theoretical one. As Hebdige reminds us, and against the gloomy scenario of nothing to say and nowhere to go, 'the "we" in Gramsci has to be *made* and re-made, actively articulated in the double sense that Stuart Hall refers to ... both "spoken" and "linked with", "combined". (It has to be at once "positioned" *and* "brought into being")' (1986, p. 95). However, in order to articulate a 'we', there must be certain conditions already in place.

We need to theorize a feminist enunciative position which could articulate a discursive space to speak from and something to say. This entails an examination of how we could put ourselves to work in theoretical contexts, in such a way as to produce both discursive and extradiscursive effects. As I have already suggested, there is something of an autobiographical turn currently taking place in cultural theory. If my tone in describing this moment is less than effusive, it is because I consider the possibilities of speaking selves to be great, and the liabilities of an untheorized return to the 'I' to be even greater. While I do not want to police uses of the personal within theory, I do think that the political and theoretical stakes at hand merit that the problematic of the self be carefully considered.

To continue on a rather negative note, I will offer some anecdotal evidence of the difficulty of speaking in the first person singular. Meaghan Morris has argued that, rather than being an expression of the personal in Jakobsen's sense of the emotive and connotative functions, anecdotes can be made to serve referential functions:

They are oriented futuristically towards the construction of a precise, local, and *social* discursive context, of which the anecdote then functions as a *mise en abyme*.

That is to say, anecdotes for me are not expressions of personal experience, but allegorical expositions of a model of the way the world can be said to be working. So anecdotes need not be true stories, but they must be functional in a given exchange (1988, p. 7).

To return to my story, several years ago I mentioned in a conference presentation that I had been anorexic as a young girl. This was my first attempt to create a discursive *abyme* and thus throw into relief some of the theories that I had been grappling with by placing them within my own social landscape. The paper was in fact on anorexia nervosa and was taken from my master's thesis, which was a feminist discursive and historical analysis of anorexia. In a way, I had stumbled across the idea of doing my thesis on anorexia. The idea had been to do a discursive analysis of the Parti Québécois' White Paper on cultural policies – a subject more evidently worthy of a master's thesis in media studies. However, as I read more and more poststructuralist theories, I found that I was using my remembrances of being anorexic as a sort of touchstone; an unthought-out problematization of some of the stricter Althusserianism in vogue at the time. In the conference paper I used Angela McRobbie's lovely analysis of the British girls' magazine *Jackie* as a springboard into my own argument:

> However, at the same time a small voice in me questioned what seemed to be the over-privileging of this particular text and the overdetermination of the reader's experience. I mean, I read *Jackie* and I didn't go around yearning for boys and clothes and despising my female friends. In fact, buying *Jackie* was part of a small site of defiance and in a way solidified the group I hung around with. At that time in pre-Thatcher Britain, all state schools provided subsidized hot mid-day meals which were, as one might imagine, rather foul. In any case it became the thing to do to keep the 10 shillings for the week's meals and sneak up to town to buy chips, smoke a cigarette and read *Jackie*. This lasted for a while but gradually the group disintegrated – one of the group was pregnant, another spent all her time studying for the O Level Exams, one switched to a tougher (and more interestingly deviant) crowd, and I became anorexic (Probyn, 1987, p. 112).

While neither the content nor the style of my paper was exactly groundbreaking, a 'postmodernist' member of the audience subsequently stated that this personal mode of enunciation made him 'nervous'. Now it is obviously difficult to say whether it was my particular discursive striptease or, more generally, a dis-ease with feminist speaking practices that most displeased this particular individual. However, following the publication of the paper I was also roundly rebuked in print by a feminist reviewer. Apart from what she called 'my weighty words' of confession (when I stated that I was anorexic), she condemned my article and argument for lacking 'sweat and blood' (Szekely, 1988). As if making postmodernists nervous and angering feminists by supposedly betraying the material weight of the female body were not enough, a mainstream sociologist recently summed up this same piece as a 'confession of anorexia', another example that in 'postmodern America, the natives are now writing their own ethnography' (Frank, 1990, pp. 148 and 146).

What I want to take from this anecdote is the way in which these three different reactions, from three different theoretical agendas, all assumed that

I was telling, or wanting to tell, the truth, in this case about the essence of my being. I found these reactions rather bewildering. First of all, and in a very general manner, anorexics (and perhaps even some ex-anorexics) are notoriously duplicitous; after all, anorexia involves living a myriad of lies (from pretending that you have eaten to reading others' horror at your body as admiration or even envy). Second, my particular argument concerned the ways in which women have historically and conjuncturally used anorexia as a way of negotiating the dominant discourses of their times (whether religious, economic, medical, or other). It was, therefore, an argument against the idea that anorexia is a modern epidemic reducible to a causal paradigm of the direct effects of media discourses on women – i.e., that anorexic women represent the sad truth of our times. Third, and perhaps most important and obvious, the experience I presented in speech was, of necessity, a representation forged for the sake of my argument (my mother's reading of the article was that I had had a happy childhood; my sister's was a little more to the point as she pointed out the academic licence involved in the descriptions).

Without overly privileging or overestimating the virtues of my paper, since the rest of the article plodded off into the usual disembodied type of argument and thus conformed to a general pattern within feminist criticism of merely using the personal at the outset of an argument (Kennard, 1981), I will use it and the reactions I raised to explore the 'problematic' of the self. In the Althusserian sense of 'une problématique', a problematic only exists in both the presence and absence of problems and concepts. If concepts cannot be found in isolation, the problematic is then a conjunctural question; it is never a universal or immutable configuration:

> it is only in the specific unity of the complex structure of the whole that we can think the concept of these so-called backwardnesses, forwardnesses, survivals and unevennesses of development which *co-exist* in the structure of the real historical present: the present of the *conjuncture* (Althusser, 1970, p. 106).

So the problematic must always be thought in its conjuncture, as necessarily structured by its conditions of possibility. It is in this sense that current uses of the self in cultural theory have neglected to consider what conditions of possibility support, displace or disarm any use of the personal within theoretical arguments. In the turn to the autobiographical as a panacea for the ills of criticism, speaking from the heart has replaced a much needed theoretical consideration of the epistemological and political stakes involved. To be quite simple about it, any contemporary use of the self within cultural theory stands among, and must contend with, the backwardnesses, forwardnesses, survivals and unevennesses of our theoretical historical present – with the theories and practices that have either written it off or celebrated it. The self has to be positioned in relation to the absence and presence of the concepts of truth, confession, experience, immanence, private and public, individual and universal, and of course, masculine and feminine as well as sex, sexuality and gender, women and men. As Marcus quite rightly asks:

> How can autobiography's emphasis on the individual, the development of the self and the confluence between author and textual 'I', be reconciled with

political and theoretical perspectives skeptical of traditional concepts of subjectivity, individualism and textual authority? (1987, p. 77).

My concern is not with the genre of autobiography but with the particular conjunctural practice of incorporating the autobiographical within cultural theory, and I am similarly concerned with the theoretical terrain organized around concepts of subjectivity and textuality. Indeed, I will argue [...] that the legacy of poststructuralist textual criticism is an evacuation of any ground upon which one could speak the self. [Here] I am particularly concerned with the conceptualizations of experience that could serve as a horizon in speaking the self, and with their erasure within cultural studies' recent past. If we are to begin to take the problematic of the self seriously, we need to look for, or remember, an epistemological basis that could support theoretical uses of the experiential.

The experience of Raymond Williams

As Lawrence Grossberg argues, 'the specific shape of cultural studies can be seen in the extremely personal form ... the problem of cultural was defined in terms of the problematic of participation' (1988a, p. 14). In particular, the experiences of Richard Hoggart and Raymond Williams as 'scholarship boys' marked early cultural studies, just as the experience of Stuart Hall as a 'marginal self' now influences contemporary cultural studies. Grossberg describes the situation of Hoggart and Williams as follows: 'caught between two worlds, two incommensurable languages, systems of relations and values, they struggled to make sense of their experience of belonging to neither fully' (p. 14).

However, the incorporation into theory of this experience of being within two incongruent worlds, was undermined by the arrival of structuralism. Hall succinctly describes the problems generated by the famous culturalist/structuralist split, as the division between a humanist Marxism and an Althusserian-inspired structuralist Marxism came to be known:

> whereas in 'culturalism', experience was the ground – the terrain of 'the lived' – where consciousness and conditions intersected, structuralism insisted that 'experience' could not, by definition, be the ground of anything, since one could only 'live' and experience one's conditions *in and through* the categories, classifications and frameworks of the culture (1980, p. 66).

The enormous influence of structuralism and post-structuralism in cultural studies can be measured, in part, by the eclipse of the category of experience. Its sway, in turn, produced, and continues to produce, a rather uncomfortable position for the cultural critic. Even if the critic is vigilant to the fact that her experience is an ideological production, the Althusserian trap still awaits:

> the men who would use an ideology purely as a means of action, as a tool, find that they have been caught by it, implicated by it, just when they are using it and believe themselves to be absolute masters of it (Althusser, cited in Slack and Whitt, 1992, p. 581).

In even more pointed terms, there is Terry Eagleton's warning to those who point 'to "experience" – as though that, precisely, were not ideology's homeland' (1976, p. 15). Unable to ground him or herself in an experiential position in relation to the structures of the social, where does the critic speak from? The quick answer is that he or she speaks from in front of texts; as Grossberg describes it, 'the cultural critic must refuse participation in order to reaffirm a reflective distanciation' (1988, p. 16).

A longer answer requires a deeper consideration of how indeed experience worked before it was written off within the 'logic of disintegration' (Dews, 1987). In thinking about critical relations other than those of the critic before the text, I cannot imagine a better place to start than in front of Hereford cathedral:

> The bus stop was outside of the cathedral. I had been looking at the Mappa Mundi, with is rivers out of Paradise, and at the chained library ... Now, across the street, a cinema advertised the *Six-Five Special* and a cartoon version of *Gulliver's Travels*. The bus arrived, with a driver and a conductress deeply absorbed in each other. We went out of the city, over the old bridge, and on through the orchards and green meadows and the fields red under the plough. Ahead were the Black Mountains ... The bus stopped, and the driver and conductress got out, still absorbed. They had done this journey so often, and seen all its stages. It is a journey, in fact, that in one form or another we have all made (Williams, 1989, p. 3).

This quotation immediately situates us before a vista of both geographical and theoretical magnitude. It is from Williams' 1958 essay, 'Culture is ordinary', a text for which I have great fondness not only because of its stunningly simple premise but also because I too grew up in the Border country, in a village that sometimes seemed to be located in between England and Wales. It is a social landscape quite extraordinary for showing, and even proving, that indeed 'culture is ordinary'. That part of Wales, unremarkable for much and for many, as the rather scrawny sheep graze amidst a mixture of Roman ruins, discarded fertilizer bags and rusting farm equipment, speaks loudly of the ways in which

> Every human society has its own shape, its own purposes, its own meanings. Every human society expresses these, in institutions, and in arts and learning. The making of a society is the finding of common meanings and directions, and its growth is an active debate and amendment under the pressures of experience, contact, and discovery, writing themselves into the land [p. 4].

Coming late as I did to that landscape, I quickly realized – was made to realize – the complex ways in which the Border Welsh cultural configurations are written into the land. Upon my father's retirement from the army, we had moved 'back' to Wales although the 'back' was after several generations of Probyns had made and lost a beer fortune in the south of England. As a worldly ex-army brat and Canadian through my mother, it took me a while to concede that my vocabulary couldn't quite keep up with the intricacies of my schoolmates' knowledge of who belonged where in the filigree of Radnorshire life. It was an early apprehension of another of Williams' statements: 'the lived is only another word, if you like, for experience: but we have to find a word for that level' (1979, p. 168). It is precisely this level of the lived that we need to explore if we are to rethink and elaborate alternative enunciative positions in cultural theory. Without those words, those riffs along the register of the experiential, we remain in our awkward positions as clumsy subjects in front of the text. Just as I was excluded at times on the playground because of my inability to speak 'the lived' of Llandrindod Wells, so too will the lack of a theory of the experiential exclude us from being within texts, from arranging them after our hearts, from using our selves within cultural theory. By returning to Williams' work, to his critical practice and his tone, we can find the beginnings of such a theory.

In thinking through the ways in which the concept of experience can be articulated with that of the self in cultural criticism, I will propose an initial heuristic distinction and contend that experience can be made to work in two registers: at an ontological level, the concept of experience posits a separate realm of existence – it testifies to the gendered, sexual and racial facticity of being in the social; it can be called an immediate experiential self. At an epistemological level, the self is revealed in its conditions of possibility; here experience is recognized as more obviously discursive and can be used overtly to politicize the ontological. Both of these levels – the experiential self and the politicization of experience – are necessary as the conditions of possibility for alternative speaking positions within cultural theory. This is to argue beyond a paradigm wherein the critic's experience can be reduced to the expression of a guarantee of authenticity, wherein the ontological is seen simply as an ideological articulation of the 'will to authority'. What I want to bring out are the ways in which these sometimes real implications of the insertion of an experiential self can be checked by using experience epistemologically to locate and problematize the conditions that articulate individuated experiences. I am not arguing that 'experience' can be simply evoked, as an invocation of an inherent 'right' to speak; indeed, as Gayatri Spivak (1988) and other feminists of colour (for example, hooks 1991; Mani 1992; Minh-ha, 1989) have forcefully argued, we know that one class's 'right' to speak of itself is based in the oppression and silencing of another's. However, it is equally important that an epistemological understanding of the self not be allowed to overwhelm the necessary ontological implications of the self. In a slightly different vein, Diana Fuss argues that the immediacy of the experiential, what she, in turn, qualifies as a necessary essentialism, must be recognized: '"Essentially speaking", we need both to theorize essentialist spaces from which to speak and, simultaneously, to deconstruct these spaces to keep them from solidifying' (1989, p. 118). In theorizing the tension within the category of experience, created in the movement between ontological and epistemological levels, we can begin to conceive of more productive uses of the critic's self.

Despite these interventions, from the standpoint of the 1990s, and in light of the various theoretical interventions that have occurred since the early 1960s, Williams' abundant use of his self and the centrality of experience are quite shocking: at times they produce an almost innocent immediacy. At the same time, his use of experience (notably in *The long revolution*) tends to be underplayed by interpreters of his work. The notable exception is Eagleton's attack in *Criticism and ideology*: 'it is precisely this insistence on experience, this passionate premium placed on the "lived", which provides one of the centrally unifying themes of Williams' *oeuvre* – which supplies at once the formidable power and drastic limitation of his work' (1976, p. 22). In a rather *ad hominem* tone, which is, I suppose, most suited to the male attack on the Father, Eagleton writes that Williams' 'ponderous pauses and stiffly rhetorical inflections, his ritualising of a cluster of key terms to the point where they seem less public concepts than private inventions, suggest the movement of an unmistakably individual voice' (22–3). Eagleton quickly reduces this possible theoretical tension to the purely idiosyncratic: 'the inert language of academicism is in fact the stage of a personal drama, the discourse of a complex, guarded self-display' (p. 23). Of course, Eagleton has since made his peace with Williams and in a footnote apologized for the 'unacceptably acerbic and ungenerous' tone of some of his remarks (1989, p. 11). Strangely enough, after his harsh words about Williams' linguistic style, it is Williams' writing ('it was quite as much "creative" and "imaginative" ... as academic work') that Eagleton most praises:

> Words for him were condensed social practices, sites of historical struggle, repositories of political wisdom or domination; he has a Celtic feel for them, for their rich texture and density, and he himself spoke pretty much as he wrote, weightily, rhetorically, constructing and composing his speech rather than slinging it provisionally together (p. 8).

While Eagleton now lauds the personal commitment to Wales and to the 'ordinary culture' of the working class, his comments verge on the nostalgic, without offering true reappraisal of the critical role of experience in Williams' theoretical project.

In the interviews that form *Politics and letters* (Williams, 1979) the questioners are more concerned with establishing the parameters of Williams' rearticulation of historical materialism than with coming to terms with the reach of his use of experience. While these interviews are central to understanding the import of Williams' theories, to my mind, the issue of experience should be understood as a major source of inspiration in his work. In other critiques, Williams' use of experience is implicitly acknowledged but it is rarely the central focus; experience is displaced into an epiphenomenal role. Typically, as in Martin Allor's account of Williams' early work, 'culture' takes centre stage:

> 'Culture' was rescued from a morass of multiple uses, and it was located as a key term: epistemologically as well as ontologically. The relations between text and social life were reframed in terms of the connections between experience and institution (1984, p. 9).

The richness of Williams' work cannot, of course, be reduced to one term, and it is precisely the explicit connections between 'text, social life, experience and institution' that make his work so productive. For Allor, the term 'culture' operates epistemologically and ontologically. It works epistemologically because it designates the relations (or to use a later term, the mediations) between individuals and social formations; it works ontologically because 'culture' also refers to the lived experience of the social formation over and above the structural elements of the social. Allor critiques Williams for this ambiguity and argues that Williams' 'cultural materialism ... covers and collapses much of the theoretical and critical space that it opens' (p. 19). Allor argues that in using 'culture' epistemologically *and* ontologically, Williams collapses the distinctions in analysis suggested by these levels.

In contrast to these critiques, I want to focus on experience as a keyword, and map the productive tension that Williams constructs between the ontological and epistemological. In other words, while experience describes the everyday, or 'the way of life', it is also the key to analysing the relations that construct that reality. Moreover, as a third term located within an epistemological/ontological tension, the experience of the critic, of her 'lived' and of its connections to an object of analysis, can be put to work to motivate alternative modes of intervention.

To hear the theoretical weight that experience can be made to carry, listen to this central passage:

> We are used to descriptions of our whole common life in political and economic terms. The emphasis on communications asserts, as a matter of experience, that men and societies are not confined to relationships of power, property and production. Their relationships, in describing, learning, persuading and exchanging experiences are seen as equally fundamental (Williams, 1979, p. 137).

We can see here Williams' unwillingness to fully subscribe to any simple version of the 'base/superstructure' metaphor. In questioning the primacy of the economic, Williams uses 'experience' in two ways: first, the materiality of day-to-day observations serves to show that 'men' are not only affected by the operations of the base; second, the structure of the relations of production becomes apparent when individuals converse about their experiences. In turn, the critic's experience is that there is something above and beyond the base's organization of everyday life, and that this something can be reached by paying attention to the exchange of individuals' experiences. What is even more striking about this passage is the tone of the first sentence: 'We are used to ... '. Here, academic awareness mingles with a sense of the very lived conditions of these descriptions. At the same time that we sense the necessity of those 'economic and political terms' as theoretical thresholds, the inhabited actuality of the economic and the political is made clear in the following sentences. It is therefore 'as a matter of experience' that individuals know both the extent and the limitation of these elements in defining their lives.

Williams admitted that his use of experience was problematic. However, he continued to maintain that there was a connection between the organization of the social formation and the lived experience of it. In fact, he went so far as to state that experience of the social formation allows us (as critics and/or individuals) to recognize that we are not solely confined and defined within an undifferentiated relationship to power and production. It is a small step to assert that the various structures of society are interrelated, that, for example, the family and the economic are not separate realms, and that they are structured and experienced very differently along lines of gender, race and sexuality. The complexities of these interrelations can be seen to be behind Williams' seemingly simple statement that 'it would be interesting to locate the historical moment when men stopped crying in public' (1989, p. 319). To answer this question of why, in general, men do not cry in public, one would need to analyse the emergence of the concepts of masculinity, public and private, in their material articulations to other structures of the social, as one simultaneously examined the experiential level of crying and not crying in public. For me, this analysis could not be disconnected from the fact that I do, at times, cry in public, and would require some investigation of how and why I can. So the experience of the articulation would (momentarily) precede, or at least be a necessary precondition of theoretical analysis: as Williams states in *Politics and letters*, 'What I said in effect was that we know this to be so about our own lives – hence we can take it as a theoretical assumption' (1979, p. 138). Here experience is seen as directly epistemologically productive; it is that which motivates a theoretical assumption, it is also that which empassions and politicizes cultural analysis. Used epistemologically, experience provides evidence of the interrelation of structural determination and individual relationships which compose the social formation. Experience is thus put to work as a theoretical first principle for the critic.

Part and parcel of this critical principle is the fact that one cares about the experiences of others. Continuing his remarks about men not crying in public, Williams goes on to note that 'the repression of tenderness and emotional response, the willingness to admit what isn't weakness – one's feeling in and through another; all this is a repression not only of women's experience but of something much more general' (1989, p. 319). While this remark flirts dangerously with an essentialist notion of Woman as nurturer, I think that we can be generous enough to recognize the sense of Williams' remark as pertaining to the historical and material situation of women. Moreover, his comment raises the necessity for caring and tenderness within cultural criticism. As theoretical battles seem to become more divisive, and as the highly competitive circumstances and the material pressures of academic jobs work to repress collective research, the edge of cultural criticism seems to be aimed at individuals. Without sounding like the 'Pollyanna' of critical theory (I have been known to participate in the guilty pleasures of conference gossip), it sometimes seems that the *raison d'être* of intellectual work gets lost in the very serious game of theoretical rivalry.

However, as I have found in the sometimes sobering experience of teaching, the absence of a reason to theorize is soon filled by students wanting to know, quite rightly, how theories about culture can help them to understand their own experiences. Put very bluntly, our experience as critics and teachers should remind us to care first about how our theoretical agendas can articulate and allow for expressions of experience, both our own and others', 'one's feeling in and through another'. One of the most memorable experiences, if not the only one, that I can recall from my undergraduate education was when a very venerable professor broke down into tears as he was lecturing about André Malraux's *La condition humaine*. As he told us of his brother's death in the Resistance, many of the young, twenty-year-old students experienced, for the first time, the interrelation of literature, war, anti-Semitism, and personal loss.

Lest there be any misunderstanding, it should also be clear that the stipulation of experience as a condition of possibility for critical enunciations cannot give way to a simple reification of either experience or the experiencer. To take experience in and of itself as the sole criterion for and in speech leads to such reifications. In fact, the experience of women certainly demonstrates that arguments based in a certain sense of experience can be the most vicious. As Williams states, 'in certain epochs it is precisely experience in its weakest form which appears to block any realization of the unity of this process, concealing the connections between the different structures' (1979, p. 138). Given the complexity of its articulations, and the fact that experience is always conjunctural, located in the backwardnesses and forwardnesses of the historical present, it is not surprising that the experience of being within certain circumscribed modes of existence sometimes serves to obscure the connections between structures. Here experience in its weakest form is vehiculed through common-sense statements. As our everyday language reminds us (when racist or homophobic comments are preceded by 'some of my best friends ...', or when a wider comprehension of the experience of sexism is precluded by 'I'm not a feminist but ...'), experience alone does not guarantee articulation with other experiences, or with the experiences of others. Indeed, 'in its weakest form', experience can also serve to mask the construction of its own ground.

From Williams, I will posit three analytic possibilities: first, that experience itself speaks of the composition of the social formation; second, that experience can be overwhelming and work to conceal the connections between the different structures; and third, that the critic's own experience can impel the analysis of his or her differentiated relations to levels of the social formation. I want to emphasize the fact that critics, like anyone else, are a part of the social and that their experience of it should be put to work theoretically; this is, then, to force back against the conclusions of experience in its simplest allusive sense, and requires 'a renewed awareness of the indissolubility of the whole social-material process' (Williams 1979, p. 138). This is not to reify the critic's experience; it is merely to recognize its positivity within a politicized theory of culture. It is to renew awareness and analysis of the indissolubility of the social because experience has already told us it is so. If the lived is to be anything more than just another mantra, another abstracted nod, then our experiences need to be put squarely in the terrain of the theoretical.

If this sounds prosaic, it is because it takes a certain amount of tenacity in the face of highly elegant arguments 'to recall an absolutely founding presumption of materialism; namely that the material world exists whether anyone signifies it or not' (Williams, 1979, p. 167). While I am certainly not advocating a wholesale rejection of theories of signification, I am arguing that we need to elaborate a theory and practice of signification which could entertain the centrality of experiences of and in the material world. Against a tendency towards a position that 'it is only in knowing that we exist at all' (p. 167), we can counter with an insistence on what I am calling the ontological level, the felt facticity of material social being. From his own experience, Williams states that one finds 'a certain kind of disturbance or unease, a particular type of tension, for which when you stand back or recall them you can sometimes find a referent' (p. 168). It is at the ontological level that we can locate 'disturbance, tension, blockage, emotional trouble [which] seems to me precisely a source of major changes in the relation between signifier and signified' (p. 168). To take but a small example, we are constantly told what the signified of 'woman' entails (a certain way of looking and being, a certain type of love, etc.). At the level of experience, this is normally confirmed, but it is also torn apart. The experience of another woman and of other women can cause disturbance, tension, blockage, and even emotional trouble, as the taken-for-granted signifying relation is changed, as the signifier and the signified are ripped apart. At an ontological level, experience speaks of a disjuncture between the articulated and the lived aspects of the social and, at an epistemological level, experience impels an analysis of the relations formulated between the articulated and the lived. These two levels are then necessary for a project of analysing people's contradictory involvement in practices that go against their own (class, gender or racial) interests. While, of course, cultural studies later used Gramsci's understanding of 'hegemony' to describe the processes through which such consent is won, in Williams' work it is experience which first articulated the ontological and epistemological conditions of the actual involvement in contradiction.

The desire to account more thoroughly for the lived relations between the articulated and the lived is at the heart of the necessity to combine both ontological and epistemological levels within any analysis. This doubled insistence is expressed more clearly in Williams' concept of 'the structure of feeling':

> it is as firm and definite as 'structure' suggests, yet it operates in the most delicate and tangible parts of our activity. In one sense, this structure of feeling is the culture of a period: it is the particular living result of all the elements in the general organisation (1979, p. 48).

The lived takes on the role of theoretical horizon as the bifurcation of experience (as both epistemological and ontological) is the condition of possibility that allows the critic to specify a structure of feeling. While the interviewers in *Politics and letters* argue that 'the concept then tends to become an epistemology for gaining a comprehension of a whole society' (1979, p. 164), their description fails to emphasize that structure of feeling designates 'the particular living result of all the elements' (1979, p. 164). Before the structure of feeling is understood as solely epistemological, it should be remembered that as a term it is always paired and held in tension with an ontological level. An acknowledgment of the ontological aspect of one's experience is necessary if one is to locate 'those specific and definable moments when very new work produces a sudden shock of *recognition*' [p. 164]. In other words, it is our experiences that enable us to construct a given structure of feeling, just as, as an analytic focus, the structure of feeling expresses and allows us to map the articulation of moments of being within structural determinations.

While structure of feeling captures the epistemological and ontological implications of experience in general, it also emphasizes the role of the critic's own experience, his or her specific shocks of recognition. While there is 'no natural seeing and therefore there cannot be a direct and unmediated contact with reality' (Williams, 1979, p. 167), experience is nonetheless the key mediating term in locating the structure of feeling. Far from designating a leap of faith on the part of the critic towards a structure of feeling, grounded in the materiality of his or her own quotidian structure of feeling, the critic accepts, as a theoretical principle, the experience of others. In acknowledging the very basic point that the experiential is part of the critical enterprise itself, we move beyond the construction of experience as an object to be passively and impersonally studied. In stating that the experiential is imbricated within a critical stance, we can begin to see how it might provide direction, and a ratifying sense of movement. It attests to a clear point of departure, even as it is partial, in the sense of being partial to (and part of) a political agenda. We are drawn to recognize and research certain experiences (as they are articulated through gender, sexuality, class or race) because we have at some level lived and experienced them ourselves. Williams' 'shock of recognition' attests to this, and in a feminist framework, we can extend this term to talk about the shock of recognition of gendered experiences. Thus, the critical stance of the feminist critic is directed by and to the experience of being gendered. It is both individual – as Rosi Braidotti puts, 'it is like *that*, I am sexed' (1989, p. 101) – and it is beyond just me: women are sexed. The shock of gendered experience thus emphasizes the duality of experience as a term: it allows for the twinned question of who am I and who is she? This doubledness of experience that the feminist critic works with and through does not necessarily mean that women are bound together in the face of their differences. Nor does the centrality of the critic's experience necessarily reify her as the organizing principle of critical discourse. It merely serves to alert the critic that there is always something else going on.

In his description of the operation of the structure of feeling, Williams raises the centrality of this 'something else':

> In the study of a period, we may be able to reconstruct, with more or less accuracy, the material life, the social organization, and to a large extent, the dominant ideas. It is not necessary to discuss here which, if any, of these aspects are determining; ... To relate a work of art to any part of that observed reality may, in varying degrees, be useful, but it is a common experience, in analysis, to realize that when one has measured the work against its separable parts, there yet remains some element for which there is no external counterpart. This element, I believe, is what I have termed the structure of feeling of a period and it is only realizable through experience of a work of art itself, as a whole (1954, 21–2).

Here we can readily see that an epistemological analysis privileges particular configurations of 'the social organization'. That is, the structure of feeling designates the relations that articulate, at any moment, 'the material life', 'the social organization' and 'the dominant ideas'. While it may not be necessary to weigh which, if any, element is determining, it is necessary to determine the particular configuration formed by these three elements. However, in addition to this analysis, there is still more to be accounted for: there 'remains some element for which there is no external counterpart'. The structure of feeling then acts to articulate the determination of the structure of feeling, it is not surprising that the critic should recognize, at the moment of analysis, that there is 'something else' going on. The critic's experience is thus integral to realizing the existence of the structure of feeling. [...]

Without reifying Williams' concept of experience as an ideal to be returned to, we can see that the way in which structuralism was taken up excluded the experiential moment in early cultural studies. In the move away from 'participation' as a theoretical framework, and to a 'semiotic–ethnographic model', the experiential aspect of the critic's involvement in theorizing is skirted as the attention turns to the distant figure of the 'audience':

> it was assumed that cultural studies had to address the question of the actual interpretations made (or at least offered) by various audience fractions, and that these differences were to be explained by the determining effects of already constituted social differences which constructed the experiential context into which individuals appropriated the text, and from which they constructed their own meanings (Grossberg, 1988, 16–17).

In this formulation of cultural studies, experience becomes an understood 'context' which allows individuals to 'negotiate' their own meanings of the text. It is, of course, an important element in the 'decoding' process; it is that which works against the masses being taken as 'cultural dupes'. Thus, 'social differences' allow for an 'experiential context' which is where 'texts' are 'read'. This experiential context is then the result of 'already constituted social differences' and as such it is an effect of the social. This sense of 'experience' is, however, located in the realm to be studied, as the critic looks on. It is this shift in perspective which differentiates an understanding of 'the experiential context' from Williams' 'structure of feeling'. Whereas the former is an important founding assumption in the theorizing of how individuals come to interpret texts, the latter goes further in describing the active relations within the structures of the social. In other words, the experiential context is a domain that remains separate from the critic – he or she must take it into account but is not necessarily implicated in it. The role of experience within the concept of structure of feeling, however, places more importance on the critic's implication – it situates where the critic stands, and speaks.

The difficulties that experience as a concept and as a category presents to cultural studies have recently resurfaced in discussions about reflexivity. Grossberg argues that the turn to reflexivity and autobiographical forms of writing is being offered as a response to the 'postmodern collapse of critical distance and the increasing uncertainty about the authority of intellectual and political voices/positions' (p. 66). He sees these reflexive writing strategies as inherently flawed:

> reflexivity demands that the author reveal his or her determining biographical and sociological conditions ... such epistemologically reflexive writing forms assume that any text is ultimately a description of the author's subjective experience of whatever he or she is writing about. Consequently, the author must either offer an interpretation of the limitations of that experience, or incorporate the voices of other experiences. This merely reinscribes, not only the

privileged place of experience, but the privileged place of the author's experience (p. 67).

Here Grossberg foregrounds the epistemological limitations of reflexivity. Reflexivity cannot be separated from the ways in which experience has come to be defined in cultural studies. Here experience is either unknowable (the determining biographical and sociological conditions cannot be known), or misleading (the interpretation turns inward with the author interpreting the limitations of his or her voice). These limitations will remain in effect as long as experience is understood as an ontological category, an essential 'beingness' that is offered up to reflexivity. Thus, if experience is unable to be the ground of anything (as in Hall's description of it within structuralism), then reflexivity can only result in 'an endless and inevitable deconstruction of the communicative relation between text and subject' [p. 67]. Reflexivity as an epistemological strategy must remain ineffective as long as experience remains a repressed and untheorized term.

Grossberg's analysis of reflexivity as one dominant mode of the autobiographical within cultural studies correctly focuses on the tendency toward solipsism. I want to ask, however, a parallel set of epistemological questions about the possibility of other modes of using the experiential within cultural analysis, as I focus on the possible enunciative positions that uses of the self may allow to emerge. In conceiving of experience as incorporated within a mode of theorizing and of speaking within theory, we are also brought to consider the ways in which its effects can be 'struggled' over. To recall Hall's definition of the ways in which articulation is an active mode of making connections is also to remember the conjunctural nature of articulation:

> [a]n articulation is thus the form of the connection that *can* make a unity of two different elements, under certain conditions. It is a linkage which is not necessary, determined, absolute and essential for all time. You have to ask, under what conditions *can* a connection be forged or made? So the so-called 'unity' of a discourse is really the articulation of different, distinct elements which can be rearticulated in different ways because they have no necessary 'belongingness'. The unity which matters is a linkage between that articulated discourse and the social forces with which it can, under certain historical conditions, but need not necessarily, be connected (Hall, 1986, p. 53).

Reconsidering experience and its use within critical practices as a form of articulation forces us beyond the culturalist/structuralist dichotomy of understanding experience. That is to say, experience may be made to work beyond either its romantic sense of 'authenticity' in the former, or its sense as an epiphenomenal product in the latter. Conceived of as an element of an enunciative practice, experience may, 'under certain conditions', make 'a unity of two different elements'. This is to emphasize, then, that the autobiographical, or the enunciation of experience, cannot be understood as a fixed condition; it may work as 'a linkage' which is not 'necessary, determined, absolute or essential for all time'. Moreover, theorized within a theory of articulation, the experiential may be pried from its commonsensical location in 'belongingness'. It then becomes possible to distance the autobiographical from a representational logic. Instead of representing a 'truth', a 'unity' or a 'belongingness', a critical use of the self may come to emphasize the 'historical conditions' involved in its *speaking*.

So I must work against traditional approaches to autobiography that stress the personal uniqueness of the (usually male) individual who writes his life, thereby guaranteeing his existence. [...] [I]n some feminist critiques of autobiography it is the unique communality of Woman which is guaranteed by the female autobiographer. In taking the autobiographical form as a representation of that which can be said to exist, these approaches severely limit the critical usefulness of experience, the autobiographical or the self. However, these tendencies can be struggled against as I work to show, through theory and through practice, that a critical enunciation of autobiographical experience has 'no necessary belongingness'. In working against a notion of experience as the possession of an entity, we can begin to recognize and theorize the different effects that an autobiographical enunciative practice may allow. In so doing, I will argue that the autobiographical must be made to work as an articulation between epistemological and ontological levels. As in Williams' use of experience, this analytic distinction is crucial in the construction of the self as a practice and as a speaking position. [...]

The stakes involved in theorizing critical uses of the self are high. Perhaps most importantly, a renewed theorization of experience sets out the conditions of possibility for the construction of a new, empowered speaking position within cultural theory. Far from being a self-indulgent affirmation, the experiential can be made to articulate both ontological and episte-mological levels of analysis. In so doing these levels are opened up for analysis as they can be made to speak of, and cut into, the conjunctural moment. This articulated analytic–critical practice emphasizes the social distinctions and experiential differentiations of gender, class, ethnicity, race, sexual preference, economics and age. However, speaking the self does not claim to represent 'differences' as fixed essences. In other words, an ontological pull is checked by the epistemological insistence precisely on the theoretical exigency and social conjuncture from and for which the self is spoken. [...] As an enunciative position within cultural theory, the self can be used to produce a radical rearticulation of the relationship of critic, experience, text, and the conjunctural moments that we construct as we speak of that within which we live.

References

Allor, M. 1984: Cinema, culture and social formation: ideology and critical practice. Unpublished dissertation. Urbana–Champaign: University of Illinois.

Althusser, L. 1970: The object of *Capital*. In Louis Althusser and Etienne Balibar *Reading capital*, translated by Ben Brewster. London: New Left Books.

Baudrillard, J. 1982: *A l'ombre des majorites silencieuses* .... Paris: Denoel/Gonthier.

Braidotti, R. 1989: The politics of ontological difference. In Brenna, T. (ed.), *Feminism and psychoanalysis*. London/New York: Routledge.

Dews, P. 1987: *Logics of disintegration: post-structuralist thought and the claims of critical theory*. London/New York: Verso.

Eagleton, T. 1976: *Criticism and ideology*. London: Verso.

Eagleton, T. 1989: Base and superstructure in Raymond Williams. In Eagleton, T. (ed.), *Raymond Williams: critical perspectives*. Cambridge: Polity Press.

Fiske, J. 1990: Ethnosemiotics: some personal and theoretical reflections. *Cultural Studies* **4** (1), 85–99.

Frank, A.W. 1990: Brining bodies back in: a decade in review. *Theory, Culture and Society* no.7, 131–62.

Fuss, D. 1989: *Essentially speaking: feminism, nature and difference*. London: Routledge.

Gallop, J. 1988: *Thinking through the body*. New York: Columbia University Press.

Grossberg, L. 1988: *It's a sin: postmodernism, politics and culture*. Sydney: Power Publications.

Hall, S. 1980: Cultural studies: two paradigms. *Media Culture and Society* **2**, 57–72.

Hall, S. 1986: On postmodernism and articulation: an interview with Stuart Hall. *Journal of Communication Inquiry* **10** (2), 45–60.

Hall, S. 1990: Cultural identity and diaspora. In Rutherford, J. (ed.), *Identity, community, culture, difference*. London: Lawrence and Wishart.

Hebdige, D. 1986: Postmodernism and 'the other side'. *Journal of Communication Inquiry* **10** (2), 78–98.

hooks, b. 1991: Narratives of struggle. in Mariani, P. (ed.), *Critical fictions: the politics of imaginative writing*. Seattle: Bay Press.

Juteau, D. and Laurin, N. 1989: From nuns to surrogate mothers: evolution of the forms of the appropriation of women. *Feminist Issues* **9** (1), 13–40 and 206.

Kennard, J.E. 1981: Personally speaking: feminist critics and the community of readers. *College English* **43** (2), 140–5.

Malette, L. and Chaloux, M. (eds) 1990: *Polytechnique, 7 decembre*. Montreal: Editions du remue-menage.

Mani, L. 1992: Cultural theory, colonial texts: reading eyewitness accounts of Wido Burning. In Grossberg, L., Nelson, C. and Treichler, P.A. (eds), *Cultural studies*. New York: Routledge.

Marcus, L. 1987: 'Enough about you, let's talk about me: recent autobiographical writing'. *New Formations* no. 1, 77–94.

Minh-ha, T.T. 1989: *Women, native, other: writing postcoloniality and feminism*. Bloomington, IN: Indiana University Press.

Morris, M. 1988: *The pirate's fiancee: feminism, reading postmodernism*. London: Verso.

Parmar, P. 1990: Black feminism: the politics of articulation. In Rutherford, J. (ed.), *Identity: community, culture, difference*. London: Lawrence and Wishart.

Probyn, E. 1987: The anorexic body. In Kroker, A. and Kroker, M. (eds), *Body invaders: panic sex in America*. Toronto: Oxford University Press.

Rutherford, J. (ed.) 1990: *Identity, community, culture, difference*. London: Lawrence and Wishart.

Slack, J.D. and Whitt, L.A. 1992: Ethics and cultural studies. In Grosverg, L., Nelson, C. and Treichler, P.A. (eds), *Cultural Studies*. New York/London: Routledge.

Spivak, G.C. 1988: Can the subaltern speak? In Nelson, C. and Grossberg, L. (eds), *Marxism and the interpretation of culture*. Urbana/University of Illinois Press.

Stuart, A. 1990: Feminism: dead or alive? In Rutherford, J. (ed.), *Identity, community, culture, difference*. London: Lawrence and Wishart.

Szekely, E. 1988: *Never too thin*. Toronto: The Women's Press.

Walkerdine, V. 1986: Video replay: families, films and fantasy. In Burgin, V., Donald, J. and Kaplan, C. (eds), *Formations of fantasy*. London: Methuen.

Williams, R. 1979: *Politics and letters*. London: Verso.

Williams, R. 1989: *Resources of hope: culture, democracy, socialism*. Gable, R. (ed.). London/New York: Verso.

28

Cultural studies from the viewpoint of cultural policy

Stuart Cunningham

Originally published in *Meanjin*, vol. 50, issue 2/3 (1991); reprinted in Graeme Turner (ed.), *Nation, culture, text – Australian cultural and media studies* (Routledge, 1993).

As cultural studies moves into a phase of consolidation and some respectability, it is being questioned from three broad directions. In placing these on a left-to-right continuum, I am mindful that one of the things at stake in the current climate is the viability of just such a political set. We might well remember the wonderful caveat issued by Jean-Luc Godard and Anne-Marie Mieville in *Numéro Deux*: 'This is not a film of the left or right, but a film of before and behind'.

To the left is a position that seeks to question the orthodoxies of academic cultural studies in the name of a more authentic critical and political practice, or in the name of a more thoroughgoing deconstruction or postmodernism. This position can invoke the powerful trope of recalling cultural studies to its origins as a brave intervention in established literary and social science orthodoxies.

Meaghan Morris's 'Banality in cultural studies',[1] for example, attacks the wilful calling into being of progressiveness in texts, and resistance in audiences – a cheerful populism that often collapses criticism into little more than fandom. She also suggests that the critical stances of the traditional humanities disciplines have not been so clearly dispelled as might once have been imagined.

On the right, emerging from the social sciences, is a position that views the recent sea changes in Eastern Europe and the USSR, the longer-term global shifts toward internationalisation and the collapse of movement politics of various kinds as calling into question the continuing relevance of the neo-Marxist 'motor' of cultural studies. From this perspective, the anti-capitalism, anti-consumerism and romanticisation of subcultural resistance embodied in the classical texts of cultural studies are no longer adequate responses to the big questions confronting the articulation of politics and culture in modern Western societies.

With these political reassessments has come a revaluation of empirical detail, aligned with a piecemeal approach to the articulation of ideology and culture. There is a 'beyond ideology' flavour about much of this work. John

Kelly's[2] discussion of Stuart Hall's key text on Left renewal in Britain, *The hard road to renewal: Thatcherism and the crisis of the Left*, is a frontal attack on a politics of grand theory that lacks credible empirics. With rhetorical naivety, Kelly poses the ultimate empirical question: 'How does Hall *know* any of these things?' (my emphasis).

The ranks of apostates from neo-Marxist orthodoxies have swelled, especially in Britain (though in the US cultural studies is still on a growth surge, and substantial questioning of the assumptions of the field from within will not come very soon or very readily). It seems that something more than a faddish search for The Next Thing is afoot.[3]

There is also a 'centrist' policy orientation. This approach seeks to position the perspectives of cultural studies within fields of public policy where academic critical protocols do not have priority. Like the 'left–humanities' position, it is aware of the limits of academic discourse. While seeking to respond to the same global concerns as the 'right–social-science' position, it is not as concerned to discredit the foundational posture of cultural studies, if that posture is distilled down to the central Enlightenment values of liberty, equality and solidarity.[4] Indeed, it seeks to revivify these core values as the central motor of reformism that can be appealed to in the public sphere of contemporary Western societies. This is the position that I wish to advance as a way forward for cultural studies.

What relations should exist between cultural studies and cultural policy? I employ the term cultural studies (or cultural criticism) as a convenient shorthand for work that treats film, the arts, media and communications, as well as lived, everyday cultures, and is driven by the many strands of neo-Marxist, structuralist, poststructuralist and postmodern thought. Cultural policy embraces the broad field of public processes involved in formulating, implementing and contesting governmental intervention in, and support of, cultural activity.

The commonsense reaction to my question, one likely to be offered by most of those outside the academy who might be inclined to consider it, would be that the former serves as a kind of 'handmaiden', developing rationales for those engaged in public policy. Theory, analysis and commentary should undergird practice; practice implements theory. On closer inspection, however, the relations are far less harmonious than this model suggests. Indeed, in many ways, contemporary practices flatly contradict received wisdom.

Cultural studies, from the viewpoint of cultural policy, is rather like the curate's egg – good in parts – but even the good parts mightn't be very good. Liz Jacka wrote recently of the 'widening gap between cultural critique and cultural policy'.[5] Taking my cue from this, I want to canvass some recent issues in Australian cultural and communications policy where practical opportunities for cultural analysis have been forgone, or worse.

Australian content on television

The Australian Broadcasting Tribunal's exhaustive inquiry into Australian Content on Commercial Television concluded its main considerations in

December 1989 with the introduction of a new Television Program Standard. The inquiry ran for about five years, with a break of three years in the mid-1980s.[6]

One of the members of the tribunal, Julie James-Bailey, commented that during the inquiry there was virtually no input from academic cultural critics and analysts.[7] There *was* one such contribution, however, from John Docker, who employed an array of contemporary theory to attack the legitimacy of regulation of Australian content on television.[8] Docker argued that regulation actually means the imposition of (British) high-cultural values onto popular culture forms whose appeal is indifferent to national variations and registrations. What viewers actively embrace in television culture, according to Docker, is the carnivalesque overturning of statist official culture and the celebration of working-class values and interests. These values and interests are transnational, and subvert state interventions to preserve national registrations of popular cultural forms.

It is probably just as well that Docker's arguments had no effect on the outcomes of the inquiry. But it is alarming that Docker's was the only significant contribution that presented any of the theoretical issues that have concerned theorists, critics and historians for decades. Docker's view of popular television and its audiences may be idiosyncratic, but it is, in Graeme Turner's words, 'directly licensed' by current strands of cultural theory.[9] To applaud Docker's irrelevance could be tantamount to applauding the irrelevance of critical and theoretical input to the policy-making process in general.

Advertising and national culture

The tribunal's inquiry addressed Australian content provisions covering all television programming, including advertising. The regulations for television advertising are different from those for other programme material. They are directed at prohibiting more than 20 per cent of any advertising being produced overseas, unless Australian crews travel overseas to obtain the footage. They constitute a very high level of protection for local content, and, because they have been in place for thirty years, they have been extremely influential in underwriting the television advertising industry in Australia.

The inquiry into foreign content in advertising has operated virtually as a sidelight to the main act. It is not hard to see why. Advertising is the unworthy discourse, as far as both criticism and policy are concerned. If there has been an outstanding consensus among critics of various persuasions it is that advertising panders to patriarchy and consumerism. This consensus sits comfortably with moves to deregulate a 'blatantly' protected industry. Regulation against foreign advertising content has been the subject of concerted attack from industry – primarily from transnational advertisers – as well as high-level economic rationalist sources of advice to government. A recent report by the Industries Assistance Commission (now the Industry Commission) attack the 'virtual embargo' on foreign-produced ads: 'the sector enjoys an extremely privileged position relative to nearly all other economic activity in Australia'.[10]

The main rationale for continued regulation has been the argument that advertising has a role in the formation of national cultural identity. The argument for making a positive connection between advertising and national culture can be mounted in two basic areas. From the viewpoint of policy, the weaker argument is the appeal to the effects of deregulation in the area of advertising on the drama production industry. It is clear that drama production could not have developed its present scope and depth without the industrial infrastructure of the Australian advertising industry. Evidence for this link is widely accepted, and pieces of it are often cited in film and television histories.[11] For this reason, if for no other, deregulating television advertising would have major cultural consequences.

The central argument, however, has to grasp the nettle – the positive contribution advertising itself may make to national culture. In its present forms, cultural studies is spectacularly unsuited to this task.

Two main patterns of criticism have remained foundational to the cultural critique of advertising. The first is diachronic, focusing on the history of advertising as an agent of American cultural imperialism. Jeremy Tunstall's *The media are American* and Mattelart and Dorfman's *How to read Donald Duck* established the parameters of this pattern, and the general critical perspective on advertising has never seriously deviated from it. The other pattern is synchronic; informed by the early semiotic guerrilla tactics of Roland Barthes's *Mythologies*, it focuses on the cultural reproduction of dominant ideological values embedded in bourgeois culture. In spite of an increasingly strong emphasis on feminism, the cultural studies approach to advertising, both in critical writing and in curricula, has not advanced significantly beyond the works of Barthes, Tunstall and Mattelart and Dorfman in the 1950s to the 1970s.

Under the umbrella of the tribunal's content regulation, Australian television advertising has developed a strong grammar of national imaging that parallels film and television fiction, but has a considerably greater permeation of the mass market. Advertising occupies an average of about three and a half hours a day on each commercial metropolitan television station, compared to recent Australian drama content of about two hours a week. By dint of repetition, saturation coverage across the most popular networks, and sophisticated textual strategies that increasingly link programmes with their commercial 'environment', advertising must be seen as having considerable cultural valence.

Such indicators of cultural permeation, though crude and problematic from a critical perspective, are important in policy formulation. The real issue is: to what extent can a positive character be imputed to them? This is not simply a question of putting the Mister Sheen gloss on what the critic has regarded as a tawdry business. It is a matter of evaluating the contribution of television advertising in terms that are not just a matter of marking ideological ticks and crosses. It is to describe the impress and influence of advertising in terms that accept that its ideologically regressive elements – its sexism, its chauvinism, its rowdy population – are bracketed within a more neutral, descriptive cultural and audiovisual history.

Such a history would focus on the central role that advertising has played in the development of a popular audiovisual 'grammar' of national identity during the 1970s and 1980s. The so-called 'new' nationalism of this period was most visibly expressed in advertising campaigns despite the large claims made for the contribution of film and television drama. These campaigns were at key moments explicit attempts at social engineering – for instance, the 'Life. Be in it' campaign and the 'Advance Australia' campaign of the late 1970s and early 1980s. This is clear in the published aims of 'Advance Australia': 'To heighten community and public awareness and pride in Australian skills, achievements and potential. To highlight the role of individual enterprise in the economy. To encourage improvements in quality design, marketing and other characteristics of Australian identity.'[12] This advertising campaign, and others that came in is wake, sought to redress what attitudinal research had identified as a widespread lack of 'pride in country' and support for Australian manufacturing.[13]

This kind of public-service advertising has had its counterparts in purely commercial campaigns, which over the last fifteen years have invented a popular audiovisual grammar of nationalism. Prestige national advertising campaigns now routinely incorporate this established repertoire of Australianist tropes. The fact that this repertoire is used for evidently contradictory purposes, from promoting health to flogging beer and tobacco, and utilises images that range from the unacceptably sexist to the innovative, even progressive, simply registers the modularity of advertising's nationalism.

There is very little substantial critical appraisal of this enormous portfolio of material, and what there is does little to articulate a position sensitive to the policy issues. There are critical exercises of the traditional kind, such as Stephen Alomee's less than trenchant putdown of the course of Australian nationalism ('from jingoism to jingle-ism') in *A nation at last?*, or Tim Rowse's critique of television populism in the 'humanity' ads.[14] But the 'sophisticated theory of consumption' called for by Kathy Myers in Britain,[15] or the magisterial descriptivist account of 'advertising as social communication' given by William Leiss, Stephen Kline and Sut Jhally in North America,[16] have no Australian counterparts. Such approaches must be applied to the question of Australian national identity in advertising if we are to advance beyond reflex ideological critique and begin to address urgent and practical policy issues.

Feminist cultural theory and bureaucratic reformism

Australia lags behind Canada and some Scandinavian nations in implementing strategies to modify sexist representations in the mass media, but in the last few years there have been significant initiatives here. The Office of the Status of Women has acted as the co-ordinating secretariat for a body called the National Working Party on the Portrayal of Women in the Media, a body consisting of representatives of the advertising industry, community groups and government departments.

To my knowledge, little or nothing arising from feminist scholars' sophisticated repertoire of theories of representation has been brought to bear on questions of bureaucratic reformism. Indeed, the most willing and effective advocates of institutional change use 'outdated', reflectionist and empiricist research to drive evidence for change, and a liberal humanist feminism to ground their campaigns.

It is not hard to see why advanced feminist theories of representation have weighed so lightly, despite the considerable body of literature that has been developed around exactly the sorts of questions that animate reformist policy initiatives. As Leiss, Kline and Jhally argue, 'representation' critiques of advertising have been subjective, non-quantitative, and have reduced the specificity of advertising to a generalised social critique.

From the viewpoint of policy, such critiques depend to an unacceptable degree on methods that are difficult to replicate without a high level of interpretative training. Semiotic method is powerful and convincing in the hands of a Barthes or a Williamson, but there has been a lot of obfuscated and redundant 'normal science' in the area. Representation critiques also depend too heavily on extrapolated pertinence – the findings are not underwritten by content analysis based on accepted sampling techniques. And they are guilty of simply using advertising, because it is arguably the most visible and most insistent form of commercialism, as a springboard into a generalised critique that is of little use within the protocols of piecemeal reformism. For all these reasons, representation accounts have been of little value in policy calculation, even for those predisposed to accept the assumptions from which they stem.

Media ownership and cultural power

Cultural studies has increasingly moved away from the orthodox political economy model's concern with questions of ownership and control of the mass media. The cultural power that is interesting now resides with audiences and, to a lesser extent, producers of media content itself. Set over against these interests are what appear to cultural theorists as rather hackneyed and predictable arguments for greater diversity and less concentration of media ownership. The calls of a David Bowman, a Paul Chadwick or an Eric Beecher appear hackneyed and predictable because they are voiced within very narrow terms of cultural debate, and partake of what Walter Benjamin memorably called 'left-wing melancholy'. This miserabilism, this prophetic nay-saying, is something that cultural studies is now resolutely rejecting.

The exercise of political and cultural power through media control, however, remains one of the blind spots of public policy in Australia. There is considerable evidence that the issue cuts through established party and factional allegiances and is beginning to create intolerable anomalies for public policy.

This issue will certainly not go away in a postmodernist flush of audience sovereignty. Indeed it will increase in centrality as media converge and narrow their focus ever more powerfully toward precise demographic and psychographic fine-tuning. Not only that, but the current theoretical fashion for championing the active audience finds an ironic echo in the rhetoric of consumer sovereignty that is offered by media owners and deregulators.

Unambiguous economic and political power will increasingly be translatable into unambiguous cultural power. Those who are best positioned to benefit from enhanced technologies of audience targeting, from the convergence of media of carriage, and from pro-competitive public policy parameters, are precisely those who now exercise enormous power through control of the traditional media. Unless it allies itself with social-democratic advocates of media reform, cultural studies could well become irrelevant in the near future.

Now, just wait a minute!

The 'handmaiden' model is easy picking for those inside the academy. Most people trained in the politics of cultural studies would view their primary role as critics of the dominant political, economic and social order. When we as cultural theorists do turn our hands to questions of policy, our command metaphors of resistance, refusal and opposition predispose us to view the policy-making process as inevitably compromised, *ad hoc*, incomplete and inadequate, controlled by people who are inexpert and ungrounded in theory and history, or who wield gross forms of political power for short-term ends. These people and processes are then called to the bar of an abstrusely formulated cultural idealism. Critical idealism would retort that mine is the mealy-mouthed voice of liberal bourgeois compromise.

A more reflective critique of the position I am advancing would raise the issue of the long-term leavening effect of critical idealism. Tomorrow's public debate and potential consensus may well issue from today's utopian, abstruse, left-of-field thinking. The clearest example of this is the 'sourcing' of femocrat reformism by feminist movement politics. Similar sourcing relationships hold between the environmental movements and green politics, or between ethnic advocacy and official discourses of multiculturalism. A more pragmatic variant of the same objection is that, if cultural studies doesn't hold to the humanities' traditional critical vocation, who will – particularly in the wake of the breakdown of more broadly based social movements?

These objections seem reasonable, so I want to respond to them carefully. First I do not wish to discount the model of prophetic critic, a role that is the essential prerequisite of critical practice. It is, however, rather disingenuous for the academy to don this mantle, as a great deal of the critical work performed within the academy cannot plausibly claim such prophetic status. The most effective public intellectuals on issues of culture in the Australian policy are not vanguard theorists, but those who work within the terms of a given (and, one might readily concede, narrow) set of public-interest, liberal-democratic and social-democratic norms. Vanguard theory, on the evidence we have to date, is less than likely to translate into prophetic criticism.

The second response proceeds from the first. To get to the nub of the problem: what is cultural studies' understanding of its political vocation? What is its vision of a better, more just, equitable, participatory, cultural order? What measures are cultural theorists and analysts taking to have this vision articulated widely? What alliances are we forming with cultural activists and policy agents and players? To what extent are we informing ourselves about the historical, existing and emergent policy agenda, and identifying where we might fit?

In an interesting interchange between John Fiske and an unnamed interlocutor, published in Fiske's *Reading the popular*, Fiske asserts that 'internal or semiotic resistance ... is an essential prerequisite of social change'.[17] This statement brings to the fore the politics of Fiske's influential model of resistive populism. The resistive strategies imputed to consumers of popular culture, by definition, are never mobilised into organisations that might seek to influence change in any institutional arrangement or professional practice by which cultural meaning is produced and delivered. The resistance Fiske champions actually undermines the strategies of organised reform movements because it sets itself against ideal standards of professional media practice and against empirical audience measurement. Both are essential if reformism is to gain some purchase in public policy processes.

The missing link is a social-democratic view of citizenship and the trainings necessary to activate and motivate it. A renewed concept of citizenship should be increasingly central to cultural studies as it moves into the 1990s. Political science, government, sociology, journalism, organisation studies, to say nothing of traditional professional trainings such as law, all have particular mobilisations of citizenship embodied in their curriculum. Despite this, the emerging evidence for an attention to citizenship in cultural studies signifies an important advance. It demonstrates that cultural studies is coming to terms with its neo-Marxist heritage as it realises that other political postures can be as radically reformist as neo-Marxism without employing a totalising and confrontational rhetoric. For this reason, the perspectives of Australian social-democratic thinkers like Hugh Stretton in social theory, Donald Horne, Peter Wilenski and H. C. Coombs in cultural and communications areas, or Francis Castles in economics, should assume as great an importance for rethinking the vocation of cultural studies as the international fathers (and mothers) of the discipline.

Replacing shop-worn revolutionary rhetoric with the new command metaphor of citizenship commits cultural studies to a reformist strategy within the terms of a social-democratic politics, and thus can connect it to the wellsprings of engagement with policy. Even though, as Ham and Hill show,[18] the policy process in modern capitalist states has arisen within a liberal pluralist problematic, it need not be limited by liberalism's underdeveloped ideas of power and of the necessity of struggle for access to decision-making processes.

This concept of citizenship does not by any means imply a politics of the status quo – a sort of primary-school civics. Donald Horne uses it to advance his Lockean notion of the 'cultural rights' of the citizen in modern social democracies. Graham Murdock and Peter Golding use it to invite thinking about information poverty in our age of increasingly privatised communications. It is also being employed to pose questions about new forms of citizenship that may embrace larger units than the individual nation-state, such as the emergent European community. Similarly, in a 1984 report to the French Ministry of Culture, Mattelart, Delcourt and Mattelart proposed a linguistic-cultural transnational community – a 'latin audio-visual space'.[19] Such concerns have been abroad for decades in the continuing debate in Unesco concerning the New World Information and Communications Order (NWICO).

Third, the greater proportion of cultural studies work is performed within academic arrangements that either prioritise vocational training or seek to marry a liberal arts education with gestures toward such training. These institutional orientations will become more established, if not necessarily accepted, under current government policies. Pragmatically then, there are powerful reasons to review the current state of cultural studies.

The calls to introduce a policy orientation into cultural studies have become louder in recent years.[20] We hear that cultural studies remains fixated on theoretical and textual orientations that provide little to equip students with knowledge and skills for citizenship and employment in the 1990s. The gap between textually based studies and policy cannot be bridged merely by further refinements in theories of representation, in new understandings of the audience or the 'progressive text', or in notions of subcultural resistance.

Indeed, two British cultural studies 'apostates', Geoff Hurd and Ian Connell, have argued that cultural critique, as a governing educational model, has actively deskilled students:

> While we accept there is a need for cultural appraisal and reconstruction, we would also suggest that the predominant view of the cultural organisations within cultural studies has been misleading and that criticism has been placed before understanding. In short, cultural studies has been critical of enterprises whose modes of operation and social significance it does not properly comprehend.[21]

Questions of policy do circulate at the margins of the traditional core curricula of cultural studies. In Trevor Barr's words, moving those marginal interests toward the centre of the curriculum ultimately has to do with 'political empowerment'.[22]

A focus on policy, if extended to both types of communications curricula – semiotics-based cultural studies on the one hand, and business communication, journalism, public relations, marketing and advertising on the other – has the potential to bridge the yawning gaps between these traditions. Its integration into liberal arts and media production programmes would encourage a firmer grasp of the social and vocational implications of cultural struggle as embodied in governmental and industrial processes. On the other hand, its integration into industry-driven courses would draw students into a broader appreciation of the politics and ethics of their vocations and the reasonable legitimacy of state intervention.

Finally, many of our protocols are disabling because they take scant account of the local conditions in which theory must be developed. It might seem a truism to state that different emphases should emerge in cultural studies in different parts of the world. Because Australia is a net importer of ideas as much as goods and services, it is crucial for an Australian cultural studies to be self-critical about is agenda, lest the agenda be set, by default, elsewhere. I can't put it better than the report of the Committee to Review

Australian Studies in Tertiary Education, which said Australianising tertiary education would prevent the intellectual cringe that slides 'between a vacuous cosmopolitan and an apologetic provincialism'.[23]

To Australianise is not to call for a form of intellectual tariff blockade. On the contrary, it implies a much stronger and more perspicacious engagement with imported traditions. And it in no way implies an a priori defence of the status quo, or a rejection of the possible benefits flowing from greater internationalisation of inquiry. It does suggest that an Australian cultural studies engaging with policy issues that affect the future of Australian culture would involve reconceptualising certain general theories, upgrading the focus on regulation as a positive underpinning of cultural production, and rethinking the politics of culture in a non-British, non-North-American setting.

Importing British cultural studies has meant privileging subcultural resistance to a repressive and class-defined state. This has much to do with Thatcherism's far-reaching influence on the agenda of the British Left, the anti-statist tone of much cultural studies and the subsequent search for positive markers of the intrinsic subversiveness of everyday life. The libertarianism implicit in this approach might find a greater echo in the United States (where the state has willingly abetted rather than mollified economic and cultural imperialism) than it ever should in Australia, or for that matter many other countries where state regulatory activity has struggled to achieve an equitable flow of economic and cultural goods and services.

Consider the perennial issue of the nation as an illustration of the importance of localism in intellectual work. The ascendant current of macro-level thought in cultural studies today lays to rest the nation-state and invites practitioners to link opportunities for internationalism with a renewed communalism. This may be appropriate for cultural thought in the present European context, but it is inappropriate in virtually any context outside the First World, including Australia.

There are high stakes involved in the arguments for internationalism and community against the nation. All the major cultural industries in Australia (film, television, the major arts and the many community-based arts programmes sponsored by the Australia Council) derive their policy justification from their being national in scope. It is too early, if indeed it will ever be politically strategic, to pit the internationalist–communalist position against the nation in Australia.

Ultimately, despite a Byzantine tripartite system of government that makes Australia one of the most 'governed' countries in the world per capita, it is at the national level that debate on cultural futures has to be staged. The future of cultural production is unavoidably bound into the future of national cultural policies. In terms of the intellectual resourcing of policy development, and in the myriad ways that local, state and subcultural sites of activity depend on national provision and support, the national arena will remain the engine room for cultural policy initiatives. For its part, cultural theory must take greater stock of its potential negative influence on progressive public policy outcomes and, if it is to orient itself in a more valuable way toward policy imperatives, must attend to the tasks of consolidating the legitimacy of policy rhetorics that sustain a national cultural infrastructure.

Implications and conclusions

Is it possible to regard a policy orientation within cultural studies as simply an add-on element, one more offering in the interdisciplinary smorgasbord? I don't think so. I have suggested that the political rhetoric undergirding cultural studies would have to be re-examined. This alone would indicate a more thoroughgoing review of the cultural studies enterprise than the smorgasbord model would permit.

Nothing in what I have said should be taken to indicate a less critical vocation for cultural studies. What would count as the critical vocation, however, would change. A cultural studies that grasps and sustains links with policy will inquire across a greatly expanded field, but with methods far less totalising and abstract, far more modest and specific, than those to which we are accustomed.

To treat cultural policy adequately from a critical perspective, it is necessary to appreciate the combined impact of economics, administrative law, cultural history, entertainment financing, government and parliamentary procedures on the development of public policy. This means a more subtle and context-sensitive re-education in the roles of the state in mixed capitalist economies, away from monolithic and wooden grand theories inspired more by critical purism than by the requirements for piecemeal reformism. Critical policy research thus implies more, rather than less, critical understanding than is found in the traditions of cultural criticism developed exclusively within humanities-based disciplines, and a significantly greater sensitivity to the extra-academic contexts within which such research must circulate for it to exercise its potential leavening function.

In summary, then, a policy orientation in cultural studies would shift its 'command metaphors' away from rhetorics of resistance, oppositionalism and anti-commercialism on the one hand, and populism on the other, toward those of access, equity, empowerment and the divination of opportunities to exercise appropriate cultural leadership. It would not necessarily discount critical strategies and priorities, but may indeed enhance and broaden them. It is not a call simply to add another 'perspective' to the academic sideboard, but would necessitate rethinking the component parts of the field from the ground up. It offers one major means of rapprochement across the critical/vocational divide that structures of academic field of cultural and communication studies. Finally, it would commit us to a genuine localism, against the abstract theoreticism that usually passes as the currency of international academic exchange.

Notes

1 Morris, M. 1990: Banality in cultural studies. In Mellencamp, P. (ed.), *Logics of television*. London: British Film Institute.

2 Kelly, J. 1988: Iron lady in a nanny's uniform. *Times Higher Education Supplement*, 840, 9 December.

3 See, for example, the British journal *Screen*'s new editorial policy (in **31**(1)), debate in that and other recent issues, and Collins, R. 1990: *Television: policy and culture*. London: Unwin Hyman.

4 See Alvarado, M. and Thompson, J.O. (eds), 1990: *The media reader*. London: British Film Institute. See also Inglis, F. 1990: *Media theory: an introduction*. Oxford: Basil Blackwell.

5 Jacka, E. 1988: Australian cinema – an anachronism in the '80s?. In Dermody, S. and Jacka, E. (eds), *The imaginary industry: Australian film in the late '80s*. Sydney: Australian Film, Television and Radio School, p. 118.

6 For discussion, see my Figuring the Australian factor. *Culture and Policy* **2**(1) (1990).

7 James-Bailey, J. 1989: Communicating with the decision makers: the role of research, scholarship and teaching in film and media studies. Staff Seminar, Griffith University, 20 October.

8 Docker, J. 1988: Popular culture versus the state: an argument against Australian content regulation for TV. Unpublished, attachment to Federation of Australian Commercial Television Stations (FACTS) submission to ABT Inquiry into Australian Content on Commercial Television, 16 August 1988 (Document D020B, ABT Inquiry File). A shorter version is published as Popular culture versus the state: an argument against Australian content regulations for TV. *Media Information Australia* **59**, (1991). For further discussion, see Cunningham, S., Craik, J., Bennett, T. and Hunter, I. 1991: Responses to Docker. *Media Information Australia* **59**.

9 Turner, G. 1992: 'It works for me': British cultural studies, Australian cultural studies, Australian film. In Grossberg, L. *et al.* (eds), *Cultural Studies*. New York: Routledge.

10 Industries Assistance Commission 1989: International trade and services. Report no. 418, AGPS, 30 June, p. 202.

11 Shirley, G. and Adams, B. 1983: *Australian cinema: the first eighty years*. Sydney: Angus & Robertson/Currency Press. Moran, A. 1985: *Images and industry: television drama production in Australia*. Sydney: Currency Press.

12 Lynch, P. 1982: Advance Australia. *Bulletin* 2 February.

13 Strugess, G. 1982: The emerging new nationalism. *Bulletin* 2 February.

14 Alomes, S. 1983: *A nation at last? The changing character of Australian nationalism 1880–1988*. Sydney: Angus & Robertson/Currency Press. Moran, A. 1984: 'Peculiarly Australian' – the political construction of cultural identity. In Encel, S. and Bryson, L. (eds), *Australian society*, 4th edn. Melbourne: Longman Cheshire. King, N. and Rowse, T. 1983: 'Typical Aussies': television and populism in Australia. *Framework* 22–3 (Autumn).

15 Myers, K. 1986: *Understains – the sense and seduction of advertising*. London: Comedia.

16 Leiss, W., Kline, S. and Jhally, S. 1986: *Advertising as social communication: persons, products and images of well-being*. Toronto: Methuen.

17 Fiske, J. 1988: *Reading the popular*. Boston: Unwin Hyman, 179.

18 Ham, C. and Hill, M. 1984: *The policy process in the modern capitalist state*. Brighton: Harvester Press.

19 Horne, D. 1988: *Think – or perish! Towards a confident and productive Australia*. Occasional Paper no. 8, Commission for the Future, June; and 1986: *The public culture*. Sydney: Pluto Press. Murdock, G. and Golding, P. 1989: Information poverty and political inequality: citizenship in the age of privatised communications. *Journal of Communications* **39** (3) (Summer), 180–95. Mattelart, A., Delcourt, X. and Mattelart, M. 1984: *International Image Markets*. London: Comedia.

20 For example, Miller, T. 1990: Film and media citizenship. *Filmnews* (February). Barr, T. 1990: Reflections on media education: the myths and realities. *Metro Media and Education Magazine* **82** (Autumn). Bennett, T. 1992: Putting policy into cultural studies. In Grossberg, L. *et al.* (eds), *Cultural studies*. New York: Routledge.

21 Hurd, G. and Connell, I. 1989: Cultural education: a revised program. *Media Information Australia* **53** (August), 23–30.

22 Barr, T. 1990: Reflections on media education: the myths and realities. *Metro Media and Education Magazine* **82** (Autumn), 16.

23 AGPS 1987: *Windows onto worlds: studying Australia at tertiary level*. Canberra.

29

European cities, the informational society, and the global economy[1]

Manuel Castells

From *New Left Review* no.204 (March–April, 1994).

An old axiom in urban sociology considers space as a reflection of society. Yet life, and cities, are always too complex to be captured in axioms. Thus the close relationship between space and society, between cities and history, is more a matter of expression than of reflection. The social matrix expresses itself into the spatial pattern through a dialectical interaction that opposes social contradictions and conflicts as trends fighting each other in an endless supersession. The result is not the coherent spatial form of an overwhelming social logic – be it the capitalist city, the pre-industrial city or the ahistorical utopia – but the tortured and disorderly, yet beautiful patchwork of human creation and suffering.

Cities are socially determined in their forms and in their processes. Some of their determinants are structural, linked to deep trends of social evolution that transcend geographic or social singularity. Others are historically and culturally specific. And all are played out, and twisted, by social actors that impose their interests and their values, to project the city of their dreams and to fight the space of their nightmares.

Sociological analysis of urban evolution must start from the theoretical standpoint of considering the complexity of these interacting trends in a given time-space context. The last twenty years of urban sociology have witnessed an evolution of thinking (including my own) from structuralism to subjectivism, then to an attempt, however imperfect, at integrating both perspectives into a structural theory of urban change that, if a label rooted in an intellectual tradition is necessary, I would call Marxian, once history has freed the Marxian theoretical tradition from the terrorist tyranny of Marxism-Leninism.

I intend to apply this theoretical perspective to the understanding of the fundamental transformations that are taking place in West European cities at the end of the second millennium. In order to understand such transformations we have to refer to major social trends that are shaking up the foundations of our existence: the coming of a technological revolution centred on information technologies, the formation of a global economy, and transition to a new society, the informational society, that – without ceasing to be capitalist or statist – replaces the industrial society as the framework of social institutions.

But this analysis has to be at the same time general and structural (if we accept that a historical transformation is under way) and specific to a given social and cultural context, such as Western Europe (with all due acknowledgement to its internal differentiation).

In recent years, a new trademark has become popular in urban theory: capitalist restructuring. Indeed it is most relevant to pinpoint the fundamental shift in policies that both governments and corporations have introduced in the 1980s to steer capitalist economies out of their 1970s crises. Yet more often than not, the theory of capitalist restructuring has missed the specificity of the process of transformation in each area of the world, as well as the variation of the cultural and political factors that shape the process of economic restructuring, and ultimately determine its outcome.

Thus the deindustrialization processes of New York and London take place at the same time that a wave of industrialization of historic proportions occurs in China and in the Asian Pacific. The rise of the informal economy and of urban dualism takes place in Los Angeles, as well as in Madrid, Miami, Moscow, Bogota and Kuala Lumpur, but the social paths and social consequences of such similarly structural processes are so different as to induce a fundamental variegation of each resulting urban structure.

I will try therefore to analyse some structural trends underlying the current transformation of European cities, while accounting for the historical and social specificity of the processes emerging from such structural transformation.

The thread of the New History

Urban life muddles through the pace of history. When this pace accelerates, cities – and their people – become confused, spaces turn threatening, and meaning escapes from experience. In such disconcerting yet magnificent times, knowledge becomes the only source to restore meaning, and thus meaningful action.

At the risk of schematism, and for the sake of clarity, I will summarize what seem to be the main trends that, together and in their interaction, provide the framework of social, economic and political life for European cities in this particular historical period.

First of all, we live in the midst of a fundamental technological revolution that is characterized by two features:

As all major technological revolutions in history, the effects are pervasive. They are not limited to industry, or to the media, or to telecommunications or transportation. New technologies, that have emerged in their applications in full strength since the mid 1970s, are transforming production and consumption, management and work, life and death, culture and warfare, communication and education, space and time. We have entered a new technological paradigm.

As the industrial revolution was based on energy (although it embraced many other technological fields) the current revolution is based upon information technologies, in the broadest sense of the concept, which includes genetic engineering (the decoding and reprogramming of the codes of living matter).

This technological informational revolution is the backbone (although not the determinant) of all other major structural transformations:

> It provides the basic infrastructure for the formation of a functionally interrelated world economic system.
>
> It becomes a crucial factor in competitiveness and productivity for countries throughout the world, ushering in a new international division of labour.
>
> It allows for the simultaneous process of centralization of messages and decentralization of their reception, creating a new communications world made up at the same time of the global village and of the incommunicability of those communities that are switched off from the global network. Thus an asymmetrical space of communication flows emerges from the uneven appropriation of a global communication system.
>
> It creates a new, intimate linkage between the productive forces of the economy and the cultural capacity of society. Because knowledge generation and information processing are at the roots of the new productivity, the ability of a society to accumulate knowledge and manipulate symbols translates into economic productivity and political–military might, anchoring the sources of wealth and power in the informational capacity of each society.

While this technological revolution does not determine per se the emergence of a social system, it is an essential component of the new social structure that characterizes our world: the informational society. By this concept, I understand a social structure where the sources of economic productivity, cultural hegemony and political–military power depend, fundamentally, on the capacity to retrieve, store, process and generate information and knowledge. Although information and knowledge have been critical for economic accumulation and political power throughout history, it is only under the current technological, social, and cultural parameters that they become directly productive forces. In other words, because of the interconnection of the whole world and the potential automation of most standard production and management functions, the generation and control of knowledge, information and technology is a necessary and sufficient condition to organize the overall social structure around the interests of the information holders. Information becomes the critical raw material of which all social processes and social organizations are made. Material production, as well as services, become subordinate to the handling of information in the system of production and in the organization of society. Empirically speaking, an ever growing majority of employment in Western European cities relates to information-processing jobs. The growing proportion of employment in service activities is not the truly distinctive feature, because of the ambiguity of the notion of 'services' (e.g. in Third World cities a majority of the population also works in 'services', although these are indeed very different kinds of activities). What is truly fundamental is the growing quantitative size and qualitative importance of information-processing activities in both goods production and services delivery. The contradictory but ineluctable emergence of the informational society shapes European cities as the onset of the industrial era marked for ever the urban and rural spaces of the nineteenth century.

A third major structural trend of our epoch is the formation of a global economy. The global economy concept must be distinguished from the notion of a world economy, which reflects a very old historical reality for most European nations, and particularly for the Netherlands, which emerged as a nation through its role as one of the nodal centres of the sixteenth century's world economy. Capitalism has accumulated, since its beginnings, on a worldwide scale. This is not to say that the capitalist economy was a global economy. It is only now becoming such.

By global economy we mean an economy that works as a unit in real time on a planetary scale. It is an economy where capital flows, labour markets, commodity markets, information, raw materials, management, and organization are internationalized and fully interdependent throughout the planet, although in an asymmetrical form, characterized by the uneven integration into the global system of different areas of the planet. Major functions of the economic system are fully internationalized and interdependent on a daily basis. But many others are segmented and unevenly structured depending upon functions, countries, and regions. Thus the global economy embraces the whole planet, but not all regions and all people on the planet. In fact, only a minority of people are truly integrated into the global economy, although all the dominant economic and political centres on which people depend are indeed integrated into the global economic networks (with the possible exception of Bhutan ...). With the disintegration of the Soviet empire, the last area of the planet that was not truly integrated into the global economy, it is restructuring itself in the most dramatic conditions to be able to reach out to the perceived avenues of prosperity of our economic model. (China already started its integration in the global capitalist economy in December 1979, while trying to preserve its statist political regime.)

This global economy increasingly concentrates wealth, technology, and power in 'the North', a vague geopolitical notion that replaces the obsolete East–West differentiation, and that roughly corresponds to the OECD countries. The East has disintegrated and is quickly becoming an economic appendage of the North. Or at least such is the avowed project of its new leaders. The 'South' is increasingly differentiated. East Asia is quickly escaping from the lands of poverty and underdevelopment to link up, in fact, with the rising sun of Japan, in a model of development that Japanese writers love to describe as 'the flying geese pattern', with Japan of course leading the way, and the other Asian nations taking off harmoniously under the technological guidance and economic support of Japan. China is at the crossroads of a potential process of substantial economic growth at a terrible human cost as hundreds of millions of peasants are uprooted without structures able to integrate them into the new urban–industrial world. South and South-East Asia struggle to survive the process of change, looking for a subordinate yet livable position in the new world order. Most of Africa, on the contrary, finds itself increasingly disconnected from the new global economy, reduced to piecemeal, secondary functions that see the continent deteriorate, with the world only waking up from time to time to the structural genocide taking place there when television images strike the moral consciousness of public opinion and affect the political interests of otherwise indifferent policy makers. Latin America, and many regions and cities around the world, struggle in the in-between land of being only partially integrated into the global economy, and then submitted to the tensions between the promise of full integration and the daily reality of a marginal existence.

In this troubled world, Western Europe has, in fact, become a fragile island of prosperity, peace, democracy, culture, science, welfare and civil rights. However, the selfish reflex of trying to preserve this heaven by erecting walls against the rest of the world may undermine the very fundamentals of European culture and democratic civilization, since the exclusion of the other is not separable from the suppression of civil liberties and a mobilization against alien cultures. Major European cities have become nodal centres of the new global economy, but they have also seen themselves transformed into magnets of attraction for millions of human beings from all around the world who want to share the peace, democracy, and prosperity of Europe in exchange for their hard labour and their commitment to a promised land. But the overcrowded and aged Western Europe of the late twentieth century does not seem as open to the world as was the young, mostly empty America of the beginning of the century. Immigrants are not welcome, as Europe tries to embark on a new stage of its common history, building the supranational Europe without renouncing its national identities. Yet the cultural isolation of the pan-European construction is inseparable from the affirmation of ethnic nationalism that will eventually turn not only against the 'alien immigrants' but against European foreigners as well. European cities will have to cope with this new global economic role while accommodating to a multi-ethnic society that emerges from the same roots that sustain the global economy.[2]

The fourth fundamental process under way in European cities is the process of European integration, into what will amount in the twenty-first century to some form of confederation of the present nation states. This is an ineluctable process for at least fifteen countries (the current twelve EC countries plus Sweden, Austria and Switzerland) regardless of the fate of the symbolic Maastricht Treaty. If, as is generally accepted, the European Community is heading toward a common market, a common resident status for all its citizens, a common technology policy, a common currency, a common defence and a common foreign policy, all the basic prerogatives of the national state will be shifted to the European institutions by the end of the century. This will certainly be a tortuous path, with the nostalgics of the past, neo-fascists, neo-communists and fundamentalists of all kinds fighting the tide of European solidarity, fuelling the fears of ignorance among people, building upon demagogy and opportunism. Yet however difficult the process, and with whatever substantial modifications to the current technocratic blueprints, Europe will come into existence: there are too many interests and too much political will at stake to see the project destroyed after having come this far.

The process of European integration will cause the internationalization of major political decision-making processes, and thus will trigger the fear of subordination of specific social interests to supranational institutions. But most of these specific interests express themselves on a regional or local basis rather than at the national level. Thus we are witnessing the renewal of the role'of regions and cities as locuses of autonomy and political decision. In particular, major cities throughout Europe constitute the nervous system of both the economy and political system of the continent. The more national states fade in their role, the more cities emerge as a driving force in the making of the new European society.

Identity and social movements

The process of historical transition experienced by Europe's cities leads to an identity crisis in its cultures and among its people, that becomes another major element of the new urban experience. This identity crisis is the result of two above mentioned processes that, however contradictory among themselves, jointly contribute to shake up the foundations of European national and local cultures. On the one hand, the march to supranationality blurs national identities and makes people uncertain about the power holders of their destiny, thus pushing them into withdrawal, either individualistic (neo-libertarianism) or collective (neo-nationalism). On the other hand, the arrival of millions of immigrants and the consolidation of multi-ethnic, multi-cultural societies in most West European countries, confronts Europe head on with the reality of a non-homogeneous culture, precisely at the moment when national identity is most threatened. There follows a crisis of cultural identity (with the corollary of collective alienation) that will mark urban processes in Europe for years to come.

More to the point: major cities will concentrate the overwhelming proportion of immigrants and ethnic-minority citizens (the immigrants' sons and daughters). Thus they will also be at the forefront of the waves of racism and xenophobia that will shake up the institutions of the new Europe even before they come into existence. As a reaction to the national identity crisis we observe the emergence of territorially defined identities at the level of the region, of the city, of the neighbourhood. European cities will be increasingly oriented toward their local culture, while increasingly distrustful of higher-order cultural identities. The issue then is to know if cities can reach out to the whole world without surrendering to a localistic, quasi-tribal reaction that will create a fundamental divide between local cultures, European institutions, and the global economy.

European cities are also affected by the rise of the social movements of the informational society, and in particular by the two central movements of the informational society: the environmental movement, and the women's movement.[3]

The environmental movement is at the origin of the rise of the ecological consciousness that has substantially affected urban policies and politics. The issue of sustainable development is indeed a fundamental theme of our civilization and a dominant topic on today's political agendas. Because major cities in Europe are at the same time nodal centres of economic growth and the living places for the most environmentally-conscious segment of the population, the battles for integration will be fought in the streets and institutions of these major cities.

The structural process of transformation of women's condition, in dialectical interaction with the rise of the feminist movement has completely changed the social fabric of cities. Labour markets have been massively feminized, resulting in a change in the conditions of work and management, of struggle and negotiation, and ultimately in the weakening of a labour movement that could not overcome its sexist tradition. This also points to the possibility of a new informational labour movement that because it will have to be based on women's rights and concerns, as well as on those of men, will be historically different from its predecessor.

At the same time, the transformation of households and the domestic division of labour is fundamentally changing the demands on collective consumption, and thus urban policy. For instance, childcare is becoming as important an issue as housing in today's cities. Transportation networks have to accommodate the demands of two workers in the family, instead of relying on the free driving service provided by the suburban housewife in the not so distant past.

Some of the new social movements, the most defensive, the most reactive, have taken and will be taking the form of territorially-based countercultures, occupying a given space to cut themselves off from the outside world, hopeless of being able to transform the society they refuse. Because such movements are likely to occur in major cities that concentrate a young, educated population, as well as marginal cultures that accommodate themselves in the cracks of the institutions, we will be witnessing a constant struggle over the occupation of meaningful space in the main European cities, with business corporations trying to appropriate the beauty and tradition for their noble quarters, and urban countercultures making a stand on the use value of the city, while local residents try to get on with their living, refusing to be bent by the alien wind of the new history.

Beyond the territorial battles between social movements and elite interests, the new marginality, unrelated to such social movements, is spreading over the urban space. Drug addicts, drug dealers and drug victims populate the back alleys of European cities, creating the unpredictable, awakening our own psychic terrors, and tarnishing the shine of civilized prosperity at the daily coming of darkness. The 'black holes' of our society, those social conditions from where there is no return, take their territory too, making cities tremble at the fear of their unavowed misery.[4]

The occupation of urban space by the new poverty and the new marginality takes two forms: the tolerated ghettoes where marginalized people are permitted to stay, out of sight of the mainstream society; the open presence in the core area of cities of 'street people', a risky strategy, but at the same time a survival technique since only there do they exist, and thus only there can they related to society, either looking for a chance or provoking a final blow.

Because the informational society concentrates wealth and power, while polarizing social groups according to their skills, unless deliberate policies correct the structural tendencies we are also witnessing the emergence of a social dualism that could ultimately lead to the formation of a dual city, a fundamental concept that I will characterize below, when considering the spatial consequences of the structural trends and social processes that I have proposed as constituting the framework that underlies the new historical dynamics of European cities.

The spatial transformation of major cities

From the trends we have described stem a number of spatial phenomena that characterize the current structure of major metropolitan centres in Western Europe. These centres are formed by the uneasy articulation of various socio-spatial forms and processes that I find useful to specify in their singularity, although it is obvious that they cannot be understood without reference to each other.

First of all, the national–international business centre is the economic engine of the city in the informational–global economy. Without it, there is no wealth to be appropriated in a given urban space, and the crisis overwhelms any other project in the city, as survival becomes the obvious priority. The business centre is made up of an infrastructure of telecommunications, communications, urban services and office space, based upon technology and educational institutions. It thrives through information-processing and control functions. It is sometimes complemented by tourism and travel facilities. It is the node of the space of flows that characterizes the dominant space of informational societies. That is, the abstract space constituted in the networks of exchange of capital flows, information flows, and decisions that link directional centres among themselves throughout the planet. Because the space of flows needs nodal points to organize its exchange, business centres and their ancillary functions constitute the localities of the space of flows. Such localities do not exist by themselves but by their connection to other similar localities organized in a network that forms the actual unit of management, innovation, and power.

Secondly, the informational society is not disincarnated. New elites make it work, although they do not necessarily base their power and wealth on majority ownership of the corporations. The new managerial–technocratic–political elite does however create exclusive spaces, as segregated and removed from the city at large as the bourgeois quarters of the industrial society. In European cities, unlike in America, the truly exclusive residential areas tend to appropriate urban culture and history, by locating in rehabilitated areas of the central city, emphasizing the basic fact that when domination is clearly established and enforced, the elite does not need to go into a suburban exile, as the weak and fearful American elite did to escape from the control of the urban population (with the significant exceptions of New York, San Francisco, and Boston).

Indeed, the suburban world of European cities is a socially diversified space, which is segmented in different peripheries around the central city. There are the traditional working-class suburbs (either blue-collar or white-collar) of the well-kept subsidized housing estates in home ownership. There are the new towns, inhabited by a young cohort of lower middle class, whose age made it difficult for them to penetrate the expensive housing market of the central city. And there are also the peripheral ghettoes of the older public-housing estates where new immigrant populations and poor working families experience their exclusion from the city.

Suburbs are also the locus of industrial production in European cities, both for traditional manufacturing and for the new high-technology industries that locate in new peripheries of the major metropolitan areas, close enough to the communication centres but removed from older industrial districts.

Central cities are still shaped by their history. Thus traditional working-class neighbourhoods, increasingly populated by service workers rather than by industrial workers, constitute a distinctive space, a space that, because it is the most vulnerable, becomes the battleground between the redevelopment efforts of business and the upper middle class, and the invasion attempts of the countercultures trying to reappropriate the use value of the city. They often become defensive spaces for workers who have only their home to fight for, while at the same time meaningful popular neighbourhoods and likely bastions of xenophobia and localism.

The new professional middle classes torn between attraction to the peaceful comfort of the boring suburbs and the excitement of a hectic, and often too expensive, urban life. The structure of the household generally determines the spatial choice. The larger the role women play in the household, the more the proximity to jobs and urban services in the city makes central urban space attractive to the new middle class, triggering the process of gentrification of the central city. On the contrary, the more patriarchal is the middle-class family, the more we are likely to observe the withdrawal to the suburb to raise children, all economic conditions being equal.

The central city is also the locus for the ghettoes of the new immigrants, linked to the underground economy, and to the networks of support and help needed to survive in a hostile society. Concentration of immigrants in some dilapidated urban areas in European cities is not the equivalent however to the experience of the American ghettoes, because the overwhelming majority of European ethnic minorities are workers, earning their living and raising their families, thus counting on a support structure that make their ghettoes strong, family-oriented communities, unlikely to be taken over by street crime.

It is in the core administrative and entertainment districts of European cities that urban marginality makes itself present. Its pervasive occupation of the busiest streets and public transport nodal points is a survival strategy deliberately designed to receive they can receive public attention or private business, be it welfare assistance, a drug transaction, a prostitution deal, or the customary police care.

Major European metropolitan centres present some variation around the structure of urban space we have outlined, depending upon their differential role in the European economy. The lower their position in the new informational network, the greater the difficulty of their transition from the industrial stage, and the more traditional will be their urban structure, with old-established neighbourhoods and commercial quarters playing the determinant role in the dynamics of the city. On the other hand, the higher their position in the competitive structure of the new European economy, the greater the role of their advanced services in the business district, and the more intense will be the restructuring of the urban space. At the same time, in those cities where the new European society reallocates functions and people throughout the space, immigration, marginality and countercultures will be the most present, fighting over control of the territory, as identities become increasingly defined by the appropriation of space.

The critical factor in the new urban processes is, however, the fact that urban space is increasingly differentiated in social terms, while being functionally interrelated beyond physical contiguity. There follows a separation between symbolic meaning, location of functions, and the social appropriation of space in the metropolitan area. The transformation of European cities is inseparable from a deeper, structural transformation that affects urban forms and processes in advanced societies: the coming of the Informational City.

The Informational City

The spatial evolution of European cities is a historically specific expression of a broader structural transformation of urban forms and processes that expresses the major social trends that I have presented as characterizing our historical epoch: the rise of the Informational City. By this concept I do *not* refer to the urban form resulting from the direct impact of information technologies on space. The Informational City is the urban expression of the whole matrix of determinations of the Informational Society, as the Industrial City was the spatial expression of the Industrial Society. The processes constituting the form and dynamics of this new urban structure, the Informational City, will be better understood by referring to the actual social and economic trends that are restructuring the territory. Thus the new international and inter-regional division of labour ushered in by the informational society leads, at the world level, to three simultaneous processes:

> The reinforcement of the metropolitan hierarchy exercised throughout the world by the main existing nodal centres, which use their informational potential and the new communication technologies to extend and deepen their global reach.
>   The decline of the old dominant industrial regions that were not able to make a successful transition to the informational economy. This does not imply however the all traditional manufacturing cities are forced to decline: the examples of Dortmund or Barcelona show the possibility to rebound from the industrial past into an advanced producer-services economy and high-technology manufacturing.
>   The emergence of new regions (such as the French Midi or Andalusia) or of new countries (e.g. the Asian Pacific) as dynamic economic centres, attracting capital, people, and commodities, thus recreating a new economic geography.[5]

In the new economy, the productivity and competitiveness of regions and cities is determined by their ability to combine informational capacity, quality of life, and connectivity to the network of major metropolitan centres at the national and international levels.

The new spatial logic, characteristic of the Informational City, is determined by the pre-eminence of the space of flows over the space of places. By space of flows I refer to the system of exchanges of information, capital, and power that structures the basic processes of societies, economies and states between different localities, regardless of localization. I call it 'space' because it does have a spatial materiality: the directional centres located in a few selected areas of a few selected localities; the tele-communication system, dependent upon telecommunication facilities and services that are unevenly distributed in the space, thus marking a telecommunicated space; the advanced transportation system, that makes such nodal points dependent on major airports and airlines services, on freeway systems, on high-speed trains; the security systems necessary to the protection of such directional spaces, surrounded by a potentially hostile world; and the symbolic marking of such spaces by the new monumentality of abstraction, making the locales of the space of flows meaningfully meaningless, both in their internal arrangement and in their architectural form. The space of flows, superseding the space of places, epitomizes the increasing differentiation between power and experience, the separation between meaning and function.[6]

The Informational City is at the same time the Global City, as it articulates the directional functions of the global economy in a network of decision-making and information-processing centres. Such globalization of urban forms and processes goes beyond the functional and the political, to influence consumption patterns, lifestyles, and formal symbolism.[7]

Finally, the Informational City is also the Dual City. This is because the informational economy has a structural tendency to generate a polarized occupational structure, according to the informational capabilities of different social groups. Informational productivity at the top may incite structural unemployment at the bottom or downgrading of the social conditions of manual labour, particularly if the control of labour unions is weakened in the process and if the institutions of the welfare state are undermined by the concerned assault of conservative politics and libertarian ideology.[8]

The filling of downgraded jobs by immigrant workers tends to reinforce the dualization of the urban social structure. In a parallel movement, the age differential between an increasingly older native population in European cities and a younger population of newcomers and immigrants forms two extreme segments of citizens polarized simultaneously along lines of education, ethnicity, and age. There follows a potential surge of social tensions.

The necessary mixing of functions in the same metropolitan area leads to the attempt to preserve social segregation and functional differentiation through planning of the spatial layout of activities and residence, sometimes by public agencies, sometimes by the influence of real-estate prices. There follows a formation of cities made up of spatially coexisting, socially exclusive groups and functions, that live in an increasingly uneasy tension vis-à-vis each other. Defensive spaces emerge as a result of the tension.

This leads to the fundamental urban dualism of our time. It opposes the cosmopolitanism of the elite, living on a daily connection to the whole world (functionally, socially, culturally), to the tribalism of local communities, retrenched in their spaces that they try to control as their last stand against the macro-forces that shape their lives out of their reach. The fundamental dividing line in our cities is the inclusion of the cosmopolitans in the making of the new history while excluding the locals from the control of the global city to which ultimately their neighbourhoods belong.

Thus the Informational City, the Global City, and the Dual City are closely interrelated, forming the background of urban processes in Europe's major metropolitan centres. The fundamental issue at stake is the increasing lack of communication between the directional functions of the economy and the informational elite that performs such functions, on the one hand, and the locally-oriented population that experiences an ever deeper identity crisis, on the other. The separation between function and meaning, translated into the tension between the space of flows and the space of places, could become a major destabilizing force in European cities, potentially ushering in a new type of urban crisis.

Back to the future?

The most important challenge to be met in European cities, as well as in major cities throughout the world, is the articulation of the globally-oriented economic functions of the city with the locally-rooted society and culture. The separation between these two levels of our new reality leads to a structural urban schizophrenia that threatens our social equilibrium and our quality of life. Furthermore, the process of European integration forces a dramatic restructuring of political institutions, as national states see their functions gradually voided of relevance, pulled from the top toward supranational institutions and from the bottom toward increasing regional and local autonomy. Paradoxically, in an increasingly global economy and with the rise of the supranational state, local governments appear to be at the forefront of the process of management of the new urban contradictions and conflicts. National states are increasingly powerless to control the global economy, and at the same time they are not flexible enough to deal specifically with the problems generated in a given local society. Local governments seem to be equally powerless vis-à-vis the global trends but much more adaptable to the changing social, economic, and functional environment of cities.

The effectiveness of the political institutions of the new Europe will depend more on their capacity for negotiation and adaptation than on the amount of power that they command, since such power will be fragmented and shared across a variety of decision-making processes and organizations. Thus instead of trying to master the whole complexity of the new European society, governments will have to deal with specific sets of problems and goals in specific local circumstances. This is why local governments, in spite of their limited power, could be in fact the most adequate instances of management of these cities, working in the world economy and living in the local cultures. The strengthening of local governments is thus a precondition for the management of European cities. But local governments can only exercise such management potential if they engage in at least three fundamental policies:

The fostering of citizen participation, on the basis of strong local communities that feed local government with information, present their demands, and lay the ground for the legitimacy of local government so that they can become respected partners of the global forces operating in their territory.

The interconnection and cooperation between local governments throughout Europe, making it difficult for the global economic forces to play one government against the other, thus forcing the cooperation of global economy and local societies in a fruitful new social contract. New information technologies should make possible a qualitative upgrading of the cooperation between local governments. A European Municipal Data Bank, and a network of instant communication between local leaders, could allow the formation of a true association of interests of the democratic representatives of the local populations. An electronically connected federation of quasi-free communes could pave the way for restoring social and political control over global powers in the informational age.

Managing the new urban contradictions at the local level by acting on the social trends that underlie such contradictions requires a vision of the new city and new society we have entered into, including the establishment of cooperative mechanisms with national governments and European institutions, beyond the natural and healthy competition of parties. The local governments of the new Europe will have to do their homework in understanding their cities, if they are to assume the historical role that the surprising evolution of society could offer them.[9]

Thus the historical specificity of European cities may be a fundamental asset in creating the conditions for managing the contradictions between the global and the local in the new context of the informational society. Because European cities have strong civil societies, rooted in an old history and a rich, diversified culture, they could stimulate citizen participation as a fundamental antidote against tribalism and alienation. And because the tradition of European cities as city states leading the pace to the modern age in much of Europe is engraved in the collective memory of their people, the revival of the city state could be the necessary complement to the expansion of a global economy and the creation of a European state. The old urban tradition of Amsterdam as a centre of politics, trade, culture and innovation, suddenly becomes more strategically important for the next stage of urban civilization than the meaningless suburban sprawl of high-technology complexes that characterize the informational space in other areas of the world.

European cities, because they are cities and not just locales, could manage the articulation between the space of flows and the space of places, between function and experience, between power and culture, thus recreating the city of the future by building on the foundations of their past.

Notes

1 This article was first given as a lecture at the Centrum voor Groontstedelijk Onderzock, Amsterdam, and is reproduced with their kind permission. It has also been presented at the Center for Social Theory and Comparative History, UCLA.

2 Castells, M. and Hall, P. 1993: *Technopoles of the world*, London. Brotchie, J.F., Hall, P. and Newton, P.W. (eds) 1987: *The spatial impact of technological change*, London.

Borja, J. *et al.* (eds) 1991: *Las grandes ciudades en la decada de los noventa*, Madrid. Throughout this article, references are given as a guide for the interested reader, and not as specific locations for arguments presented.

3   Castells, M. 1983: *The city and the grassroots: a cross-cultural theory of urban social movements*, Berkeley, CA.

4   Portes, A. *et al*, (eds) 1988: *The informal economy*, Baltimore, MD.

5   On this subject, see Castells, M. 1989: *The Informational City*, Oxford. Carnoy, M., Castells, M., Cohen, S. and Cardoso, F.H. 1993: *The new world economy in the information age*, University Park, PA.

6   Hall, P. and Preston, P. 1988: *The carrier wave: new information technology and the geography of innovation, 1846–2003*, London.

7   Sassen, S. 1991: *The global city: New York, London and Tokyo*, Princeton, NJ.

8   Mollenkopf, J. and Castells, M. (eds) 1991: *Dual city: restructuring New York*, New York.

9   Judd, D. and Parkinson, M. (eds) 1990: *Leadership and urban regeneration: cities in North America and Europe*, Newbury Park, CA. Campos, Venuti G. 1991: *L'urbanistica del riformismo*, Rome. Kings, D.S. and Pierres, J. (eds) 1990: *Challenged to local government*, London.

30

An invitation to a sociology of stories

Ken Plummer

From his *Telling sexual stories – power, change and social worlds* (Routledge, 1995).

[...] 'Stories' have recently moved centre stage in social thought. In anthropology, they are seen as the pathways to understanding culture. In psychology, they are the bases of identity. In history, they provide the tropes for making sense of the past. In psychoanalysis, they provide 'narrative truths' for analysis. In philosophy they are the bases for new forms of 'world-making' and the key to creating communities. Even economics has recognised its 'storied character'. Everywhere, it seems, there is an interest in stories, and social scientists have now finally grasped this point. Sociologists may be the last to enter this field explicitly, although much of their work over the past century has in one way or the other implicitly been concerned both with the gathering of other people's stories (through interviews and the like) as well as telling their own stories (of modernity, of class, of the degradation of work). But a clear 'narrative moment' has now been sensed. Sociology is bound up both with obtaining stories and telling stories. At the extreme, Patricia Ticineto Clough (1992) has argued that 'all factual representations of empirical reality, even statistical representations, are narratively constructed', whilst David Maines (1993) has presented an agenda for narrative research, arguing that 'nearly anything a sociologist might want to investigate can be done so from the narrative approach'.

[...] I am concerned with helping develop a sociology of stories, but I do it at an angle. I take as my topic *the personal experience narratives of the intimate* – a story that haunts us everywhere today in ways it did not in the recent past. I have in mind the stories told by men and women of coming out as gay and lesbian; of women who discover they 'love too much'; of the tales told by the survivors of abortion, rape and incest; of the 'new men' who are rediscovering their newly masculine roots through mythical stories. And many others. This book is about the proliferation of personal narratives of the intimate in the late twentieth century. *But the ideas in this book could be applied to any story telling process: the focus on sexuality is merely one instance.* This chapter is hence concerned with laying out some of the contours of a sociology of stories with wider applicability than just the intimate.

Maines and others in their proposal for a 'narrative turn' in sociology have focused primarily upon narrative structures. Thus key elements of narrative have a concern with the way 'events are selected from the past'; with the 'story elements' of 'plot, setting and characterization'; and with the creation of a 'temporal ordering'. But for me, a sociology of stories should be less concerned with analysing the formal structures of stories or narratives (as literary theory might), and more interested in inspecting the social role of stories: the ways they are produced, the ways they are read, the work they perform in the wider social order, how they change, and their role in the political process. Whilst I have taken as my 'case' the distinctly modern quest to provide personal narratives around the sexual life, much of what will be said could be applied to other genres of story work. Although recent developments in literary theory and cultural studies will prove useful, and there is indeed a need for analysing the formal properties of stories, I will constantly return to the social work they perform in cultures. *It is time to go beyond the text.* [...] Here the task is to see stories in two linked and critical ways: as symbolic interactions and as political processes. [...]

Whilst sociology may provide many roots into the study of stories, this study takes a symbolic interactionist view. Briefly, this century-old and now revitalising position takes as its baseline the view that the social world for human beings can be helpfully viewed as a vast flow of ever-changing symbolic interactions in which we are set actively adrift in a never-ending stream of practical activities. Isolated individuals and abstracted societies are there none. We human beings are social world-makers, though we do not make our social worlds in conditions of our own choosing. Through symbols and languages, we are able to reflect upon ourselves and others, and we cannot but help acting in, on and through the world. We work and worry, pray and play, love and hate; and *all the time we are telling stories* about our pasts, our presents and our futures. We are constantly doing things together – no person is an island: even when alone, especially when alone, there is an awareness of others. We are constantly writing the story of the world around us: its periods and places, its purposes and programmes, its people and plots. We invent identities for ourselves and others and locate ourselves in these imagined maps. We create communities of concern and arenas of activity where we can make our religions, tend to our 'families', practise our politics, get on with our work. We experience our bodies and our feelings, as well as our behaviours and talk. And everywhere we go, we are charged with telling stories and making meaning – giving sense to ourselves and the world around us. And the meanings we invoke and the worlds we craft mesh and flow, but remain emergent: never fixed, always indeterminate, ceaselessly contested. Change is ubiquitous: we are always becoming, never arriving; and the social order heaves as a vast negotiated web of dialogue and conversation. So-called social science is not cut off from this activity but is itself very much part of it: it is simply an occasion of more systematic reflection and story telling upon the world. It too is a stream of practical activities – doing things together, immersing ourselves in the world, facing problems, creating working solutions, making meanings to make a difference. It too is a flow requiring constant change, more adjustment, equivocation and contest. Truth which emerges as helpful for one time may not be so at another. Active problem-solving is required anew of each group. And all the time it is itself a vast symbolic enterprise, feeding on the world as much as shaping it.

Story telling can be placed at the heart of our symbolic interactions. The focus here is neither on the solitary individual life (which is in principle unknown and unknowable), nor on the text (which means nothing standing on its own), but on *the interactions which emerge around story telling*. Stories can be seen as *joint actions*. [...] People may be seen as engaged in fitting together lines of activity around stories; they are engaged in *story actions*.

Some of the folk engaging in joint actions may be seen as *producers* of sexual stories: these are the sexual *story tellers* who write lengthy autobiographies exploring their inner sexual natures. They are the sexual story tellers who produce voluminous correspondence or diaries which display the minutiae of their erotic lives. These are the people who provide life histories of sociologists, oral histories for oral historians and case studies for psychologists and clinicians. They even, and more complexly, can *perform* their stories – not just in words and scripts but as emotionally charged bodies in action.

Closely allied to these tellers are a second kind of producer: *the coaxers, coachers and coercers*. These folk possess the power, at least momentarily, to provoke stories from people. Their line of activity is to seduce stories: coaxers become listeners and questioners. They probe, interview, and interrogate. They send out questionnaires and solicit 'problem letters'. Sometimes they gather in groups to make others tell their stories and sometimes as individuals they just simply clasp their hands, smile and listen. They are the Sigmund Freuds, the Oprah Winfreys, the Shere Hites who poke and probe for the personal narrative. They are even the parents demanding to know what their child has been up to. They are the courtroom interrogators, the doctors, the therapists, the tabloid journalists. They coax, coach and coerce people to tell their stories. My own role as a sociologist conducting research into the lives of the sexually different in the 1970s turned me into a coaxer: bringing people to the edge of telling a story they might never have told before, and coaching them to tell it in a certain way. My questions, my style, my theory meant that the story they told me did not emerge as it did a century before in the hands of a Krafft-Ebing. Whereas he looked for – and found – pathological tales, I looked for – and found – tales of normalcy. Coaxers can play a crucial role in shifting the nature of the stories that are told.

Another major group are the *consumers, readers, audiences* of sexual stories: their line of activity is to consume, to interpret and make sense of all these stories. These are the viewers who watch the documentary of a transvestite life on prime-time TV; the bookworms who consume the biographies of Rock Hudson, Jan Morris, Magic Johnson, Woody Allen, Madonna or the latest 'sexual scandals'; the control agents who scour a person's tale for the sexual signs; the student who is compelled for her course to read the biography of Herculine Barbine, Jane Fry or Dora. Just how these 'readers' interpret the story is a crucial process in understanding stories. Sometimes they are brought to outrage and sometimes to better understanding. Sometimes such consumption becomes a passionate hobby and sometimes it is all a matter of great indifference. Sometimes it is a tool-kit and manual for guidance and sometimes it is a source where a person can literally find themselves in the text. Sometimes a text is read in relative isolation and sometimes it is read through a social world or an imagined community – of class, of race, of gender, of experience, of taste. Sometimes people hear so lightly what others say so intensely, and sometimes people hear so intensely what others say so lightly.

All these people – producers, coaxers, consumers – are engaged in assembling life story actions *around* lives, events and happenings – although they cannot grasp the *actual* life. At the centre of much of this action emerge the story *products*: the objects which harbour the meanings that have to be handled through interaction. These congeal or freeze already preconstituted moments of a life from the *story teller* and the *coaxer* and await the handling of a *reader* or *consumer*. The meanings of stories are never fixed but emerge out of a ceaselessly changing stream of interaction between producers and readers in shifting *contexts*. They may, of course, become habitualised and stable; but always and everywhere the meaning of stories shift and sway in the contexts to which they are linked.

Stories get told and read in different ways in different contexts. The consuming of a tale centres upon the different *social worlds* and *interpretive communities* who can hear the story in certain ways and hence not others and who may come to produce their own shared 'memories'. [...] The stories of people with HIV infection feed into some communities where support, love and care is offered; but into others where exclusion, stigma and fear is the interpretive frame. Hence these communities are more than just cognitive or symbolic units (though they are that), they are also emotional worlds. More, such communities are not permanent and fixed: when, for instance, the US basketball player Magic Johnson announced his HIV status in 1991, his story became accepted in the same youthful communities (where he was an established hero) that had previously shown enmity to Aids stories. Prior rage and hostility amongst the young turned to tears and bafflement. Youthful communities may lend support to the telling of some tales but not others. Adult stories may not easily be heard in youthful worlds, and youthful stories may not be heard easily in adult worlds. Stories of young mums with no husbands may be heard very differently in black ghettoes and white suburbia. Further, these communities themselves are part of wider *habitual or recurring networks of collective activity*. Stories do not float around abstractly but are grounded in historically evolving communities of memory, structured through age, class, race, gender and sexual preference. There is often an organised pattern behind many of the tales that are heard: audience studies of television for instance suggest that the reception of television programmes may be strongly gendered – with men exerting more control over what is watched, focusing more upon 'newsworthy' and public stories and being more silent in their watchings than women – who talk more, and watch in a less focused manner (often because they are so distracted by family matters such as the children or the ironing!). Likewise with age: teenage girls, for example, look for their stories in teenage girl magazines – in the UK magazines like *Jackie* and *Just Seventeen*. The magazines bring together a community of girls bonded through the common reading process. But again, they are not consumed in any straightforward fashion – reading is a complex but highly social process. As Angela McRobbie [1991] says of *Jackie* readers:

> Reading routines vary enormously according to time, place and other available activities. [Girls] flick through *Jackie*, they read it in segments, they read it voraciously to cut off from the family noise around them, and they read the same issue again when they have nothing else to do. *Jackie* makes sense to them as a weekly ritual. It punctuates the end of the week and thus creates a feeling of security. This is reinforced by its repetition and its continuity. The stories that seem to go on forever and the features which are the same over the years also fulfil this function of reassuring sameness.

Finally, the *mechanisms* through which the story is told will matter: 'the media is the message.' Telling a story face to face around a log fire is very different from telling a story through a pulp-paperback book, telling a story to a therapy group that engulfs you in its twelve-step programme, or to telling your story in full frontal glare on *Kilroy* or *Oprah*! These are the differences between oral, print and electronic cultures – creating very different modes of story telling. Whereas sexual stories were most surely told in the oral narratives modes of folklore and myth, increasingly sexual stories have become a part of the 'mediasation' of society. They have been engulfed as most of modern life has – in the permeation of symbolic forms through media technologies. It is not true to suggest, as Walter Benjamin [1970] and others have, that story telling is in decline: rather the channels for telling stories have changed. For many, film has become the narrative medium of the twentieth century. And the solitary verbal tale has now become the public media tale.

Figure 30.1 puts all this simply in schematic form. It suggests there is much in common with recent developments in linguistic, literary and media

Figure 30.1 Stories as joint actions.

theory, but goes beyond this to sense the fully social nature of story telling as joint actions. From this it is possible to see that the telling of a story has no simple, unitary or fixed character. For setting it out like this deconstructs, decentres and destabilises the story. Stories depend upon a constant flow of joint actions circulating between tellers, coaxers, texts, readers and the contexts in which the stories are told: tellers can only select, coaxers can only sift, texts can only sieve and readers can only interpret. Each of these processes compounds the others till the link between reality and the story become very fragile. There is much in common here with what is often called postmodern social theory except that this sociological approach offers distinctive advantages because it does not stay at the level of textual analysis: it insists that story production and consumption is an empirical social process involving a stream of joint actions in local contexts themselves bound into wider negotiated social worlds. Texts are connected to lives, actions, contexts and society. It is not a question of 'hyperrealities' and 'simulacra' but of practical activities, daily doings and contested truths.

With all this in mind, several questions can now be asked of sexual stories. The first concerns *the nature of stories*. This is the classic question of literary theory, asking about the genres and tropes of stories. What common forms do stories take? How are they organised – through plot and time? What are the metaphors embedded within them? Much of such analysis aims to detect underlying structural forms, the formal properties for instance of tragedy, comedy or romance. As such it has a root in some sociology which seeks the underlying structures of social order. The morphology of story telling meets structural sociology.

Thus, for instance, in this book I have chosen one genre of story to analyse: that of the personal experience narrative – the tale told by a person about the self. This is only one kind of sexual story – others might include the pornographic tale, the fictional tale, the scientific tale. And within these sub-classifications, more classical genres may be examined: in looking at Aids narratives, for instance, Judith Williamson has detected their affinity to gothic and melodramatic forms of story telling, whilst Linda Williams's (1989) analysis of pornographic movies over the past century keeps detecting shifting links to other genres – most intriguingly to the musical! The task here is to unpack the types, the languages, the tropes at work inside the text of a sexual story. But for the sociologist it must go further. The genres and structures of story telling may also link to the generic social processes and structures at work in social life. [. . .]

A second question concerns *the social processes of producing and consuming stories*. These are the questions that have been of prime concern to media theorists, but they are centrally sociology of knowledge questions. How do stories get produced: what brings people to the brink of tellings? How do people come to construct their particular stories (and possess them as their own)? Further, what might silence them, and what might bring people to the *emotional* brink of revealing all? Some of the stories told trip lightly off the tongue: but for others there is immense emotional work involved. And why do they tell this particular kind of story rather than another – where does the story they tell come from?

But tellings cannot be in isolation from hearings, readings, consumings.

When can a story be heard, and most especially how is it heard? A voice with no listener is a silence. How might a reader interpret a text and what role might the story play in the consumer's life? How do some readers find themselves emotionally in a text, whilst others may readily dismiss it? And how might such readings connect to the social worlds – real, imagined, interpretive, symbolic – in which they are read? Further, producing and reading should not be seen as separate events. There is a flow of action and producers become consumers whilst consumers become producers. What, then, are the links between the story and the flow of production and consumption? How does one feed into and upon the other such that the making and consuming of stories are closely bound together?

A clear example of this is to be found in the work of Constance Penley [1992]. Her feminist research interests led her, curiously, to focus upon the TV stories of *Star Trek* and a large group of women who, since the early 1970s, have been avid fans. Starting off their lives as consumers of this popular product, these women turned increasingly to a rewriting of the stories so that the lead male characters became sexualised and gay. Rereading the original texts (and turning them into something almost resembling 'gay porn'), they moved from consuming to producing in a highly active writing spiral – making their own fanzines, magazines, books and holding major conventions. Here, production and consumptoin became part of a continuous active spiral. [. . .]

A third question concerns *the social role that stories play*. Once told, what functions might such stories serve in the lives of people and societies? How might stories work to perform conservative functions maintaining dominant orders, and how might they be used to resist or transform lives and cultures? Stories seem a prominent feature of all societies, though their shape and content shift. Sexual stories are also common as a type, as any review of legend and mythology through history would show – highlighting universal themes of passion and desire. But in the modern world, the workings of personal confessions – in the press, in biography, on chat shows, in paperbacks, in therapy groups, in social sciences – seem to have taken on an especially important role in highlighting a key aspect of culture. [. . .]

Finally, a fourth question should address issues of *change, history and culture*. What are the links between stories and the wider social world – the contextual conditions for stories to be told and for stories to be received? What brings people to give voice to a story at a particular historical moment? What are the different social worlds' interpretive communities that enable stories to be told and heard in different ways? And as the historical moment shifts, perhaps into a late modern world, what stories may lose their significance, and what stories may gain in tellability? [. . .]

Stories are not just practical and symbolic actions: they are also part of the political process. Sexual stories ooze through the political stream. Power is not so much an all or nothing phenomenon, which people either have or don't have, and which resides either here or there. Rather, it is best viewed as a flow, a process, a pulsate – oscillating and undulating throughout the social world and working to pattern the degree of control people experience and have over their lives. Power is the process which shifts outcomes and distributes control and regulation. It affects hierarchy, patterns of domination and the distribution of resources. It connects processes which make a difference to the conduct of life. Power is not a simple attribute or a capacity, but a flow of negotiations and shifting outcomes. As electricity is to the physical world, so power may be to the social world: it is the conduit through which much life gets enacted. But its shapes and forms are immensely varied. Like the air we breathe, or the blood that flows through our veins, it is omnipresent. It is not a property of people *per se*, nor is it zero-sum: we do not either have it or not have it. Instead it flows through all interaction, though in starkly different ways. It is both *negative* – repressing, oppressing, depressing – and *positive* – constructive, creative, constitutive. It flows into *lives* making some abundant in capacity (empowered, actualised) and others diminished (inferiorised, marginalised, weak, victims). It flows into *situations*, making some open, flexible and participatory and others closed, rigid and limiting. It flows through the *habitual networks of social activity*, making some alive with possibilities (democratic, participatory) and others infused with oppression and dominance (hierarchic, authoritarian). And ultimately it flows through the whole *negotiated social order* – controlling and empowering, closing and opening, making some things possible and others things impossible. Power is a process that weaves its way through embodied, passionate social life and everything in its wake. *Sexual stories live in this flow of power. The power to tell a story, or indeed to not tell a story, under the conditions of one's own choosing, is part of the political process.*

To put this more concretely: what allows a 'rape story' to be told, to be felt, to be heard, to be legitimated? When can a traumatised raped woman tell herself this story? When can she give public voice to it, and indeed to which public will she voice it: her partner, her child, her parent, the police, the media, the court, a rape hot line, the defendant? When will it be a credible voice, and when will it be an incredible one? This entire process of opening up and closing down the spaces for her talk and the acceptance of her talk can be seen as a political flow. A quarter of a century ago few women could speak of rape, and even fewer would believe such stories once said: the political flow stopped even self-recognition. Today, at least for some women under some circumstances, in many parts of the western world, talk is more possible and belief a little more likely. It may be easiest for wealthy, white women with access to resources and hardest for poor, black women: matters such as literacy, economic security and resources shape the capacity to tell the story. But [...] rape stories have become politically both more feasible and more plausible. *Lives* have become empowered as (some) women have come to tell their story and, with increased emotional strength, see themselves as active survivors. *Situations* have become transformed as a new set of spaces have been created for women to come together and talk, for police and courts to shift their practices from the past, for a greater possibility to see how rape impacts on women's lives. And at the broadest level of *social order*, a new set of challenging understandings about rape have started shifting a little of the patriarchal hierarchies, the dominant stories of sexuality which have silently terrorised many women's lives in the past.

The same is true of 'gay and lesbian stories'. To speak of being gay or lesbian in the early part of the twentieth century in the western world was to invite dramatic social exclusion in all its forms: incarceration in concentration camps, criminal sanctions and imprisonment, medicalisation – treatments and therapies of all sorts, religious banishment, community ostracism and mockery. Not only did the person not tell the 'other', frequently they could not even tell the self. With feelings denied and personal control reduced, a politics of emotion was at work. An organising feature of gay and lesbian life may be seen as the 'Closet'. Here secrecy keeps any story of lesbian and gay life from public view.

But what makes people empowered enough to tell their coming out stories? What enables people first to tell themselves the gay story of their lives; then to tell another – a friend, a lover, a member of the family; then to tell more and more people; and then – for many throughout the 1980s – to shout it passionately from the street corner or the gay parade? And finally, to anticipate a future that may not even be possible, to exhaust the story: to feel it no longer needs to be said. All this is about the flow of power. Here are hierarchy and patterns of domination which facilitate the ability to tell the story of 'being gay': both personal power that allows stories to be told or withheld; and social power which creates spaces or closes down space for stories to be voiced. Here, then, is a flow of negotiations and shifting outcomes, enabling gay life stories to be told at one moment and not another. As gay life story telling has increased, so has the power some gays and lesbians feel over their lives: in the recent past, most lacked this power and even today, in the early 1990s, many may feel powerless to tell their story to self or other. Likewise, some social orders refuse any space at all for such stories to be told – most schools for example, and until very recently, the military. The ability to tell the story of being gay shifts in different 'arenas' of interaction: economic, religious, work, home, media, government. To tell the story of being gay may well be linked to the ability to take the role of others (local, specific and 'significant' as well as wider, abstract and 'generalised'); to the kinds of reference groups and social world perspectives assumed. Likewise, gay story telling is never fixed or final: there will be moments it can be told, moments it is precarious, and moments when it is best kept quiet! The outcome of telling a story is never clear in advance but always under different degrees of contestation and conflict. Emerging everywhere, telling a gay story will open up some possibilities and close down others. It is positive and negative, both releasing capacities in a life whilst also closing down others. Telling gay and lesbian stories does not float around in some heavenly void: it is an everyday and grounded matter. It works its way through practical everyday experience: the child at school who hears peers mock gays will soon realise that this is a story of danger that cannot be safely told to (m)any; the woman in her office may hear jokes about lesbians that make her segregate her worlds to those where she can tell her lesbian story and those where she remains silent. And now there is 'outing': where relatively empowered 'out' gays and lesbians elect to tell the story of privileged (powerful) others without their consent. Power is everywhere in sexual stories.

This power is strongly connected to emotion: shame may prevent a story being told, pride may lead to it being shouted. The telling (and not telling) of stories is usually accompanied by strong feelings [...]. Power cannot easily be grasped without sensing its links to feeling – or not feeling. Many writers on Aids, for instance, speak simultaneously of emotional pains which lead to blocking any ability to tell their Aids stories, but also of the emotional empowerment that flows from telling [Williamson, 1989]. John Preston (1989) in the introduction to a series of personal testaments and stories around Aids, reveals both how emotion can work to bring a story together and how it can work to keep a story silent. On learning of his own HIV status, he writes:

> In 1987 ... I learned that I was infected with the disease myself. It was then that I truly understood the difficulties that many other writers had with their stories, and I became all the more admiring of those who would tell their truths. Because I couldn't do it. Not for well over a year. The manuscript sat on a shelf in my study, something too raw for me to read, too difficult. The epidemic became more immediate, became suffocating, became the way I learned of my lover's and friends' deaths. Now the book seemed, in its own strange way, to become the harbinger of my own infection. Faced with pressing medical decisions and a sense of dread about the repercussions of having Aids in today's society, it seemed there was not time to create a book, there was no relief from the oppression of the illness. How could one reflect on what was happening *when it was happening now?*
>
> But, in fact, this collection (of stories) was one of the means I had at my disposal to come back to life. These articles had helped me fight the feeling that Aids was overwhelming me.

Stories, then, can often not be easily told, and they are always embedded in the political flow. Every part of the interactionist story telling model presented above needs to be placed in this political flow. And so another series of questions arises:

1 *The nature of stories* Which kinds of narratives work to empower people and which degrade, control and dominate? Some stories may work to pathologise voices, or turn them into victims with little control over their lives; other stories may sense human agency and survival, giving the voice a power to transform and empower. Stories may also be told in different ways by different groups – giving some kinds of stories much more credibility than others? Talk from 'below' may be marginalised and excluded, whilst 'expert' talk from above may be given priority and more credibility.

2 *The making of stories* What strategies enable stories to be told, how are spaces created for them, and how are voices silenced? How do stories feed into the wider networks of routine power? Does a coaxer, for example, facilitate stories (enabling new voices to be heard) or entrap stories, into a wider story of his or her own? In a famous instance, Arthur Munby, the Victorian gentleman of letters with a sexual turn-on by the 'dirty work' of housemaids – amongst other things he got his servant to go up the chimney naked! – coaxed his servant Hannah Cullwick to write her diary and reveal her sexual life – 'he told me not to forget to put them things down what I'd been telling him'. When stories are told under such circumstances how might it shape them? Are they really the authentic voices of women, or do men speak through these women's voices? Likewise, in the great parade of sexual survey research, how far does the coaxing role of the interviewer have a part to play, even to the extent that many are more like the researchers' stories than the subjects'?

3 *The consuming of stories* Who has access to stories? Where is the reader located in the political spectrum? How far can one gain access to a story on television, hear it on a radio, buy it in a book, read it in a newspaper, find it in a library? Can one afford to buy it? Does one know where to look? What cultural and economic resources – literacy, knowledge, money, time, space – are needed to consume a story? And how interconnected are these consumers? Although some stories may be told, they may not have the space to be told widely, and they may be told in ways which restrict them to narrow groups. It is quite likely, for instance, that the black feminist lesbian biography which now has a voice is only really read by black lesbian feminists, to whom it makes a big difference. But it has no wider audience than that. How might the consumption of stories be extended?

4 *The strategies of story telling* How might various strategies of talk be implicated in this story telling? Issues of role-taking, turn-taking, impression management, pausing, body gesture, spatial arrangements, shame spirals and the like help 'open' stories or 'close' them down? For instance, some have suggested that some women may speak 'in a different voice' – one that is much less formally rational, linear and abstract than 'male voices', more prone to particularities, interconnections and 'care'. In this view, women's stories may actually be told in a different way – and have a different outcome. They may 'stumble' more, be told with less assuredness and boldness, be more qualified and hesitant, and hence (initially) sound less convincing. Women may generally find it harder to consider their stories as possessing 'authority', harder to express themselves in public, harder to believe that others will respect their story. There is almost certainly a massive gender skew to sexual story telling.

5 *Stories in the wider world* How do stories sit with the wider frameworks of power? The story telling process flows through social acts of domination, hierarchy, marginalisation and inequality. Some voices – who claim to dominate, who top the hierarchy, who claim the centre, who possess resources – are not only heard much more readily than others, but also are capable of framing the questions, setting the agendas, establishing the rhetorics much more readily than the others. These social acts become habitual networks of domination congealing around gender, race, age, economic opportunity and sexuality: certain stories hence are silenced from a saying. Children, for instance, are usually denied access to sexual stories; the elderly who speak of their desires may be looked at suspiciously; 'black voices' around single motherhood and alternative voices may be co-opted into white voices talking of pathology; 'underclass' sexualities are silenced. The importance of 'finding a voice' and 'telling one's story' has been well recognised in the politics of the new social movements over the last decade, and it is an important backdrop to this study. As bell hooks [1989] so tellingly has remarked: 'Oppressed people resist by identifying themselves as subjects, by defining their reality, shaping their new identity, naming their history, *telling their story.*' There are many political processes involved in story telling in general, but in looking at 'sexual stories' a sexual hierarchy needs to be made clear. Gayle Rubin [1984] in a much celebrated and discussed article, has outlined what this means and it is worth quoting her in full:

Modern Western societies appraise sex acts according to a hierarchical system of sex value. Marital, reproductive, heterosexuals are alone at the top of the pyramid [i.e. their stories are heard loud and clear]. Clamouring below are unmarried monogamous heterosexuals in couples, followed by most other heterosexuals. Solitary sex floats ambiguously. The powerful nineteenth-century stigma on masturbation lingers in less potent, modified forms as an inferior substitute for partnered encounters. Stable, long-term lesbian and gay male couples are verging on respectability, but bar dykes and promiscuous gay men are hovering just above the groups at the very bottom of the pyramid. The most despised sexual castes currently include transexuals, transvestites, fetishists, sadomasochists, sex workers such as prostitutes and porn models, and the lowliest of all, those whose eroticism transgresses generational boundaries.

Those at the bottom of the hierarchy have stories that cannot easily be told, and this book will in part be investigating how some of these voices are slowly being heard. But many stories, whose nature at present we can only guess at, are not being told. Such a hierarchy needs to be criss-crossed with gender (which is probably why rape is not on Rubin's list of those low on this hierarchy!), class and race (which would make the black, working-class drag queens and sex workers a pretty low-down, marginalised story!).

An image of a 'gendered heterosexism' may also help reveal the hierarchy of sexual stories. This notion refers to a set of acts which are organised around the divisions of men and women, and through which heterosexual relations – usually leading to some kind of heterosexual coitus, potential reproduction and coupling/marriage – are given priority. Gendered heterosexism takes on many historically varying forms, but here it will mean that those stories that will be most readily said and heard will be those which facilitate standard gender divisions and the paramountcy of heterosexual relations. Again, they will be criss-crossed with class, race and age. Stories which fall outside of this, or worse, challenge this, will have a much harder time being said and heard. [...]

This chapter has been much less concerned with sexual stories *per se* than it has been with providing a wider agenda of questions for the newly emerging sociology of story telling. It should be clear that for sociology, the world of stories is much larger than a mere focus on narrative – overflowing to the social and political conditions that generate some stories and not others, enabling some to be heard and not others. A sociology of stories seeks to understand the role of stories in social life. [...]

References

Benjamin, W. 1970: The storyteller. In Arendt, H. (ed.), *Illuminations*. London: Jonathan Cape.

Clough, P.T. 1992: *The end(s) of ethnography*. London: Sage.

hooks, b. 1989: *Talking back: thinking feminist, thinking black*. Boston, MA: South End Press.

McRobbie, A. 1991: *Feminism and youth culture: from Jackie to Just Seventeen*. London: Macmillan.

Maines, D.R. 1993: Narrative's moment and sociology's phenomena: toward a narrative sociology. *Sociological Quarterly*, **34**(1), 17–38.

Penley, C. 1992: Feminism, psychoanalysis and the study of popular culture. In Grossberg, L., Nelson, C. and Treichler, P. (eds), *Cultural studies*. London: Routledge, 479–94.

Preston, J. (ed.) 1989: *Personal dispatches: writers confront Aids*. New York: St. Martin's Press, p. xii and xviii.

Rubin, G. 1984: Thinking sex: notes for a radical theory of the politics of sexuality. In Carole, V. (ed.), *Pleasure and danger*. London: Routledge, 267–319.

Williams, L. 1989: *Hard core: power, pleasure and the frenzy of the visible*. Berkeley, CA: University of California Press.

Williamson, J. 1989: Every virus tells a story: the meanings of HIV and Aids. In Carter, E. and Watney, S. (eds), *Taking liberties*. London: Serpent's Tail, 69–80.

31

Empowering technology

Julian Stallabrass

From *Gargantua – manufactured mass culture* (Verso, 1996).

[...] The environment in which all digitized media promise to combine and be exchanged is called cyberspace. It is a curious subject, because as yet it barely exists. Nevertheless, this has not hindered previews of its concepts and ideals being played out constantly in theory and fiction; these writings, which took to technology to fulfil their wishes, visions and nightmares, promise no less than a fundamental remaking of human relations to machines and information, and with it a remaking of humanity itself.

The component parts of cyberspace – virtual reality and computer networking – are already with us; the first, in a crude form, can already be seen in the video arcades, while the second is a rapidly growing global infrastructure. Until now, however, the heady marriage of the two, which is the ideal of cyberspace, has been described only in theory and science fiction. The typical vision is as follows:

> From vast databases that constitute the culture's deposited wealth, every document is available, every recording is playable, and every picture is viewable. Around this: a laboratory, an instrumental bridge; taking no space, a home presiding over a world.[1]

The user is immersed in a world of data which is present either as we would normally see it (perhaps a simulation of a printed page), or represented graphically (a dynamic three-dimensional graph of financial movements on the stock exchange). The massive number of sites or specialisms which this data comprises could be presented as different geographical areas between which the user would virtually travel. A number of old bourgeois dreams are encompassed in the promise of this technology: to survey the world from one's livingroom, to grasp the totality of all data within a single frame, and to recapture a unified knowledge and experience. It also holds out the vision of an eternal archive which will persist long after the physical objects from which it was taken have crumbled; paintings may crack and photographs fade but digital records permit their colours and surfaces to remain forever pristine, while the exact trajectory of the object's decline is plotted. Artefacts and even species which have been lost may be reconstructed; in a computer simulation, at least, we can wander about the Acropolis in its prime, or see dinosaurs stamp the virtual earth. Of course to write about *the* culture's 'wealth' assumes a community of interest among users before this process starts, and that cultural riches are simply out there to be grasped and codified. Yet this is in fact widely assumed: to the renewed liaison between technology and culture, the developers of cyberspace bring both a charming naivety and much commercial acumen. Microsoft is buying up the digital rights to what its founder, Bill Gates, calls the million most fascinating images in the world.[2]

The ideal of cyberspace takes in more than just the sum of all human knowledge. It is also an electronic agora in which isolated, anomic but presumably rather well informed individuals may once more come together, without risk of violence or infection, to engage in debate, exchange information or merely chew the fat. Both data and conversation are potentially accessible from anywhere; to be able to 'chat' instantaneously with a neighbour on the other side of the world certainly changes notions of distance and locality. Cyberspace seems to offer simultaneously the advantages of privacy and cultural wealth, self-sufficiency and opportunities for sociability.

Yet, despite all the attention it has been receiving, cyberspace as a technological development has a strange status, not only because it has not yet been realized, but also because it is a concept which has its origins in fiction, particularly in the cyberpunk novels of William Gibson. Programmers and engineers are acting on fictional blueprints and, since these are naturally extremely vague, the very concept and the details of its implementation are up for grabs. The whole affair is even more curious because the fictional vision of cyberspace and the world which surrounds it is hardly positive: what has been taken up so enthusiastically is not so much a technical proposal as a dystopian vision of the future. Of the very term itself, Gibson admits that he 'Assembled the word *cyberspace* from small and readily available components of language. Neologic spasm: the primal act of pop poetics. Preceded any concept whatever. Slick and hollow – awaiting received meaning'.[3] In Gibson's books cyberspace is a dizzying, dangerous 'place', where experience is so intense that it exceeds anything likely to be encountered in real life. It is dominated by leviathan corporations for whose operations it exists, but the system has exceeded them, producing mysterious creatures of mythical abilities, and encompassing such enormous complexity that there are many opportunities for daring Net frontiersmen, who make money by breaking security systems and copying confidential information. Above all, cyberspace is a visual environment in which, while deception is sometimes a feature, things generally look much like what they are: large databases look large, corporations look powerful, military complexes look remote and dangerous, electronic countermeasures look threatening, and as they operate their workings are graphically represented. There is, as we shall see, some sense to this. The transparency of meaning in cyberspace, the absolute match between concept and appearance, is a utopian feature which stands in marked contrast to the real world of meaningless detail and redundant matter.

These descriptions should be contrasted with the reality of computer networking today for, while there are certainly opportunities for hackers, the interface is largely text-based and highly technical. Visceral experiences and reactions are absent – unless boredom counts. If computer networks are eventually to present themselves through graphical systems, there is no particular rule to say that there will be any resemblance between 'what they are' and what they look like, although there will no doubt be a tendency to link looks with the image an entity wishes to project. Yet links between data and its representation cannot be entirely arbitrary, because the major advantage of cyberspace is that everyday perceptual skills would be employed in understanding and manipulating complex information; people are generally much better at picking up an anomaly in a visual representation of data than from a raw mass of figures. The development of computer systems is also certainly running in the direction of Gibson's vision: as Michael Benedikt points out, the 'evolution' of systems, from typed command to menu to Graphical User Interface (for instance, the Macintosh operating system copied in *Windows*) is that of making implicit navigation data visible and marrying it to content.[4] The idea of an apparently immersive, three-dimensional cyberspace is another step in this direction.

What, then, are the details of this fictional vision to which many technicians, parts of the mass media and a portion of the public, have subscribed? There is little common agreement about the definition or extent of cyberpunk. However, its main features are easy to characterize, as Istvan Csicsery-Ronay Jr, a writer about science fiction, rather wearily demonstrates:

> how many formulaic tales can one wade through in which a self-destructive but sensitive young protagonist with an (implant/prosthesis/telechtronic talent) that makes the evil (megacorporations/police states/criminal underworlds) pursue him through (wasted urban landscapes/elite luxury enclaves/eccentric space stations) full of grotesque (haircuts/clothes/self-mutilations/rock music/sexual hobbies/designer drugs/telechtronic gadgets/nasty new weapons/exteriorized hallucinations) representing the (mores/fashions) of modern civilization in terminal decline, ultimately hooks up with rebellious and tough-talking (youth/artificial intelligence/rock cults) who offer the alternative, not of (community/socialism/traditional values/transcendental vision), but of supreme, life-affirming *hipness*, going with the flow which now flows in the machine, against the spectre of a world-subverting (artificial intelligence/multinational corporate web/evil genius)?[5]

Despite all this, he goes on to argue that the genre is worthy of attention because it explores links between four levels of information-processing: the individual's biological processes and personality, the totality of social life, mechanical artificial intelligences and finally new, 'living' entities, created out of these AIs.[6] Cyberspace jockeys in these fictions do not just wear virtual-reality headsets but undergo surgery so that they may interface directly with the Net. There is an air of telepathy about the way they experience, if not understand, the sublime complexity of the world's data, and the most fortunate may hope for mystical contact with artificial super-beings. In the connection of the individual and the social, there is a dialectical move in which opposed qualities find resolution in a higher unity, and we shall see that this is typical of writing about cyberspace in fiction and non-fiction. For the moment note the strange combination of hi-tech and grunge, of the laboratory and the street (or at least a suburban boy's idea of the street), of social critique and unreconstructed heroism. Cyberpunk sports a Gothic technophilia.

The cyberpunk vision is not simply negative, but it is not a happy one. Gibson's first novel, *Neuromancer* (a great success and the book which, more than any other, defined the genre), is set in the wake of a worldwide nuclear conflict. After the reconstruction, the rich are fabulously so, while everyone else scrapes by in an environmentally degraded world of drugs, violence and conspiracy, aided by bizarre mental and physical prostheses. The hero:

> slept in the cheapest coffins, the ones nearest the port, beneath the quartz-halogen floods that lit the docks all night like vast stages; where you couldn't see the lights of Tokyo for the glare of the television sky, not even the towering hologram logo of the Fuji Electric Company, and Tokyo Bay was a black expanse where gulls wheeled above drifting shoals of styrofoam. Behind the port lay the city, factory domes dominated by the vast cubes of corporate arcologies. Port and city were divided by a narrow borderland of older streets, an area with no official name. ... By day, the bars down Ninsei were shuttered and featureless, the neon dead, the holograms inert, waiting, under the poisoned silver sky.[7]

The real world is in a perhaps terminal decline, and threatens to bury its inhabitants beneath obsolete consumer goods, an ever-rising tide of trash. People turn their backs on reality, into drugs, into cyberspace, or, for the less active, into an enveloping form of television which directly imparts the sensory experiences of its stars. Cyberspace is at once an ideological inverse image of this world, and a tool which helps to maintain the power of those who govern. Nevertheless, for those who regularly inhabit it, even the real world comes to seem like cyberspace, as the virtual takes on a reality which often has material effects, and the material acquires an unreal virtuality.[8] Given this scenario, a question naturally arises: why does anyone want to develop dystopia? Among the reasons which immediately spring to mind are its supposed technical inevitability, coupled with dissatisfaction with currently fixed identities and activities; also perhaps that there might be a career in it. Most of all, though, because fictional cyberspace has a fascination as a glossy technophiles' dystopia, which contains some curiously utopian elements. In cyberspace, as it appears in novels at least, the world seems to make transparent sense, if only for the god-like entities which haunt its highest margins. Rising up beyond the mundane, messy everyday world of gross matter, it is a wondrous vision of dazzling complexity, a visual manifestation of the spirit of a higher order. Yet beyond even this, there is a resolutely positive vision of cyberspace, very much at odds with its face in fiction, which is at once highly congruent with current intellectual fashions and with powerful commercial interests.

A phone book is a material object containing data; this data is abstract and can be understood only by those who know how to read it; the book itself is a piece of matter and has to be put in the appropriate place and sometimes moved around. In cyberspace both of these conditions may be changed: data is extracted from its material support and purified so that it can be in many places at once, and sent at near the speed of light. Cyberspace also promises to restore a sensorial form to data without its losing utility or fungibility.

Furthermore, this data can be directly linked into a functioning system: such a telephone system may still work with numbers but the regular user would never need to deal with them.

The representation of data within cyberspace is generally thought of as visual and strictly organized in space. Michael Benedikt, a professor of architecture, writes of 'cyberspace architects' who will visualize the 'intrinsically nonphysical' and so give 'inhabitable visible form to society's most intricate abstractions, processes, and organisms of information'.[9] Cyberspace, then, will be a unified field in which the real is abstracted and the abstract is solidified, in which data, extracted from real purposes, is reconstituted into apparently solid, immediately comprehensible forms, stripped of all actuality. Within this neat schema, the status of representations is equivocal. While data gains physicality, representations in cyberspace lose it, floating free in the digital environment, but as pieces of data which already have a form, they are not manipulable in quite the same way as, say, numbers. They are hard nuggets of discrete information among a shifting mass, manipulable by position and presentation, but not so much (except on the whim of the individual) in terms of form or content, nor changeable in response to shifts in the values of external data. Old, fixed representations, then, might become an important anomaly within the dematerialized visual arena of cyberspace.

[...] The simultaneous dematerialization of data and its transformation into readily understood visual forms have been used as the basis for much metaphysical speculation about the nature of cyberspace. At times this has amounted to the exercise of a hi-tech Hegelianism. Cyberspace is often presented as a new realm between the material and the mental: 'Cyberspace becomes another venue for consciousness itself. And this emergence, proliferation, and complexification [*sic*] of consciousness must surely be this universe's project'.[10] Its materialization of information, the gift of form to data, is also a Platonic dream come true:

> Cyberspace is Platonism as a working product. ... The computer recycles ancient Platonism by injecting the ideal content of cognition with empirical specifics. ... The computer clothes the details of empirical experience so that they seem to share the ideality of the stable knowledge of Forms.[11]

Rather than see cyberspace simply as a halfway house between various pre-existing concepts, the temptation is to view it as a Hegelian synthesis. If for Hegel the real was ideal, in cyberspace the ideal is made virtually real. Very often theories about cyberspace encompass a grand historical sweep, taking on a Hegelian tone as the technology is seen as the means of achieving a sublation of previously opposed fundamental forces or qualities. Cyberspace becomes the conclusion of a wondrous and harmonious historical pageant, a story of human technical and cultural evolution sweeping forwards from cave-painting to computer science. So Benedikt, for instance, argues that it ushers in a '*post* literate era' which unites the advantages of pre-literate physical activity with literate symbolic activity.[12] Or it may be seen as the sublation of the 'monadological' body and the community,[13] body and mind, art and science and no doubt quite a few other combinations. Two self-proclaimed, networked media-philosophers,

Mark Taylor and Esa Saarinen, spell out the nature of the attraction clearly:

> According to Hegel, the concept is actually embodied in time and space. In different terms, objectivity is actually conceptual or the real is the idea. In the society of spectacle, the idea becomes the image and the real is imaginary. For Hegel, it is concept all the way down; for the society of the spectacle, it is image all the way down. In the twentieth century, the Hegelian concept becomes real in electronic telecommunications. The net wires the world for Hegelian *Geist*.[14]

The Hegelianism of the cyberphiles is not one of process, a form of becoming – in fact there is a general assumption that what is technically possible will inevitably be implemented. Rather, the cyberspace utopia is a fixed state in which the end of history and the total realization of mind is finally achieved in a fixed Platonic form. Yet cyberspace is to be more than a pretty picture; it must also be an operational system. Data, which must be handled in the visual arena of cyberspace, like numbers on the stockmarket, has already been abstracted from the real world and made fungible. Its particularity has already been stripped away in its reduction to number. In cyberspace, where it is given an apprehensible form, this data must be constantly animated, as if in a movie. Given that the function of virtual representation is tied to movement, a fixed perfection, like that of architecture, will certainly elude these forms. Further, even these clean, mobile cyberspace forms can never show the material suffering behind a row of financial figures, for this has been stripped away long ago in the very collection of the data. When form is restored to this data, the 'reality' it adopts is utterly cleansed of anything that cannot be exchanged.

Perhaps we should try to stand Hegel on his head for a while. 'Empowering technology' is the new buzz phrase of the informatics enthusiasts, and it has a revealing ambiguity to it. The cyberphiles have generally had an easy time of it in the mass media, which are owned by the very companies that are buying up rights to data for virtual distribution. Here fundamental questions about the direction in which the technology is being taken are rarely asked. A basic assumption behind the acceptance of cyberspace underlies that of the information society as a whole: Andrew Ross has rightly argued that 'the technical *fact* of communication itself is celebrated as an inherent good', without any discussion of the 'resulting shape of the community that is wired up in this way'. New Age dreams of universal, seamless networking are oddly congruent with features of a modern corporate communications ideology.[15] Cyberspace is also allied with an unashamed consumerism: 'We are present at the apotheosis of commercial culture. Commerce is the ocean that information swims in. [...] the means of exchange in commercial culture is now *pure information*'.[16] Vivian Sobchack has analysed the mix of New Age spiritualism and New Edge technophilia in which sixties political activism and social consciousness have been resolved into 'a particularly privileged, selfish, consumer-oriented and technologically dependent libertarianism', which fulfils 'the dreams of "mondoids" who, by day, sit at computer consoles working for (and becoming) corporate America'.[17] It is cyberspace which will allow this becoming to complete itself, uniting the worlds of work and leisure in an environment plied by virtual alter-egos. In this light, cyberspace appears as less the end of history than the ultimate business environment, being stockmarket, warehouse and shopping centre all in one.

Aside from commercial interests, there is also an unholy alliance of postmodern disintegration theorists and wide-eyed New Agers, producing a ludicrous image of the world immersed in a great, shifting sea of data, each person jacking in and finding exactly what they want, in their own personalized order and format. People will live intensely in this digital utopia, forgetting their grosser material needs in an affective, intellectual search for companionship and knowledge. In this ostensibly democratic forum, the chairman of some Western conglomerate and an impoverished peasant in Central Africa will both use a device, about the size of a Walkman, to communicate by satellite with a panoply of open information systems.

As soon as this utopian vision of global information sharing is baldly stated, its stupidity becomes obvious. It is not a matter of doubting the capabilities of the technology, which has already been developed and is becoming cheaper all the time. One should be deeply sceptical, however, about who will control the information, how much it will cost, and to whom it will be sold. Technological revolutions of the past parade their many broken utopian promises. As Herbert Schiller has shown, similar arguments have been rehearsed about all manner of new technologies in order to prepare for their acceptance, and in all cases the liberatory effects have been negligible. Desktop publishing is one example, as is cable television which, although it was much touted as the guarantor of pluralism, has rapidly succumbed to homogeneous corporate dominance.[18] Indeed, at its inception, even the standard technology of television was supposed to offer equal exchange between broadcaster and viewer and access to universal knowledge.[19] Domestic computer technology provides another striking example of the marketing of a rapidly improving technology. Computers have indeed become much cheaper, but only in a certain sense. Average systems still cost a considerable amount of money and, while they are far more powerful, their basic price has not fallen for many years; in fact it may be that the average system has become more expensive in real terms.[20] Software developments which, like cameras, do not always develop in a strictly functional manner, push the minimum acceptable machine ever upward into new areas of speed and sophistication. Below a certain price level, there is little money to be made selling these goods, unless they can be shifted in vast amounts. There is no interest in selling electronic commodities at the price the world's poor can afford, nor is there likely to be. The idea that high-band global networking will become truly universal in a world where only a fifth of the population currently have even telephones is laughable.[21] Even in the highly improbable event of the hardware price sinking to that of a can of Coke, there are still insuperable obstacles for the impoverished. The technology requires that end-users are connected by satellites or a network of specialized terrestrial cabling, the 'Information Super-Highway' in which the United States government is currently investing much money. Already there is an awareness that the placement of the cables may be a means of discriminating against the less wealthy. Without the cabling, and without expensive, advanced modems to receive the data, transfer is much slower, to the point of being either impractical or, since online charges are much like telephone calls, too expensive. Then there is the whole vexed issue of copyright, which will certainly add further charges for the access of 'intellectual property'. Large companies are actively buying the digital rights to all kinds of data, from financial records to pop records; they are not doing this to distribute them free of charge.

The emergence of cyberspace as the main information channel is worrying because it will not necessarily be seen as complementary to existing media. If the Net becomes the only way of receiving certain kinds of information, it may be more restrictive than current systems. Schiller puts the broad issue clearly:

> Transforming information into a saleable good, available only to those with the ability to pay for it, changes the goal of information access from an egalitarian to a privileged condition. The consequence of this is that the essential under-pinning of a democratic order is seriously, if not fatally, damaged.[22]

Now of course, access to certain kinds of information has always been difficult and time-consuming, and what appears in the mass media has always been strictly controlled; in one sense, and perhaps as it exists today, networking can provide a minority with the means to receive information and opinions from diverse sources, yet in another, pay-as-you-go cyberspace threatens to add another powerful disincentive on top of the controls which already exist.

Far from closing down access to information, cyberphiles have generally seen the Net as evolving into an open, global forum to which anybody can contribute, in which information and data are shared and weighty issues discussed. Communities, often sundered in the real world by traffic, the threat of violence or by the self-sufficiency encouraged by modern domestic appliances, will be reborn in the ether, as people with the same interests, but who are perhaps geographically distant, virtually meet. Roy Ascott, for instance, has stressed the dialogic nature of the new telematic media:

> Interactive telecommunications – telematic technology ... speaks a language of cooperation, creativity and transformation. It is the technology not of monologue but of conversation. It feeds fecund open-endedness rather than an aesthetics of closure and completion.[23]

This is not to forge the way for a society of the kind described by Habermas, in which government is founded on reasoned conversation, but something far more fractured and postmodern; not so much dialogue as a cacophony of separate, atomistic voices. For Ascott, and this is a very common association, it has its philosophical basis in the writings of Nietzsche, Bateson, Weiner, Derrida and Rorty. Ascott, speaking now of art on the Net, continues:

> Art is no longer seen as a linear affair, dealing in harmony, completion, resolution, closure – a composed and ordered finality. Instead it is open-ended, even fugitive, fleeting, tentative, virtual. Forming rather than formed, it celebrates process, embodies system, embraces chaos.[24]

On the face of it, there would seem to be some contradiction between building a community, which must have a basis in some agreed terms, and the supposed ever-shifting fluidity of postmodern discourse. Yet people on the Net, despite their differences, have managed to build something of a community, though as we shall see it is of quite a particular kind.

Until very recently, many of the advantages of networking were derived from its very exclusiveness: it was open only to people who had access to a computer and a modem, and using these was quite a technical matter. In Britain especially, the social composition of participants on the Net was very narrow, in part because of high telephone charges, being dominated by young computer professionals and academics, often scientists, who gained access through the free university network. In all countries, the restricted social make-up of those on the Net, and the fact that they were all technically competent, encouraged a good deal of solidarity. The great increase in the number of new users, however, has led old hands to complain that the pleasures of discovery are being obstructed by the high number of learners and 'party-goers'. Theodore Roszak, writing of Bulletin Board Systems where people can post computer messages, describes part of the problem:

> In most of the BBS [Bulletin Board System] hard copy I have seen, the gems of thought lie scattered through a dense thicker of trivia, cute limericks, snippets of opinion, off-the-wall outbursts, illegible fragments. I would be inclined to see much of this as simply another source of data glut, requiring more time to sort through and glean than it is worth. Is networking really better than gathering of an evening at a nearby coffeehouse, or pub, or café to make conversation?[25]

Even those who are enthusiastic about the potential of the Net have to admit that most BBS discussion is 'mundane or puerile or esoteric', having something in common with homemade fanzines.[26] Net conversations are often theatrical, featuring well-known regular participants who are thoroughly informed about networking etiquette, and are greatly outnumbered by silent listeners.[27] Various intellectuals hang around this world, in the hope that a little of its street cred might rub off. Some have cultivated a cool but apocalyptic mode of writing, replete with neologisms and oxymorons. This is a passage from Arthur Kroker and Michael Weinstein's aptly named book, *Data trash*, in which the authors are careful to parade their pretensions in detail:

> I am sitting in Foufounes Electrique, an underground cyberpunk music bar in Montreal. I've a shooter in my hand, copies of Bruce Sterling's *Crystal Express* and Nietzsche's *Will to Power* in my data bag, and my cyber-flesh is taking direct hits from the sound force-field of *Fuzzy Logic*, a group of digital music hackers.[28]

And so it proceeds interminably.

Aside from the danger that meaningful discourse may be buried by trivia and, increasingly, advertising, there is a postmodern dilemma which the Net faces, and which is very much linked with the philosophical work of Rorty *et al*. Howard Rheingold, who has been very active in building a local network in San Francisco, notes that the Net's diversity of dialogue and porous boundaries 'might be an artifact of the early stages of the medium – fragmentation, hierarchization, rigidifying social boundaries, and single-niche colonies of people who share intolerances could become prevalent in the future'.[29] The idea that there is a 'true' structure of information is one of the most pervasive myths of cyberspace, notes Erik Davis,[30] and it is likely to be eroded as people begin to disagree about what constitutes trivia, or how special-interest groups are structured and represented, or as fascists and religious fundamentalists increasingly use the Net to push views which would deny the rights of others. The consensual environment of cyberspace must try to satisfy many competing demands.

These incipient communities also have to face active vandalism. This may take the form of hacking into the operating system to cause disruption or bypassing security measures in order to read private mail and credit-card numbers. Beyond this, forums may be attacked merely by the content of the messages. Rheingold notes:

> One of the great problems with the atmosphere of free expression now tolerated on the Net is the fragility of communities and their susceptibility to disruption. The only alternative to imposing potentially dangerous restrictions on freedom of expression is to develop norms, folklore, ways of acceptable behaviour that are widely modelled, taught, and valued, that can give the citizens of cyberspace clear ideas of what they can and cannot do with the medium, how they can gain leverage, and where they must beware of pitfalls in the medium, if we intend to use it for community-building.[31]

He gives one example of a community Bulletin Board System which was destroyed by a group of young males choking the system with obscene postings.[32] Such tales point to a fundamental problem: to function successfully, the virtual community demands that a real one lie behind it. The propensity for trying to make virtual communities is comment enough on the debility of real ones, but also on the need for them. If virtual communities flourish now, this is due to the relatively closed nature of the Net, which means that it is hardly the identity-free utopia that some claim. People are defined at least by the fact that they are there.

Postmodern critics who praise Net-speak for its diversity are reluctant to raise questions of judgement about its quality. The central argument of Roszak's book, *The cult of information*, is that there is no necessary connection between the mere amount of data available and the quality of thought brought to bear on it. There is also the question of whether the computer itself has any effect on the quality of thought produced in its presence. At first sight, it would seem that the answer must be no; the computer is a universal machine, capable of simulating the action of any other machine, so its operation need do little to change our previous habits and predilections. Yet the actual form which it has taken is highly specific, and very much determined by the fact that it must be marketed and sold to businesses and consumers, and this particular form does seem to encourage certain types of relationship to the content it displays. In part, this may be to do with the system of navigation; effortless and unlimited jumps lead to skimming, while the lack of hierarchy in presentation and the equality of access to each area give the impression that all pieces of information are equivalent. There is a propensity to travel but never to arrive. Benedikt is aware of the difficulty:

> If instant access to people and information were to become endemic to cyberspace, gone would be the process of progressive revelation inherent in

closing the distance between self and object, and gone would be a major armature in the structuring of human narratives: the narrative of *travel*. Destinations would all be certain, like conclusions foregone. Time and history, narrativity and memorability, the unfolding of situations, the distance between objects of desire and ourselves – the distance, indeed, that creates desire and the whole ontology of eroticism ... – would be collapsed, thrown back, to existing in *this* physical world only, and only as lame, metaphorical constructions, here and there, in that one.[33]

This is not mere speculation. Theodore Roszak has commented on the diminished attention span encouraged by 'edutainment', arguing:

There is something about all computerised activities that is worrisome in this respect, something built into the physical posture, emotional affect, and perceptual action of sitting at a video terminal, entering data, scrolling through, revealing snippets of this and that.[34]

If this seems exaggerated, it may be because we have already been affected: Adorno wrote of the abbreviated thought which takes place with pencil in hand, so what would he have made of the insistently flashing cursor?[35] Even the best multimedia programs encourage constant flicking from screen to screen, partly because the options for moving on are always present, awaiting the next click of the mouse, but mostly because of the paucity of the material offered. One might gaze at a painting by Poussin for quite some time, but not at the little images in 256 colours provided in Microsoft's *Art Gallery*. The flattening of information and representation into a single field tends to erode the significance of the unusual. Again, as in digital photography, this amounts to a retrospective justification of postmodern views, in this case of extreme relativism.

The rise of digital media has encouraged the propagation of a 'theory' which lauds these very qualities of shallowness and dispersal as a new form of radicalism. The beginnings of a theoretical attack on print itself are evident, working in the interests of those corporations which have invested in multimedia. A symptomatic example is *Imagologies*, to which I have already referred, which is about a videolinked seminar on networking and the new media conducted between Finland and the United States. This book is somewhat embarrassed to be a book, and seeks to convince the reader by its layout (which uses multiple parallel texts and words printed in different directions and in different typefaces, rather in the style of an up-market student rag magazine) that it goes beyond the mundane, linear reasoning associated with the reading of mere print. Matching the layout, there are few passages of sustained argument, the stress being rather on sequences of dispersed soundbites and unsupported statements. The cover sports the phrase 'If you read books, justify it'. Of course, unlike transitory musings over the ether, this book is an object and a commodity, one that might even appeal to masochistic bibliophiles. The alliance with deconstruction is made quite explicit:

While marking the closure of the western metaphysical tradition, deconstruction also signals the opening of post-print culture. Deconstruction remains bound to and by the world of print that it nonetheless calls into question. What comes after deconstruction? Imagology. To realize what deconstruction has made possible, it is necessary to move into the world of telecommunications technology. The notion of textuality cannot be radicalized until it is transformed from print to other media. To perform dissemination is to electrify the signifier.[36]

To show that this alliance is not what it seems will involve a staid recourse to analyse and a dissatisfaction with dwelling on the surface of things. Taylor and Saarinen argue for naivety and plain speaking in the face of ecological catastrophe a few pages later,[37] and neither quality might be thought to match the electronic apotheosis of deconstruction. The general argument, however, is that meaning itself involves an authoritarian closure, and that, in any case, no one has much time in this age of television and telecommunications to read a whole book from cover to cover or develop an argument, so we have no option but to celebrate the liberatory potential of fragmentary thought, hypertextual skipping, and the merely tactical use of the media in highly transitory situations. Obviously, in such a situation, contradiction may be borne lightly.

The greatest freedom cyberspace promises is that of recasting the self: from static beings, bound by the body and betrayed by appearances, Net-surfers may reconstruct themselves in a multiplicity of dazzling roles, changing from moment to moment according to whim. From being restricted to a single time and place, the Net being may distribute itself over the wired-up globe and make its acts and statements eternal. The new technology offers us freedom of the most fundamental and necessary kind, from identity itself:

> The technology of these transformative systems fulfils a profound human desire: to transcend the limits of the human body, time and space; to escape language, to defeat the metaphors of self and identity that alienate and isolate, that imprison the mind in solipsistic systems. Our need is to fly, to reach out, to touch, connect – to expand our consciousness by a dissemination of our presence, to distribute self into a larger society of mind.[38]

As it currently exists, this utopian anonymity has been founded on text, in fact on the technical limitations of the interface. Identity can be fluid in virtual communication where accent, looks, wealth, posture and gender are screened out in text-only dialogue; this is not likely to last long, and in fact the degree to which it happens even now may be exaggerated.[39] Such playing of roles goes back to Alan Turing's gender game, in which a man and a woman in separate rooms conversing only with written messages try to convince each other that they are both women.[40] Turing of course also devised a similar test for machine intelligence. When video rather than text is exchanged the conventional boundaries of identity may be re-established. Images could be modified, of course, but only by deliberate falsification. On the other hand, representations of the self in cyberspace may be thought of as deliberate fictions, and gender-swapping seems to be one of those most in demand, to the extent that in the Lucas films virtual world, *Habitat*, there is a 'Change-o-matic' object which switches the virtual gender of its user. The Humean kit form of identity change is likely to be the most open to most users: true fluidity being beyond all but the independent programmer. Yet the extreme mutability and multiplication of identity possible in cyberspace collides with the desire to build communities based upon honest communication with people of diverse backgrounds and interests. Role-playing, and the potential for dishonesty which goes with it, militates against community.[41] [...]

The hope is that the shiny new world of cyberspace will be a free, public space where the environmental depredations and commercial white noise of the real world can be avoided. In the United States, it is often described as the new Frontier. For those rugged, libertarian individuals who dare to venture there, the realm of cyberspace will reactivate the lost magic of a mythological past. For Timothy Leary, who retired from recommending designer drugs to take up proselytizing, the benefits of computer net-working, cyberpunks are strong, stubborn individuals who have inherited the mantle of the early explorers, mavericks, ronin and free-thinkers everywhere.[42] Certainly some of the hackers and legitimate Net-surfers do understand their experience in this way, largely because the networks are still difficult to navigate. When and if this space really does become as public and as immediate as television, what is to say that it will not become as cluttered and full of commercial garbage as anywhere else? A comparable example is the previously unsullied world of computer games which has succumbed to 'product placement' within the past few years.

Two descriptions of cyberspace skies elucidate this situation: for Gibson they are a 'monochrome nonspace where the only stars are dense concentrations of information, and high above it all burn corporate galaxies and the cold spiral arms of military systems'.[43] A bleak vision of some frozen frontier, then, forbidding but at least not crass. For Benedikt, by contrast, the skies are alive with the images of their travellers, hurtling through space, and 'alive with entities licensed to inhabit this public realm, floating like ribbons, hot-air balloons, jellyfish, clouds, but in wonderful, unlikely shapes, constrained only (1) to represent information systems in the public interest, and (2) to be mostly transparent. There would be a thousand words and images, a din of voices and music (and, yes, advertisements are possible).[44] They are far more than just possible. Benedikt also recommends that travel in cyberspace have a monetary cost, and speculates about various sources of cyberspace profit, from virtual 'real estate' in cyberspace, which might be leased to advertisers, to connection charges for the system.[45]

So the radical and exclusive position of the Net is fragile. Howard Rheingold correctly argues that the Net offers liberatory potential just because it is still largely outside the control of the mass media. Using Ben Bagdikian's analysis of the media monopoly, he argues that the 'new media lords ... are not likely to encourage their privately owned and controlled networks to be the willing conduits for all kinds of information that unfettered citizens and nongovernmental organizations tend to disseminate'.[46] The commercialization of the Net will raise questions of pricing, access, censorship and copyright, of 'intellectual property' in short, which the owners will take action to protect. In 'Operation Sun Devil', FBI agents arrested hackers not for causing damage but merely for gaining free access to information.[47] Here the open-door ideology of the network founders collides with the commercial ethos of the society in which they live. The United States government's support of the networking infrastructure is founded on connecting supercomputers, and gaining advantage in international technological competition, rather than on some experiment in networked democracy.[48] Rheingold, analysing this process of commodification, warns that, 'this transition might render moot many of the fantasies of today's true believers in electronic democracy and global online culture'.[49] Commercialization and political control are entangled issues.

Cyberspace will be highly complex, so people will need guidance through it, and this is where corporations step in, providing regular and assured channels of access. As Microsoft has shown again and again, in an industry where common standards are usually of more importance than quality, the big players have most of the advantages. The nineties have seen various powerful mergers and alliances between large companies which are trying to dominate this technology, including the agreement between Microsoft, Telecommunications Inc. (the largest cable television company) and Time-Warner. Such corporations are limbering up for the control of a medium which would serve as a substitute for movies, newspapers, magazines and even shops. The virtual world is also the ideal arena for public relations exercises: 'Perhaps the most dramatic opportunity cyberspace provides for a corporation is a dynamic and exciting public face. Public visits to the corporation will provide intimate interactions with company products either simulated or real'. Best of all, information flows both ways for, as the potential customer gathers information about the product, the corporation will gather data about its customers 'for instant measurements of acceptance'.[50] [...]

Dreams of a networked utopia will come up against hard commercial reality. Cyberspace is of course flexible enough to incorporate areas for both; where it is used for recreation, some freedom and flexibility will be permitted, and when it is used practically and is connected to the real world, strict rules will no doubt apply and access will be restricted. To illustrate the contrast, it is enough to think of teleworking on the Net, where the actions of isolated and unprotected workers, remotely linked to their employer, are monitored from moment to moment. Primarily cyberspace will be a working environment, virtual but with very real consequences. Its solipsism will be that not of the pioneer but of the worker as monad:

> Absolute solitude, the violent turning inward on the self, whose whole being consists in the mastery of material and in the monotonous rhythm of work, is the specter which outlines the existence of man in the modern world.[51]

Cyberspace is a way of literally enforcing this solitude and concealing it virtually. Systems will enforce behaviour, in the workspace, and in the very acquisition of knowledge itself.

Although misgivings about the economics of cyberspace are rarely expressed, despite much discussion there is also little agreement about its likely cultural effect. From the overview given so far, it is obvious that there is a basic contrast between utopian theory and dystopian fiction, a fundamental difference over whether the new technology will bear us to heaven or send us to hell. [...]

When we see the operation of another sort of intelligence in computer art, we become aware of a power which is hard to define or hold steady in the mind, yet which is felt as a presence, like the fleeting, protean artificial minds of Gibson's novels. Goethe wrote of a force of nature which is:

> both animated and inanimate, both souled and soulless, something which manifested itself only in contradictions and could not therefore be formulated in concepts, let alone in words. It was not divine, for it seemed irrational; not human, for it had no understanding; not diabolical, for it was beneficent; not angelic, for it often betrayed *Schadenfreude.* It was like chance in its inconsequentiality; like Providence in the inter-relationships it revealed. Everything that has limits for us seemed to it penetrable; it seemed wilfully to recombine the most necessary elements of our existence, eclipsing time and extending space.... This being, which seemed to interpose itself between all the others, to sunder or unite them, I called the *Demonic.*[52]

Goethe's natural force is surely what we now call emergent order, that force which somehow forges complex pattern from unthinkable chaos, a force which we have begun to know only through computer simulation. It is notable that it is described as demonic, notable also that it is harnessed now to control real or virtual robots, or artificial life.[53] Such order is apparent not merely in nature, but in many complex systems; if in computer forms we find a disturbing recognition of some alien order, then what we see is an image of the operation of economic markets, of apparently obscure and inhuman forces which control every detail of our lives. A cold order is wrought from the immensely complex flows of funds (now largely electronic signals), material, jobs and – finally – people that are flung across the globe, gathering and dispersing at the whim of this power, incessantly building and wrecking hopes, raising and lowering the death-rate as it goes. The computer can, then, act as an 'analogue' of these forces, revealing an image of the demon of Capital.

Although most descriptions of cyberspace stress its dizzying complexity, they also emphasize the empowerment of the user, who flies through the virtual sky, or swims through its depths. The fantasies are always the same:

> Sometimes I linger on a pattern for the sake of its strangeness, and as it becomes familiar I grow into another self. I wonder how much richer the patterns I can recognize can become, and surprise myself by scanning faster and faster regions in times shorter and shorter. Like a bird of prey my acuity allows me to glide high above the planes of information, seeking jewels among the grains, seeking knowledge.[54]

New Agers make computer simulations of flying through fractal landscapes at great speed which are transferred to video and marketed as 'cyberspace' experiences. About this new sea of capital in which millions of punters swim, the question arises: aside from their own personal experience of immersive travel, what will be their relation to the leviathan corporations, and how will they treat each other?

Horkheimer and Adorno argued that at the heart of Enlightenment there was a secularized version of the belief that God controlled the world. People thus confronted nature as an inferior, external other, a world of lifeless, fungible atoms, open to manipulation, and without conceiving of an interpenetration of subject and object.[55] In one sense, then, cyberspace may be seen as the final act of the Enlightenment, in which the interface of nature disappears, replaced by a more evidently divine other. Although subject and object are most certainly entwined, the subject's attributes become definitively open to exchange. Some time before the age of intelligent machines, Aldous Huxley described virtual reality pornography, his 'feelies': 'then suddenly, dazzling and incomparably more solid-looking than they would have seemed in actual flesh and blood, far more real than reality, there stood the stereoscopic images'.[56] While each solipsistic user may feel empowered, every other being is prepared for use. Cyberspace is an ideal realization of Lukács's 'second nature', entangling the subjective and objective, and since, unlike the transformation of the real world by Capital, it evolves without direct material destruction, the speed of development (and mental destruction) can be all the more dizzying.

Cyberspace is also likely to be, in flagrant contradiction to its postmodern apologists, the embodiment of the totalizing system of capital. Again, Adorno and Horkheimer are relevant here: 'For the Enlightenment whatever does not conform to the rules of computation and utility is suspect ... Enlightenment is totalitarian.'[57] It aims at a principle of scientific unity in which the 'multiplicity of forms is reduced to position and arrangement, history to fact, things to matter'.[58] If we replace 'matter' with 'data' then this passage can be directly applied to cyberspace. Douglas Kellner notes that 'Such quantitative modes of thought presuppose an identity between concept and object, word and thing, and privilege mathematical logic as alone capable of grasping the essence of things.'[59] The invention of cyberspace is, then, the attempt to create a world where to perceive is the same as to understand, where 'objects' are entirely adequate to their concepts, and are even, through their dematerialization, identical with them. Despite the sport of fictional demons within cyberspace, the impetus of the system is towards the reduction of everything to the calculable; for this 'the Net' is indeed an apt name.

So technophiliac enthusiasts are stitching up a totalizing, brave new world based on an Enlightenment paradigm but defended by postmodern theory. Adorno, and others following him, have been much concerned to argue that there is a negative and liberatory charge in objects exceeding their concepts. It is this which cyberspace promises to abolish. This virtual space threatens to form the ultimate illusion of a unified understanding, not by surmounting contradiction, but by remaking the world in specious harmony. As a universal system of data, however, cyberspace will have to contain representations of pictures, texts and photographs. While these will have lost all materiality, at least their fixed forms will challenge the homogeneity of the system. History and its representations will become resistant islands of unchangeable data, reminders of the other of reality, of process and finally of humanity.

In the extraordinary situation in which a new technology of profound importance is being created, there is a curious parallel between the associated confusion, bloated claims, predicted utopian dystopias and vice versa, and what Benjamin described in his analysis of Germany during the great inflation of the twenties. He noted that within accounts of widespread decline, accommodations were always made to justify specific personal positions and activities:

> A blind determination to save the prestige of personal existence, rather than, through an impartial disdain for its importance and entanglement, at least to detach it from the background of universal delusion, is triumphing almost everywhere. That is why the air is so thick with life theories and world views, and why in this country they cut so preposterous a figure, for almost always they finally serve to sanction some wholly trivial private situation. For just the same reason the air is so full of phantoms, mirages of a glorious cultural future breaking upon us overnight in spite of all, for everyone is committed to the optical illusions of his isolated standpoint.[40]

This passage illuminates the solipsism of cyberspace, which is merely a literal expression of the situation of the individual in contemporary society, and more specifically of business people and their camp followers (from engineers to intellectuals) spinning universalizing fantasies out of their desire to ride the next commercial wave. This wondrous but specious technology threatens to act as another curtain between those who consume it and the condition of the world: as the poor are excluded from cyberspace, and will appear on it only as objects, never as subjects with their own voices, there is a danger that they recede even further from the consciousness of the comfortable. As the real world is left to decline, the air once again becomes full of phantoms, this time digital, promising at the last moment to pluck utopia from apocalypse. [...]

Notes

1 Benedikt, M. 1991: Introduction. In Benedikt, M. (ed.), *Cyberspace. First Steps.* Cambridge, MA, p. 2.
2 Gates has founded a new company, Continuum, to form a massive visual database. See Bill Gates' Mega-database of World Art, *The Art Newspaper* (December 1994), supplement on publishing, i–ii. The first fruit of this has been a CD-ROM catalogue of the paintings in the National Gallery, London, which Microsoft has marketed under the name *Art Gallery*.
3 Gibson, W. 1991: Academy leader. In Benedikt, M. (ed.), *Cyberspace*, p. 27.
4 Benedikt, M. 1991: 'Cyberspace. Some proposals', in Benedikt, M. (ed.), *Cyberspace*, p. 174.
5 Csicsery-Ronay, Jr, I. 1991: Cyberpunk and neuromanticism. In McCaffery, L. (ed.), *Storming the reality studio. A casebook of cyperpunk and postmodern fiction.* Durham, NC, p. 184.
6 Csicsery-Ronay, Jr, I. 1991: Cyberpunk and neuromanticism. In McCaffery, L. (ed.), *Storming the reality studio. A casebook of cyperpunk and postmodern fiction.* Durham, NC, p. 190.
7 Gibson, W. 1984: *Neuromancer*. London, p. 13.
8 For the similarities between electronic matrices and physical reality in Neuromancer, see Bukatman, S. 1993: *Terminal identity. The virtual subject in postmodern science fiction.* Durham, NC, p. 148.
9 Benedikt, M. 1991: Introduction. In Benedikt, M. (ed.), *Cyberspace*, p. 18.
10 Benedikt, M. 1991: Cyberspace: some proposals. In Benedikt, M. (ed.), *Cyberspace*, p. 124.
11 Heim, M. 1991: The erotic ontology of cyberspace. In Benedikt, M. (ed.), *Cyberspace*, p. 64.

12 Benedikt, M. 1991: Introduction. In Benedikt, M. (ed.), *Cyberspace*, p. 12.
13 Stone, A.R. 1991: Will the real body please stand up? Boundary stories about virtual cultures. In Benedikt, M. (ed.), *Cyberspace*, p. 101.
14 Taylor, M.C. and Saarinen, E. 1994: *Imagologies. Media philosophy*. London, Simcult, p. 3 (each chapter of this book is paginated separately).
15 Ross, A. 1991: *Strange weather: culture, science and technology in the age of limits*. London, p. 35.
16 Sirius, R.U. 1992: A user's guide to using this guide. In Rucker, R., Sirius, R.U. and Queen Mu (eds), *Mondo 2000: a user's guide to the new edge*. New York, p. 16; cited in Vivian Sobchack 1993: New age mutant ninja hackers. Reading *Mondo 2000*. *South Atlantic Quarterly*, **92**(4), Fall, p. 583.
17 Sobchack 1993: New age mutant ninja hackers, p. 574.
18 Schiller, H.I. 1989: *Culture Inc., The corporate takeover of public expression*. Oxford, p. 51.
19 See Dienst, R. 1994: *Still life in real time: theory after television*. Durham, NC, p. 5.
20 The price of a usable machine in the early eighties was considerably less than the £1000 paid for an average 486 system today. See Rockman, S. 1995: Back to the future. *Personal Computer World* (March), p. 533.
21 See Crary, J. 1994: Critical reflections. *Artforum* (February), p. 59.
22 Schiller 1989: *Culture Inc.*, p. 75.
23 Ascott, R. 1991: Connectivity: art and interactive communications. *Leonardo*, **24**(2), p. 115.
24 Ascott, R. 1991: Connectivity, p. 116.
25 Roszak, T. 1994: *The cult of information. A neo-Luddite treatise on high-tech, artificial intelligence and the true art of thinking*. Berkeley, p. 171. This is also the repeated complaint of a former proselytizer of the Net, Clifford Stoll, in his recent book, *Silicon snake oil. Second thoughts on the information highway*. London, 1995.
26 Rheingold, H. 1994: *The virtual community. Finding connection in a computerized world*. London, p. 132.
27 Rheingold, H. 1994: *The virtual community*, p. 61.
28 Kroker, A. and Weinstein, M.A. 1994: *Data trash. The theory of the virtual class*. Montreal, p. 105.
29 Rheingold, H. 1994: *The virtual community*, p. 207.
30 Davis, E. 1993: Techgnosis: magic, memory, and the angels of information. *South Atlantic Quarterly*, **92**(4), Fall, p. 601.
31 Rheingold, H. 1994: *The virtual community*, p. 64.
32 This cautionary tale is recounted in Rheingold, H. 1994: *The virtual community*, p. 135.
33 Benedikt, M. 1991: Cyberspace: some proposals, p. 170.
34 Roszak, T. 1994: *The cult of information*, p. 197.
35 Adorno, T.W. 1992: The curious realist: on Siegfried Kracauer. In *Notes to Literature*, trans. Shierry Weber Nicholsen, vol. II, New York, p. 61.
36 Taylor and Saarinen, *Imagologies*, Style, p. 5.
37 Taylor and Saarinen, *Imagologies*, Naivete, p. 4.
38 Ascott, R. 1991: Connectivity, p. 116.
39 See Balsamo, A. 1993: Feminism for the incurably informed. *South Atlantic Quarterly*, **92**(4), Fall, p. 698.
40 See Woolley, B. 1993: *Virtual worlds. A journey in hype and hyperreality*. London, p. 105.
41 Rheingold, H. describes the outrage which followed the revelation that a de facto agony aunt on the Net, who claimed to be disabled, disfigured, mute and female, was actually a New York psychiatrist with none of these attributes. Rheingold, H. 1994: *The virtual community*, 164–5.
42 Leary, T. The cyberpunk: the individual as reality pilot. In McCaffery, L. (ed.),

Storming the reality studio, 245–58. For more on Leary's computer enthusiasms and uncritical responses to virtual reality and networking in general see Bukatman, S., *Terminal identity*, 189f.

43 Gibson, W. 1993: *Burning chrome*. London, p. 197. The first edition was New York, 1986.
44 Benedikt, M. 1991: Cyberspace: some proposals, p. 205.
45 Benedikt, M. 1991: Cyberspace: some proposals, p. 219.
46 Rheingold, H. 1994: *The virtual community*, pp. 5, 14.
47 Rheingold, H. 1994: *The virtual community*, 251f.
48 Rheingold, H. 1994: *The virtual community*, p. 84.
49 Rheingold, H. 1994: *The virtual community*, p. 273.
50 See Pruitt, S. and Barrett, T. 1991: Corporate virtual workspace. In Benedikt (ed.), *Cyberspace*, p. 405.
51 Adorno, T. and Horkheimer, M. 1973: *Dialectic of enlightenment*, trans. John Cumming. London, p. 226.
52 Goethe 1950: *Dichtung und Warheit*. Zurich, pp. 839–40; cited in Jameson, F. 1971: *Marxism and form. Twentieth century dialectical theories of literature*. Princeton, 129–30. Jameson uses this passage to describe creative production.
53 The term 'demon' is appropriately used by programmers to describe an algorithm, which is of course defined by and devoted exclusively to its task.
54 Novak, M. 1991: Liquid architectures in cyberspace. In Benedikt, M. (ed.) *Cyberspace*, p. 230.
55 Adorno, T. and Horkheimer, M. 1973: *Dialektik der Aufklärung*, p. 41; cited in Jay, M. 1973: *The dialectical imagination. A history of the Frankfurt School and the Institute of Social Research, 1923–1950*. Boston, p. 260.
56 Huxley, A. 1955: *Brave new world*. Harmondsworth, p. 134.
57 Adorno, T. and Horkheimer, M. 1973: *Dialectic of enlightenment*, p. 6.
58 Adorno, T. and Horkheimer, M. 1973: *Dialectic of enlightenment*, p. 7.
59 Kellner, D. 1989: *Critical theory, marxism and modernity*. Cambridge, p. 96.
60 Benjamin, W. 1979: Imperial panorama. A tour of the German inflation. In *One way street and other writings*, trans. Jephcott, E. and Shorter, K., London, p. 58.

Index